# LOW-WAGE WORK IN THE UNITED KINGDOM

# LOW-WAGE WORK IN THE UNITED KINGDOM

Caroline Lloyd, Geoff Mason,
and Ken Mayhew,
Editors

The Russell Sage Foundation Case Studies of Job
Quality in Advanced Economies

Russell Sage Foundation • New York

# The Russell Sage Foundation

The Russell Sage Foundation, one of the oldest of America's general purpose foundations, was established in 1907 by Mrs. Margaret Olivia Sage for "the improvement of social and living conditions in the United States." The Foundation seeks to fulfill this mandate by fostering the development and dissemination of knowledge about the country's political, social, and economic problems. While the Foundation endeavors to assure the accuracy and objectivity of each book it publishes, the conclusions and interpretations in Russell Sage Foundation publications are those of the authors and not of the Foundation, its Trustees, or its staff. Publication by Russell Sage, therefore, does not imply Foundation endorsement.

**Library of Congress Cataloging-in-Publication Data**
Low-wage work in the United Kingdom / Caroline Lloyd, Geoff Mason, and Ken Mayhew, editors.
    p. cm. — (The Russell Sage Foundation case studies of job quality in advanced economies)
  ISBN 978-0-87154-563-3
  1. Unskilled labor—Great Britain.  2. Wages—Great Britain.  3. Minimum wage—Great Britain.  4. Labor market—Great Britain.  I. Lloyd, Caroline, 1965–  II. Mason, Geoff, 1949–  III. Mayhew, Ken.
  HD8391.L676  2008
  331.7'980941—dc22                            2007045928

Text design by Suzanne Nichols.

RUSSELL SAGE FOUNDATION
112 East 64th Street, New York, New York 10021
10 9 8 7 6 5 4 3 2 1

# Contents

# About the Authors

CAROLINE LLOYD is senior research fellow at the Economic and Social Research Council Centre on Skills, Knowledge, and Organisational Performance (SKOPE) and senior lecturer at the School of Social Sciences at Cardiff University.

GEOFF MASON is Senior Research Fellow at the National Institute of Economic and Social Research, London.

KEN MAYHEW is Fellow in Economics at Pembroke College, Oxford, and director of SKOPE.

MARILYN CARROLL is a research associate in the European Work and Employment Research Centre at the University of Manchester.

JOHANNA COMMANDER is a research assistant at the Scottish Centre for Employment Research at the University of Strathclyde.

ELI DUTTON is research fellow in the School of Health and Social Care at Glasgow Caledonian University.

DAMIAN GRIMSHAW is Professor of Employment Studies at the University of Manchester and director of the European Work and Employment Research Centre.

SUSAN JAMES is a SKOPE Research Fellow and Leverhulme Early Career Development Fellow at the Department of Economics, University of Oxford.

DENNIS NICKSON is Reader in Human Resource Management and Service Work and co-director of the Scottish Centre for Employment Research in the Department of Human Resource Managment, University of Strathclyde.

MATTHEW OSBORNE works as an economist at the UK Financial Services Authority, and was formerly a research officer at the National Institute of Economic and Social Research, London.

JONATHAN PAYNE is a senior researcher with the ESRC's Centre for Skills, Knowledge, and Organisational Performance (SKOPE) and is based at Cardiff University's School of Social Sciences.

ROBERT SOLOW is Institute Professor Emeritus at the Massachusetts Institute of Technology and a Nobel laureate in economics.

PHILIP STEVENS is Chief Advisor, Economic Strategy, at the Ministry of Economic Development in Wellington, New Zealand, and a visiting fellow at the National Institute of Economic and Social Research in London.

CHRIS WARHURST is Professor of Labour Studies and co-director of the Scottish Centre for Employment Research at the University of Strathclyde in Glasgow, and co-editor of the British Sociological Association journal *Work, Employment and Society*.

# INTRODUCTION

## The United Kingdom Story

*Robert Solow*

By any reasonable standard definition of "low-wage work," about a quarter of American wage earners are low-wage workers. The corresponding figure is smaller, sometimes much smaller, in other comparable advanced capitalist countries. This fact is not very good for the self-image of Americans. It does not seem to be what is meant by "crown(ing) thy good with brotherhood, from sea to shining sea." The paradox, if that is the right word, is the starting point for the extensive study of which this book is an important part. What are the comparative facts, what do they mean, and why do they turn out that way?

A foundation dedicated from its beginning to "the improvement of social and living conditions in the United States of America" has to be interested in the nature of poverty, its causes, changes, consequences and possible reduction. Low-wage work is not the same thing as poverty, still less lifelong poverty. Some low-wage workers live in families with several earners, and share a common standard of living, so they may not be poor even while working such jobs. Some low-wage workers are on a reasonably secure track that will eventually move them to better paid jobs, so they are not poor in a lifetime sense. But some low-wage workers are stuck with very low income for a meaningful length of time. For them, low-wage work does mean poverty in the midst of plenty.

Of course, the incidence of poverty can be reduced by transfer payments outside the labor market. Nevertheless, in a society that values self-reliance, and in which productive work confers identity and self-respect as well as the respect of others, income redistribution unconnected or wrongly connected with work is not the best solution except in special cases. In that kind of society, ours for instance, the persistence of low-wage work is felt as a social problem on its own. It first has to be understood if we are to find satisfactory ways to diminish its incidence or alleviate its effects.

One obvious basis for low-wage work is low productivity, which may be primarily a characteristic of the worker, as is often simply assumed, or may be primarily a characteristic of the job. If it inheres in the job, equity could be achieved by passing the job around, so to speak, like boring committee assignments or military service, but that would have no aggregate effect. Wherever low pay originates, however, raising productivity provides a double benefit: it diminishes the amount of low-wage work to be done, and it increases the useful output of the whole economy.

Low productivity, and therefore low-wage work, tends to reproduce itself from generation to generation. This is an important additional reason why a high incidence of low-wage work is a "social condition" that needs to be improved. Growing up in a chronically low-wage family limits access to good education, good health care, and to other ladders to social mobility. So a persistent high incidence of low-wage work, when confined to a relatively small group, contravenes the widely accepted social goal of equal opportunity.

These are among the reasons why, in 1994, the Russell Sage Foundation inaugurated a major program of research on the nature, causes, and consequences of low-wage work and the prospects of low-wage workers. This initiative replaced a successful but more conventional program of research on poverty. It was called, rather grandly, *The Future of Work*. One of its key motivations was the need to understand how poorly educated, unskilled workers could cope with an economy in which most jobs were becoming technologically advanced, and therefore more demanding of cognitive power and refined skills.

This formulation was intended to call attention both to workers and to jobs, the natural subtext being that low-end jobs might be disappearing faster than low-skilled workers. This potential disparity presented the danger that low-wage workers could be stranded in an economy that had no use for them. The research mandate was interpreted quite broadly.

*The Future of Work* program was, as a matter of course, focused on the United States. It produced a large body of useful and original research, some of which was collected and summarized in the 2003 volume *Low-Wage America: How Employers Are Reshaping Opportunity in the Workplace*, edited by Eileen Appelbaum, Annette Bernhardt, and Richard Murnane. One of the refreshing aspects of these studies was precisely that the needs and capacities of employers shared the stage in the low-wage labor market with the abilities and motivations of workers.

One interesting hypothesis that emerged from this work was the notion that employers have significant discretion about the way they organize their use of low-skilled workers and the value they put on the continuity and productivity of their work force. The extreme versions came to be labeled "low-road" and "high-road" modes of organization. At the low-road extreme lie employers such as the typical car-wash, whose workers are regarded as casual labor, interchangeable parts that can be picked up off the street freely under normal labor-market conditions. There is no advantage in doing otherwise. At the other extreme are employers who regard their unskilled workers as an asset whose productive value can be increased by more training and longer attachment to the firm.

The point of this distinction was the belief that in some market situations both styles can be viable. An employer's place on the continuum is not uniquely determined by technology and the intensity of competition in the product market. Satisfactory profits can be earned by somewhat higher- and somewhat lower-road modes of organization; in some industries, examples of both can be found coexisting.

Of course, the nature of the technology and the competitive intensity in the industry are important determinants of labor-market outcomes. That is not in doubt. In some situations, however, there may be scope for several levels of wages and job quality for unskilled workers. It is important here to note that job quality covers much more than the current wage and benefits paid; it includes the length and slope of the internal wage scale, the degree of job security, the training offered and the possibilities of promotion within the firm, small creature comforts, the pace of the work itself, the autonomy and ergonomic character of the work, and so on. Each of these has a cost to the firm and a value to the workers, and the two are not always the same.

It hardly needs arguing that these elements of job quality can be important for the satisfaction and self-respect attached to a job. It then becomes important to the researcher to understand the broad factors that govern the typical choices made by employers. These may include historical precedents, legislation, the working of the educational system, collective bargaining, and other "institutional" biases.

At this stage of the argument, the advantages of a comparative cross-country study stand out. Most of those broadly institutional factors cannot be studied empirically within the United States because they change so slowly in time, and because there is not much locational variation. One cannot actually see them at work in a still snapshot. One can speculate and make thought-experiments, but that is not the same thing. So the idea sprouted within the Russell Sage Foundation in 2003 that it might be very useful to observe systematically how the fate of low-wage labor differs across a sample of European countries. Not any countries will do: one wants countries with somewhat different but not radically different political and institutional histories; but they must be at the same level of economic development as the United States if lessons are to be learned that could be useful in the United States. In the end, the countries chosen included the three indispensable large countries—France, Germany, and the United Kingdom—and two small northern European countries—Denmark and the Netherlands. The choice was consciously limited to Europe in order to avoid the complication of drastically different sociopolitical systems. A competition was held, and a local team selected for each of these five countries.

The planners of the project framed it in such a way that would sharpen the inferences that could be made from cross-country comparisons. Most centrally, five target jobs were chosen as objects of close study, the same five in each country. They were nurses' assistants and cleaners in hospitals, housekeepers in hotels, checkout clerks and related occupations in supermarkets and retail stores specializing in electrical goods, packagers, machine tenders and other unskilled occupations in two branches of food processing, namely confectionary and meat products, and low-skilled operators in call centers. (This last choice took advantage of an already ongoing international study of the call-center industry.) These are all low-wage jobs in the United States. The fact that some of them are not low-wage jobs in some of the five countries is an example of the value of cross-country comparisons. The simple fact invites, or rather compels, the question: Why not?

Each national team was asked to compile a statistical overview of low-wage work in its country, with special but not exclusive attention to the five target jobs. The team was also asked to complement the routine data with a survey of the historical, legislative, educational and other institutional infrastructure that is believed to underlie its own particular ways of dealing with low-end jobs and low-skilled workers. The final part of each country report is a series of case studies of each of the target jobs, including interviews with em-

ployers, managers, workers, union representatives and other participants. (When temporary work agencies were used to provide some or
all of the relevant workers, they were included in the interviews
wherever possible.) The national teams met and coordinated their
work in the course of the research. This book is the report of the
United Kingdom team.

There will be one more stage to complete the project. A six-coun-
try group of participants, including Americans, will prepare an ex-
plicitly comparative volume, job by job. They will try to fathom what
deeper attitudinal, institutional, and circumstantial factors might explain the sometimes dramatic differences in the way these six modern nations engage with the problem of low-wage work.

One big, somewhat unexpected, finding is the one mentioned in
the first paragraph of this introduction. The six countries differ substantially in the incidence of low-wage work. ("Incidence" is defined
as the fraction of all workers, in the country or in a specific sector,
who fall into the low-wage category.)

There is an interesting and important definitional issue that arises
immediately. Uniformly in Europe (and elsewhere), a low-wage
worker is anyone who earns less than two-thirds of the national median wage (usually the gross hourly wage, if only for data-availability
reasons). This obviously makes the incidence of low-wage work an
index of the inequality or dispersion of the wage distribution: multi-
plying or dividing everyone's wage by ten leaves the number of low-
wage workers unchanged. The same applies to the measurement of
poverty. In the United States, the poverty line is an absolute income.
It was initially chosen as an empirical compromise, never entirely
appropriate and less so as time passes, but nevertheless an absolute
income. The United States has no corresponding definition for low-
wage work, but the same approach could be taken. There are arguments to be made on both sides of this issue; for the purposes of this
project, the choice of a low-wage threshold makes little practical difference. We use the European definition because that is the way their
data are collected.

There is yet another practical reason to use the European definition. As noted, the two-thirds-of-median index simply reflects the degree of wage dispersion: a low incidence of low-wage work means a
relatively compressed wage distribution, at least in the lower tail.
This measure makes international comparisons more meaningful.
Comparing absolute real wages between the United States and other

countries is problematic because pensions, health care, payroll taxes, employer contributions and other such benefits and deductions are handled differently in different systems. Relative comparisons are subject to similar distortions, but considerably less so.

Here are the basic facts. In 2005, the incidence of low-wage work was 25 percent in the United States, 22.1 percent in the United Kingdom, 20.8 percent in Germany (2004), 18.2 percent in the Netherlands (2004), 12.7 percent in France (2002) and 8.5 percent in Denmark. The range is obviously very wide.

In a way, that is helpful, because figures like this can not be interpreted to the last decimal. Here is one interesting example of an unexpected twist. It turns out that the Dutch are the part-time champions among these countries, with a significantly larger fraction of part-time workers than elsewhere. This appears to be a voluntary choice, not something compelled by the unavailability of full-time work. Part-time workers tend to be paid lower hourly wages than full-time workers in the same or similar jobs, even in countries where it is against the law to discriminate against part-timers. The incidence measures given in the preceding paragraph are based on a head-count: 18 percent of all Dutch workers earn less than the low-wage threshold. One could with reason ask instead what fraction of the hours worked in the Netherlands falls into the low-wage category; the answer is about 16 percent. The fact that the hours-based incidence is lower would be common in all countries, but the difference is particularly large in the Netherlands.

A key issue is the degree of mobility out of low-wage work that characterizes each country's system. The seriousness of the "problem" turns almost entirely on the transitory nature of low-wage work. It is impossible to be precise about inter-country differences, because the data are sketchy and definitions vary. It is clear, however, that there are substantial differences among the countries, although mobility is fairly substantial everywhere, if only because younger workers eventually propel themselves into better jobs. The Danes appear to have the shortest residence times in low-wage work. For Americans the take-away lesson is that the self-image of an extremely mobile society is not valid, at least not in this respect.

Of course, there are many uniformities—often just what you would expect—among these countries in the pattern of low-wage work. The "concentration" of low-wage work in any subgroup of the population is defined as the incidence in that subgroup divided by the incidence among all workers. For instance, any subgroup with a higher incidence than the country at large will have a concentration index bigger than 1. This is the case for workers in the service sector of the economy, for women, for young people, for part-timers, and for those with little education. In most instances, the particular sectors we have picked out for study have a high concentration index; together, retail trade and "hotels and catering" have a concentration ratio of about 3 in the Netherlands. The categories mentioned obviously overlap, but the data do not permit us to zero in statistically on young part-time secondary-school-only women working in supermarkets. Nevertheless, the odds are very high that they fall into the low-wage category.

The cross-country differences are more interesting, however, because they at least offer the possibility that we can find explanations for them in the circumstances, institutions, attitudes and policies of these basically similar economies. It is important that these are basically similar economic systems with broadly similar labor markets. They differ in certain historically established social norms, institutions and policies. One can hope to figure out which of these fairly small differences underlie the observed variation in the conditions of low-wage work. This would be difficult or even meaningless if we were comparing radically different economic systems.

Here is one example of commonality that illustrates the point. In some of the target jobs, in several instances and several countries, there has been a noticeable increase in the intensity of competition in the relevant product market. Low-cost German chains compete with Dutch food retailers. Large food retailers, domestic and foreign, put pressure on meat processing and confectionary prices in every country. The spread of international hotel chains—along with the availability of exhaustive price comparisons on the internet—has made the hotel business more competitive. In all such instances, business firms respond to intensified competition by trying to lower their own unit costs (as well as by product differentiation, quality improvement, and other devices).

The urgent need to reduce costs seems almost invariably—though not exclusively—to involve particular pressure on the wages of low-skilled workers. It is not hard to understand why this should happen in every country, precisely because they are all advanced capitalist market economies. The main reason is that low-wage workers usually have very little "firm-specific human capital." That is to say, since they have few skills of any kind, they have few skills that are difficult to replace for the firm that employs them. If they quit in response to wage reductions, they can be replaced with little cost, especially in a slack labor market. Low-wage workers have few alternatives, so they cannot defend themselves well. For similar reasons, they have little political power and usually little clout with their trade unions, if they have any union protection at all. Firms seeking profit will respond similarly, though not identically in every detail. Country-specific institutions can modify the response, but not entirely.

A closely related common factor has to do with "flexibility." Partly because technology now permits it, and partly because a globalized market now demands it, business firms find that their level of production has to fluctuate seasonally, cyclically and erratically. Sometimes it is not so much the total but the composition of production that has to change, often with short notice. Under those circumstances, it is an advantage if the firm can vary its employment more or less at will; otherwise, underutilized labor constitutes an unproductive cost. The low-end labor force is likely to bear the brunt of this adjustment, for the same reasons already mentioned in connection with wage pressure. Low-wage workers cannot do much to defend themselves against or prepare themselves for these vicissitudes, other than to try for even lower-wage part-time jobs or to resort to public assistance.

There is always a possibility that observed cross-country variation in low-wage employment practices are somehow "natural," in the sense that they can be traced to underlying differences that were not chosen and could not be changed, such as geographical or topographical characteristics, resource availability, or perhaps even some irreversible bit of historical evolution. That does not seem to be what is happening in these six countries. In many instances, cross-country differences are the result of legislation, with minimum wage laws being an obvious example. A more unusual example, at least to Americans, is the fact that many European governments, such as those in France and the Netherlands, can and do extend certain collective bargaining agreements to cover employers and workers in the industry who were not parties to the bargaining itself. In this way, even comparatively small union density can lead to much broader coverage by union agreements.

This need not be an unalloyed benefit to workers. Companies have been known to arrange to bargain with a small, weak union and then press for the resulting favorable agreement to be generalized. But the practice may also reflect a desire by employers to eliminate large wage differentials as a factor in inter-firm competition. It is interesting that when the abolition of this practice of extending collective bargaining agreements was proposed in the Netherlands, the employers' federation opposed the proposal. It is a toss-up which event seems more outlandish to an American: the practice of mandatory extension or that employers should oppose abolishing it.

Explicit legislation is not the only source of institutional differences that affect the low-wage labor market. All sorts of behavioral norms, attitudes, and traditions on both sides of the labor market can have persistent effects. The country narratives describe many such influences. For example, the German report outlines a distinctive system of wage determination and labor relations, based on diversified high-quality, high-value-added industrial production, along with "patient," mostly bank-provided, capital, and participation of employee representatives in company supervisory boards.

This system may be coming to an end, undermined by international competition—especially from the ex-communist countries of eastern Europe, including the reunification of Germany—and shifts in public opinion and political power. It is still a matter of controversy among specialists whether the traditional system had become unsustainable or simply unsustained. The German "mini-job," low wage, frequently incurring lower non-wage employment costs in practice, and limited to very short hours per month, is an example of a device to encourage both demand and supply for certain kinds of low-wage work.

This introduction is not the place for a detailed description of each national system. The individual country narratives will provide that. It is important, however, to underline the fact that the components of each national system often hang together in some way. It may not be possible to single out one component and think: "That looks clever; why don't we try it in our country?" The German mini-job, for example, is occupied mostly by women, and may work the way it does because the social welfare apparatus in Germany is still organized around the notion of the single-breadwinner family. The concept of a labor relations "system" may suggest tighter-fitting than the facts justify; a word like "pattern" might be more accurate. But the basic point remains.

The four continental countries in the study correspond in a general way to the common notion of a "European social model" in contrast with the more individual-responsibility oriented approach of the United States. The post-Thatcher United Kingdom probably falls somewhere in between. It would be a bad mistake, however, to ignore the differences among Denmark, France, Germany, and the Netherlands. To do so would be to miss the variety of conditions for low-wage labor that is possible for advanced capitalist market economies. Only the briefest characterization is possible here, but the individual reports are quite complete.

The Danish "flexicurity" system has achieved the status of a buzzword. The idea is to allow wages and job quality to be determined in an unregulated labor market (except for considerations of health and safety, of course) but to combine this flexibility with a very generous safety net, so that "no Dane should suffer economic hardship." For this system to be workable, the rules of the safety net have to push most recipients into whatever jobs are available. Even so, the system is likely to be expensive. Apparently the *lowest* marginal income tax rate is 44 percent (which is higher than the *highest* rate in the U.S.). One would need to know more about the details of the tax system in order to understand the content of any such comparison, but the details are unlikely to reverse the presumption that Danes are less tax-averse than some others.

To describe the Danish labor market as "unregulated" means only that there is very little intervention by the government. In fact, the labor market is regulated through centralized negotiations between representatives of employers and employees, who have very wide scope. For example, there is no statutory minimum wage, but a minimum labor scale is negotiated by the "social partners." It (almost) goes without saying that there is some evasion of this scale in traditional low-wage sectors, including some covered in the case studies. One reason why this is tolerated is that many of the affected workers are young people, especially students, who are only engaged in low-wage part-time work as a transitory phase. Denmark is a country that is low on university enrollments but high on vocationally-oriented post-secondary, non-university education.

There is a neat contrast here with France, which lives up to its reputation as a rather bureaucratically organized society. As the French report says, "Low hourly wages are fixed in France—perhaps more than in any other country—at the political level, not through collective bargaining agreements, and these wage rates are set in a centralized, not decentralized, manner. Thus, the legal minimum wage plays a crucial role in France." Since 1970, the SMIC (minimum inter-branch growth wage) is indexed not only to inflation but also to the growth of overall productivity and wages. The intent was specifically to resist what was felt to be a tendency in the market toward excessive wage inequality.

The SMIC has been set at a fairly high level, and one consequence of this has been the disappearance of some unskilled jobs, to be replaced by unemployment (especially long-term unemployment), participation in active labor market policies, and withdrawal from the labor force. Other forces have been at work, however—urban land-use regulation in food retailing, for example—so the simple-minded causal connection between the SMIC and high unemployment is not exact. France is also distinguished by having a trade union movement that is rather strong at the national level, but has very little presence on the shop floor. This may account for some evasion of labor market regulations at the low end.

The low-wage labor market in the United Kingdom is especially interesting because it is an example of changes in institutions and outcomes brought about in a relatively short time by deliberate acts of policy. The Thatcher government chose as a matter of principle to weaken or eliminate preexisting supports for the occupants of low-quality jobs, and to undermine the ability of the trade union movement to compress the wage distribution. As a result, the incidence of low-wage work increased in the late 1970s and after. The Blair government, looking for a work-based solution to the problem of poverty, undertook measures to increase the supply of low-wage workers, but it also introduced a (fairly low) National Minimum Wage in 1999. The net outcome appears to have been a steady increase in the incidence of low-wage work from the late 1970s until the mid-1990s, and a leveling-off since then.

In effect, the United Kingdom has changed from a system rather like the other continental European countries to something much closer to the United States. The incidence of low-wage work has then followed the same trajectory. Of course, other economic factors, common to many countries, were also at work.

The Netherlands occupies a position somewhere between the Nordic model and the United States model, but not in a simple average sense. Many of the institutions are peculiarly Dutch; together they are described as the "Polder" model. One of its features is the important extent to which organizations representing employers, the government, and labor act jointly to regulate the labor market and much else, sometimes in a very detailed way. For instance, the minimum wage for young workers is substantially lower than for adults. The proliferation of part-time jobs, many of them occupied by students and young people, may be a consequence of this in part, though it may have other roots as well.

It is striking to an outsider that these tripartite institutions are more than merely regulatory. They are described as "deliberative," and apparently much of the serious public discussion of issues underlying socioeconomic policy takes place within them. This fact may make fairly tight regulation palatable to the Dutch public. The system has had considerable success; for example, the national unemployment rate fell from over 10 percent in 1984 to under 4 percent in 2001, when the widespread recession supervened. As will be seen in the Dutch report, however, it has its problems.

The purpose of these brief vignettes is definitely not to provide a summary of the pattern evolved in each of these countries with respect to low-wage job quality. That information is to be found in each of the separate country studies. The goal of this introduction is to illustrate the important general point that there are several viable systems of labor-market governance, including the mode of management of the low-wage labor market. The issue is not uniquely determined by the needs of a functioning market economy, or by technology, or by the imperatives of efficient organization. The system in place in each country has evolved in response to historical circumstances, cultural preferences, political styles and fashion in economic and social ideas. One cannot avoid noticing that relatively small countries, like Denmark and the Netherlands in our sample, and the other Nordic countries, Austria and perhaps Ireland outside it, seem more able than large countries to create and maintain the amount of trust that is needed for tripartite cooperation. This observation begs the question as to whether successful policy aimed at improving the relative status of low-wage workers may require a degree of social solidarity and trust that may be beyond larger, more diverse populations.

There are certainly many common influences as well: the response to intensified competition; the role of women, immigrants, and minorities; limitations on productivity; and so on. But there is no unique or best pattern. It even seems likely that the same "principles" of organization, applied in different institutional contexts, would eventuate in quite different practices. Some of this may emerge in the detailed comparative volume that is still to come.

The United Kingdom story is one of the influence of broad policy on wage inequality, and also the limitations of policy. Before the Thatcher era, the United Kingdom was more like the large continental European economies in its social model. The relevant Thatcher policies—weakening the labor unions, deregulating the labor market, and making unemployment insurance and other redistributive transfers less accessible and less generous—were followed by an increase in the incidence of low-wage work and a general widening of income inequality. This was not unexpected by observers.

The Blair "New Labour" government moved in the opposite direction in some respects. It instituted a modest National Minimum Wage, along with an in-work benefit loosely modeled on the earned income tax credit in the United States, though not so narrowly bound to families with children. Unions were allowed more scope in organizing and collective bargaining. On the other side, Blair's emphasis on tying benefits to work, something like welfare reform in the United States, had the effect of increasing the absolute and relative supply of potentially low-wage labor. The net result was little, if any, reduction in the incidence of low-wage work. There must also have been downward pressure on the relative wage of low-end workers. In these key respects, the United Kingdom is now much more like the United States than the Continent. One possible inference is that it takes drastic shifts in policy to create meaningful changes in these labor market characteristics; Thatcher certainly acted more drastically than Blair did.

It is very noticeable that the United Kingdom, unlike the United States, has a lower level of labor productivity than the other large European countries. This helps to explain its lower average real wage, but there is no arithmetical reason why a lower average wage should go along with wider wage dispersion in the lower tail.

The United Kingdom study suggests, however, an indirect mechanism through which generally lower productivity could reinforce and sustain a drift to predominantly low-wage work. The existence of low average productivity—or of the underlying forces that push in that direction—could induce a substantial fraction of British industry to adopt a pattern of production that focuses more on lower-quality, medium- to low-technology sectors and products than on more demanding, high-quality, high-tech sectors and products, whether material goods or services. The causal circle is closed if that pattern of employment then discourages workers from acquiring higher-level skills and also discourages employers from providing training aimed at raising skill levels.

It is always a difficult question whether low productivity and low wages inhere more in the worker or in the job. The United Kingdom may be a case in which the answer is "both," each deficiency reinforcing the other. Existing skill levels, adaptive business strategies, and the educational system may interact to create and sustain a sector that practices the opposite of the German system of diversified, high-quality production. This is a more subtle version of multiple equilibria than the simple high road/low road dichotomy.

The United Kingdom study notes that while there is some mobility out of low-wage work, there are also signs of a tendency among many workers to stay in that category for long periods. The team also observes what they call a low pay/no pay cycle, in which workers alternate between periods of low-wage work and inactivity. These phases also have the potential to reinforce each other, and perhaps also to validate the strategy of low-complexity, low-value-added production.

The report also raises the question of whether the United Kingdom could successfully disengage from this pattern of production and employment. One speculation is that a revived trade union movement might be able to restore the earlier degree of wage compression and thus induce industry to aim at higher-quality production. But such a revival is unlikely to happen autonomously. In the meanwhile, low-end labor in the United Kingdom is increasingly exposed to competition from immigrants from eastern Europe, where wage levels are even lower; these immigrants can easily fill the jobs available in low-complexity production. The difficulty is that the low-productivity, low-complexity, low-wage pattern is one equilibrium situation, even if not the only possible one.

# CHAPTER 1

# Low-Paid Work in the United Kingdom: An Overview

*Geoff Mason, Ken Mayhew, and Matthew Osborne*

During the nineteen years of Conservative government (1979 to 1997), the United Kingdom experienced rising levels of income disparities and poverty and a growing proportion of low-paid workers. With an economic approach that shunned labor market regulations and trade unions, Britain appeared to be shifting further away from the "European social model" and toward the more free market approach of the United States. With the election of the New Labour government in 1997, the reduction of the extremely high levels of household poverty (especially child poverty) was given a priority, alongside the provision of a floor to pay rates at the bottom end of the labor market through the introduction and subsequent annual uprating of the national minimum wage (NMW).

Yet, if we take a standard definition of "low pay"—gross hourly earnings below two-thirds of the median hourly wage for all employees—international comparisons suggest that its incidence in the United Kingdom is still one of the highest in Europe. In 2005 an estimated 22.1 percent of employees in the United Kingdom fell below this low pay threshold, not far above the 20.8 percent incidence of low pay in Germany in 2004, but high compared to 17.6 percent in the Netherlands in 2005, 12.7 percent in France in 2002, and 8.5 percent in Denmark in 2005.[1] Furthermore, it is striking that, in spite of the NMW and government efforts to reduce household poverty, this high incidence of low pay has remained unaltered for the last decade. As shown in figure 1.1, the proportion of the United Kingdom's workforce that was low-paid rose sharply between the late 1970s and the mid-1990s; since that period, it has continued at a level that is far higher than thirty years ago. Though the proportion of women who are low-paid is still significantly higher than the proportion of men, much of the increase in the incidence of low pay reflects the changing fortunes of male workers.

Figure 1.1   Proportion of United Kingdom Workforce that Falls Below the Low-Pay Threshold, 1975 to 2005

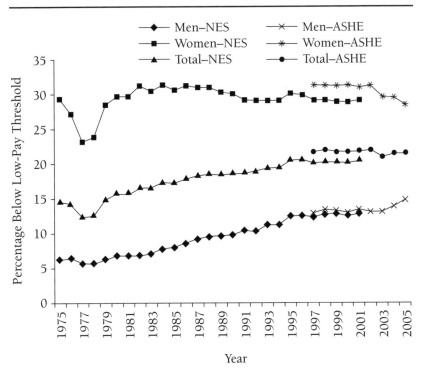

*Sources:* New Earnings Survey (NES) Panel Dataset (1975 to 2001) and Annual Survey of Hours and Earnings (ASHE) (1997 to 2005).

*Notes:* The discontinuity and overlap in the time series reflects the introduction in 2004 of the Annual Survey of Hours and Earnings, which differs from the former New Earnings Survey, in several respects, in particular, in improved coverage of low-paid employees. The ASHE estimates for 1997 to 2003 are based on a reworking of NES data for those years using ASHE imputation and weighting procedures. However, the 1997 to 2003 ASHE estimates do not take account of the improved coverage of low-paid employees.

For further details, see http://www.statistics.gov.uk/statbase/Product.asp?vlnk =13291&More=Y.

In this context, an investigation of the employer strategies, labor market institutions, and government policies that have contributed to low pay in the United Kingdom's economy is long overdue. This book starts with a brief overview of the distinctive features of the United Kingdom labor market as compared to other countries and of the evolution of its pay distribution over the last thirty years before considering the links between low pay and household poverty. In chapter 2, we explore the determinants of low pay and analyze the impact of United Kingdom labor market institutions and policies on the number, composition, and nature of low-wage jobs in Britain. We then go on to present a series of workplace case studies that allow us to investigate the relationships between the competitive environment, the institutional framework, and the quality of employment in depth. Chapters 3 through 7 focus in turn on six occupational groups that are potentially vulnerable to low pay: hotel room attendants, retail sales assistants, hospital cleaners and nursing auxiliaries, food-processing operators, and call center agents. Chapter 8 summarizes our main findings and assesses their implications for policymakers in the United Kingdom.

## THE UNITED KINGDOM'S ECONOMY AND LABOR MARKET IN COMPARATIVE PERSPECTIVE

At the macroeconomic level, the United Kingdom has performed well on some dimensions relative to other industrialized economies in recent years. Of the six countries compared in table 1.1, it recorded the second-highest growth rates in GDP between 1993 and 2005 (row 2), and its unemployment rate in 2005 was the lowest of the six countries, though very close to those in Denmark and the Netherlands (row 3). However, in spite of some improvement in relative labor productivity performance over this period, average labor productivity per hour worked in Britain remains well below that of the other five countries (row 1). Growth accounting estimates suggest that the proximate causes of this productivity gap include lower levels of physical capital–intensity in Britain than is typically found in the United States and continental Europe and deficiencies in measured skills relative to countries such as Germany (O'Mahony and de Boer 2002).

The United Kingdom has seen a steady growth in participation levels in employment over the last decade, with the overall employment-population (EPOP) ratio up by almost four percentage points between 1994 and 2005. However, it was not alone in this trend: the Netherlands, France, and Denmark also showed significant growth over this period (row 4). The 2005 EPOP ratios of the six countries cover a fairly large range, with Denmark at 76 percent, the United Kingdom, the United States, and the Netherlands at 72 to 73 percent,

Table 1.1  Indicators of Macroeconomic and Labor Market Performance, Denmark, France, Germany, Netherlands, the United Kingdom and the United States, Various Years

| | | Year | Denmark | France | Germany | Nether-lands[a] | United Kingdom | United States |
|---|---|---|---|---|---|---|---|---|
| 1 | Average labor productivity per worker (index numbers: U.S. = 100) | 2002 | — | 88 | 80 | 78 | 74 | 100 |
| 2 | Average labor productivity (per hour worked) (U.S. = 100) | 2002 | — | 103 | 101 | 106 | 79 | 100 |
| | Average annual growth in GDP | 1993 to 2005 | 2.5% | 2.1% | 1.5% | 2.4% | 2.9% | 3.3% |
| 3 | Standardized unemployment rate as a percentage of civilian labor force | 1994 | 7.7 | 11.7 | 8.3 | 6.8 | 9.3 | 6.1 |
| | | 2005 | 4.8 | 9.5 | 9.5 | 4.8 | 4.7 | 5.1 |
| 4 | Employment/population ratio, persons age fifteen to sixty-four | 1994 | 72 | 58 | 65 | 64 | 69 | 72 |
| | | 2005 | 76 | 62 | 66 | 72 | 73 | 72 |
| 5 | Employment/population ratio, men age fifteen to twenty-four | 1994 | 65 | 25 | 54 | 56 | 61 | 61 |
| | | 2005 | 66 | 29 | 45 | 64 | 60 | 55 |
| 6 | Employment/population ratio, men age twenty-five to fifty-four | 1994 | 86 | 86 | 87 | 88 | 84 | 87 |
| | | 2005 | 88 | 87 | 84 | 89 | 88 | 87 |
| 7 | Employment/population ratio, men age fifty-five to sixty-four | 1994 | 60 | 39 | 48 | 41 | 57 | 63 |
| | | 2005 | 67 | 44 | 54 | 56 | 66 | 67 |
| 8 | Employment/population ratio, women age fifteen to twenty-four | 1994 | 59 | 19 | 49 | 55 | 57 | 55 |
| | | 2005 | 58 | 23 | 40 | 63 | 57 | 53 |
| 9 | Employment/population ratio, women age twenty-five to fifty-four | 1994 | 75 | 67 | 65 | 59 | 69 | 72 |
| | | 2005 | 80 | 73 | 71 | 74 | 75 | 72 |
| 10 | Employment/population ratio, women age fifty-five to sixty-four | 1994 | 40 | 28 | 25 | 18 | 39 | 47 |
| | | 2005 | 53 | 38 | 38 | 33 | 48 | 55 |

| | | Year | | | | | | |
|---|---|---|---|---|---|---|---|---|
| 11 | Part-time employment as a proportion of total employment, men only | 1994 | 10 | 5 | 3 | 11 | 7 | 9 |
| | | 2005 | 12 | 5 | 7 | 15 | 10 | 8 |
| 12 | Part-time employment as a proportion of total employment, women only | 1994 | 26 | 25 | 28 | 55 | 41 | 20 |
| | | 2005 | 25 | 23 | 39 | 61 | 39 | 18 |
| 13 | Average annual hours actually worked, per person in employment | 1994 | 1,494 | 1,676 | 1,543 | 1,362 | 1,737 | 1,842 |
| | | 2005 | 1,551 | 1,535 | 1,435 | 1,367 | 1,672 | 1,804 |
| 14 | Long term-unemployment (six months or more) as a percentage of total unemployment | 1994 | 54% | 62% | 64% | 78% | 63% | 20% |
| | | 2005 | 44 | 61 | 71 | 60 | 38 | 20 |
| 15 | Long term-unemployment (twelve months or more) as a percentage of total unemployment | 1994 | 32 | 39 | 44 | 49 | 45 | 12 |
| | | 2005 | 26 | 43 | 54 | 40 | 22 | 12 |
| 16 | Initial net replacement rate (unemployment benefit as a percentage of net earnings in work)[b] | 2004 | 70 | 75 | 69 | 74 | 54 | 54 |
| 17 | Unemployment insurance benefit duration (months, equivalent initial rate) | 2004 | — | 30 | 12 | 24 | 6 | 6 |
| 18 | Average of net replacement rates over sixty months of unemployment (percentage of net earnings in work)[c] | 2004 | 70 | 57 (+4) | 66 (−3) | 66 | 53 (−1) | 36 (−6) |
| 19 | Indices of strictness of employment protection legislation:[d] Protection of regular workers against (individual) dismissal | 2003 | 0.61 | 1.03 | 1.12 | 1.27 | 0.46 | 0.07 |

# Table 1.1 (Continued)

| | Year | Denmark | France | Germany | Netherlands[a] | United Kingdom | United States |
|---|---|---|---|---|---|---|---|
| 20 Specific requirements for collective dismissal | 2003 | 0.65 | 0.35 | 0.63 | 0.50 | 0.48 | 0.48 |
| 21 Regulation on temporary forms of employment | 2003 | 0.57 | 1.51 | 0.73 | 0.49 | 0.16 | 0.10 |
| Summary (0–6 scale) | 2003 | 1.83 | 2.89 | 2.48 | 2.26 | 1.10 | 0.65 |

*Sources*: 1: Artus and Cette (2004); 2: OECD, *Economic Outlook* 79 (May 2006); 3–15: OECD, *Employment Outlook* (2006); 16–18: OECD, *Benefits and Wages: OECD Indicators* (2004a); 19–21: OECD, *Employment Outlook* (2004b).

[a] Netherlands data on employment/population ratios in the later year refer to 2004, not 2005.

[b] Initial net replacement rate is an average of cases of a single person and a one-earner married couple, an average of cases with no children and with two children, and an average of cases with previous earnings in work 67 percent of average production worker (APW) level, 100 percent of APW level, and 150 percent of APW level. Typical-case calculations relate to a forty-year-old worker who has been making contributions continuously since age eighteen. Net income out of work includes means-tested benefits (housing benefits are calculated assuming housing costs are 20 percent of APW earnings) where relevant but not noncategorical social assistance benefits. Taxes payable are determined in relation to annualized benefit values (monthly values multiplied by twelve), even if the maximum benefit duration is shorter than twelve months. See OECD, *Benefits and Wages* (2004a) for further details.

[c] As described in note b, except that the net replacement rates are averaged over five years of unemployment, the three previous earnings levels considered are 67 percent, 100 percent, and 150 percent of the average wage (all workers), and noncategorical social assistance benefits are included in out-of-work net income. Values in brackets are percentage-point changes between 1995 and 2004.

[d] Assessed on a 0 to 6 point scale where higher scores indicate a higher degree of strictness of employment protection legislation.

Germany at 66 percent, and France at 62 percent. The United Kingdom has relatively high rates of participation by older men and women (rows 7 and 10) and by the younger age group (rows 5 and 8). Some 39 percent of employed women in the United Kingdom worked part-time in 2005, a rate that was substantially higher than in the United States (18 percent) and that was equaled or exceeded only by Germany and the Netherlands among the European countries under consideration.

Where the United Kingdom's labor market performance has been distinctive in the last decade has been the substantial decline in unemployment, down from 9.3 percent in 1994 to 4.7 percent in 2005 (row 3). Over the same period, long-term unemployment rates (unemployed for six to twelve months or more) have also fallen to levels not found in any of the four continental European countries, though they are still not as low as in the United States (rows 14 and 15). Significantly, this decline in unemployment rates has coincided with relatively low levels of price inflation. Stephen Nickell and Glenda Quintini (2002) attribute a large part of the apparent reduction in the equilibrium rate of unemployment (the rate consistent with stable inflation) to labor market reforms initiated by Conservative governments in the 1980s. These included legislation and other developments that reduced the bargaining power and organizing capability of trade unions. At the same time, changes in the social security system reduced the ratio of benefits to earnings quite substantially over time and tightened rules on the duration of benefits for those thought capable of working. These changes in the administration of social security were consolidated and in some cases extended by subsequent governments.

Many features of the United Kingdom labor market that are relevant to performance on unemployment emerge clearly in recent cross-country comparisons. For example, the Organization for Economic Cooperation and Development (OECD) estimates of the ratio of unemployment benefits to previous wage incomes after tax (the "net replacement rate") suggest that Britain is now at parity with the United States on this measure and well below any of the four continental European countries (table 1.1, rows 16 to 18). The relative fluidity of the United Kingdom labor market is also shown by OECD measures of the tightness of employment protection legislation (for example, regulation on temporary forms of employment), which show Britain to be closer to the United States on this dimension than to most continental European countries (rows 19 to 22).

In short, over the last decade the United Kingdom labor market has seen sustained growth in employment rates and a substantial decline in the level of unemployment. The growth in employment rates has been equaled or exceeded in some other parts of Europe, but Britain stands out for its sharp reduction in unemployment rates. In addition, cross-country evidence suggests that Britain now tends to resemble the United States rather than continental Europe in providing economic incentives for individuals to take up paid work at the bottom end of the labor market. These developments may well have contributed to the continued high incidence of low pay in the United Kingdom labor market. To assess their relative importance, we now briefly review trends in labor force participation, wage inequality, and the policy and institutional changes within the United Kingdom that have helped foster the growth of low-paid work in the last thirty years.

## TRENDS IN LABOR FORCE PARTICIPATION

On the face of it, employment, unemployment, and inactivity rates among the working-age population in the United Kingdom are much the same today as they were thirty years ago (figure 1.2). However, these figures conceal marked differences in the ways in which male and female labor force participation rates have evolved over this period. While the male inactivity rate increased from 16 percent in 1971 to 29 percent in 2004, the female inactivity rate declined from 55 percent to 44 percent (figures 1.3 and 1.4). From about 1970 until 1993, there was a particularly noteworthy decline in the participation rates of men age fifty or older, although this trend has since reversed (Hotopp 2005).

As shown in figure 1.2, the overall unemployment rate fell throughout the late 1980s until it reached 6 percent in 1990. It then rose to reach a new peak of 10 percent in 1993. Since then, it has fallen consistently until the present-day levels of just under 5 percent. What was unusual about the recession in the early 1990s was that it hit men particularly hard. During the recession in the early 1980s, male and female unemployment rates were broadly similar. During the early 1990s recession, the unemployment rate for women rose only slightly, from 4 percent to 5 percent. That for men, however, soared, from 5 percent to 12 percent.

These higher rates of male unemployment appear to have con-

## Figure 1.2 Employment, Unemployment, and Inactivity Rates for All Persons in the United Kingdom Age Sixteen and Over, 1971 to 2004

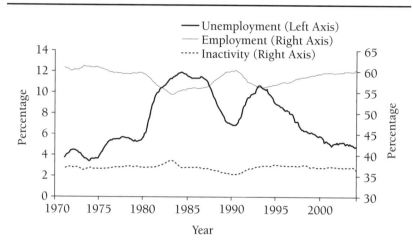

*Source:* "Labour Force Survey Summary by Sex," in Labour Market Statistics First Release Historical Supplement, accessed at http://www.statistics.gov.uk/OnlineProducts/LMS_FR_HS.asp.

## Figure 1.3 Employment, Unemployment, and Economic Inactivity Rates for All Women in the United Kingdom Age Sixteen and Over, 1971 to 2004

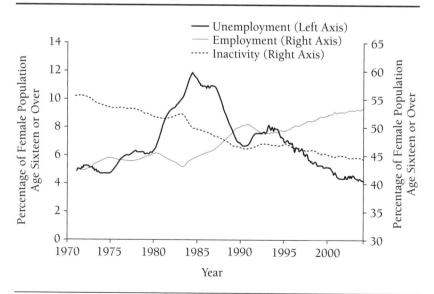

*Source:* Office of National Statistics (ONS).

Figure 1.4  Employment, Unemployment, and Economic
Inactivity Rates for All Men in the United
Kingdom Age Sixteen and Over, 1971 to 2004

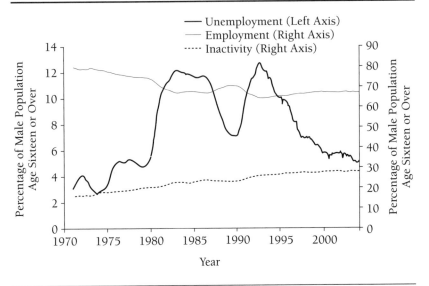

*Source:* Office of National Statistics (ONS).
*Notes:* All rates are seasonally adjusted. Unemployment is calculated on the International Labor Office (ILO) measure. Post-1992, the ILO measure was produced from the Labour Force Survey (LFS); pre-1992, the data have been estimated by ONS (see Lindsay 2005).

tributed to higher rates of male inactivity in subsequent years, in part because of the "scarring" effects of non-employment caused by factors such as depreciating skills, increasing irrelevance of experience, and loss of motivation (Arulampalam, Gregg, and Gregory 2001). Accompanying these developments was a fall in the relative demand for less-educated labor over the last twenty years (Berman, Bound, and Machin 1998). Giulia Faggio and Stephen Nickell (2003) estimate that among prime-age men (ages twenty-five to fifty-four), the less-educated are three or four times more likely than other men to be inactive. Indeed, 50 to 60 percent of inactive men in this age group are in the bottom skill quartile.

At the same time, however, female inactivity has declined, reflecting in particular the growth of part-time employment among married women (Robinson 2003). Some of the factors underlying this trend are an increase in demand for low-skilled workers in the service industries that have traditionally employed more women than manufacturing industries, coupled with shortcomings in the availability of child care, which make it difficult for women with children to combine full-time work with domestic responsibilities (see chapter 2).

Inactivity is now heavily associated with chronic illness or disability. The number of people reporting this condition is now substantially higher than in the 1970s, and the proportion of this group who are inactive has increased by three- or fourfold. Faggio and Nickell (2003) cite evidence that during the 1980s and the early 1990s the Employment Service tended to move those with a chronic illness or disability on to invalidity benefit if finding a job for them proved difficult. Once an individual was on invalidity benefit (now incapacity benefit), there was, until recently, less incentive to rejoin the labor market, since incapacity benefits were somewhat more generous than benefits for the unemployed.[2]

Since 1993, however, the flow from inactivity into employment has risen above the flow out of inactivity and into unemployment (McIntyre 2002). In part this is explained by increasing tightness in the labor market. At the same time, the shift toward in-work benefits has been designed to discourage economic inactivity (see chapter 2).

Accompanying these trends in United Kingdom labor force participation is substantial inequality in the distribution of work across households. In 2002 an estimated one in six households of working age were "workless"—that is, they had no employed adult present. This is a much higher proportion than in the United States, but on a par with Germany and France (Gregg and Wadsworth 2003).

## EARNINGS INEQUALITY AND UNITED KINGDOM LABOR MARKET INSTITUTIONS SINCE THE 1970s

As in other countries, low pay in the United Kingdom is strongly associated with female employment, part-time work, and low-skilled occupations. However, in chapter 2 we show that during the period when the incidence of low pay consistently increased (between the early 1980s and mid-1990s), the proportion of low-paid rose among males, among full-time workers, and in all age groups (including prime-age workers). This development was part of a general increase in earnings inequality in the United Kingdom economy during this same period. As shown in table 1.2, during the 1980s and the first half of the 1990s, the 90/10 pay ratio grew much faster than the 75/25 ratio, suggesting that much of the increase in inequality was accounted for by changes at the very top and bottom ends of the distribution. From the mid-1990s, levels of earnings inequality increased at a much slower rate, culminating in a more or less stable picture over the last five years.

The increase in inequality in the United Kingdom has been variously ascribed to the increase in labor market flexibility achieved through institutional reforms during the Thatcher era in the 1980s (Prasad 2002), to the impact of global trade, and to skill-biased technical change (De Santis 2003). These are not mutually exclusive explanations, nor do they provide an exhaustive list of possibilities. Some argue that there has been an increase in the relative demand for more-educated workers (Machin 2003) and that the increase in this demand has outstripped increases in supply, reflected in the rise in educational pay differentials. However, other evidence suggests that there are growing levels of overqualification within the workforce (see Felstead, Gallie, and Green 2002).

Eswar Prasad (2002) has found that much of the increase in inequality over the last twenty-five years reflected an increase in within-group inequality (such as within-gender, -occupation, or -industry groups).[3] Inequality was much higher within nonmanual occupations (high-skill managerial and professional workers, low-skill nonmanual) than among manual occupations (skilled manual, unskilled manual), perhaps because the lingering effects of higher unionization rates among manual workers has kept wages more compressed in these occupational groups. Another, more likely, explanation is that nonmanual groups span a larger range of occupations.

The change in within-group inequality was markedly lower for women than men. However, the overall change in inequality was similar for men and women, suggesting that shifts in the occupational or sectoral distributions of employment accounted for more of the growth in inequality among women. For both sexes, a substantial proportion of the increase in inequality was accounted for by a shift toward sectors with higher within-group earnings dispersion. For example, over the last twenty-five years there has been a marked shift in employment from manufacturing to services, where there is greater wage dispersion. On the basis of such evidence, Roberto De Santis

Table 1.2  Percentile Differentials of Gross Hourly Wages,
            1976 to 2004

|      | 90/10 | 90/50 | 50/10 | 75/25 | 75/50 | 50/25 |
|------|-------|-------|-------|-------|-------|-------|
| 1976 | 2.92  | 1.77  | 1.65  | 1.69  | 1.31  | 1.29  |
| 1981 | 3.13  | 1.88  | 1.66  | 1.79  | 1.36  | 1.32  |
| 1986 | 3.30  | 1.95  | 1.69  | 1.88  | 1.39  | 1.35  |
| 1991 | 3.62  | 2.06  | 1.76  | 1.98  | 1.45  | 1.37  |
| 1996 | 3.89  | 2.15  | 1.81  | 2.08  | 1.48  | 1.41  |
| 2001 | 3.94  | 2.20  | 1.79  | 2.12  | 1.51  | 1.41  |
| 1998 | 3.99  | 2.17  | 1.84  | 2.17  | 1.51  | 1.43  |
| 2001 | 4.03  | 2.21  | 1.83  | 2.18  | 1.52  | 1.43  |
| 2004 | 4.01  | 2.23  | 1.80  | 2.19  | 1.53  | 1.43  |

Sources: Derived from New Earnings Survey (NES) (1976 to 2001) and the Annual
Survey of Hours and Earnings (ASHE) (1998, 2001, and 2004). See notes to table 1.1
for further details of these surveys.

(2003) suggests that *sector-biased*, rather than skill-biased, technical
change can be considered a significant contributor to the increasing
premium attached to many educational qualifications.

However, even if sector- and skill-biased technical change can be
shown to be important in the United Kingdom, the question as to why
their effects on wage inequality were so much stronger there than in
many continental European nations remains unanswered. That answer does not seem to lie in a relatively slow increase in the supply of
skills in the United Kingdom, since the late 1980s saw a rapid transition from elite higher education to mass higher education (Mason
2002). As we now go on to show, the most likely explanation is that
the impact of sector- and skill-biased technical change occurred at a
time when the influence of the institutions that had traditionally encouraged wage compression was sharply declining and the various
government policies that had played a similar role were eroding.

As discussed in chapter 2, union density in the United Kingdom
reached its peak in 1979, after which there was a sustained fall, accompanied by a decline in the proportion of the workforce covered by
collective bargaining. Today, even where firms recognize unions for
bargaining purposes, the balance of power has moved significantly
against unions. By 2004 negotiation over pay took place in only 18
percent of workplaces. Not only did trade unions become much less
powerful, but the structure of collective bargaining changed in the

private sector, which now accounts for a much larger proportion of total employment as a consequence of the privatizations of the Thatcher and post-Thatcher eras. Though local bargaining (at the company and even the establishment level) increased in importance through the post–World War II years, multi-employer collective agreements, which set minimum terms and conditions for an industry or sector, were still a feature of many industries and sectors at the end of the 1970s, particularly in manufacturing. This higher-level bargaining disappeared almost entirely in the 1980s. Today pay-setting in the private sector occurs at the company or establishment level, and indeed, a large proportion of employment contracts are now "individualized"—that is, they are determined mainly through negotiations between individuals and their employers. In the public sector, there is also some evidence of more localized and individualized pay-setting, though important recent changes in local government and health care have contributed to a consolidation of national coordinated bargaining (see chapter 5).

Compared with its continental neighbors, Britain never had a highly regulated labor market. However, the Conservative governments of 1979 to 1997 loosened what regulation there was. This was heralded as an important element of Thatcher's supply-side revolution. The stress was on enhancing "static efficiency" (the effectiveness of existing factors of production) by reducing elements of monopoly power, taking steps to improve information and mobility, and removing as much red tape as possible. Unfair dismissal and redundancy legislation had been a relatively recent introduction, starting in the mid-1960s. The Thatcher and Major governments significantly loosened such provisions. Various statutory forms of low pay protection, details of which are given in chapter 2, had a longer history. Virtually all such forms of protection had been removed by the time the Labour government entered office in 1997. Though there were many reasons for union decline, a contribution was made by sustained legislation. This legislation made it more difficult to recruit and retain members, to establish and sustain bargaining relationships with employers, and to start and pursue industrial action.

The post-1997 "New Labour" government continued the rhetoric of free and competitive labor markets and of "flexibility"—functional, temporal, and numerical. New legislation has provided small boosts to unions' ability to obtain recognition from employers and to negotiate with them on some issues, but the industrial relations framework created by previous Conservative governments remains essentially intact (chapter 2). However, as noted earlier, some important New Labour policy initiatives have affected labor markets. The NMW was introduced in 1999. A welfare-to-work policy was also unveiled in the form of a series of "New Deals" for different groups, the two most important of which were for the young unemployed and for long-term unemployed adults. Essentially the New Deals made social security benefits more conditional on actively seeking ways out of unemployment, whether into a regular or subsidized job or through a variety of work experience schemes or education and training. Failure to respond positively to guidance and then to offers of labor market opportunities could lead to the loss of social security benefits.

The New Deal policy seems to have had two rationales. The first was that even if initially there was no net increase in jobs and therefore no net reduction in unemployment, the durational distribution of the unemployed would change, with the proportion of the long-term unemployed falling and the proportion of the short-term unemployed rising. As shown in table 1.1, this objective has largely been achieved. It was argued that, since those who had not been unemployed for long could put more pressure on the real wages of those with jobs than could those who had been unemployed for longer, this "churning" would discipline the labor market in such a way as to contribute eventually to a fall in the non-accelerating inflation rate of unemployment.[4]

The second rationale was that it was important to get the unemployed back into contact with the world of work, even if this meant that they received very modest pay. If, for some individuals, low pay led to poverty, this could be tackled with generous in-work benefits. Thus, the period since 1997 has seen a major change in emphasis within the social security system, with more stress placed on in-work benefits and less on out-of-work benefits (chapter 2). This shift has been accompanied by government efforts to promote paid work and to reduce the number of workless households, with the stated belief that work is "the best form of welfare" for people of working age (DSS 1998). Given that other forms of low pay protection had been abolished in the United Kingdom, the NMW was expected to provide some safeguard against the worst kinds of employer exploitation and to prevent employers from reducing the wages of employees who were eligible for top-ups through the social security and tax systems. Great faith was also placed in improving literacy, numeracy, and other basic skills, whether in the formal education system or through workplace training; a variety of training and education subsidies have been made available for both workers and employers. For the unemployed, renewing contact with the world of work and upgrading one's skills were seen as the routes to improving one's longer-term labor market prospects.

In the event, after a modest start, the NMW was uprated faster than the growth in average earnings between 2003 and 2006 and has begun to have an impact for the first time on the wage-setting behavior of large employers in sectors such as retailing (see chapter 4). The overall impact of the NMW on the incidence of low pay since 1999, however, seems to have been partly offset by the substantial growth in low-paid employment, which other elements of New Labour policy, such as in-work benefits, have been designed to encourage (chapter 2). At the same time, the government's efforts to upgrade the skills of low-paid workers have met with mixed success. Though there is evidence that average school attainment has been improving in recent years, a large proportion of school leavers in the United Kingdom still display deficiencies in numeracy and literacy skills. Similarly, the various schemes for adults already in the labor market have only had modest success (see chapter 2).

This perspective on New Labour policies helps to explain why the rise in the incidence of low pay in the United Kingdom economy has been halted since the mid-1990s but not forced into reverse, and why the incidence of low pay has stabilized at a historically high level. Other factors contributing to this state of affairs are covered in the remainder of this book, including the evolution of employers' human resource strategies in the context of market competition, the growth of outsourcing, changes in the labor supply (such as the increased availability of migrant labor), and continuing weaknesses in vocational education and training. Where New Labour has been more successful in reversing the impact of previous Conservative governments on living standards is in reducing household poverty. However, as we go on to show, measures adopted in the context of the United Kingdom to help reduce household poverty do not necessarily help to reduce the incidence of low-paid work.

## THE "DISCONNECT" BETWEEN LOW PAY AND HOUSEHOLD POVERTY

In the 1980s and early 1990s, the rapid growth in earnings inequality and a sharp increase in the number of workless households in the United Kingdom led to a substantial increase in household poverty and, in particular, child poverty (Burgess and Propper 1999; Dickens and Ellwood 2003; Nickell 2004). In 1999, less than two years after coming to power, Prime Minister Tony Blair committed the government to eradicating child poverty by 2020, and this announcement was followed by interim targets to cut child poverty by one-quarter by 2004 and by one-half by 2010. Among the key policies intended to achieve this objective were those described earlier: the minimum wage combined with tougher administration of out-of-work benefits and increased provision of in-work benefits to those who needed them.

Using a standard measure of household poverty—defined as the proportion of households with net equivalent incomes before housing costs that are below 60 percent of the median for all households[5]—the new policy regime has contributed to a fall in relative poverty: the proportion of individuals living in poor households declined from 18.4 percent in 1996–1997 to 16.1 percent in 2004–2005, with most of this reduction occurring since 1999–2000. The proportion of children in poverty also fell during this period, from 33.3 percent to 27.2 percent, although this reduction was not sufficient to meet the government's target of reducing child poverty by one-quarter by 2004–2005 (Brewer et al. 2006).

However, there are a number of reasons why New Labour's focus on poverty reduction could not be expected to contribute to a lower incidence of low-paid work. First, household poverty is still a particular problem for workless households rather than for households that contain at least one adult who works.[6] Given the low skills and lack of recent work experience of most currently unemployed or inactive people, policies designed to encourage more of them to take up paid employment almost presuppose that the jobs in question will be relatively low-skilled and low-paid in nature.

Second, there is only a very partial overlap between household poverty and low-paid work in the United Kingdom. On the one hand, the "working poor"—that is, households classified as poor by the definition used here, but with at least one member working—accounted for 57 percent of all poor households in 2004–2005 (DWP 2006, table 5.4). Almost half of the 3 million children in poverty live in households that have a working member (Kenway 2005). On the other hand, the low-paid workers in these poor households represent only a small proportion of all low-paid workers. Using data from the Family Expenditure Survey, Jane Millar and Karen Gardiner (2004) estimate that out of approximately 5.4 million low-paid workers in Britain in 2000–2001, 14 percent were living in poor households, up from 11 percent in 1995 and 3 to 4 percent in the 1970s and early 1980s.[7] This leaves 86 percent of low-paid workers in Britain who were not living in household poverty. The prime reason for this "disconnect" between low pay and poverty is that many low-paid individuals avoid poverty by living in households with access to additional incomes (through working partners, parents, and/or adult children) or by securing access to additional benefits or tax credits (Millar and Gardiner 2004).

As the case studies reported in this book show, living on low pay is difficult even for households that are not officially classified as "poor." This is particularly the case for low-paid workers who have financial dependents or who wish to purchase a house. Furthermore, there is strong evidence of a cycle of "low pay, no pay" in the United Kingdom labor market whereby many low-paid workers are likely to find themselves moving temporarily into and out of paid employment, with damaging consequences for their lifetime earnings capabilities (chapter 2) and their ability to avoid poverty in old age.

Therefore, pointing out the limited overlap between official definitions of low pay and household poverty is not intended to dismiss the social problems attached to low-paid work. Rather, it is important to identify this disconnect in order to better understand why the incidence of low-paid work has remained at historically high levels under a New Labour policy regime that has focused on reducing household poverty.

Another important implication of the disconnect is that employers in the United Kingdom have access to a large pool of employees who can survive on low wages for long periods of time without actually entering poverty. This may well contribute to existing incentive structures that encourage many employers to engage in low-pay, low-skill product strategies and work practices.[8] New evidence on the extent and nature of business strategies and work practices of this kind is presented in chapters 3 through 7 of this book.

## SUMMARY AND ASSESSMENT: IS THERE A CONFLICT BETWEEN EMPLOYMENT AND EQUALITY OBJECTIVES?

Low-paid employment constitutes a sizable share of total employment in the United Kingdom (22 percent in 2005). This proportion rose sharply between the late 1970s and the mid-1990s, since when it has leveled off at a rate that is relatively high by European standards. The growth in low-paid employment in the 1980s and early 1990s occurred at a time when there was a general increase in earnings inequality. Some of the factors that may have contributed to this growth in inequality were common to many countries, such as the impact of skill-biased technical change and the shift in the composition of employment from manufacturing to service industries with higher within-group earnings inequality. What seems to have been distinctive about the United Kingdom during this period was the extent of the reduction in the bargaining power and organizing capability of trade unions and the removal of legislation and institutions (such as wages councils) that had previously provided some protection for low earners.

Since 1997, New Labour policies have tended to reinforce the growth of low-paid employment by promoting higher rates of labor force participation and encouraging a "paid work" route out of poverty (for example, through in-work benefits). This helps to explain why the rise in the incidence of low pay in the United Kingdom's economy has been halted since the mid-1990s but not forced into reverse. Low-paid employment has tended to stabilize at what is a historically high level in the United Kingdom. Cross-country comparisons suggest that it now tends to resemble the United States rather than continental Europe in its rate of unemployment, average duration of unemployment, and economic incentives for individuals to take up paid work at the bottom end of the labor market.

Continued high levels of low pay in the United Kingdom are therefore associated with the country's relative success in reducing unemployment and achieving high rates of employment among groups, such as women, youth, and older people, who have traditionally enjoyed less favorable employment prospects than prime-age males. In this context, it is a valid question for debate whether some kind of policy and institutional trade-off exists between the objective of maximizing employment and the objective of reducing income inequality. Consider, for example, the role of unions. In chapter 2, we identify the declining influence of unions in Britain as a key factor contributing to higher wage inequality and the growth of low-paid work during the 1980s and early 1990s. Examining the impact of unions from a different angle, however, Giuseppe Bertola, Francine Blau, and Lawrence Kahn (2002)'s analysis of data from seventeen OECD countries, including the United Kingdom, suggests that the stronger the influence of unions in wage-setting procedures, the lower the employment rates for the young and old relative to prime-age workers. They also find that union influence is associated with relatively high unemployment for women.

More generally, a number of research studies since the 1980s—surveyed most recently by Olivier Blanchard (2006)—have pointed to "labor market rigidities" (for example, employment protection legislation and long-duration unemployment benefits) as key factors contributing to relatively high rates of growth in and persistence of unemployment in continental European economies such as France, Germany, Spain, and Italy.[9] In the wake of this research, the OECD (1994) "Jobs Study" report was influential in its advocacy of reform of unemployment insurance, employment protection, collective bargaining procedures, and other labor market institutions, with a view to reducing "rigidities" and thus unemployment rates.

Many recent government policy initiatives and outcomes can be seen as consistent with this policy prescription, and on the face of it, our own assessment of the factors contributing to the persistence of low pay in the United Kingdom might be interpreted as supporting the idea of a policy and institutional trade-off between employment and equity objectives. However, if we turn to cross-country comparisons, there is little evidence of such a trade-off. According to recent OECD (2006, 175) analyses, there is "no systematic relationship [across countries] between changes in unemployment rates since 1994 and changes in low-pay incidence." In addition, if we turn to evidence on levels rather than changes, then measures of income inequality are negatively correlated with labor force participation and employment rates, and are positively correlated with unemployment rates (165).[10]

In the light of evidence of this kind, Andrew Glyn, David Howell, and John Schmitt (2006) argue that no case has been made for dismantling the social institutions associated with labor market "rigidities" that provide important social and economic benefits to citizens (for example, greater job security and democratic representation in the workplace). Blanchard (2006, 45) also concedes the mixed nature of the evidence on the links between labor market institutions and employment rates, but argues that "while there is a trade-off between efficiency [in resource allocation] and [social] insurance, the experience of the successful European economies suggests it need not be very steep."

One aim of this book is to present policy recommendations that would help improve pay levels and job quality at the bottom end of the United Kingdom labor market while minimizing any adverse effects on employment rates. To be successful, such recommendations need to be rooted in an understanding of what determines employer strategies for labor deployment and remuneration in the United Kingdom. With this objective in mind, we consider in chapter 2 how employer behavior in relation to currently low-paid workers is influenced by United Kingdom labor market institutions and government policies. In chapters 3 through 7, we present new evidence based on case studies in retail, hotels, hospitals, food processing, and call centers that focus on a range of interrelated factors affecting employer behavior in respect of pay and job quality for workers in selected occupations. As a preliminary guide to the reader, these factors can be categorized as follows:

1.  Employer strategies and processes, including product and production strategies that influence human resource management practices and employer demand for skills. Product market and production strategies are in turn influenced, among other things, by product market competition and by technological developments.

2.  Factors affecting the labor supply at the lower end of the labor market, such as immigration, demographic developments, and tax and social security incentives and disincentives.

3.  Institutions, such as trade unions and the structure and content of collective bargaining and the legislative environment affecting the relative bargaining power of employers and workers.

4.  Government policies that impinge on all of the above—for example, minimum wage legislation, active labor market interventions, immigration rules, education and training measures (all of which affect the quantity and quality of the labor supply), product market legislation, and employment and industrial relations legislation.

We use the evidence derived from the case studies, along with our analysis of labor market data and institutional developments in chapter 2, to inform the policy recommendations we make in chapter 8.

---

We are grateful to John Forth, Damian Grimshaw, Caroline Lloyd, Martin Weale, participants in National Institute of Economic and Social Research seminars, and the Russell Sage Foundation referees and project participants for helpful comments on previous versions of this chapter. We are also grateful to the Office of National Statistics for access to the Annual Survey of Hours and Earnings through the Virtual Microdata Laboratory. Responsibility for any errors is ours alone.

## NOTES

1.  The German, Dutch, French, and Danish estimates are taken, respectively, from Gerhard Bosch and Thorsten Kalina (2008), Wiemer Salverda (2008), Ève Caroli, Jérôme Gautié, and Philippe Askenazy (2008), and Niels Westergaard-Nielsen (2008). For Germany, the Netherlands, and Denmark, low pay thresholds are defined as two-thirds of the median gross hourly wage for all employees, as is the case for the United Kingdom low pay threshold in this chapter. For France, the threshold is defined as two-thirds of the median *before-tax* hourly wage (net of social contributions) for all employees, excluding apprentices. The proportion of workers in the United Kingdom earning below the low pay threshold changed very little between 2002 and 2005: 22.1 percent in 2002, 21.1 percent in 2003, 21.6 percent in 2004, and 21.7 percent in 2005 (estimates based on Annual Survey of Hourly Earnings data).

2.  In general, the incidence of inactivity has been geographically concentrated: there are much higher rates of inactivity (and unemployment) in northeastern England than in southeastern and eastern England. However, unemployment and inactivity rates may vary sharply *within* regions as well as between them, so much so that some authors argue

that unemployment black spots are at least as much a localized problem (particularly in inner cities) as a regional problem (Turok and Edge 1999).

3.  Note that similar evidence of increased wage inequality within different age, gender, and education groups has been found in the United States (Juhn, Murphy, and Pierce 1993; Katz and Murphy 1992).

4.  A further rationale for reducing average unemployment duration is that it enables public expenditure on unemployment to be spread across a larger number of people.

5.  This is the definition of household poverty used by the government in setting its child poverty reduction targets.

6.  The Department of Work and Pensions (DWP 2006) reports that in 2004–2005 some 48 percent of workless households were below 60 percent of the median income, compared with 18 percent of households with at least one adult (but not all) working and 8 percent of households with all adults working.

7.  By contrast, only 2 percent of non-low-paid workers were living in household poverty in 2001.

8.  International comparisons have suggested that in many sectors the proportion of firms in the United Kingdom engaged in relatively low value-added, less skill-intensive production is greater than in countries such as Germany and the Netherlands (Prais 1995). Lower average value added per hour worked in United Kingdom market sectors compared to Germany and France is associated with relatively low levels of physical capital per hour worked and workforce skills in the United Kingdom (O'Mahony and de Boer 2002).

9.  For a review of contradictory findings on the effects of employment protection legislation, see OECD, *Employment Outlook* (2004b).

10. The measure of low pay in OECD, *Employment Outlook* (2006), is the proportion of full-time wage earners earning less than two-thirds of the median wage of full-time wage earners. The measures of income inequality referred to are Gini coefficients and ninth/first wage decile ratios.

# REFERENCES

Artus, Patrick, and Gilbert Cette. 2004. *Productivité et croissance* [*Productivity and Growth*]. Paris: Rapport au Conseil d'Analyse Economique.

Arulampalam, Wiji, Paul Gregg, and Mary Gregory. 2001. "Unemployment Scarring." *The Economic Journal* 111(475): 577-84.

Berman, Eli, John Bound, and Stephen Machin. 1998. "Implications of Skill-based Technological Change: International Evidence." *Quarterly Journal of Economics* 113(4): 1245-79.

Bertola, Giuseppe, Francine D. Blau, and Lawrence M. Kahn. 2002. "Labor

Market Institutions and Demographic Employment Patterns." Working paper 9043. Cambridge, Mass.: National Bureau of Economic Research (July).

Blanchard, Olivier. 2006. "European Unemployment: The Evolution of Facts and Ideas." *Economic Policy* 21(45): 5–59.

Bosch, Gerhard, and Thorsten Kalina. 2008. "Low-Wage Work in Germany: An Overview." In *Low-Wage Work in Germany*, edited by Gerhard Bosch and Claudia Weinkopf. New York: Russell Sage Foundation.

Brewer, Mike, Alissa Goodman, Jonathan Shaw, and Luke Sibieta. 2006. "Poverty and Inequality in Britain: 2006." Commentary 101. London: Institute for Fiscal Studies.

Burgess, Simon, and Carol Propper. 1999. "Poverty in Britain." In *The State of Working Britain*, edited by Paul Gregg and Jonathan Wadsworth. Manchester, U.K.: Manchester University Press.

Caroli, Ève, Jérôme Gautié, and Philippe Askenazy. 2008. "Low-Wage Work and Labor Market Institutions in France." In *Low-Wage Work in France*, edited by Ève Caroli and Jérôme Gautié. New York: Russell Sage Foundation.

Department of Social Security (DSS). 1998. *New Ambitions for Our Country: A New Contract for Welfare*. Command 3805. London: DSS.

Department of Work and Pensions (DWP). 2006. "Households Below Average Income (HBAI), 1994–1995 to 2004–2005." Accessed at http://www.dwp.gov.uk/asd/hbai/hbai2005/contents.asp.

De Santis, Roberto A. 2003. "Wage Inequality in the U.K.: Trade and/or Technology?" *World Economy* 26(6): 893-909.

Dickens, Richard, and David T. Ellwood. 2003. "Child Poverty in Britain and the United States." *Economic Journal* 113(488): 219–39.

Faggio, Giulia, and Stephen Nickell. 2003. "The Rise in Inactivity Among Adult Men." In *The Labour Market Under New Labour*, edited by Richard Dickens, Paul Gregg, and Jonathan Wadsworth. London: Palgrave Macmillan.

Felstead, Alan, Duncan Gallie, and Francis Green. 2002. *Work Skills in Britain*. London: Department for Education and Skills (DfES).

Glyn, Andrew, David R. Howell, and John Schmitt. 2006. "Labor Market Reforms: The Evidence Does Not Tell the Orthodox Tale." *Challenge* 49(2): 5–22.

Gregg, Paul, and Jonathan Wadsworth. 2003. "Workless Households and the Recovery." In *The Labour Market Under New Labour*, edited by Richard Dickens, Paul Gregg, and Jonathan Wadsworth. London: Palgrave Macmillan.

Hotopp, Ulrike. 2005. "The Employment Rate of Older Workers." *Labour Market Trends* 113(2): 73-88.

Juhn, Chinhui, Kevin M. Murphy, and Brooks Pierce. 1993. "Wage Inequality and the Rise in Returns to Skill." *Journal of Political Economy* 101(3): 410–42.

Katz, Lawrence F., and Kevin M. Murphy. 1992. "Changes in Relative Wages, 1963–1887: Supply and Demand Factors." *Quarterly Journal of Economics* 107(1): 35–78.

Kenway, Peter. 2005. "In-Work Child Poverty." *Poverty* 122: 13–15.

Lindsay, Craig. 2005. "Employment and Unemployment Estimates for 1971 to 1991." *Labour Market Trends* 13(1): 15-19.

Machin, Stephen. 2003. "Wage Inequality Since 1975." In *The Labour Market Under New Labour*, edited by Richard Dickens, Paul Gregg, and Jonathan Wadsworth. London: Palgrave Macmillan.

Mason, Geoff. 2002. "High Skills Utilization Under Mass Higher Education: Graduate Employment in Service Industries in Britain." *Journal of Education and Work* 15(4): 427–56.

McIntyre, Andrew. 2002. "People Leaving Economic Inactivity: Characteristics and Flaws." *Labour Market Trends* 10(4): 187-94.

Millar, Jane, and Karen Gardiner. 2004. *Low Pay, Household Resources, and Poverty*. Joseph Rowntree Foundation 64. Accessed at Center for the Analysis of Social Policy, http://www.jrf.org.uk/bookshop/eBooks/1859352588.pdf.

Nickell, Stephen. 2004. "Poverty and Worklessness in Britain." *Economic Journal* 114(March): C1–25.

Nickell, Stephen, and Glenda Quintini. 2002. "The Recent Performance of the U.K. Labor Market." *Oxford Review of Economic Policy* 18(2): 202–20.

O'Mahony, Mary, and Willem de Boer. 2002. "Britain's Relative Productivity Performance: Updates to 1999." London: National Institute of Economic and Social Research.

Organization for Economic Cooperation and Development (OECD). 1994. *The OECD Jobs Study: Facts, Analysis, Strategies*. Paris: OECD.

———. 2004a. *Benefits and Wages*. Paris: OECD.

———. 2004b. *Employment Outlook*. Paris: OECD.

———. 2006. *Employment Outlook*. Paris: OECD.

Prais, Sigbert John. 1995. *Productivity, Education, and Training*. Cambridge: Cambridge University Press.

Prasad, Eswar. 2002. "Wage Inequality in the United Kingdom, 1975-1999." Discussion paper no. 510, Forschungsinstitut zur Zukunft der Arbeit (IZA), Bonn, Germany.

Robinson, Helen. 2003. "Gender and Labour Market Performance in the Recovery." In *The Labour Market Under New Labour*, edited by Richard Dickens, Paul Gregg, and Jonathan Wadsworth. London: Palgrave Macmillan.

Salverda, Wiemer. 2008. "Low-Wage Work and the Economy." In *Low-Wage Work in the Netherlands*, edited by Wiemer Salverda, Maarten van Klaveren, and Marc van der Meer. New York: Russell Sage Foundation.

Turok, Ivan, and Nicola Edge. 1999. *The Jobs Gap in Britain's Cities: Employment Loss and Labour Market Consequences*. Bristol, U.K.: The Policy Press.

Westergaard-Nielsen, Niels. 2008. "Low-Wage Work in Denmark." In *Low-Wage Work in Denmark*, edited by Niels Westergaard-Nielsen. New York: Russell Sage Foundation.

# CHAPTER 2

# Low Pay, Labor Market Institutions, and Job Quality in the United Kingdom

*Geoff Mason, Ken Mayhew, Matthew Osborne, and Philip Stevens*

In chapter 1, we identified a high proportion of low-wage workers in the United Kingdom as compared to other European countries. In this chapter, we explore the reasons why this high incidence of low pay has persisted despite the introduction of a national minimum wage (NMW) in 1999. In particular, we investigate the number, composition, and nature of low-paid jobs in the United Kingdom's economy and outline the economic and institutional context in which employers are operating and in which the wages and working conditions of low-paid jobs have evolved.

In the next section, we investigate the extent to which low-wage employment in the United Kingdom is associated with gender, ethnicity, skill levels, and other personal characteristics, paying particular attention to the jobs and sectors covered in chapters 3 through 7. Then we explore the reasons why there are so many low-paid workers in the United Kingdom, focusing on the declining influence of the institutions that have traditionally helped to shore up wages at the bottom end of the labor market; the diverse forms by which workers are encouraged to participate in the workforce even if low-wage employment is all that is available to them; deficiencies in workforce skills and associated employer product strategies that make use of low-skilled, low-paid labor; and the recent impact of immigration on the pay and conditions of workers in low-wage employment. In the following section, we assess trends in job and life quality in low-paid work in the United Kingdom (for example, hours worked, insecurity of employment, maternity leave provision, and sick pay), taking account of the impact of the national minimum wage, the implementation of European Union directives affecting pay and conditions, and other relevant components of legislation in the United Kingdom. We conclude with an assessment of the extent to which individuals in low-paid employment may over time be able to escape such employment and find their way to higher-paying jobs.

## WHO AND WHERE ARE THE LOW-PAID?

In 2005 some 22 percent of employees in the United Kingdom were engaged in low-paid work, according to the Annual Survey of Hours and Earnings (ASHE). For women, the low-paid share of employment was 29 percent, while for men it was 13 percent. Figure 2.1 captures this gender split in more detail while also highlighting the particular problems of part-timers. Thus, for example, male part-timers earn consistently less per hour than women full-timers at all points on the distribution. However, among part-timers there is little differ-

Figure 2.1 The United Kingdom Earnings Distribution, 2005

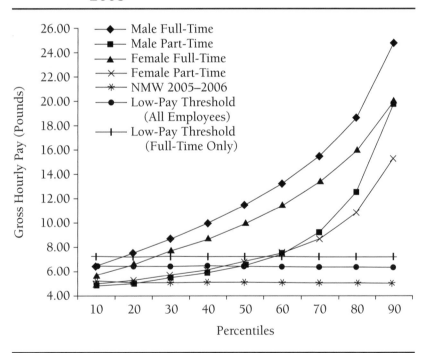

Source: Annual Survey of Hours and Earnings (ASHE).
Note: The ASHE is an annual survey that is administered through employers and collects data on a sample of 1 percent of employees.

ence between male and female pay below the seventieth percentile. Some 50 percent of all part-timers earn below the low-pay threshold—defined as two-thirds of the median hourly pay of all employees. This proportion rises to about 57 percent if the threshold is defined in terms of median full-time hourly earnings. For women full-timers, the equivalent proportions are 15 and 25 percent, respectively, depending on the definition of the low-pay threshold, while for male full-timers they are 10 and 20 percent.

Low-paid employment is heavily concentrated by sector, with just over half of all low-paid workers found in three sectors: retail, health services, and hotels. Although hotels have the highest incidence of low-paid workers among their employees (59 percent), it is the much larger retail sector that has the largest number of low-paid workers in absolute terms, accounting for just over one-quarter of all the low-paid workers in the United Kingdom's economy (table 2.1).

Estimates based on Labour Force Survey (LFS) data (table 2.2) confirm these findings with respect to gender and full-time/part-time status and also show that low-wage employment is strongly related to age, with 49 percent of workers in the sixteen- to twenty-four-year-old age group classified as low-paid in 2005, up slightly from 47 percent in 1995. At the other end of the age spectrum, there is an above-average incidence of low pay among those over the age of sixty, albeit slightly reduced from the levels prevailing ten years earlier. Other characteristics associated with low pay are having relatively low levels of qualifications (below national vocational qualification, level three [NVQ3]—equivalent to a craft apprentice standard); working in personal service, sales, or operator occupations; and working on a temporary contract. Foreign nationals as a whole are only slightly more likely than United Kingdom nationals to be low-paid, but there is a wide disparity in skills and earnings potential within this group.

Some caution needs to be attached to all results concerning ethnicity because of relatively small cell sizes for some minority groups. That said, workers of Pakistani, Bangladeshi, Chinese, and black African origin appear to be clearly disadvantaged relative to other ethnic groups in terms of pay.[1] By contrast, less-than-average proportions of workers of Indian and black Caribbean origin were below the low pay threshold in both 1995 and 2005. The fact that Indian workers in the United Kingdom are noted for their relatively high levels of formal education helps to explain why a below-average proportion of

### Table 2.1 Distribution of Low-Paid Employment in the UK Economy, 2005, Analyzed by Sector

| SIC Code | Sector | Total Low-Paid Employees in UK Economy | Employees in Sector Earning Below Low-Pay Threshold |
|---|---|---|---|
| 52 | Retail | 26% | 49% |
| 85 | Health services | 13 | 18 |
| 55 | Hotels and restaurants | 12 | 59 |
| 15–37 | Manufacturing | 9 | 13 |
| 80 | Education | 8 | 16 |
| 90–93 | Social and community services | 7 | 29 |
| 74 | Cleaning, security, and miscellaneous business services | 6 | 18 |
| 60–64 | Transport and communications | 5 | 13 |
| 50–51 | Wholesale | 5 | 22 |
| 45 | Construction | 3 | 13 |
| 65–73 | Other private services | 3 | 8 |
| 75 | Public administration | 2 | 6 |
| 01–14; 40–41 | Other industries | 1 | 15 |
| | Total | 100 | 21 |

*Source:* Labour Force Survey (LFS).
*Note:* The LFS is a quarterly survey of 60,000 households and the individuals within those households. It differs substantially from the Annual Survey of Hours and Earnings, which is administered through employers (see figure 2.1 note).

them are low-paid (Blackaby et al. 2002, table 1). Although at first sight the findings for black Caribbeans may appear surprising, there are a number of factors that, taken together, help to explain them. First, the discrimination encountered by this ethnic group often results in restricted opportunities to enter any form of employment (Blackaby et al. 1994, 2002). Second, while the mean hourly pay of black Caribbean workers in 2005 was some 3 percent below that for white workers, this difference largely reflects the more restricted opportunities for black Caribbeans at the upper end of the pay scale, not a greater concentration of them below the low pay threshold. Third, there are marked differences between black Caribbean men and women in comparison to the differences between white men and women: while the mean hourly pay for black Caribbean men in 2005 was some 11 percent below that of white men, the mean hourly pay

Table 2.2  Incidence of Low-Paid Employment in the U.K.
Economy, 2005, Analyzed by Gender, Age
Group, Ethnic Origin, Nationality, Nature of
Employment Contract, Highest Qualification
Attained, and Occupational Category

|  | 1995 | 2005 | 1995 | 2005 |
|---|---|---|---|---|
| Total | 22.0% | 20.8% | 36,770 | 55,982 |
| Gender |  |  |  |  |
| Male | 14.3 | 15.1 | 18,182 | 26,709 |
| Female | 30.2 | 26.6 | 18,588 | 29,273 |
| Age group |  |  |  |  |
| Sixteen to twenty-four | 46.6 | 49.4 | 5,413 | 6,565 |
| Twenty-five to twenty-nine | 17.1 | 16.1 | 4,714 | 5,543 |
| Thirty to thirty-nine | 15.4 | 13.9 | 10,201 | 14,070 |
| Forty to forty-nine | 15.5 | 13.9 | 9,179 | 14,965 |
| Fifty to fifty-nine | 20.1 | 16.2 | 5,783 | 11,588 |
| Sixty to sixty-four | 24.5 | 24.1 | 1,115 | 2,427 |
| Sixty-five or older | 45.2 | 40.6 | 365 | 824 |
| Ethnic origin |  |  |  |  |
| White | 21.8 | 20.6 | 34,590 | 51,090 |
| Black Caribbean | 16.8 | 17.0 | 241 | 454 |
| Black African | 21.6 | 23.1 | 112 | 429 |
| Indian | 27.4 | 19.0 | 406 | 939 |
| Pakistani | 31.1 | 26.9 | 112 | 302 |
| Bangladeshi |  | 30.3 |  | 95 |
| Other Asian | 19.3 | 26.4 | 156 | 526 |
| Other ethnic | 19.4 | 22.9 | 172 | 606 |
| Nationality |  |  |  |  |
| United Kingdom national | 22.1 | 21.1 | 35,614 | 39,028 |
| Foreign national | 20.7 | 23.0 | 1,156 | 3,235 |
| Nature of employment contract |  |  |  |  |
| Full-time (thirty hours or more per week) | 15.5 | 14.0 | 27,529 | 42,061 |
| Part-time | 43.1 | 42.5 | 9,216 | 13,901 |
| Permanent | 21.2 | 20.1 | 34,100 | 53,136 |
| Temporary | 32.7 | 32.6 | 2,663 | 2,834 |
| Highest qualification attained[a] |  |  |  |  |
| Bachelor degree or higher | 4.1 | 5.2 | 5,278 | 12,032 |
| Other NVQ4 | 8.2 | 8.9 | 3,893 | 6,012 |
| NVQ3 | 18.0 | 20.1 | 8,531 | 13,249 |

Table 2.2 (*Continued*)

|  | 1995 | 2005 | 1995 | 2005 |
|---|---|---|---|---|
| NVQ2 | 27.5 | 28.7 | 8,093 | 13,128 |
| NVQ1 | 34.1 | 32.7 | 2,812 | 2,659 |
| Other qualifications | 23.3 | 28.2 | 2,782 | 3,765 |
| No qualifications | 40.6 | 41.5 | 5,352 | 4,941 |
| Occupational category |  |  |  |  |
| Manager | 6.7 | 5.0 | 5,315 | 8,222 |
| Professional | 2.8 | 2.5 | 3,867 | 7,335 |
| Associate professional | 5.7 | 5.0 | 3,475 | 7,989 |
| Administrative and secretarial | 16.4 | 14.2 | 6,310 | 7,916 |
| Skilled trades | 17.9 | 18.1 | 3,536 | 4,372 |
| Personal services | 40.0 | 35.9 | 4,264 | 4,693 |
| Sales occupations | 49.8 | 54.0 | 3,135 | 4,629 |
| Operators | 22.8 | 21.6 | 3,572 | 4,075 |
| Other occupations | 50.9 | 51.2 | 3,229 | 6,736 |

*Source:* Labour Force Survey (LFS).
*Notes:* See table 2.1 note.
[a] NVQ4 includes Business and Technician Education Council (BTEC) higher national and teaching and nursing qualifications and equivalent; NVQ3 includes A levels, trade apprenticeships, and the equivalent; NVQ2 includes General Certificate of Secondary Education (GCSE) grades A to C, city and guilds craft, General National Vocational Qualification (GNVQ) intermediate, and the equivalent.

for black Caribbean women was 9 percent above that for white women, apparently reflecting the greater concentration of black Caribbean women in occupations such as nursing (Blackwell and Guinea-Martin 2005) and a lower incidence of part-time employment among them (Modood et al. 1997).

To explore the interrelationships between gender, age group, ethnicity, and other characteristics, table 2.3 reports the results of a logistic regression analysis of the probability of being low-paid in 2005. Equation 2.1 confirms that the likelihood of being low-paid is significantly and positively related to being female, being either relatively young or old (especially being younger than twenty-five or age sixty or older), and being of Pakistani, Bangladeshi, or Chinese origin.[2] The association of Pakistani, Bangladeshi, and Chinese workers with low pay partly reflects their above-average representation in low-paid occupations such as sales assistants (Pakistani men and women, Bangladeshi and Chinese women) and restaurant workers (Chinese men and women, Bangladeshi men) (Blackwell and Guinea-Martin 2005).

Nearly all the gender, age, and ethnic results remain significant when controls are introduced for nationality and qualification level (table 2.3, equation 2). The gender and age results are also robust to the inclusion of job-related characteristics such as occupation, working part-time, and working on a temporary contract (equation 3) and establishment characteristics such as sector, region, and size of establishment (equation 4). Workers in the "Chinese/other Asian" group are in the only ethnic minority group that is significantly more likely than white workers to fall below the low pay threshold after controlling for occupation and sector.[3]

Although low pay in the United Kingdom is strongly associated with being female, working part-time, and being young, analysis of New Earnings Survey (NES) data for the period when the incidence of low pay consistently increased (between the early 1980s and mid-1990s) shows that the proportion of low-paid rose during this period among males and in all age groups (tables 2.4 and 2.5). It actually fell somewhat for female full-timers. Overall, these developments reflected the general increase in wage inequality over this period (chapter 1).

As shown in table 2.2, low-paid employment is concentrated in relatively low-skilled occupational groups such as personal services, sales, and operative occupations. These groups include some of the occupations covered in chapters 3 through 7, such as retail sales assistants (75 percent of whom earned below the low pay threshold in 2005), hotel cleaners, and food-processing workers (table 2.6). Of particular significance is that for all of these occupations, mean gross hourly earnings in the early 2000s were significantly lower relative to all occupations than they had been ten years earlier. This decline in relative earnings occurred for both full-time and part-time employees (table 2.7). Logistic regression analysis of the probability of falling below the low pay threshold in the selected occupations highlights the extent to which some workers may be particularly disadvantaged if they are female, are in the younger or older age group, work part-time or on a temporary contract, or hold either no qualifications or low qualifications (table 2.8).

Table 2.3 Logistic Regression Estimates of the Probability of Being Low-Paid, 2005: Marginal Effects (Evaluated at Sample Means)

| | Equation 1: Individual Characteristics | Equation 2: Individual Characteristics, Including Nationality and Education | Equation 3: Plus Job-Related Characteristics | Equation 4: Plus Establishment Characteristics |
|---|---|---|---|---|
| Female | 0.12*** | 0.12*** | 0.08*** | 0.07*** |
| Reference age category: age forty to forty-nine | | | | |
| Age sixteen to twenty-four | 0.39*** | 0.42*** | 0.26*** | 0.21*** |
| Age twenty-five to twenty-nine | 0.01** | 0.06*** | 0.04*** | 0.03*** |
| Age thirty to thirty-nine | 0.00 | 0.02*** | 0.01** | 0.01 |
| Age fifty to fifty-nine | 0.03*** | 0.01 | 0.01 | 0.01 |
| Age sixty plus | 0.19*** | 0.12*** | 0.07*** | 0.05*** |
| Reference ethnic category: white | | | | |
| Black Caribbean | -0.04** | -0.03* | -0.02 | 0.00 |
| Black African | 0.02 | -0.01 | -0.04** | -0.02 |
| Indian | 0.01 | 0.00 | 0.00 | 0.02 |
| Pakistani | 0.05** | 0.01 | 0.00 | 0.00 |
| Bangladeshi | 0.09* | 0.11** | 0.07 | 0.05 |
| Chinese/other Asian | 0.08*** | 0.09*** | 0.07*** | 0.07*** |
| Other ethnic minority | 0.02 | -0.02 | -0.02 | 0.00 |
| Foreign national | | -0.02*** | 0.00 | 0.00 |
| Reference skill category: intermediate qualifications (such as craft or technician qualifications) | | | | |
| Graduate | | -0.15*** | -0.05*** | -0.04*** |
| Low qualifications | | 0.16*** | 0.06*** | 0.06*** |

| | | | | |
|---|---|---|---|---|
| Reference occupational category: skilled trades | | | | |
| Managerial occupations | | | −0.10*** | −0.10*** |
| Professional occupations | | | −0.13*** | −0.11*** |
| Associate professional occupations | | | −0.12*** | −0.10*** |
| Administrative and secretarial occupations | | | −0.08*** | −0.06*** |
| Personal services occupations | | | 0.01* | 0.03*** |
| Sales occupations | | | 0.09*** | 0.05*** |
| Operator occupations | | | 0.02*** | 0.05*** |
| Other occupations | | | 0.11*** | 0.12*** |
| Part-time (less than thirty hours per week) | | | 0.10*** | 0.07*** |
| Temporary | | | 0.06*** | 0.06*** |
| Establishment size dummies | No | No | No | Yes |
| Sector dummies | No | No | No | Yes |
| Regional dummies | No | No | No | Yes |
| Observations | 54,543 | 41,005 | 40,912 | 39,466 |
| Pseudo R-squared | 0.10 | 0.17 | 0.29 | 0.32 |

*Source*: Labour Force Survey (LFS).
* significant at 10%; ** significant at 5%; *** significant at 1%

Table 2.4 Proportion of Employees Earning Less Than Two-Thirds
of Median Hourly Wages, 1976 to 2001

|      | Full-Time | | Part-Time | | | | | | |
|------|------|--------|------|--------|------|--------|-----------|-----------|-------|
|      | Male | Female | Male | Female | Male | Female | Part-Time | Full-Time | Total |
| 1976 | 6%   | 26%    | 41%  | 33%    | 6%   | 27%    | 34%       | 12%       | 14%   |
| 1981 | 6    | 24     | 42   | 46     | 7    | 30     | 46        | 12        | 16    |
| 1986 | 8    | 24     | 54   | 52     | 9    | 31     | 52        | 13        | 18    |
| 1991 | 9    | 22     | 53   | 50     | 10   | 29     | 50        | 14        | 19    |
| 1996 | 11   | 22     | 54   | 50     | 13   | 30     | 51        | 15        | 21    |
| 2001 | 11   | 20     | 54   | 49     | 13   | 29     | 50        | 15        | 21    |

*Source:* New Earnings Survey (NES) panel dataset.

## WHY ARE THERE SO MANY LOW-PAID PEOPLE IN THE UNITED KINGDOM?

We now turn to a more detailed discussion of the reasons for the relatively high incidence of low-wage employment in the United Kingdom. We start with an appraisal of the decline in union bargaining power and organizing ability, then move on to consider the extent and nature of wage protection for low-paid workers, recent developments in policy affecting labor force participation, the links between workforce skills and employer product strategies, and the impact of recent trends in immigration.

### THE REDUCTION IN TRADE UNION INFLUENCE AND COLLECTIVE BARGAINING

Historically, trade unions provided significant protection for many workers at the low end of the labor market. Union density (the percentage of employed workers who are members of a union) peaked at about 53 percent in 1979, when membership stood at 11.7 million and there were nearly 450 unions. This peak was followed by a sustained decline, precipitated initially by the severe macroeconomic recession at the end of the 1970s and beginning of the 1980s; the decline continued, however, in each successive year, long after economic activity picked up. Since the late 1990s, there have been some signs that the decline has been halted, but not reversed. Today union density in the United Kingdom stands at about 29 percent,

Table 2.5 Proportion of Employees Earning Less Than Two-Thirds of Median Hourly Wages, 1976 to 2001, by Age Group

| | Sixteen to Twenty-four | Twenty-five to Twenty-nine | Thirty to Thirty-nine | Forty to Forty-nine | Fifty to Fifty-nine | Sixty or Older | Total |
|---|---|---|---|---|---|---|---|
| 1976 | 31% | 7% | 9% | 10% | 10% | 18% | 14% |
| 1981 | 30 | 7 | 10 | 13 | 14 | 21 | 16 |
| 1986 | 35 | 10 | 12 | 14 | 15 | 22 | 18 |
| 1991 | 35 | 12 | 13 | 16 | 18 | 29 | 19 |
| 1996 | 44 | 16 | 15 | 16 | 21 | 34 | 21 |
| 2001 | 46 | 16 | 15 | 16 | 20 | 35 | 21 |

*Source:* National Earnings Survey (NES) panel dataset.

Table 2.6  Employees Earning Less Than Two-Thirds of
          Median Hourly Wages, 1991, 1996, and 2005,
          by Selected Occupational Group

| New Earnings Survey (SOC 1990 code) | | 1991 | 1996 | 2001 |
|---|---|---|---|---|
| 640 | Assistant nurses, nursing auxiliaries | 14% | 17% | 15% |
| 641 | Hospital ward assistants | 31 | 33 | 39 |
| 720 | Sales assistants | 66 | 66 | 66 |
| 721 | Retail cash desk and check-out operators | 65 | 74 | 78 |
| 800 | Bakery, confectionery process operatives | 41 | 38 | 46 |
| 809 | Other food, drink and tobacco process operatives | 23 | 23 | 25 |
| 958 | Cleaners, domestics | 67 | 73 | 76 |
| Annual Survey of Hours and Earnings (SOC 2000 code) | | | | 2005 |
| 6111 | Nursing auxiliaries and assistants | | | 19 |
| 7111 | Sales and retail assistants | | | 75 |
| 7112 | Retail cashiers and check-out operators | | | 78 |
| 7211 | Call center agents and operators | | | 27 |
| 8111 | Food, drink and tobacco process operatives | | | 31 |
| 9233 | Cleaners, domestics | | | 76 |

*Source:* New Earnings Survey, Annual Survey of Hours and Earnings.

representing a membership of about 7.5 million in slightly more than 200 unions. As in most other developed countries, public sector workers are more unionized than those in the private sector, manual workers more than nonmanual workers, and those in manufacturing more than those in services. One compositional feature that has changed in recent years is that women are now at least as likely to be unionized as men.

In 1979, when density was 53 percent, about 78 percent of the workforce was covered by collective agreements. Today, with density at 29 percent, only 36 percent of the workforce is covered by collective agreements. The main reason for the smaller gap between membership and coverage is the death of the multi-employer agreement (to be discussed later). It is noteworthy that about 25 percent of union members are not covered by collective bargaining.[4]

Results for the 2004 Workplace Employment Relations Survey (Kersley et al. 2006) show that negotiation over pay now takes place in only 18 percent of workplaces (with ten or more employees). In another 12 percent, employers formally "inform" or "consult" the

Table 2.7  Mean Gross Hourly Earnings for Selected Occupations in the United Kingdom, Relative to "All Occupations," 1992 and 2002 (Index Numbers: All Occupations = 100)

| SOC 1990 Code | | Men, Full-Time | | Women, Full-Time | | Women, Part-Time | |
|---|---|---|---|---|---|---|---|
| | | 1992 | 2002 | 1992 | 2002 | 1992 | 2002 |
| 620 | Chefs and cooks | 63 | 58 | 67 | 60 | 81 | 75 |
| | Counterhands and catering assistants | — | 45 | 59 | 54 | 75 | 68 |
| 958 | Cleaners and domestics | 55 | 46 | 61 | 53 | 77 | 69 |
| 720 | Sales assistants | — | — | 61 | 55 | 77 | 70 |
| 721 | Retail cash desk and check out operators | — | — | 60 | 52 | 80 | 70 |
| 72 | Sales assistants and retail cash desk and check out operators | 56 | 53 | — | — | — | — |
| 800 | Bakery, confectionery process operatives | 59 | 51 | — | — | — | — |
| 809 | Other food, drink, and tobacco process operatives | 69 | 60 | — | — | — | — |
| 80 | Food, drink, and tobacco process operatives | — | — | 71 | 63 | 94 | 75 |
| 640 | Assistant nurses, and nursing auxiliaries | 67 | 56 | 78 | 70 | 107 | 98 |
| 641 | Hospital ward assistants | — | — | 69 | 58 | 91 | 81 |
| | All manual occupations | 73 | 65 | 66 | 61 | 79 | 75 |
| | All non-manual occupations | 126 | 125 | 108 | 107 | 112 | 109 |
| | All occupations | 100 | 100 | 100 | 100 | 100 | 100 |

*Source:* National Earnings Survey (NES).

workforce about pay. In the remaining 70 percent of workplaces, pay is a matter of management fiat. The corresponding percentages for workplaces where unions are recognized are 61, 23, and 16. After pay, the items that are most frequently the objects of negotiation are hours (16 percent for all workplaces and 53 percent for unionized ones), holidays (15 percent and 52 percent), and pensions (10 percent and 36 percent). The bottom line is that in the vast majority of

Table 2.8  Logistic Regression Analysis of the Probability of
Being Low-Paid in Selected Occupations, 2003
to 2005

| SOC 2000 Code | Occupation | Below Low-Pay Threshold | Variables Positively and Significantly Related to Low Pay[a] | Number of Observations |
|---|---|---|---|---|
| 7111, 7112 | Sales and check-out occupations | 66% | Female Age sixteen to twenty-four Age fifty to fifty-nine Age sixty or older Part-time Low qualifications | 4,897 |
| 9233 | Cleaners and domestics (including hotel and hospital cleaners) | 66 | Female Part-time | 1,973 |
| 8111 | Food, drink, and tobacco process operatives | 37 | Female Age sixteen to twenty-four Age twenty-five to twenty-nine Part-time Temporary Low qualifications | 499 |
| 7211 | Call center agents | 18 | Temporary Low qualifications | 293 |
| 6111 | Nursing auxiliaries and assistants | 21 | Age sixteen to twenty-four Temporary | 749 |

*Source:* Labour Force Survey (LFS).
[a] Refers to significance at the 5 percent level or better in logistic regression for each occupation group where the independent variables are: female, age group (reference category: age forty to forty-nine), ethnic group (reference category: white), qualifications group (reference category: intermediate qualifications, such as craft and technician level), foreign nationality, part-time working (defined as working fewer than thirty hours per week), temporary contract status, and two year dummies. Based on pooled LFS data for three years, 2003 to 2005, with analysis confined to pay observations for wave 1 respondents in each year. Full results available from authors upon request.

workplaces (70 percent or more) there is no negotiation or consultation regarding pay and conditions. Even in unionized workplaces, there is substantial use of managerial prerogative. Joint consultative committees, which might have compensated to some extent for less bargaining, have not increased much in significance. Indeed, they were to be found in only 14 percent of workplaces in 2004, as compared to 20 percent in 1998 (Kersley et al. 2006).

Unsurprisingly, these developments are reflected in the changing impact of unions on the overall earnings distribution. A consensus has recently emerged that a "within-group" effect (by which unions act to compress wages within, for example, an industry) dominates any "between-group" effect (such as unions in one sector using their bargaining power to garner wage gains relative to other sectors). David Card, Thomas Lemieux, and Craig Riddell (2004) find that this holds for the United Kingdom, with the net effect being that unions have reduced wage inequality over the last two decades. However, the "steady erosion of the equalizing effects of unions . . . explains a significant fraction of the growth in wage inequality in the . . . United Kingdom" (Card, Lemieux, and Riddell 2004, 22). There has been a decline in the union wage premium, which was virtually nonexistent in Britain for many types of workers by the end of the twentieth century (Blanchflower and Bryson 2004).

To obtain a broader view of the changing role of unions, it is necessary to describe briefly the evolution of collective bargaining institutions and arrangements. In contrast to some other Western European economies, there was never a single all-embracing *system* of industrial relations in the United Kingdom. That said, in the early post–World War II period much of private manufacturing was covered by multi-employer collective agreements. As with the vast majority of collective agreements in the United Kingdom, these agreements carried no legal force. However, it was a requirement of membership of the relevant employers' association that a firm offered at least the nationally agreed terms and conditions. Thus, membership compliance was usually 100 percent. The minority of firms in any given industry that were not members usually followed the national agreement. This kind of bargaining was less common in private services, though it was not unknown. Retail banking, for example, had a multi-employer agreement. In most parts of the public sector, including the then-nationalized industries, bargaining and pay-fixing were normally conducted at the national level, with some regional supplements for high-cost areas. Bargaining arrangements such as these provided substantial de facto protection for many of those in the lower reaches of the workforce.

Where multi-employer agreements existed, it was always open to individual employers to offer better terms and conditions, whether determined unilaterally or through bargaining. As the postwar years wore on, however, the importance of localized bargaining increased greatly, especially in the 1960s and 1970s. The literature of the time dubbed these changes "the rise of plant bargaining," reflecting the fact that in many larger firms decentralization extended even to individual plants and establishments. By the end of the 1970s, for the majority of private sector workers the most significant level at which pay—and to a lesser extent other terms and conditions—were determined was the company or establishment. Multi-employer agreements remained, but more and more they were seen as floors, especially for pay. In the public sector, national bargaining continued for each activity—schoolteaching, mining, steel, civil service, and so on.

These changes were accompanied by a shift of power within the union movement—from the full-time national and local officials to local shop stewards.[5] As local bargaining became more prominent, it was often the shop stewards who initiated and led it, sometimes without the knowledge, or even against the wishes, of the formal union hierarchy. The reasons for the rise of plant bargaining are complex, but it reflected a degree of employee assertiveness in the workplace that now has almost disappeared.

During the 1960s and 1970s, successive British governments became concerned that the country's relatively slow growth was in part the consequence of an industrial relations system that was contributing to rapid wage inflation and slow productivity growth. The Conservative government's Industrial Relations Act of 1971 represented a failed attempt to use the law more directly to regulate the conduct of industrial relations. The rest of that decade saw attempts at voluntary reform of the industrial relations system to make bargaining more cooperative and less confrontational.

However, the arrival of Margaret Thatcher as prime minister in 1979 led to a significant upheaval in the United Kingdom industrial relations framework. A series of new laws introduced periodically right up until the mid-1990s reduced the scope of unions to act effectively in the following dimensions:

- Calling and prosecuting strikes
- Recruiting and retaining members
- Disciplining and controlling members
- Establishing and maintaining the closed shop, which finally was effectively made illegal in a 1993 act

This legislation contributed to an environment in which many employers were able to withdraw recognition from trade unions or, more often, to negotiate new agreements with or impose new arrangements on unions that were more to employers' liking (Brown, Deakin, and Ryan 1997). New workplaces were also significantly less likely than existing ones to recognize unions (Millward, Bryson, and Forth 2000). As a result, a large proportion of employment contracts in the United Kingdom may now be described as "individualized," and employer efforts to link pay increases to individual performance are widespread (Brown et al. 1998, 2000).

The role of the law in reducing union power remains a controversial issue—a prolonged labor market recession lasting from 1979 until 1986 and union leadership's failure to confront the new realities were at least as significant (see Brown and Wadhwani 1990; Brown, Deakin, and Ryan 1997). It is also important to stress a major difference in collective labor law between Britain and other countries. Going back to the early years of the last century, unions in the United Kingdom benefited from a series of immunities from civil action for "torts" committed in contemplation or furtherance of a trade dispute. They were not the beneficiaries of specific legal rights, nor were they subject to specific obligations. Although this situation has changed somewhat since the early 1970s, the legal basis of the union position remains one of immunity from action in tort. However, the effective range of these immunities has been much reduced.

Since the New Labour government came to power in 1997, more union-friendly legislation has been introduced. The Employment Relations Act of 1999 set out new procedures requiring unions to be recognized by employers if a number of fairly stringent conditions were met—for example, a majority of employees in the bargaining unit were union members or a majority (and at least 40 percent of those eligible to vote) voted in favor in a secret ballot. The evidence suggests that this legislation has resulted in a significant increase in recognition agreements, although the scope of many of the new agreements is limited, in particular with respect to pay negotiations (Blanden, Machin, and Van Reenen 2006; Gall 2004; Oxenbridge et al. 2003). The Employment Relations Act of 2004 was also more union-friendly, giving, for example, somewhat greater protection against unfair dismissal to workers engaged in a legally called strike. Although the New Labour approach to industrial relations legislation has been characterized by some critics as "embodying employers' wishes at almost every turn" (Smith and Morton 2001, 124), the new laws have widened the scope for unions to negotiate with employers on a number of issues and given more employment protection to individual workers. Despite this impact, the Labour government's legislation has really only chipped away at the edges of the profound changes to the framework of industrial relations and employment law engineered during the eighteen years of Conservative governments.

Thus, for example, in sectors such as retail (chapter 4), one of our case studies provides an example of a workplace where a union had recently been "recognized," but not to the point where it could engage in pay bargaining on behalf of its members. Similarly, in local government and other parts of the traditional public sector, pressure has been maintained to contract out services to private firms in ways that often lead to deterioration in the terms and conditions of the workers carrying out those jobs. Unions, however, have been successful in pushing for an agreement to bring in equal treatment for contracted workers within the health service (see chapter 5).

Overall, therefore, the reduction in trade union influence and organizing ability during the 1980s and 1990s contributed substantially to workers' inability to resist increasing inequality in the pay distribution, and this situation has been only partially alleviated under the New Labour government. By contrast, however, New Labour did move quickly to introduce minimum wage legislation, which was expected to offset some of the effects of reduced union involvement in pay-setting. We now assess the effects of this new legislation.

## Low Pay Protection and the National Minimum Wage

Until 1999, the United Kingdom did not have a national minimum wage. However, there had been other forms of low pay protection. Dating back in its modern form to the late 1940s, though having its origins in the late nineteenth century, the Fair Wages Resolution applied to private firms tendering for government contracts. Essentially a tender would be considered only if a fair wage was being paid for the jobs involved. A fair wage was defined as the minimum rate set in the relevant industrial multi-employer agreement, or, if no such agreement existed, as the going rate for similar work in the geographical area concerned. Schedule 11 of the 1975 Employment Protection Act extended the Fair Wages Resolution to *cover all employers*. The post-1979 Conservative government abolished both Schedule 11 and the Fair Wages Resolution shortly after coming into office.

The United Kingdom also had a system of wages councils, originating in the 1909 Trade Boards Act. In terms of the number of workers covered, the councils were at their height in 1953, when sixty-six councils covered roughly 15 percent of the total workforce in a range of different industries. Each council had three members who established minimum terms and conditions for their industry or subindustry—an independent, a union representative, and an employer representative. The orders of all the wages councils were enforced by the Wages Inspectorate. By the late 1980s, there were twenty-six wages councils covering over 2 million employees, the vast majority of whom were employed in retailing, miscellaneous services (especially hairdressing), and clothing. The range of matters over which wages councils could issue orders was severely curtailed by the Conservative government in 1986, and the councils were abolished altogether by a later Conservative government in 1993, leaving the Agricultural Wages Board as the only statutory instrument that set minimum wages. In addition to these various forms of statutory protection for the low-paid, industry-wide collective agreements provided a floor for the large numbers of workers covered by them. As explained earlier, these had effectively disappeared in the private sector by the end of the 1980s.

Thus, when the New Labour government entered office in 1997, the British system was more bereft of low pay protection than it had been at any time since the Second World War. At its introduction in 1999, the NMW was worth £3.60 (US$7.35)[6] for "adult" workers (age twenty-two and older) and £3.00 (US$6.12) for young workers (age eighteen to twenty-one). The latter is sometimes known as the development rate, since it can also be paid to adult workers in the first six months of a new job with a new employer if they are receiving accredited training. In 2004 a third rate was introduced for six-teen- and seventeen-year-olds.

The Low Pay Commission coordinates research on the impact of the NMW and makes recommendations on future increases in the level of the minimum, while the final decision on up-ratings rests with the government. Early forecasts that the NMW would initially affect about 9 percent of the workforce proved to be overestimates, largely owing to deficiencies in the data available; in fact, only 6 to 7 percent of workers were affected (Dickens and Manning 2004). The NMW adult rate initially fell as a proportion of adult median earn-ings, from 47.6 percent in 1999 to 45.2 percent in 2001. As a result of subsequent up-ratings in excess of average earnings growth, the rela-tive value of the NMW recovered to 48.9 percent of median earnings in 2005 (figure 2.2).[7] Thus, the estimated gap between the NMW and the low pay threshold still remains as high as seventeen to eighteen percentage points.

Comparisons of the degree of inequality before and after the intro-duction of the NMW show the bottom third of the wage distribution experiencing above-median growth in wages (Butcher 2005), though it is difficult to isolate the specific impact of the NMW. The NMW ap-pears to have had a greater impact on women than on men. One study, for example, found that the effects of the NMW on male wage inequality were indiscernible at the fifth and tenth percentiles, while there was a significant impact on the female wage distribution, pulling wages at the fifth and tenth percentiles up by sixty pence and nineteen pence an hour, respectively, and bringing female wage inequality into line with male wage inequality (Gosling and Lemieux 2004). This is consistent with other studies showing the NMW to have contributed, albeit in a moderate way, to reducing the gender wage gap at the bot-tom of the wage distribution (Robinson 2002, 2003).

Early evidence indicated that this positive impact at the bottom of the wage distribution was achieved largely without the adverse ef-fects on employment predicted by the NMW's opponents (Draca and Vaitilingam 2006). Mark Stewart (2004) found no such effects from the introduction of the NMW or subsequent up-ratings in 2000 and 2001, while a review by David Metcalf (2004) found that the NMW resulted in a "large boost" for lower-paid earners, with no harmful consequences for jobs. However, the NMW may have reduced em-ployment opportunities in some industries with very high propor-tions of low-paid workers, as shown by one study of the home care

Figure 2.2  Adult Minimum Wage as a Proportion of
           Median and Mean Gross Hourly Earnings
           (Excluding Overtime), All Employee Jobs,
           1999 to 2005

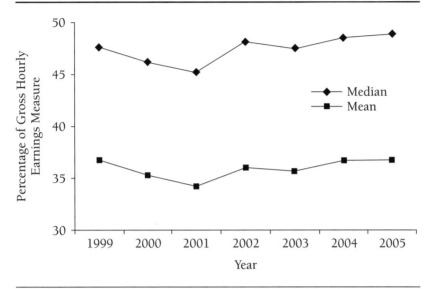

*Source:* 1999 to 2004: Low Pay Commission (LPC) (2005, table 2.5); 2005: National Institute of Economic and Social Research (NIESR) estimates.

sector (Machin and Wilson 2004). Another study suggested that employment growth was lower in the regions and sectors that were most exposed to the impact of the NMW (Galindo-Rueda and Pereira 2004).

More positively, there is evidence that some employers may respond to a minimum wage by seeking to improve the productivity of low-wage workers. For example, Wiji Arulampalam, Alison Booth, and Mark Bryan (2004) found that increases in the level of the NMW in the period 1998 to 2000 increased the probability that the affected workers would receive training by eight to eleven percentage points. In a study by Ed Cronin and Michael Thewlis (2004), 23 percent of small businesses surveyed reported a positive effect on training in response to the minimum wage. This is consistent with an analysis based on the 1998 Workplace Employment Relations Survey (WERS) by Filipe Almeida-Santos and Karen Mumford (2004), who found that higher levels of wage compression were positively related to training. In some cases, this may come about as a result of firms reviewing their human resource policies in response to NMW up-ratings (Rainbird, Holly, and Leisten 2002).

In addition, some employers reported that their approach to coping with the minimum wage was to cut costs by improving productivity, changing suppliers, or diversifying into new areas (Cronin and Thewlis 2004). Similarly, Damian Grimshaw and Marilyn Carroll (2006) found evidence of some firms opting for a higher-quality, higher-paid form of customer service in response to the NMW, and some had also begun to offer new services and enter new markets. In both of these studies, however, the proportion of firms in which the NMW was linked to a change in product market or human resource strategies was small. Grimshaw and Carroll argue that this is because many firms have long-established cost-minimizing employment practices (for example, a lack of training or pay progression; long working hours) that inhibit them from pursuing innovative product strategies.

Overall, the introduction of the NMW has not succeeded in reducing the proportion of workers in the United Kingdom below the low pay threshold. As noted earlier, there is still a substantial gap between this threshold and the NMW, and many organizations have found ways of complying with minimum wage legislation that effectively reduce the terms and conditions of employment for many low-wage employees. For example, firm-level assessments by Incomes Data Services (2004) indicate that many employers have responded to the minimum wage by reducing differentials between wage rates at the bottom of the wage structure. In some cases, firms have restructured wages, collapsing starter grades and low grades into a smaller number of wage bands. A number of large retailers have responded by introducing new contracts that remove or reduce fringe payments, such as bonuses and premiums for working unsociable hours or overtime, and replace them with a higher basic rate that complies with the NMW (for examples from our retail case studies, see chapter 4).

## Increased Labor Market Participation at Low-Wage Rates

The battery of policies available to help bring the unemployed into employment can have a variety of impacts on low-paid work. Here we consider the effects, in particular, of active labor market policy and the shift toward in-work benefits. We also assess the impact of the growing student labor supply.

*Active Labor Market Policies for the Unemployed*    The battery of policies available to help bring the unemployed into employment can have a variety of impacts on low-paid work. Currently in the United Kingdom, active labor market policy for the unemployed revolves around a series of so-called New Deals for the young (age eighteen to twenty-four) unemployed, for those age twenty-five and older, for those over fifty, for the disabled, for lone parents, and for the partners of unemployed people. The largest of these, the New Deal for Young People (NDYP), had 1.2 million participants between 1998 and 2004 (Brewer and Shephard 2005). The program is compulsory for all young people age eighteen to twenty-four who have been on Job-Seeker's Allowance (JSA), an unemployment benefit, for six months. Participants are given four months of intensive support to help them find a job, and if by the end of this time they have not succeeded, they are offered four options for further support: education, subsidized job placement with training, voluntary work, and environmental work. Of these options, subsidized employment has been found to be the most effective in reducing unemployment (Dorsett 2004). Studies have shown that the NDYP has increased the probability of young people finding jobs by around five percentage points, representing around 17,000 job placements (Blundell et al. 2003). Michael White and Rebecca Riley (2002) found an overall reduction in youth unemployment of 35,000 to 40,000, an estimate supported by the findings of David Wilkinson (2003). This is in line with evaluations of similar schemes in Sweden, Switzerland, and East Germany (Dorsett 2004). Despite high expenditure per participant (around £19,000 (US$38,791), according to Brewer and Shephard 2005), cost-benefit analysis suggests that the scheme has created substantial welfare gains (White and Riley 2002; Van Reenen 2003).

The New Deal for 25 Plus is the second-largest program, with 720,000 individuals having passed through it between 1998 and 2004. It is focused on the long-term unemployed, people who have claimed JSA for eighteen out of the last twenty-one months, and the program works in a very similar way to the NDYP. The New Deal for Lone Parents (NDLP) is a very different kind of program. It is voluntary, and participation is by invitation. The support consists of assistance with job search and child care provision. By the end of 2004,

700,000 people had been through the NDLP program, and 320,000 of these participants had gained a job.

*Increased Emphasis on In-Work Benefits*    The origins of the United Kingdom's present social security system lie in the Beveridge-designed welfare state at the end of the Second World War. The driving principle behind this system was not simply the narrow aim of poverty relief, but the wider one of social insurance. Thus, the main benefits were state-contingent. Anyone who fell into a defined state of "misfortune" was entitled to such benefits regardless of means. These misfortunes included unemployment, long-term sickness and disability, and old age. A second class of benefits, which were means-tested, was for poverty relief. These were meant to be available for those who had slipped through the social insurance net, most often because they had not worked for long enough to have made sufficient national insurance contributions to qualify for the state-contingent benefits.

Thus, the initial aim of the system was for state-contingent benefits to be higher than, or at least as high as, means-tested benefits. However, this imposed a severe financial strain on the public finances, not least because the designers of the original system had not anticipated future high levels of unemployment and inactivity, and most importantly of all because they had not anticipated the rapid increase in longevity. Inevitably, therefore, the system became more and more driven by means-tested benefits, whose value now comfortably exceeds those of state-contingent benefits.

The unemployment benefit was a state-contingent benefit. In the 1980s, its generosity was eroded in a variety of respects. Its value relative to median earnings fell; the earnings-related supplement was withdrawn; it became taxable. In its later years, only those who were out of work for less than a year qualified. Thereafter, if an individual remained unemployed, he or she went on income support, a broader-based, means-tested benefit available also to those out of the labor market. In 1996 the unemployment benefit was abolished, and the Job-Seeker's Allowance was introduced in its stead. As the authorities put it, a claimant had to "be capable of, available for and actively seeking work."

Over the years, the administration of the unemployment benefit and subsequently the Job-Seeker's Allowance and income support has become tougher. Although there was not a strict maximum duration of social security support, government officials became more aggressive in attempting to persuade people into jobs and were more likely to withhold benefits from those who refused to take up job offers. The New Deal policy of the present Labour government has continued this theme of compulsion by making participation in the New Deal compulsory for the young and prime-age adult unemployed. At the same time, there has been increased scrutiny of those on the incapacity benefit. Potentially this could increase the supply of labor at the bottom end of the market, putting further downward pressure on pay.

A very significant change introduced by the present government has been an increased stress on in-work benefits. Broadly speaking, the evidence suggests that this has increased work incentives for lone parents and the primary earners in couples, but that it may have slightly reduced work incentives for secondary earners in couples (for a review see Brewer and Browne 2006).

The Working Families Tax Credit (WFTC), which was introduced in 1999, provided support for those who were working and who had dependent children. It also had a large child care supplement. Following substantial increases in generosity, the WFTC was replaced in 2003 by the Working Tax Credit (WTC) and the Child Tax Credit (CTC). The WTC is significant in that it is not limited to those with dependent children. The CTC is available to those with children whether they are working or not, providing a bridge of support that does not change according to economic activity. The stated aim of the tax credits is to "make work pay" for families and provide a "minimum income, above and beyond the minimum wage" (HM Treasury 1998). The emphasis on increasing the incomes of families with children is an important part of the government's plan to reduce child poverty (see chapter 1). A distinctive feature of the tax credits is that they have a relatively low withdrawal rate as recipients earn more, so as to minimize adverse impacts on labor supply (Hills and Waldfogel 2004; McKay 2003).

The WFTC rapidly became a major source of income for a large number of families: a survey of families with children found that 21 percent of those with a parent working over sixteen hours per week were receiving the WFTC in 2001 (McKay 2003). Around two-thirds of those who had moved into work (of more than sixteen hours per week) since the previous year were receiving the WFTC. According to one comparative study, the WFTC had the most generous payouts of in-work benefits in any OECD country (OECD 2005).

The evidence suggests that the overall impact of the WFTC was to raise the labor force participation rates and number of hours worked by lone parents while at the same time slightly reducing the participation rates of second-income earners (for example, married women) owing to income effects on the household as a whole. Overall, the impact on participation appears to have been positive (Brewer and Browne 2006). A recent study by Ian Mulheirn and Mario Pisani (2006) found that the 2003 WTC regime has had similar effects. They estimate an overall positive impact on participation of between 1.9 and 2.9 percentage points, with a very small reduction in the number of hours supplied. Much of this increase in participation is in low-wage jobs, since these are often the most readily available form of employment for people who are reentering the labor force after a period of unemployment or inactivity.[8]

*The Growth in Student Labor*　Another factor contributing to the prevalence of low-wage labor in recent years has been the increasing pressure on students to work part-time while at school, college, or university. There used to be a time when British commentators thought of "working your way through college" as a North American phenomenon. However, the situation has changed rapidly in the United Kingdom. A recent survey by the Royal Bank of Scotland claims that almost half of university students in the United Kingdom take on paid work during term time—an average of sixteen hours per week (McGillivray 2006). Twenty percent of students are reported to work more than twenty hours per week.

A number of authors (see, for example, Dustmann et al. 1996; Hibbett and Beatson 1995) have documented the growing presence of students in the United Kingdom's labor market. A study by the Employment Policy Institute (1997) showed that 45 percent of the increase in part-time female employment (and 50 percent of the increase in part-time male employment) in the United Kingdom was accounted for by students. Angela Canny (2002) reminds us that it is not just university students in this age group who are working more. Typically, a British youth enters university at eighteen, but compulsory schooling ends at sixteen. Canny studied the sixteen- to nineteen-year-old age group, which includes not only young university students but also those who are in any full-time education, predominantly in secondary schools and sixth-form colleges. She finds that the percentage of this age group engaged in full-time education who were also employed rose from 36 to 41 percent between 1992 and 2000. On average, they worked thirteen hours per week in 1992 and sixteen hours per week in 2000. Just twelve occupations accounted for student employment, with the most common being sales assistants, waiters or waitresses, and retail checkout operators. The sectors most affected, therefore, were retail, hotels, and restaurants (see chapters 3 and 4).

One important reason for these developments has been changes in government funding arrangements for university students. Progressively over the last twenty-five years, student maintenance grants (to cover living expenses) have disappeared, except for those going to students from the poorest families, while more recently "top-up" fees have been introduced: students themselves now have to pay a proportion of their tuition fees, as opposed to the government bearing the whole funding burden.[9] Though a government-backed system of student loans has been introduced, these loans are limited in size, and it is reported that students from poorer families are averse to taking on debt.

Obviously these new financial arrangements for university students cannot explain the increased labor force participation of college and school students. It is conjectured that part of the explanation is related to a massive increase in staying-on rates after sixteen. Young people who in earlier years would have gone into paid employment now stay on in full-time education but contribute to the household budget by undertaking part-time jobs. The scale of this growth in student labor implies a significant increase in the labor supply at the lower end of the labor market, making it easier for employers to offer low wages and almost certainly displacing workers from other demographic groups.

## WORKFORCE SKILLS AND EMPLOYER PRODUCT STRATEGIES

In policy circles, great emphasis is placed upon skill upgrading as a route out of low-paid work. However, as we show in this section, there still appears to be a relatively high level of employer demand for low-skilled labor in the United Kingdom.

The architecture of the United Kingdom's education and training system has changed so considerably in the last couple of decades that it can be bewildering even to the native reader. Therefore, we introduce the section with a brief route map. In the last ten years, political devolution has made it increasingly difficult to talk about a single system in the United Kingdom. The Scottish system has long had significant differences from the English one, but in recent years the Welsh and Northern Irish systems have started to develop more features of their own as well. In what follows, we describe the English system, which covers about 80 percent of the United Kingdom's population.

Children start secondary school at the age of eleven. Successful students take the General Certificate of Secondary Education (GCSE) after five years. After another two years at school, they take advanced-level exams (A level). It is performance at A levels that primarily determines whether students obtain a university place and at how good a university. Until 1992, higher education could be obtained in universities or polytechnics.[10] After 1992, the polytechnics became universities. Less successful students leave the formal education system at some earlier stage. The minimum school leaving age is sixteen (fifteen until 1972), and historically many children used to leave at this point, often with few or no qualifications.

Some of these individuals received work-based training from their employers. In the post–World War II years, there was a well-developed apprenticeship system, associated largely, but not entirely, with traditional manufacturing. A small percentage of school-leavers were lucky enough to obtain apprenticeships. As for the rest, if they received training at all, it was of much shorter duration and more ad hoc. A wide array of vocational work-based qualifications were available from a variety of awarding bodies, though uncertified training was a common feature of the scene. The traditional apprenticeship system was largely collapsed in the 1980s, and since then successive governments have been trying to rebuild and widen a satisfactory system of work-based training.

Meanwhile, in the 1980s, the Thatcher government sought to develop a unified and comparable system of qualifications, and out of this effort emerged national vocational qualifications (NVQs). There are five levels of NVQs: level 5 equates to a postgraduate degree, level 4 to a bachelor's degree, level 3 to a reasonable performance at A level, and level 2 to a reasonable performance at GCSE. There is an equivalence scale for vocational qualifications, whether acquired at the workplace or in formal education. Most such vocational qualifications are at NVQ levels 1 to 3.

Figure 2.3  Proportions of Individuals Age Sixteen to Sixty-Five with a University Degree or Higher Qualifications or with No Qualifications

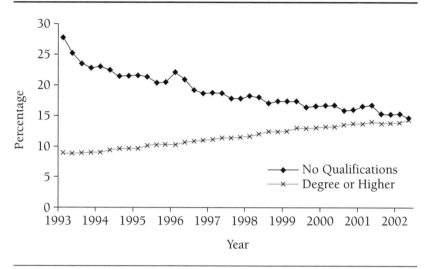

Source: Labour Force Survey (LFS).

On many criteria, the performance of the United Kingdom's formal education system has improved dramatically over the last twenty years: the proportion of school pupils staying on after the minimum school-leaving age of sixteen has gone up, and the proportion of the population lacking formal qualifications has declined steadily (figure 2.3). In the late 1980s and early 1990s, the previously elite system of higher education transformed into a mass higher education system, and the government has now set a target for some 50 percent of the relevant age cohort to participate in higher education by 2010.

However, the economic and distributional implications of this expansion remain a matter of controversy (Keep and Mayhew 2004). The United Kingdom government justifies the expansion by arguing that it will not only lead to greater national economic success in terms of international competitiveness and growth, but also be an instrument for increasing social justice by giving students from less-well-off families easier access to higher education, thereby increasing the likelihood that they will obtain better jobs. Both presumptions have been questioned. Greater national economic success, it is argued, will result only if a whole series of other conditions, such as an increase in the average quality of production in the United Kingdom, are fulfilled (Wolf 2002). At the same time, expansion may have perverse consequences for young people from families in lower socio-economic groups unless more direct measures are taken to improve access to universities (Mayhew, Deer, and Dua 2004). Despite the move to mass higher education, the percentage of university students originating from the three lowest of the six socioeconomic groups remains much the same as it was forty years ago, while students from this background are disproportionately represented at the "new" universities (the former polytechnics) and have more limited prospects for high-paid employment.

Given these doubts, questions are raised as to whether some of the public money currently being devoted to higher education might not be better spent elsewhere in the education system—for example, at junior schools (to tackle emerging learning problems earlier and more effectively) or on post-sixteen subdegree education and training to prepare young people more adequately for the types of jobs currently on offer.

At the bottom end of the labor market is widespread evidence of continuing problems with deficiencies in basic skills such as numeracy and literacy (DfES 2005). The results of the 1998 International Adult Literacy Survey confirmed the country's relatively low standing in this regard. The 2000 Program for International Student Assessment (PISA) study of fifteen-year-olds showed the United Kingdom in a more favorable comparative light. This led some parts of the government to believe that the lack of basic skills would flush out of the system via an age cohort effect. However, the unofficial results of the more recent 2003 PISA study (the response rate was too low for the United Kingdom to be included in the official results) were much less promising.[11]

In terms of workforce skills and training, the United Kingdom is noted for its relative lack of intermediate or NVQ3 (level 3) skills (Prais 1995). As described earlier, the apprenticeship system went into steep decline during the early 1980s recession, and successive government attempts to rebuild it have had limited success. Available evidence now points to an increase in the number of people receiving work-based training and an increase in the amount of this training that leads to a qualification (Leitch 2005). Insofar as international comparisons are reliable in this area, it would appear that British employers spend more than most others on adult training. However, this training is generally short in duration, low-level, and often defensive (for example, to meet health and safety requirements). It is also unevenly distributed, with lower-skilled, part-time, and older workers receiving relatively little training.

Thus, in a workforce that has generally received more education and training than it used to and is more qualified than it used to be, there remains a substantial bottom layer that lacks basic skills, receives little real training and development, and is heavily represented in low-wage employment. As noted in chapter 1, the existence of this relatively large low-skilled, low-paid section of the workforce may well reinforce existing incentives for many employers in the United Kingdom to engage in low-skill, low-pay product strategies and work practices and thus to add to the demand for workers who fit this description.

Research evidence on the links between employer product strategies and workforce skills has included international comparisons of matched samples of establishments in which British producers were typically found to specialize in less elaborate, less complex types of product than are commonly made in other countries such as Germany. Lower value-added product strategies in the majority of British establishments were in turn linked to lower levels of workforce skills in a number of different industries such as clothing, food processing, and automotive components (Steedman and Wagner 1989; Mason, van Ark, and Wagner 1994; Mason and Wagner 2002). Within the United Kingdom, establishment-level multivariate analysis based on Employer Skills Survey data has found a high level of correlation between a summary measure of product strategy (incorporating information on product complexity, product quality, and innovation leadership) and a mean skills measure based on a wage-weighted qualifications index (Mason 2004).

Other research has identified a sizable number of employers in the United Kingdom that demand workers with no qualifications at all (see, for example, Felstead, Gallie, and Green 2002). Such employers tend to be producers of low-specification products and services with relatively low skill requirements. Their work organization and job design also imply lack of informal training and development. By increasing demand for low-skilled workers, the prevalence of product strategies of this kind has contributed to the relatively large share of employees in the United Kingdom that fall below the low pay threshold.

IMMIGRATION

Any exogenous increase in the supply of labor emanating from net migration is likely to hold down pay levels in those segments of the labor market in which immigrants compete. At least since the mid-1970s there has been a long-term positive trend in net migration. Both immigration and emigration have increased since 1993, and net immigration has remained positive since 1994 (see figure 2.4, where the numbers cover migration for all purposes and not just for work). As David Coleman and Robert Rowthorn (2004) point out, in 1997 there was a major change in United Kingdom immigration policy. Until then, the emphasis had been on "minimizing settlement," whereas thereafter "large scale immigration was seen as essential for the UK's economic well-being." Since then, there has been a substantial increase in migrants coming to the United Kingdom for work from within and outside the European Union. Immigration from outside the European Union is controlled through a work permits system, supplemented by a variety of special schemes (covering, for example, highly skilled migrants, seasonal agricultural workers, and low-skilled workers in "labor shortage" sectors such as hospitality and food processing; see chapters 3 and 6). May 2004 marked a major watershed: citizens of ten new member states of the European Union were allowed what were effectively unrestricted working rights in the United Kingdom.

Christian Dustmann and his colleagues (2005), using Labour Force Survey data for 1983 to 2000, found that the skill distribution of immigrants was pretty similar to that of the indigenous population. They could find few "overall" effects on the aggregate employment, participation, unemployment, or wages of indigenous workers, though they tentatively concluded that indigenous workers with intermediate levels of education may have suffered negative employment effects. By contrast, Coleman and Rowthorn (2004) agree that the aggregate economic effects of immigration, good or bad, are likely to be negligible, but they highlight the possibility of significant negative effects of competition from unskilled migrants on labor market outcomes for unskilled workers in the United Kingdom. This seems most likely to occur if the migrant workers are relatively high-skilled but nonetheless willing to compete for low-skilled jobs. Both these studies were conducted on data that predate the entry of large num-

Figure 2.4 International Migration

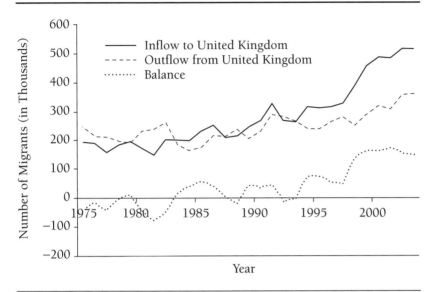

*Notes:* Data for 1975 to 1990 are based on the International Passenger Survey (IPS) only. Data for 1991 to 2003 are based mainly on IPS data. Includes adjustments for those whose intended length of stay changes so that their migrant status changes; asylum-seekers and their dependents not identified by the IPS; and flows between the United Kingdom and the Republic of Ireland.

bers of Central and Eastern European immigrants following European Union enlargement.

By the nature of things, it is difficult to estimate the number of illegal immigrants, but there is a general perception that this is a growing problem in the United Kingdom. Jo Woodbridge (2005) estimates that 430,000 illegal immigrants were present in the United Kingdom in 2001—representing about 0.7 percent of the total population. It is believed that more of these are people who "overstay" their visa rather than people who enter clandestinely (IPPR 2006). The majority of illegal migrants who work are thought to be employed in low-paying sectors such as food processing and agriculture.

Legal migrant workers are more widely dispersed across a range of jobs, but many are competing with indigenous workers at the bottom end of the market—and indeed, in some areas of skilled work as well, for example, central European workers in construction trades.[12] Bridget Anderson and her colleagues (2006) discovered many "high-quality" migrants in low-quality jobs, while Sally Dench and others (2006) found employers welcoming migrants as a means of filling vacancies without having to push up pay. Some of these employers also stated that they preferred the "work ethic" and "general attitude" of migrants. However, concerns that further competition for low-skilled workers seeking employment could cause social problems led even some employers' organizations, such as the British Chambers of Commerce and the Confederation of British Industry, to call for restricted entry for migrants from Romania and Bulgaria before those two countries joined the European Union in 2007 (*Financial Times*, August 18, 2006). Some of our case study research reported in chapters 3 and 6 suggests that recent immigrants have added greatly to the supply of workers competing for low-wage jobs in, for example, hotels and food processing. According to a recent study published by the Bank of England, the influx of new immigrants since 2004 may well have contributed to slower growth in nominal wages (Saleheen and Shadforth 2006).

## JOB AND LIFE QUALITY IN LOW-WAGE EMPLOYMENT

The case study evidence presented in chapters 3 through 7 highlights a number of ways in which low-wage employment can have negative effects on life quality—for example, by requiring workers to work long hours or unsociable hours; making it difficult for workers to meet their parental responsibilities; imposing strict monitoring of absence from work; creating feelings of job insecurity; and limiting access to sick pay, holidays, and pension entitlements. In recent years, however, new legislation, some of it based on European Union directives, has sought to rectify some of these problems—for example, by bringing terms and conditions for part-time workers into line with those covering full-time workers. In this section, we explore the impact of some of this legislation and address the question of whether the job and life quality associated with low-wage employment is getting better or worse.

### TRENDS IN WORKING HOURS

The average weekly hours of men in full-time work in the United Kingdom have fallen slightly, from 40.9 in 1996 to 39.1 in 2002, and those of women have fallen from 33.4 to 33.1 (Green 2003). This represents a continuation of a downward trend throughout the postwar years (Green 2001). Nonetheless, the United Kingdom remains distinctive among European Union member states in the degree to which hours are unstandardized and polarized between the top and bottom of the distribution (Kodz et al. 2003). Average annual hours worked per employee are also long compared to other European countries (though not compared to the United States).[13] On the one hand, there has been continued growth in reduced-hours flexible working arrangements (Kersley et al. 2006). On the other hand, some 29 percent of men and 9 percent of women continued to work long hours (forty-five hours per week or more) in 2005, although these proportions had declined slightly in the preceding five years (Grimshaw and Marchington 2006).

In the United Kingdom the regulation of working time has historically taken place through collective bargaining rather than through legislation. This changed when, in 1998, the government of the United Kingdom adopted a set of working time regulations that implemented the European Commission's 1993 "Working Time Directive." The regulations limited working time to forty-eight hours per week over a seventeen-week reference period and guaranteed set rest periods and days off. The United Kingdom was the only country to make use of the "opt-out" clause negotiated in the 1993 directive, which allowed employees to agree not to be subject to the forty-eight-hour limit, although other countries have since implemented similar provisos. Catherine Barnard, Simon Deakins, and Richard Hobbs (2004) report substantial use of the opt-out in the health, hotels and catering, manufacturing and engineering, and legal and financial sectors. A 2001 survey found that an estimated 13 percent of all employees "usually" worked more than forty-eight hours per week (BMRB 2001). According to a European Commission report, many firms in the United Kingdom ask prospective employees to sign a declaration alongside their employment contracts as a matter of routine, and in some cases inadequate records are kept of hours worked per week in excess of forty-eight (European Commission 2004). Attempts to amend the directive by applying stricter controls to the opt-out have so far made little progress.

The directive also ensured a minimum number of paid holidays (four weeks) for all employees, a subject that had previously been regulated only by collective bargaining. Women in part-time jobs, in particular, benefited. According to Francis Green (2003), the proportion of female employees deprived of any such entitlements fell from 15 percent in 1996 to 6 percent in 2001.

For low-paid workers, any moves to reduce working hours may be a mixed blessing. On the one hand, shorter working hours may be beneficial for health and for family and personal life. On the other hand, workers may be deprived of a means of securing a living wage. We return to this issue in chapter 8.

## Implementation of European Union Directives

Much other legislation with direct relevance to low-paid jobs has been enacted as a result of the Labour government implementing certain European Union directives—for example, those covering part-time and fixed-term employment. Thus, the "Part-time Workers (Prevention of Less Favorable Treatment) Regulations 2000" require part-timers to be treated the same as comparable full-timers with respect to:

- Hourly rates of pay

- Access to company pension schemes

- Entitlements to annual leave and maternity/parental leave on a pro rata basis

- Entitlement to contractual sick pay

- Access to training

Similar protection for temporary employees is provided by the "Fixed-term Employees (Prevention of Less Favorable Treatment) Regulations," which were introduced in 2002. However, these regulations do not apply to agency workers who are not directly employed by the company for which they do their work.

In 2000 the British government reluctantly implemented the European works council directive. However, works councils have never been a significant part of the British scene, and research suggests that this directive has had little impact on employment relations in the United Kingdom to date (Terry 2003). The "Information and Consultation Regulations," which came into force in April 2005, apply to organizations with 150 or more employees and are more likely to make an impact in the British context, but it is hard to imagine this having a significant effect on the terms and conditions of the low-paid.

## Temporary Employment

The United Kingdom has a relatively low incidence of temporary work compared to most other European countries. In part, this reflects low levels of employment protection for permanent workers. The proportion of employees engaged in temporary work has fluctuated between 5 and 7 percent over the last ten years, with a slight downward trend since 1997 (figure 2.5). The biggest change over this period has been in the sort of temporary work being done. Agency work has increased substantially, from 7 percent of all temporary employees in 1992 to 16 percent in 2004, while the proportions employed on a fixed contract, on a casual basis, or in seasonal work have

## Figure 2.5  Temporary Employment, 1990 to 2005

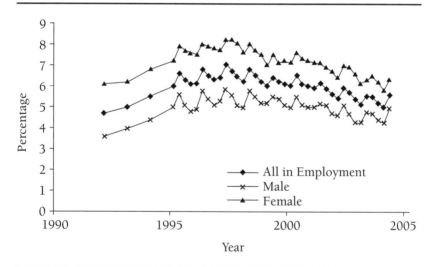

*Source:* Labour Force Survey (LFS), taken from the Office of National Statistics (ONS) website, http://www.statistics.gov.uk.

*Notes:* "Temporary" employees in the LFS are defined as those who say that their main job is nonpermanent for one of the following reasons: fixed-period contracting, agency temping, casual work, seasonal work, or other. Figures include part-time temporary employees. Data are not seasonally adjusted. Estimates are based on the revised population estimates published in October 2004.

all gradually declined.[14] However, the United Kingdom remains distinctive in the lack of regulation covering temporary agency workers compared to other countries (Purcell and Cam 2002). The legal position of agency workers is ambiguous in Britain, since in the so-called triangular employment relationship, the absence of a contract can mean that temporary workers are deemed not to be employed either by the user firm or by the agency (Davidov 2004).

On average, temporary workers report lower levels of job satisfaction, receive less job-related training, and are less well paid than their permanent counterparts (Booth, Francesconi, and Frank 2002). However, there is evidence that temporary jobs can act as a stepping-stone to more permanent work, with the median transition time being between eighteen months and three and a half years, depending on the contract type (seasonal or fixed-term) and gender (Booth, Francesconi, and Frank 2002). As described in chapter 7 on call centers, some employers that in the past have relied heavily on temporary agency workers are now under pressure to upgrade more of these jobs to permanent status in order to attract and retain the type of person needed to meet service quality standards. In other sectors, such as food processing and hotels, agency workers are overwhelmingly migrants with pay and conditions at or even below the statutory minimums (see chapters 3 and 6).

## Employment Security

An important aspect of any job is the degree of employment security, an issue addressed in the case study chapters. Employment protection legislation has an important role to play in this regard.

Legislation concerning dismissal has changed periodically over the decades, swinging between more and less generosity to the employee. Currently, a worker has to have been in a job for at least a year to be covered by the law. Part-timers have the same rights as full-timers. Not only does due cause have to be proved, but strict warning procedures have to be followed, with time given to improve against specific targets, before a dismissal can be deemed to be fair. Many unfair dismissal cases are concluded by informal agreements between the parties, but if such an agreement is not possible, the case is heard by an industrial tribunal (a lay court). Compensation is related to the pay and length of service of the employee, though rigid formulas are not always applied unless the case comes to court. In general, the procedural requirements relating to dismissal are demanding, but the financial penalties with which employers are threatened are usually not great. Similarly with legislation concerning redundancy, the procedural requirements are strict, but penalties for failing to follow them are not large, nor is the scale of statutory compensation to which workers are entitled. There are few legal restrictions on group dismissals or entire establishment closures, beyond those that apply on an individual basis to each of the affected workers (Dickens and Hall 2003).

## Antidiscrimination Legislation

This legislation has important implications for the incidence of low pay since low-paid work has traditionally been associated with women and with some racial minorities.

Legislation against both gender and racial discrimination has been a feature of the United Kingdom scene since the early 1970s. The Equal Pay Act of 1970 required employers to offer the same pay terms to men and women doing the same job within their organization. This was thought to be so revolutionary that employers were given until 1975 to become fully compliant. In 1975 the Sex Discrimination Act made it illegal to discriminate against women in recruitment and promotion. The Equal Opportunities Commission was established to monitor this legislation and also to promote various forms of affirmative action to advance the position of women in the labor market. The principle of positive discrimination has never been generally accepted in the United Kingdom. In the 1980s, under pressure from the European Court of Justice, the principle of equal pay for work of equal value was adopted and the provisions of the 1970 act amended accordingly. The precise details of the legislation were changed from time to time but remained essentially unaltered.

In 1970 the median female earner received about half of what the median male earned. The same percentage comparison applied point to point on the male-to-female earnings distributions. This earnings disadvantage could be decomposed into occupational disadvantage (women being crowded into low-paying occupations) and pay disadvantage (women being relatively badly paid within any occupation). Either form of disadvantage could be the consequence either of specific acts of labor market discrimination or of possession of relatively poor productive characteristics. In the latter case, these characteristics could themselves be in part the consequence of prior acts of discrimination in the labor market or outside the labor market. Today the 50 percent figure for female/male earnings has increased to about 81 percent for full-timers, but to only 59 percent for part-timers (Equal Opportunities Commission 2005). These gender pay gaps vary considerably from occupation to occupation and from sector to sector, but overall they have changed very little since the mid-1990s. The consensus of opinion among researchers is that specific acts of discrimination in the labor market have fallen over time. However, it seems clear that after rapid improvements in the position of women in the 1970s, progress slowed significantly thereafter.

Legislation against racial discrimination was first comprehensively introduced in the Race Relations Act of 1976. As a consequence the Commission for Racial Equality was established. The commission implements the legislation and engages in affirmative action programs. Nonwhite racial minorities comprise between 7 and 8 percent of the population. Before the early 1950s, the nonwhite population of the country was tiny. The first large waves of immigrants, predominantly Afro-Caribbeans and Pakistanis, were encouraged to move to the United Kingdom to help employers cope with extremely tight labor markets. Later-entering groups were Indians, East African Asians, and Chinese. United Kingdom law makes it illegal to discriminate on the grounds of racial or ethnic origin in hiring, promotion, or the award of terms and conditions. The research consensus is that specific acts of labor market discrimination have been significantly reduced over time but by no means eliminated.

Nonwhites as a whole do less well in the labor market than do whites. They have lower employment rates, higher unemployment rates, lower occupational attainment, and lower earnings. However, as noted earlier, the labor market fortunes of different racial groups differ significantly. On most measures Pakistani and Bangladeshi men and women and Afro-Caribbean men do worst. Indians and East African Asians tend to fare better, and on some measures, such as occupational attainment, they are higher-placed than indigenous whites (Clarke and Speeden 2001). It is the groups that entered the United Kingdom earliest that do worst two and three generations later. These early entrants were generally less well educated than later entrants, who were subject to tighter immigration regulations that favored those with more education. That the children and grandchildren of the early entrants continue to fare badly in the labor market appears to testify to the intergenerational transmission of disadvantage.

## Maternity Leave Provision and Child Care Arrangements

Before the Labour government entered office in 1997, there was limited child care provision in the United Kingdom, and the child care facilities that did exist tended to be extremely expensive while maternity pay was low. This caused many women to leave the labor market after having children and, on their return, to enter part-time jobs in low-paying sectors.

In line with its declared "family-friendly" policies, the present Labour government has increased assistance for child care. One measure in particular is of help to lower-paid workers. If a parent is working more than sixteen hours a week and qualifies for the Working Families Tax Credit, the state will cover up to 80 percent of approved child care costs. Other initiatives are not specifically directed at the low-paid. For example, there is now a statutory right to a limited amount of time off as parental leave for each child under five years of age, but the employer is not obliged to pay for this leave. Similarly, an employee has the right to request "flexible working patterns" if he or she is responsible for the upbringing of a child under six, but again, the employer is not obliged to grant the request.

Other policy improvements have come in the area of maternity leave. An employee is entitled to twenty-six weeks of maternity leave irrespective of her length of service with the employer. However, the qualifying conditions for obtaining statutory maternity pay are rather more stringent. She must have been working for her employer for at least six months, and her earnings must have exceeded a certain very low minimum level—£87 (US$177) per week in 2005-06. If these conditions are met, the employee is entitled to six weeks at 90 percent of her average weekly earnings and then up to twenty weeks at a flat rate of £106 (US$216) or 90 percent of her average weekly earning, whichever is the lower. A woman who does not qualify for statutory maternity pay may be entitled to a maternity allowance. To qualify for this, she must have been self-employed or employed for at least twenty-six weeks of the sixty-six weeks before her confinement, and she must have been earning an average of £30 (US$61.25) per week. The maternity allowance was £106 in 2005-2006, or 90 percent of previous average earnings, whichever was the lower.

These statutory provisions, in and of themselves, do not impose a major financial burden on employers, which can reclaim the vast bulk of the cost from the government. Nevertheless, there are some ways in which workers at the lower end of the labor market may lose out. They may find it difficult to meet the qualifying conditions—obviously this is a particular potential problem for temporary workers. They are also less likely than other workers to be working for employers whose maternity leave policy is better than the statutory requirements. Equally important, the statutory payments do imply a significant loss of income, which may be harder to sustain for those who had previously been low earners. The United Kingdom has very limited provision for paternity leave.

Although improvements in maternity and child care provision have occurred, they have done little to break the pattern of women leaving the labor market to have children and then returning to part-time employment. Many female workers still find it necessary to stay in low-paid part-time jobs in order to be able to combine family commitments with paid employment. In our retail case studies, for example, there were very few opportunities for female employees to be promoted unless they were willing and able to work full-time (chapter 4).

## WHAT ARE THE PROSPECTS FOR ESCAPING LOW-WAGE EMPLOYMENT?

In counting the personal and social cost of being low-paid, it is important that we determine how long people have remained in that state and whether periods of low pay have harmful consequences for subsequent labor market outcomes.

A number of studies have estimated the probability that a low-paid worker will continue to be low-paid in a subsequent period. For example, Mark Stewart (1999a) finds that the probability of being low-paid in the current year given low pay in the previous year is 0.68; this rises to 0.79 after two years, rises again to 0.84 after three years, and falls slightly to 0.83 after four years. The probability of becoming low-paid also declines the longer an individual avoids that state. Similar evidence has been reported by Lorenzo Cappellari and Stephen Jenkins (2003).[15]

Several factors have been linked to a high probability of remaining in low pay from one year to the next. According to Mark Stewart and Joanna Swaffield (1999), these include being female and having relatively little education; establishment-level factors include a lack of union coverage and employing fewer than twenty-five workers. However, much of the persistence is explained by endogenous factors ("state dependence"), indicating that the experience of low pay itself is damaging to subsequent earnings prospects. There could be several reasons for this: employers may take low pay in previous jobs to be an indicator of low productivity; low-paying jobs may provide fewer opportunities for human capital accumulation; or the experience of low pay may reduce employees' aspirations or motivation to seek better jobs (Stewart and Swaffield 1999).

There is also evidence of the existence of a "low pay, no pay" cycle in which the experience of low pay increases the probability of subsequently becoming unemployed, while unemployment has a similar effect on the probability of later finding low-paid work (Stewart 1999b). Cappellari and Jenkins (2003) found that the probability of obtaining a low-paid job was over three times higher for an unemployed person than for a person chosen at random, and other studies have confirmed the strong link between non-employed states and subsequent low pay (Arranz, Davia, and García-Serrano 2005; Dickens 1999). The transition from unemployment to low-paid work is found to be associated with poor qualification levels (Cappellari and Jenkins 2003), and the duration of a spell of non-employment is found to be positively associated with the wage penalty upon reentry (Arranz, Davia, and García-Serrano 2005).

Drawing on New Earnings Survey panel data, Abigail McKnight (2000) investigated the progress over a six-year period of individuals age twenty-five to forty-nine who were identified as being in the bottom quarter of the wage distribution in 1991. She found that 52.4 percent were still low-paid in the second year, gradually reducing in succeeding years to 20.3 percent in 1997. However, in keeping with the "low pay, no pay" cycle, many of these low-paid workers left the labor force in each period. By the end of the six years, 47 percent of those who had started out low-paid in 1991 were no longer in employment and another 20 percent were still low-paid. This left only one in three who had stayed in employment and raised themselves above the lower pay quartile. Only 8.7 percent had achieved pay rates in the third and upper quartiles (table 2.9).

## Table 2.9 Progression of Low-Paid Workers, 1991 to 1997

| | 1991 | 1992 | 1993 | 1994 | 1995 | 1996 | 1997 |
|---|---|---|---|---|---|---|---|
| Quartile 1 | 100% | 52.4% | 41.9% | 31.5% | 27.8% | 27.8% | 20.3% |
| Quartile 2 | | 10 | 12.6 | 13.9 | 16 | 18.1 | 21.6 |
| Quartile 3 | | 1.5 | 2.1 | 3 | 4 | 5.5 | 7.2 |
| Quartile 4 | | 0.5 | 0.5 | 0.7 | 1 | 1.2 | 1.5 |
| Unemployed | | 4.3 | 5.6 | 5 | 4.2 | 3.9 | 2.9 |
| Other leavers | | 31.4 | 37.3 | 41.4 | 43.3 | 43.6 | 46.6 |
| Base (100 percent) | 35,283 | 35,283 | 35,283 | 35,283 | 35,283 | 35,283 | 35,283 |

*Source:* McKnight (2000).

Comparing the 1991 to 1997 period with two earlier six-year periods, McKnight found that earnings progression had improved over time for women but not for men (table 2.10). However, *long-term earnings inequality* had risen for both men and women, reflecting the overall increase in earnings inequality that had occurred over this period and the greater propensity of low-paid people to experience periods of unemployment or inactivity. Thus, low pay tends to be a persistent phenomenon for significant numbers of workers in the United Kingdom.

## Summary and Assessment

Low pay in the United Kingdom is heavily concentrated among part-time, temporary, and female employees, among younger (age sixteen to twenty-five) and older (sixty or older) age groups, and among employees holding low or no vocational qualifications. Over half of all low-paid workers are found in just three sectors (retail, health services, and hotels) and in three relatively unskilled occupational groups: personal services, sales, and operators.

Compared to many other European countries, the United Kingdom is distinctive for the way in which long working hours (forty-five or more per week) persist among sections of the population (29 percent of men and 9 percent of women in 2005), while part-time work has grown among men in recent years (10 percent in 2005) and remains high among women (39 percent). Temporary work accounts for only 6 percent of employees, but within this category the importance of agency work has increased substantially in recent years, reflecting the relative lack of regulation covering temporary agency

Table 2.10  Earnings Experience of Workers in the Lowest
Quartile (Q1) of the Earnings Distribution in
1977, 1984, and 1991

|  | 1977 to 1983 | 1984 to 1990 | 1991 to 1997 |
|---|---|---|---|
| All persons in Q1 in year 1 who were still employed and still in Q1 in year 7 | 50.9% | 49.6% | 40.1% |
| All persons in Q1 in year 1 who were still employed and still in either Q1 or Q2 in year 7 | 79.6 | 79.8 | 82.8 |
| Males in Q1 in year 1 who were still employed and still in Q1 in year 7 | 28.0 | 33.8 | 29.8 |
| Males in Q1 in year 1 who were still employed and still in either Q1 or Q2 in year 7 | 61.4 | 66.4 | 74.4 |
| Females in Q1 in year 1 who were still employed and still in Q1 in year 7 | 83.1 | 56.9 | 45.3 |
| Females in Q1 in year 1 who were still employed and still in either Q1 or Q2 in year 7 | 97.6 | 86.0 | 87.1 |

*Source:* McKnight (2000, tables 6.4 to 6.6).

workers in the United Kingdom compared to many other European countries.

Following a marked reduction in trade union influence during the 1980s and early 1990s, only 29 percent of employees in the United Kingdom are union members, and only 36 percent have their pay covered by collective agreements (down from 53 percent and 78 percent, respectively, in 1979). In private sector workplaces, trade union density is 18 percent, compared to 59 percent in the public sector. Employers now negotiate with unions over pay in only 18 percent of workplaces with more than ten employees. A large proportion of employment contracts in the United Kingdom are now effectively "individualized," and employer efforts to link pay increases to individual performance are widespread.

Since New Labour came to power, there have been few substantive changes to the industrial relations framework bequeathed by the previous Conservative governments. However, some terms and conditions relating to part-time employment, temporary employment, and maternity and paternity leave have been improved as a result of new regulations, many of them inspired by European Union directives. A national minimum wage (NMW) was introduced in 1999 following several decades when other forms of low pay protection had been abolished or weakened. This has contributed to above-median growth in earnings for employees toward the bottom of the pay distribution, particularly female employees. However, the newest NMW adult rates still amount to less than 50 percent of median gross hourly earnings across the economy as a whole. In some cases, employers have cut back on overtime premiums and premiums for working unsociable hours in order to introduce a higher basic wage rate that complies with the NMW.

The generosity of unemployment benefits was greatly eroded during the 1980s, and over the years the administration of such benefits has become tougher, with benefits likely to be withheld from people who refuse to take up job offers. Since 1997 the New Labour government has put increased emphasis on in-work benefits for low-paid employees. These have contributed to small increases in labor force participation among lone parents and primary earners in couples. The active labor market policy of the Labour government has been dominated by a desire to get people into jobs and to try to ensure that pay pressures do not hinder this endeavor. If low pay leads to poverty for some people, then in-work benefits are designed to alleviate this problem.

The likelihood of being in low-paid employment is strongly correlated with low levels of formal education, while those in low-paid work generally receive less work-based training than the workforce as a whole. The United Kingdom's education and training system has changed massively in recent years. There has been a transformation of elite higher education into mass higher education since the late 1980s, while there have been rapid increases in educational staying-on rates accompanied by a sharp decline in the proportion of the workforce who lack formal educational qualifications of some kind. However, there remain widespread deficiencies in basic skills (numeracy and literacy) among sections of the workforce. At the same time efforts to rebuild a craft apprenticeship training system have met with limited success. By international standards, Britain's levels of spending on adult training are comparatively high, but this training is generally short in duration and unevenly distributed, with less-skilled adult workers receiving relatively little training. In other words, the vocational education and training system still serves badly those who are in the lower reaches of the pay distribution.

On balance, these trends in labor force participation and in the evolution of the United Kingdom labor market and educational institutions have contributed to the present circumstances whereby sizable proportions of the workforce are low-skilled and low-paid. The evidence on wage mobility suggests that many such employees are essentially trapped in low-paid work, partly as a result of a "low pay, no pay" cycle in which individuals may end up alternating between periods of low pay and unemployment.

In general, our knowledge and understanding of the quality of low-paid jobs, the backgrounds and circumstances of those who work in them, and their aspirations and prospects is limited. The new case study evidence reported in the following chapters goes some way toward filling this gap.

In particular we explore in detail the factors determining pay and job quality in low-paid jobs, with a view to learning more about how the product strategies and pay and employment practices pursued by employers are influenced by United Kingdom labor market institutions and government policies.

## NOTES

1.  Pakistani, Bangladeshi, and Chinese workers, in particular, tend to be concentrated in poorly paid sales and restaurant jobs.
2.  Table 2.3 reports the marginal effects of each independent variable, taking a value of one as compared to a value of zero, evaluated at the means of independent variables in each equation. Thus, to take two examples, in equation 1 of table 2.3, the estimated probability of females being low-paid is twelve percentage points higher than it is for males (after controlling for age and ethnicity). In equation 2, the probability of graduates being low-paid is fifteen percentage points lower than it is for the reference group (skilled trades workers), while the probability of people with qualifications below the skilled trades level being low-paid is sixteen percentage points higher than it is for the reference group (after controlling for gender, age, ethnicity, and nationality).
3.  Note that the relationship between ethnicity and the probability of being paid below the low pay threshold is quite different from the relationship between ethnicity and pay levels in general. In standard OLS regressions of log hourly pay on gender, age group, qualifications

group, nationality, part-time working, temporary contract, occupation, sector, region, establishment size, and ethnic group (with whites as the reference ethnic category), the coefficients attached to five ethnic minority groups are negatively signed and statistically significant: black Caribbeans, black Africans, Indians, Bangladeshis, and Chinese/other Asian. The coefficients attached to Pakistanis and the residual "other" ethnic minority group are negatively signed but not significantly different from zero. These results are available from the authors on request.

4.  At the same time, as David Metcalf (2005) points out, almost 40 percent of workers covered by collective bargaining are *not* union members. In his estimate, this proportion of "free-riders" is four times higher than in the United States.

5.  "Shop steward" is a generic term for an "ordinary" worker who takes on the duties of union representative at the establishment.

6.  All currency conversions noted in this volume were made at the prevailing rate for September, 2007.

7.  Note that, as a proportion of mean earnings, the NMW adult rate was no higher in 2005 than it had been in 1999 (figure 2.2).

8.  The success of United Kingdom tax credits in raising participation rates and contributing to higher incomes for families with children has been clouded somewhat by flaws in the administration of the system. One distinctive feature of the tax credits is that they are paid via the wage packet, with much of the responsibility for administering the system devolved to employers. However, there is little evidence that paying through the wage packet increases take-up, and there is evidence of employers making claims difficult for employees and even firing those who try to make claims (Brewer and Shephard 2004; OECD 2005). More recently, the system has been criticized for being slow in adjusting to changes in income and for computer failures that have resulted in many families having to pay back excess payments.

9.  In the last ten years, the Scottish university funding system has diverged somewhat from that of the rest of the United Kingdom. In particular, as discussed in the next section, the Scots have not introduced top-up fees.

10. Historically, polytechnics specialized in more vocational subjects than universities and also provided a range of subdegree-level courses.

11. See OECD Program for International Student Assessment at http://www.pisa.oecd.org.

12. Recent legislation has sought to tighten the regulation of "gangmasters," the organizations that provide casual labor in the food and agriculture sectors (Grimshaw and Marchington 2006).

13. In 2003, employees in the United Kingdom worked on average 1,610

hours per year, compared with 1,354 in Germany, 1,443 in France, and 1,787 in the United States (Groningen Growth and Development Center 2006).

14. According to the Labour Force Survey, in the spring of 2004, 47 percent of temporary workers were employed on fixed-period contracts, 16 percent were agency temps, 21 percent were engaged in casual work, 4 percent were doing seasonal work, and 11 percent were classified as engaged in other forms of temporary employment. In the spring of 1992, the respective proportions were 48, 7, 22, 7, and 17 percent.

15. Both the Stewart (1999a) and Cappellari and Jenkins (2003) studies include younger workers (age eighteen to twenty-five), who might be expected to be more mobile than those in older age groups.

# REFERENCES

Almeida-Santos, Filipe, and Karen Mumford. 2004. "Employee Training and Wage Compression in Britain." Discussion paper 04/11. York, U.K.: Department of Economics, University of York.

Anderson, Bridget, Martin Ruhs, Ben Rogaly, and Sarah Spencer. 2006. "Fair Enough? Central and East European Migrants in Low-Wage Employment in the U.K." Oxford: COMPAS (May 1).

Arranz, José M., María A. Davia, and Carlos García-Serrano. 2005. "Labor Market Transitions and Wage Dynamics in Europe." Working paper 2005-17. Colchester, U.K.: Institute for Social and Economic Research, University of Essex.

Arulampalam, Wiji, Alison L. Booth, and Mark L. Bryan. 2004. "Training and the New Minimum Wage." *Economic Journal* 114(494): C87–C94.

Barnard, Catherine, Simon Deakin, and Richard Hobbs. 2004. "Opting Out of the Forty-eight-Hour Week—Employer Necessity or Individual Choice? An Empirical Study of the Operation of Article 18(1)(b) of the Working Time Directive in the U.K." Working paper 282. Cambridge: Economic and Social Research Council (ESRC) Centre for Business Research, University of Cambridge.

Blackaby, David, Ken Clark, Derek Leslie, and Philip Murphy. 1994. "Black-White Male Earnings and Employment Prospects in the 1970s and 1980s: Evidence for Britain." *Economics Letters* 46(3): 273–9.

Blackaby, David, Derek Leslie, Philip Murphy, and Nigel O'Leary. 2002. "White/Ethnic Minority Earnings and Employment Differentials in Britain: Evidence from the LFS." *Oxford Economic Papers* 54(2): 270–97.

Blackwell, Louisa, and Daniel Guinea-Martin. 2005. "Occupational Segregation by Sex and Ethnicity in England and Wales, 1991 to 2001." *Labour Market Trends* 113(12): 501–16.

Blanchflower, David G., and Alex Bryson. 2004. "The Union Wage Premium in the U.S. and U.K." Discussion paper 0612. London: Centre for Economic Performance, London School of Economics.

Blanden, Jo, Stephen Machin, and John Van Reenen. 2006. "Have Unions Turned the Corner? New Evidence on Recent Trends in Union Recognition in U.K. Firms." *British Journal of Industrial Relations* 44(2): 169–90.

Blundell, Richard, Howard Reed, John Van Reenen, and Andrew Shephard. 2003. "The Impact of the New Deal for Young People on the Labor Market: A Four-Year Assessment." In *The Labor Market Under New Labour: The State of Working Britain*, edited by Richard Dickens, Paul Gregg, and Jonathan Wadsworth. London: Palgrave Macmillan.

Booth, Alison L., Marco Francesconi, and Jeff Frank. 2002. "Temporary Jobs: Stepping Stones or Dead Ends?" *Economic Journal* 112(480): F189.

Brewer, Mike, and James Browne. 2006. "The Effect of the Working Families Tax Credit on Labor Market Participation." Briefing note 69. London: Institute for Fiscal Studies.

Brewer, Mike, and Andrew Shephard. 2004. *Has Labour Made Work Pay?* York, U.K.: Joseph Rowntree Foundation.

———. 2005. "Employment and the Labor Market." Election briefing 2005. London: Institute for Fiscal Studies.

British Market Research Bureau (BMRB). 2001. "A Survey of Workers' Experiences of the Working Time Regulations." BMRB Social Research, Employment Relations Series 31. London: Department of Trade and Industry (November).

Brown, William, and Sushil Wadhwani. 1990. "The Economic Effects of Industrial Relations Legislation." *National Institute Economic Review* 131(1): 57–70.

Brown, William, Simon Deakin, and Paul Ryan. 1997. "The Effects of British Industrial Relations Legislation." *National Institute Economic Review* 161(1): 69–83.

Brown, William, Simon Deakin, David Nash, and Sarah Oxenbridge. 2000. "The Employment Contract: From Collective Procedures to Individual Rights." *British Journal of Industrial Relations* 38(4): 611–29.

Brown, William, Simon Deakin, Maria Hudson, Cliff Pratten, and Paul Ryan. 1998. "The Individualization of Employment Contracts in Britain." Research paper for the Department of Trade and Industry. London: DTI.

Butcher, Tim. 2005. "The Hourly Earnings Distribution Before and After the National Minimum Wage." *Labour Market Trends* 113(10): 427–34.

Canny, Angela. 2002. "Flexible Labor? The Growth of Student Employment in the U.K." *Journal of Education and Work* 15(3): 277–301.

Cappellari, Lorenzo, and Stephen P. Jenkins. 2003. "Transitions Between Unemployment and Low Pay." Paper presented to British Household Panel Survey users' conference, Colchester, Essex, U.K.

Card, David, Thomas Lemieux, and W. Craig Riddell. 2004. "Unions and Wage Inequality." *Journal of Labor Research* 25(4): 519–59.

Clarke, Julian, and Stuart Speeden. 2001. *Then and Now: Change for the Better?* London: Commission for Racial Equality.

Coleman, David, and Robert Rowthorn. 2004. "The Economic Effects of Immigration into the U.K." *Population and Development Review* 30(4): 579–624.

Cronin, Ed, and Michael Thewlis. 2004. "Qualitative Evidence on Firms' Adjustments to the National Minimum Wage: Final Report to the Low Pay Commission." Accessed at IRS Research, http://www.lowpay.gov.uk/lowpay/research/pdf/tOIDZGQO.pdf.

Davidov, Guy. 2004. "Joint Employer Status in Triangular Employment Relationships." *British Journal of Industrial Relations* 42(4): 727–46.

Dench, Sally, Jennifer Hurstfield, Darcy Hill, and Karen Akroyd. 2006. *Employers' Use of Migrant Labor*. London: Home Office (April).

Department for Education and Skills (DfES). 2005. *Skills: Getting on in Business, Getting on at Work*. White paper. London: HM Government.

Dickens, Linda, and Mark Hall. 2003. "Labor Law and Industrial Relations: A New Settlement?" In *Industrial Relations: Theory and Practice in Britain*, 2nd edition, edited by Paul Edwards. Oxford: Blackwell.

Dickens, Richard. 1999. "Wage Mobility in Great Britain." In *The State of Working Britain*, edited by Paul Gregg and Jonathan Wadsworth. Manchester, U.K.: Manchester University Press.

Dickens, Richard, and Alan Manning. 2004. "Has the National Minimum Wage Reduced U.K. Wage Inequality?" *Journal of the Royal Statistical Society* 167(4): 613–26.

Dorsett, Richard. 2004. "The New Deal for Young People: Effect of the Options on the Labor Market Status of Young Men." London: Policy Studies Institute.

Draca, Mirko, and Romesh Vaitilingam. 2006. "The National Minimum Wage: The Evidence of Its Effect on Jobs and Inequality." Briefing paper. London: Centre for Economic Performance, London School of Economics.

Dustmann, Christian, Francesca Fabbri, and Ian Preston. 2005. "The Impact of Immigration on the British Labor Market." *Economic Journal* 115(507): F324–41.

Dustmann, Christian, John Micklewright, Najma Rajah, and Stephen Smith. 1996. "Earnings and Learning: Educational Policy and the Growth of Part-time Work by Full-time Pupils." *Fiscal Studies* 17(1): 79–103.

Employment Policy Institute. 1997. *Employment Audit 5*. London: Employment Policy Institute.

Equal Opportunities Commission. 2005. "Annual Report 2004-05." Accessed at http://www.eoc.org.uk/PDF/annual_report_2004_05.pdf.

European Commission. 2004. "Communication from the Commission to the Council, the European Parliament, the European Economic and Social Committee, and the Committee of the Regions Concerning the Re-exam of Directive 93/104/EC Concerning Certain Aspects of the Organization of Working Time." Brussels: European Commission.

Felstead, Alan, Duncan Gallie, and Francis Green. 2002. *Work Skills in Britain*. London: Department for Education and Skills.

Galindo-Rueda, Fernando, and Sonia Pereira. 2004. "The Impact of the National Minimum Wage on British Firms: Final Report to the Low Pay Commission on the Econometric Evidence from Annual Respondents Database." Accessed at http://www.lowpay.gov.uk/lowpay/research/pdf/t0Z2NTSH.pdf.

Gall, Gregor. 2004. "Trade Union Recognition 1995–2002: Turning a Corner?" *Industrial Relations Journal* 35(3): 249–70.

Gosling, Amanda, and Thomas Lemieux. 2004. "Labor Market Reforms and Changes in Wage Inequality in the United Kingdom and the United States." In *Seeking a Premier Economy: The Economic Effects of British Economic Reforms 1980–2000*, edited by David Card, Richard Blundell, and Richard B. Freeman. Chicago, Ill.: University of Chicago Press.

Green, Francis. 2001. "'It's Been a Hard Day's Night': The Concentration and Intensification of Work in Late Twentieth-Century Britain." *British Journal of Industrial Relations* 39(1): 53–80.

———. 2003. "The Demands of Work." In *The Labor Market Under New Labour*, edited by Richard Dickens, Paul Gregg, and Jonathan Wadsworth. London: Palgrave Macmillan.

Grimshaw, Damian, and Lorrie Marchington. 2006. "Employment Trends in the U.K.: Vulnerable Work and Vulnerable Workers." Report to the International Labor Organization. Manchester, U.K.: European Work and Employment Research Centre, University of Manchester.

Grimshaw, Daniel P., and Marilyn Carroll. 2006. "Adjusting to the NMW: Constraints and Incentives to Change in Six Low-Paying Sectors." *Industrial Relations Journal*, 37(1): 22–47.

Groningen Growth and Development Center. 2006. "Industry Growth Accounting Database" (September). Accessed at http://www.ggdc.net/dseries/iga.html.

Hibbett, Angelika, and Mark Beatson. 1995. "Young People at Work." *Employment Gazette* 103(4): 169–77.

Hills, John, and Jane Waldfogel. 2004. "A 'Third Way' in Welfare Reform? Evidence from the United Kingdom." *Journal of Policy Analysis and Management* 23(4): 765–88.

HM Treasury. 1998. "The Working Families Tax Credit and Work Incentives: The Modernization of Britain's Tax and Benefit System." Accessed at http://www.hm-treasury.gov.uk/media/5/1/wftc.pdf.

Incomes Data Services (IDS). 2004. "Report to the Low Pay Commission on the Impact of the National Minimum Wage: A Research Report." Accessed at http://www.lowpay.gov.uk/lowpay/research/pdf/IDS_report_September _2004.pdf.

Institute for Public Policy Research (IPPR). 2006. *Irregular Migration in the U.K.* London: IPPR.

Keep, Ewart, and Ken Mayhew. 2004. "The Economic and Distributional Implications of the Expansion of Higher Education." *Oxford Review of Economic Policy* 20(4): 298–314.

Kersley, Barbara, Sarah Oxenbridge, Gill Dix, Helen Bewley, Alex Bryson, John Forth, and Carmen Alpin. 2006. *Inside the Workplace: Findings from the 2004 Workplace Employment Relations Survey.* London: Department of Trade and Industry.

Kodz, Jenny, Sara Davis, David Lain, Marie Strebler, Jo Rick, Peter Bates, John Cummings, and Nigel Meager. 2003. *Working Long Hours: A Review of the Evidence*, Volume 1. Employment Relations Research Series 16. London: Department of Trade and Industry.

Leitch, Sandy. 2005. *Leitch Review of Skills: Skills in the U.K.: The Long-Term Challenge.* London: HM Treasury.

Low Pay Commission (LPC). 2005. *National Minimum Wage: Low Pay Commission Report 2005.* London: Low Pay Commission.

Machin, Stephen, and Joan Wilson. 2004. "Minimum Wages in a Low-Wage Labor Market: Care Homes in the U.K." *Economic Journal* 114(494): C102–9.

Mason, Geoff. 2004. *Enterprise Product Strategies and Employer Demand for Skills in Britain: Evidence from Employers Skill Surveys.* Working paper 50. Oxford: Economic and Social Research Council (ESRC) Centre on Skills, Knowledge, and Organizational Performance (SKOPE), Universities of Oxford and Warwick.

Mason, Geoff, and Karin Wagner. 2002. *Skills, Performance, and New Technologies in the British and German Automotive Components Industries.* Research report SPN1. London: Department for Education and Skills.

Mason, Geoff, Bart van Ark, and Karin Wagner. 1994. "Productivity, Product Quality, and Workforce Skills: Food Processing in Four European Countries." *National Institute Economic Review* 147(1): 62–83.

Mayhew, Ken, Cecile Deer, and Mehak Dua. 2004. "The Move to Mass Higher Education in the U.K." *Oxford Review of Education* 30(1): 65–82.

McGillivray, Anne. 2006. *Student Living Index 2005.* Edinburgh: Royal Bank of Scotland.

McKay, Stephen. 2003. "Working Families' Tax Credit in 2001." Research report 181. London: Department for Work and Pensions.

McKnight, Abigail. 2000. "Trends in Earnings Inequality and Earnings Mobility, 1977 to 1999: The Impact of Mobility on Long-Term Inequality."

Employment Relations Research Series 8. London: Department of Trade and Industry.

Metcalf, David. 2004. "The Impact of the National Minimum Wage on the Pay Distribution, Employment, and Training." *Economic Journal* 114(494): 84–87.

———. 2005. *British Unions: Resurgence or Perdition?* London: Work Foundation.

Millward, Neil, Alex Bryson, and John Forth. 2000. *All Change at Work? British Employment Relations 1980–1998, as Portrayed by the Workplace Industrial Relations Survey Series.* London: Routledge.

Modood, Tariq, Richard Berthoud, Jane Lakey, James Nazroo, Patten Smith, Satnam Virdee, and Sharon Beishon. 1997. *Ethnic Minorities in Britain: Diversity and Disadvantage.* London: Policy Studies Institute.

Mulheirn, Ian, and Mario Pisani. 2006. "The Labor Supply Effect of the Working Tax Credit: A Quasi-Experimental Evaluation." Paper presented to the Work, Pensions and Labour Economics Study Group (WPEG) Conference. July 10-12, 2006, University of Kent, Canterbury, U.K.

Organization for Economic Cooperation and Development (OECD). 2005. "Increasing Financial Incentives to Work: The Role of In-Work Benefits." *Employment Outlook.* Paris: OECD

Oxenbridge, Sarah, William Brown, Simon Deakin, and Cliff Pratten. 2003. "Initial Responses to the Statutory Recognition Procedures of the Employment Relations Act 1999." *British Journal of Industrial Relations* 41(2): 315–34.

Prais, Sigbert. 1995. *Productivity, Education, and Training.* Cambridge: Cambridge University Press.

Purcell, Kate, and Surhan Cam. 2002. "Employment Intermediaries in the U.K.: Who Uses Them?" Working paper 7. Bristol, U.K.: Bristol Business School, Employment Studies Research Unit, University of the West of England.

Rainbird, Helen, Lesley Holly, and Ruchira Leisten. 2002. "The National Minimum Wage and Training." Research report for the Low Pay Commission. Northampton, U.K.: University College Northampton, Centre for Research in Employment, Work, and Training (October). Accessed at http://www.lowpay.gov.uk/lowpay/research/research1_01.shtml.

Robinson, Helen. 2002. "Wrong Side of the Track? The Impact of the Minimum Wage on Gender Pay Gaps in Britain." *Oxford Bulletin of Economics and Statistics* 65(5): 417–48.

———. 2003. "Gender and Labor Market Performance in the Recovery." In *The Labor Market Under New Labour*, edited by Richard Dickens, Paul Gregg, and Jonathan Wadsworth. London: Palgrave Macmillan.

Saleheen, Jumana, and Chris Shadforth. 2006. "The Economic Characteristics of Immigrants and Their Impact on Supply." *Bank of England Quarterly Bulletin* 2006(Q4): 374–85.

Smith, Paul, and Gary Morton. 2001. "New Labour's Reform of Britain's Employment Law: The Devil Is Not Only in the Detail but in the Values and Policy Too." *British Journal of Industrial Relations* 39(1): 119–38.

Steedman, Hilary, and Karin Wagner. 1989. "Productivity, Machinery, and Skills: Clothing Manufacture in Britain and Germany." *National Institute Economic Review* 128(1): 40-57.

Stewart, Mark. 1999a. "Low Pay in Britain." In *The State of Working Britain*, edited by Paul Gregg and Jonathan Wadsworth. Manchester, U.K.: Manchester University Press.

———. 1999b. "Low Pay, No Pay Dynamics." In *Persistent Poverty and Lifetime Inequality*, HM Treasury occasional paper 10. London: HM Treasury.

———. 2004. "The Employment Effects of the National Minimum Wage." *Economic Journal* 114(494): C110–16.

Stewart, Mark B., and Joanna K. Swaffield. 1999. "Low Pay Dynamics and Transition Probabilities." *Economica* 66(261): 23–42.

Terry, Michael. 2003. "Employee Representation: Shop Stewards and the New Legal Framework." In *Industrial Relations: Theory and Practice*, edited by Paul Edwards. Oxford: Blackwell.

Van Reenen, John Michael. 2003. "Active Labor Market Policies and the British New Deal for Young Unemployed in Context." In *Seeking a Premier Economy: The Economic Effects of British Economic Reforms 1980–2000*, edited by David Card, Richard Blundell, and Richard B. Freeman. Chicago, Ill.: Chicago University Press.

White, Michael, and Rebecca Riley. 2002. "Findings from the Macro Evaluation of the New Deal for Young People." Research report 168. London: Department for Work and Pensions. Accessed at http://www.dwp.gov.uk/asd/asd5/168summ.asp.

Wilkinson, David. 2003. *New Deal for Young People: Evaluation of Unemployment Flows*. London: Policy Studies Institute.

Wolf, Alison. 2002. *Does Education Matter? Myths About Education and Economic Growth*. London: Penguin.

Woodbridge, Jo. 2005. "Sizing the Unauthorized (Illegal) Migrant Population in the United Kingdom in 2001." Home Office report 29/05. London: Home Office.

# CHAPTER 3

# "Just Like the Elves in Harry Potter": Room Attendants in United Kingdom Hotels

*Eli Dutton, Chris Warhurst, Caroline Lloyd,
Susan James, Johanna Commander,
and Dennis Nickson*

As part of the hospitality sector, the hotel industry is a significant contributor to the United Kingdom's economy. Although estimates are difficult because of a lack of definitive statistics, the hotel industry's annual turnover was as high as £27 billion (US$52.5 billion) in 2006, according to the British Hospitality Association (*Caterer and Hotelkeeper* 2006). The industry is diverse, including bed-and-breakfast establishments, budget, midrange, and luxury hotels. Because of volatile markets and intense competition over recent years, it has undergone significant change, with ownership internationalizing, companies restructuring, and market segmentation deepening. Significantly, mergers and acquisitions have created an industry increasingly shaped by branded national and international hotels.

Around 1.2 percent of all jobs in the United Kingdom are in the hotel industry, with total employment estimated at 309,000 (*Labour Market Trends* 2006). The hotel industry has the highest incidence of low-wage employment in the United Kingdom (see table 2.1). Roy Wood (1997, 69) claims that this situation is a result of employers' "ruthless" pursuit of "low-pay strategies."

Curiously, academic attention in the United Kingdom has tended to focus only on particular occupations within the industry—usually those associated with food and beverage—and these occupations have come to constitute "a dominant research paradigm" (Lennon and Wood 1989, 227; see also Hunter-Powell and Watson 2006). Much less is known about workers engaged in "accommodation work," such as receptionists, porters, and cleaners (Lennon and Wood 1989). Of these occupations, room attendants—those workers who clean and "make up" rooms in hotels for guests' use—"are amongst the least skilled of all hotel staff," John Lennon and Roy Wood (1989, 229) claim, and their jobs are "physically demanding and dirty . . . repetitive and limited in variety and scope." Even the industry tends to overlook these jobs. The national employers' organization, the British Hospitality Association, omits room attendants from its head count of the industry (see BHA 2005, 53). Room attendants are imperceptible, even to the guests whom they service: "I liken my staff to the elves in Harry Potter—beds are made, work is done, but no one sees anyone, the majority of the work is done behind the scenes and staff are more or less invisible," said one executive housekeeper (quoted in Hunter-Powell 2005, 14).

Recent journalistic investigations of low-wage jobs in the United States (Ehrenreich 2001), the United Kingdom (Toynbee 2003), and Australia (Wynhausen 2005) have also overlooked room attendants.[1] This neglect is puzzling given that room attendants are hit by a double income whammy (IDS 2005): they receive the lowest total remuneration in a low-wage industry because, in addition to being low-paid, they tend not to receive the tips given to other industry workers, such as front-of-house staff in food and beverage.

American research by Annette Bernhardt, Laura Dresser, and Erin Hatton (2003a, 1) has recently focused academic attention on these workers and has also sought to suggest "model solutions" for the industry to lift it out of its current "low-wage and low investment equilibrium." Our research has similar objectives. Drawing on primary, qualitative research generated from eight case studies of hotels from two major cities in the south and north of the United Kingdom—London and Glasgow, respectively—our analysis focuses on the work and employment, including the pay, of these jobs and discusses ways in which room attendant job quality could be improved.

The next section presents an overview of the United Kingdom hotel industry and explains the selection of case studies. Following a short outline of the research design and methods, we then present the findings. The chapter continues with a short section that summarizes the findings and raises a number of conceptual and policy issues. The research reveals that room attendants are marginalized workers undertaking hard work for little financial reward and lacking realistic job mobility opportunities. Significantly, unlike the American research of Bernhardt and her colleagues, which focused only on hotels in the upper market segment, the United Kingdom research included both the upper and middle product market segments. This difference proved significant because the United Kingdom research also reveals that room attendants' job characteristics vary little across the different market segments of the hotel industry; thus, labor strategies, in this industry at least, may not be as tightly coupled to product market strategies as in some other industries where product service quality is positively related to workforce skills (Finegold and Soskice 1988). It is for this reason that we argue for the need to use other strategies in the hotel industry besides labor strategies if job quality is to be improved.

## AN OVERVIEW OF THE UNITED KINGDOM HOTEL INDUSTRY

### Industry Organization and Performance

The total number of hotels in the United Kingdom is difficult to calculate because the industry is diverse, hotels are not obliged to register with tourist boards, and the data collected are not standardized. The overwhelming majority of hotels in the industry are small—the industry average is twenty bedrooms—and most hotels are independent (*Caterer and Hotelkeeper* 2006). People1st, the industry's skills council, cites 12,425 hotels as registered with national tourist boards in the United Kingdom (People1st 2006); the British Hospitality Association (2005) cites a figure of 14,609 hotels in 2004, although this figure includes registered inns as well as hotels. Including nonregistered establishments, small hotels, guesthouses, and bed-and-breakfast establishments would push the number up much higher: close to 30,000 (People1st 2006) and as high as 50,000 to 60,000 (BHA 2005). The hotel rating scheme in the United Kingdom uses the star (*) classification system, with hotels awarded more stars—from one to five—as they offer higher standards. Facilities and services are limited in one-star and two-star hotels, whereas five-star hotels are expected to offer a wider and better range of facilities and services to guests. However, the star rating system was until recently not uniform, with different accreditation bodies involved. In 2006 a uniform method of assessing and rating was introduced, but registration is not compulsory (Key Note 2005).

Although fragmented, there are developments and trends that are identifiable across the hotel industry. It is particularly susceptible to

## Table 3.1 United Kingdom Hotel Performance, 2000 to 2005

| | 2000 | 2001 | 2002 | 2003 | 2004 | 2005[a] | Change from 2003 to 2005 |
|---|---|---|---|---|---|---|---|
| Occupancy | 74.0% | 71.8% | 72.2 % | 71.7% | 73.5% | 77.8%[a] | +3.8% |
| Room rate | £69.70 | £70.05 | £68.38 | £67.86 | £70.87 | £77.51 | +11.2 |
| RevPAR[b] | £51.54 | £50.32 | £49.36 | £48.66 | £52.07 | £60.29 | +17.0 |

*Source:* Mintel (2005).
[a] For the half-year to June 2005.
[b] RevPAR (revenue per available room) is the commonly used measure of financial performance in the industry.

economic cycles, political troubles, and other external events that cause fluctuations in the numbers of international and domestic tourists (People1st 2005). Significant revenue reductions occurred as a result of the early 1990s recession in the United Kingdom, the global economic downturn from 2001 to 2004, the foot-and-mouth disease crisis, 9/11, the Iraq war, and the outbreak of SARS in the Far East. These events had a severe impact on the industry. Despite the range of facilities and services offered by hotels—such as meeting room hire and food and beverage—most revenue (56 percent) is still accrued through the sale of bedrooms (BHA 2005, 37). Recently, signs of recovery are evident: the volume of overseas visitors to the United Kingdom has been higher, and performance levels have improved as a result of higher room rates (see table 3.1). After "three years of bad news," there is now "solid evidence of recovery," states the hospitality consultant Jonathan Langston (quoted in BHA 2005, 13).

Three main trends can be identified over this period as hotel companies have responded to competitive pressures. First, hotels generally are trying to improve customer service by offering more personalized service—particularly in upper market segment hotels—or by diversifying and upgrading product offerings to cater to the differing needs of guests. For example, some budget brands are responding with "amenities creep"—adding air conditioning, satellite TV, bar facilities, or twenty-four-hour reception—in order to compete with the growing number of hotels in the two- and three-star market segments (*Caterer and Hotelkeeper* 2005). Branded budget hotels with low, fixed pricing structures are the growth phenomenon of the last decade. These hotels are not rated within existing schemes but are generally considered to have the same facilities as the midmarket two- and three-star hotels, which, in response to this pressure from the branded budget hotels, are themselves adding facilities, such as banqueting and health clubs, to broaden their customer base to include local nonresidents. This amenities "creep" has become, as it is in the United States, an amenities "war," whereby hotels

> are rolling out super thick mattresses, mountains of new pillows, extra sheets and hefty duvet covers in a competition to create the most restful sleep experience. Even the budget chains are joining the fray, upgrading the room with a rainbow of soaps, shampoos, teas and speciality coffees. (Avila 2005, 13)

Second, branding has become more important generally as employers use standardized products in an effort to guarantee quality and create brand loyalty (Mintel 2005). In this respect, amenities creep is accompanied by clear standard operating procedures for the presentation of rooms. Curtain pleats have to be a regular width, the angle of chairs in rooms is stipulated, and stationery has to lie properly on desks; "everything has to be just so," states Zaiba Malik (2006, 51). International hotel companies such as Marriott and Hilton have particularly strong, recognizable brands. The top five branded United Kingdom hotel companies are shown in table 3.2. Although they account for only around one-third of hotel rooms in Britain, these hotel companies are shaping the industry, according to Mintel (2004), driving a new, third trend: the separation of "bricks and brains"—property investment and hotel operations. "What matters more to hoteliers than sales figures," according to Jonathan Langston, "is profitability" (BHA 2005, 13). The big corporates have struggled to improve profitability while retaining sizable property interests. Hotel chains such as InterContinental, Whitbread, and the Hilton Group have all recently sold their property assets to release capital tied up in property management. These companies then lease back the hotels through management contracts that allow brand operations to continue without the additional building and maintenance costs, putting cost pressures on the small independent operators (BHA 2005).

## Employment in the Industry

Because the hotel industry is seasonal, employment levels fluctuate throughout the year to meet demand. In addition, the number of

Table 3.2  Top Five United Kingdom Hotel Companies, 2005

| Company | Number of Hotels | Brand | Number of Bedrooms |
|---|---|---|---|
| Whitbread | 460+ | Premier Travel Inn | 28,000+ |
| Intercontinental | 227 | InterContinental (1), Crowne Plaza (13), Holiday Inn (111), Express by Holiday Inn (102) | 31,909 |
| Hilton International, London | 70 | Hilton | 15,282 |
| Permira | 270+ | Travelodge | 15,000+ |
| Marriott International, London | 72 | Renaissance (7), Marriott (54), Courtyard by Marriott (11) | 12,000+ |

*Source:* British Hospitality Association (BHA) (2005).

workers varies depending on hotel service provision and use of technology, with hotels in the upper market segment tending to be more labor intensive (Key Note 2003). To cope with the varying patterns of demand, the industry tends to employ what Wood (1997) has described as "marginal workers"—women, the young, casuals, part-timers, students, and migrant workers. Between 56 and 59 percent of hotel workers are women, one-third are female part-timers, 11 percent are from ethnic minorities, and nearly 40 percent are between the ages of sixteen and twenty-four. The workforce is generally low-qualified, with 15 percent having no qualifications at all (People1st 2006). Nearly half of all hotel employees work in elementary occupations, with cleaning and domestic staff estimated at nearly 29,000 (People1st 2006). According to the Labour Force Survey, 95 percent of cleaners are women, and 72 percent work less than thirty hours per week. There is also a disproportionately high number of workers under the age of twenty. Room attendants' work requires little formal training and qualifications (Wood 1997), a point borne out by the predominance of the lowest NVQ level—level 1—among housekeeping staff who do have job-related qualifications (BHA 2005). Such a low qualification requirement for this type of job is common in the

United Kingdom (for details on this point with regard to hospital cleaners, see chapter 6).

Employment as a hotel room attendant is characterized by low pay, poor working conditions, shift work and unsociable hours, and high labor turnover (Lucas 2004; Nickson et al. 2002). The labor intensity of the work makes hotel labor costs high. In the upper market segment, labor costs can be even higher, not because of higher rates of pay but because the ratio of employees to guests is higher. Nevertheless, pay in the industry is low in relative terms—it is one of the three industries that comprise over half of all low-wage jobs in the United Kingdom (see table 2.1 in chapter 2)—and is often cited as the main reason for leaving. Room attendants receive the least total remuneration; only waitstaff and luggage porters are paid less than room attendants, but workers in these occupations can typically enhance their earnings with tips (IDS 2005). Labour Force Survey data show that pay rates for hotel cleaners are lower than for any of the other occupations investigated in this book. As figure 3.1 shows, 76 percent earn below the low pay threshold (LPT), with rates for the majority set at or just above the minimum wage.[2] There is also little prospect of earning much above the LPT: only 10 percent are paid over £6.50 (US$13.11) per hour. Figure 3.1 also reveals that over one-quarter were paid below the October 2003 adult national minimum wage (NMW) rate of £4.50 (US$9.08) per hour (applicable until October 2004). This "underpayment" is likely to be a result of the widespread use of youth and of training rates and/or illegal underpayment. Interestingly, even though industry profitability is highest in London, pay and related expenses as a percentage of total expenses in London are markedly below the United Kingdom average (BHA 2005, 36, 37), suggesting that even when hotels are more profitable, there is not necessarily any greater distributive outcome for hotel employees.

To continue to be able to recruit at such low levels of pay, hotels, particularly in London and the Southeast of England, have looked beyond the local labor market, recruiting from overseas and, in some cases, offering accommodation that is offset against wages. A sectors-based work permit scheme was introduced in 2003 to address shortages in lower-skilled occupations in the United Kingdom. Ten thousand permits were available yearly, with almost three-quarters approved for the hospitality and catering sector in 2004 (Salt and Millar 2006). In 2005, however, the hospitality sector was excluded from the scheme because European Union (EU) enlargement, combined with the de-

Figure 3.1  Pay Distribution for Hotel Cleaners, Combined 2004 and 2005

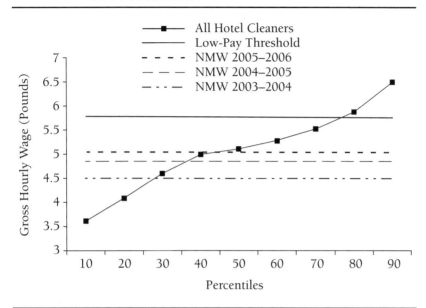

*Source:* Analysis of Labour Force Survey (LFS) data conducted by Matthew Osborne at the National Institute for Economic and Social Research (NIESR).

cision to open the United Kingdom labor market to workers from the new accession countries (the Czech Republic, Estonia, Hungary, Latvia, Lithuania, Poland, Slovakia, and Slovenia), rapidly expanded the number of migrant workers. The decision to end the scheme caused particular consternation in the hospitality industry, and the Home Office (2006, 29) noted the view from the industry that low-skilled migration was an "essential support" to the sector "in the absence of U.K. workers prepared to do these jobs."

At just 4 percent—well below the national average of 29 percent (DTI 2006)—trade union membership is low in United Kingdom hotels. A number of reasons have been put forward to explain this low union density. First it is suggested that a culture of conservatism and individualism prevails among the workforce, consolidated by reliance on informal rewards and employee preference for self-representation in negotiations with management. Combined, these practices create a workforce culture that is antipathetic to trade unions (McCauley and Wood 1992). Additionally, the predominance of small hotels and their wide geographical dispersion pose considerable challenges to trade union organizing, while the "family culture" of many of these small hotels compounds the barriers to union organizing. Rosemary Lucas (2004), interrogating the 1998 Workplace Employee Relations Survey (WERS) data, found that hospitality employees in very small workplaces were more likely to endorse their manager's style of management.

The structure of the workforce also contributes to low levels of union membership: the industry has a high number of young, student, part-time, and migrant workers, groups that traditionally have been less involved with unions. High labor turnover among workers further undermines union recruitment and retention. There is also evidence of management hostility toward trade unions (Aslan and Wood 1993; Wills 2005). Unionization and collective bargaining are mainly restricted to a minority of corporate chains, for example, Thistle and Jarvis (IDS 1999). Finally, trade unions themselves are part of the problem. Notwithstanding recent initiatives by the T&GWU and GMB, it is generally acknowledged that trade unions have long failed to develop effective strategies for organizing workers in the industry.

## RESEARCH DESIGN AND METHODS

The research design featured qualitative methods, supplemented by quantitative, performance-related data from some of the hotel case studies. Two main factors influenced the selection of the case studies: hotel market segment and labor market location. We selected hotels that allowed comparison between high- and middle-quality product offerings—four- and five-star deluxe hotels, on the one hand, and two- and three-star hotels and budget hotels, on the other. Upper market hotels offered twenty-four-hour service, high-quality restaurants, and fitness or health clubs. The midmarket hotels commonly offered bar and restaurant facilities.

The case studies focused on larger hotels—that is, those with a minimum of thirty staff—in order to ensure a reasonable number of interviews and to allow an exploration of room attendants' opportunities for progression within the hotel to positions that are generally not available in smaller establishments. Cases featured a mix of chain and independent hotels that catered predominantly to the business market (although the majority of business hotels cater to the leisure

## Table 3.3 The Case Study Hotels

| Location | Upper Market | Middle Market |
|---|---|---|
| London | | |
| City | H1—International chain | H2—International chain |
| Greater | H8—Independently owned group | H3—National budget chain |
| Glasgow | | |
| City | H4—International chain | H5—Independently owned group |
| Greater | H6—International chain | H7—Independently owned group |

*Source:* Authors' compilation.

trade at the weekends). This approach thus took into account the diversity of hotels within the industry as well as different business strategies.

As in the American research of Bernhardt and her colleagues (2003a), the case study hotels were located in different and contrasting regional labor markets, primarily in two major cities in the south and north of the United Kingdom—London and Glasgow. Although average unemployment rates for the two cities were similar and, compared to the rest of the United Kingdom, relatively high during the period of study at between 7 and 8 percent (ONS 2006), there were differences between the two cities' labor markets for room attendants; the Glasgow hotels drew predominantly upon local labor, while the London hotels employed mainly migrant labor. In terms of supply, however, the quantity and quality of this labor was of concern to all of the case study hotels. Within these two locations, the labor markets could be further differentiated between city-center and outer-city hotels. Of the four Glasgow case studies, two were hotels located in the city center and two were in greater Glasgow. Of the four London hotels, two were in the city center and two were in greater London. The case studies are outlined in table 3.3.

In each hotel, we interviewed managers responsible for operations, human resources, and housekeeping as well as housekeeping supervisors and room attendants. In some cases, we also interviewed the hotel owner or general manager. In addition, we gathered quantitative data from management on hotel performance and employment figures. In some cases, these data were patchy because of managerial turnover in the industry. Commercial confidentiality was also sometimes cited as an issue. We conducted seventy-six interviews directly related to the eight case studies; thirty-five of those were with room attendants. The hotels H1, H2, and H8 used temporary work agencies (TWAs) to supply staff, and we conducted interviews with three TWAs in central London that were linked to two of these hotels. H2 also used a contract cleaning company, and we interviewed the operations director and two contract managers from this company. In addition, we conducted five interviews with a number of organizations related to the industry: a sector careers promotion organization, one trade union, and two low-wage campaign groups. The latter two sets of interviews were deemed necessary because, again, unlike the American research, all of the United Kingdom case studies were nonunionized, which is a general tendency of the industry. There were thus eighty-one interviews in total, with empirical data collected over the period 2005 to 2007. We have made all hotels and individual participants anonymous.

## RESEARCH FINDINGS

### BUSINESS AND HUMAN RESOURCE STRATEGIES

The upper market (four- and five-star) hotels offered high-quality service with larger and differently configured rooms, had more amenities in each room, and provided an extensive range of complementary products. By contrast, the middle market (two- and three-star and budget) hotels offered basic rooms with limited amenities. In the branded hotels, rooms and amenities were standardized with identical layouts; independent hotel room layouts could vary, though rooms still had basic fixtures and fittings. All hotels were profitable; although H7 had experienced losses recently, its performance was improving owing to a change in business strategy from cheap-rate group tours to individual guests paying higher room rates. The majority of the hotels had occupancy rates above the national average of 73.5 percent (Mintel 2005), although for all hotels occupancy rates varied seasonally throughout the year.

Generally, the hotels faced fierce competition, and the budget hotels in particular were concerned about price wars. Budget hotels offered transparent pricing strategies with fixed room rates, making it more difficult to compete against the independent midmarket hotels, which offered flexible price rates for rooms. Typically hotels with flexible pricing charged less than their publicly stated room rates. Upper market hotels also had flexible room rates that could vary considerably both by location and by hotel, depending on the volume of demand.

To cope with reduced business levels, hotels adopted different employment strategies. The low hotel occupancy levels after 9/11 resulted in a period of redundancies. As the operations director of the contract cleaning company for H2 explained: "Hotels changed their philosophy about what they wanted to provide. They had to provide the bare bones really and cut back on the service." Other strategies included asking room attendants to take holidays during the quieter months or adopting multitasking so that room attendants could make up their hours by working across departments. As the H5 general manager recognized:

> In the five years that I've been here, I've refused to lay people off because then you are constantly searching for new staff and there is no stability for them. We had a very, very dark period from January to March [2003]. . . . We had to do something, so most of the staff went to either reduced hours or a four-day week. . . . Eleven weeks is a long time when you are on weekly pay and you've still got your bills to meet, but I think we more than made up for it by multitasking, so if anybody left, then [the others] would do multitasking to keep their hours.

## Room Attendant Demographics

Room attendant demographics typically reflected the location of the hotels. In Glasgow, room attendants tended to be female and slightly older, usually either women returning to the labor market or working mothers with few or no formal qualifications. These workers were usually recruited by both formal (job centers) and informal (word of mouth) means. As workers with domestic or child care responsibilities, these women found that the hours of work and the job demands suited their schedules. In London local working mothers were also hired as room attendants, but most workers tended to be migrant laborers of a wider age range, and they were often from the countries of Southern Europe and the new accession countries. A living wage campaigner noted that

> the Polish factor is a big factor in London right now. Britain has opened the door completely to Polish labor, which was a strategy supported by the government largely because the business community very much supported it because it's fantastic for business. It is great for the hotel industry to have the labor market flooded with desperate, exploitable Polish women.

This migrant labor tended to cluster by nationality in particular hotels. For example, in one case study hotel, 75 percent of the staff were Portuguese; in another, all the staff were Eastern European. This clustering was an outcome of formal and informal recruitment methods, such as recruitment agencies and word of mouth. Clustering is useful for hotels because it eases language communication within housekeeping departments, but as noted later, clustering can have negative consequences for individual workers. Hotels, however, appreciated the quality of this labor: "They are educated, they've got brains in their heads, and they can think. The Polish immigrants are of a high standard—the ones we've touched, they're all very good. . . . [They] make British people look sick," claimed the owner of H7. Indeed, some of these workers were overqualified for the job of room attendant, with some qualified to degree level.

The use of migrant labor is becoming more widespread across the United Kingdom, including Scotland (see Meiklem 2004). Its use in London hotels, however, is not new but rather an established practice. The operations director of the contract cleaning company explained that in the past room attendants in London would have been Afro-Caribbean in origin. In London the hotel industry has welcomed the influx of new migrant labor, and hotels in other parts of the United Kingdom seem to be doing likewise, as the comment of the owner of H7 quoted earlier indicated. However, the use of migrant labor can be problematic for hotels. Because many migrant workers speak English only as a second language, problems have emerged with health and safety, for example. To counteract these problems, various measures have been introduced in hotels, such as the color coding of cleaning fluids (People1st 2004).

For migrant workers, room attendant jobs provide entry into the

United Kingdom labor market, and many of them assume that they could move from there to better jobs—in offices, for example: "I think most of them are using this as a bridge, as a way forward to make money. . . . [They] work a certain period of time in order for them to settle and then start looking maybe for something else," said the recruitment consultant for H2. This desire was most obvious in migrant workers who were overqualified, as one such worker explained: "My aspirations are much higher because I've now graduated [from] my studies, so I don't want [to be cleaning rooms] for the rest of my life." However, internal or external job mobility was contingent on having appropriate language skills, most obviously proficiency in English, which migrants often lacked: "If she can't speak very good English or understand, what else can she do really?" a contract cleaning company manager for H2 explained. "There are some here that don't speak any English, but that doesn't really matter because they're cleaning rooms, they don't have to." Given that the job is socially isolated and employers typically do not provide language lessons, migrant workers' capacity to improve their English and so advance in the labor market is therefore limited.

## Working Patterns

There were differences between the upper and midmarket hotels in terms of employment contracts and working patterns. Guaranteed working hours were limited to the upper market hotels, where room attendants tended to be full-time and permanent, though they were supplemented by part-time casuals on variable hours contracts.

In London, these casual staff were employed through TWAs that provided numerical flexibility to meet varying levels of demand and a way of quality assurance—those workers who did not perform to the required standard could be easily replaced. Thus, TWA staff lacked not only guaranteed hours but also job security. TWA use, however, was not without problems for the hotels. The general manager at H2 recognized that agency staff were not as loyal, needed a lot of training, and that turnover among them was high; he claimed, however, as other managers did, that agency staff were needed to meet the fluctuating labor demand of the industry and that the local labor force was reluctant to work as room attendants. "I suppose they think it's very low for them," the head housekeeper at H2 commented. This point was emphasized by the operations director for the contract cleaning company: "It's filling that void that the indigenous race just don't want to do that sort or work. . . . Hotels have sort of taken the benefits of the movement of migrants." By contrast, in Scotland, despite having the same labor demands, managers preferred not to use TWAs. One operations manager even stated that "I would clean the rooms myself before I would use them [agency staff]." It may be that in London there are more alternative opportunities for British workers, such that the low rates of pay and hard working conditions on offer are just not attractive. In contrast, Glasgow may have fewer jobs available for low-qualified women with domestic responsibilities.

In midmarket hotels, jobs were part-time, and room attendants were normally on variable hours contracts. They might be contracted to work a minimum of twenty hours per week, with hours above this number varying according to room occupancy rates. In H2, room cleaning had been outsourced to contract cleaners as part of a national agreement within the chain. The hotel had difficulties recruiting room attendants and felt that outsourcing was a cheap solution. However, the hotel also used TWAs because the contract cleaner could not supply extra staff when needed. H3 had used a contract cleaning company in response to recruitment problems and the perceived low quality of the local workforce, which had "attitude problems"; however, the function was brought back in-house as the cost of contract cleaning rose dramatically. These new jobs were permanent, part-time, and almost wholly held by migrant labor. In Glasgow, the midmarket hotels also employed room attendants on permanent part-time contracts with long job tenure, as one general manager explained:

> It's women who are bringing up young families—they need part-time work because they need the money, and it then becomes habitual and they get themselves into the stage where all of a sudden they are fifty. . . . They don't think they can move, they don't think they can do something else.

Working times tended to be stable, even permanent, for workers in the upper market segment. However, given that these were low-wage jobs, part-time and even some full-time workers needed more than one job to earn a living. As a London-based contract cleaner explained, "It's not enough to work in only one [job], because London is very expensive." Some room attendants could manage on the low wages by, for example, having another wage-earner in the household, claiming child tax credit (if a lone parent), or not having a mortgage and living instead in rented accommodation. Because overtime that was an extension of the normal working day was not paid, workers had to finish their cleaning targets within their shift or else work longer and unpaid. Room attendants could also be called in for paid additional hours, or rostering could be changed to cover the absence of other workers, both at short notice. This type of overtime was paid, but either at the normal rate or for a day off. Such unforeseen changes in working patterns could be financially disruptive, as one room attendant in H7 explained:

> After that [Christmas], it's very quiet, it's like two people [in the whole] hotel. . . . It goes downhill, and it's not very good for us because we are not set hours, and it affects our money, which is quite the downfall of the job, you know, it's not set hours.

In addition, during the working day in some of the hotels, breaks had been removed without explanation by management, and during busy working times employees worked long hours illegally without breaks. In H8, formal breaks were scheduled but often not taken because of work pressures: "I usually don't take my last break because of the amount of rooms we have," said a room attendant. This work intensification was acknowledged by management: "They are expected to do the work in their own hours, so the usual eight to ten rooms then become twelve rooms, but they still do it within the hours that they're allocated to work," one human resource manager stated openly. One room attendant at this hotel claimed that up to sixteen rooms might require cleaning during a shift.

## WORK ORGANIZATION

Room attendant work is important to the functioning of any hotel. The main tasks are cleaning rooms and replenishing amenities—for example, changing bed linen, cleaning beds and bathrooms, and restocking room items and minibars. Room attendants also clean corridors in their rooms' section and have supplementary daily or weekly tasks that might include, for example, deep-cleaning carpets and changing shower curtains.

Despite the rhetoric of teamwork in housekeeping departments, work is in fact organized so that most room attendants usually work alone for long periods of time. This isolated work organization was one reason why some room attendants left the job: "It's a very solo job. . . . You are working on your own most of the time, and it doesn't fit with a lot of people's personality," said one general manager. However, for those attendants who stay, it can provide welcome autonomy: "You can get on with it and [have] nobody on your back saying, 'Right, you need to do this and you will need to do that.' You can get it done a lot better, I think," said one room attendant. Some workers who were experienced and trusted by supervisors were able to finish their shift after completing their cleaning target. Supervisors would still check this work, but in two hotels a few such workers could be promoted to "self-checkers" who received additional payment. In upper market hotels, monitoring was stringent, with daily and additional spot-checks to ensure adherence to the prescribed standards: "I feel to not let the standards slip you've got to keep your checking power there," said one head housekeeper. In branded hotels, regardless of star rating, rooms were also tightly monitored for cleanliness by supervisors. Only in the midmarket independent hotels was monitoring light, with occasional spot-checks.

In all of the case study hotels, room attendants had a target number of rooms to clean per shift, though the number varied depending on the type of hotel. In the upper market segment, room attendants were expected to clean between ten and fourteen rooms during an eight-hour shift. In midmarket hotels, workers were expected to clean between nine and eighteen rooms in a four- or five-hour shift. Significantly, the time that it takes to clean a room varies depending on the hotel's market segment because of the varying size of rooms and the different level and range of in-room amenities. Managers in the upper market segment stated that the average time to clean a room was thirty-two to thirty-three minutes; in the middle market, managers cited fifteen to sixteen minutes as the norm. However, room attendants suggested that cleaning could take longer for a number of reasons: differences in the state of the rooms; whether the room was an "occupied" or a "departure"; and whether the guests had stayed for a weekday or a weekend. The housekeeping supervisor in the upper market H8 said that some rooms could take an hour and a half to clean, and another in the midmarket H3 stated that it could take up to forty minutes to clean particularly messy rooms. Interviewees noted that it was easier to clean a weekday occupied room compared to a weekend departure; midweek business guests might stay more than one night without making extensive use of the facilities, whereas weekend guests tended to leave rooms messy. The repetitive demands of a routine job were described by one general manager:

> I've seen that lady do twenty rooms. To clean twenty rooms is such a phenomenal feat, it is really hard. It's what I call *Groundhog Day*—you know the film *Groundhog Day*. Every day's the same, every room they open is trashed in the same way, and they've got to bring it back to the standard you expect.

The job is regarded as low-skilled, and the "skills" that are required are really personal attributes and capacities—the ability to work hard, stamina, flexibility in terms of working hours, and attention to detail (Grugulis, Warhurst, and Keep 2004). The questionability of these attributes and capacities as skills was recognized by a number of interviewees. One room attendant in an upper market hotel commented that "you don't need skills to dust or hoover." Another in a midmarket hotel suggested that "it's common sense mostly, common sense and basic housework, what you would do at home." Thus, room attendants were doubly invisible, with their work not only unseen but also unrecognized as "real work" because of its association with "women's work": "It's one of those jobs. You don't really need to be trained. Most people know how to make a bed, and obviously, being a housewife, you know how to clean toilets, so it was basically an easy option," explained a head housekeeper. This lack of recognition is common in perceptions of "women's work" (the debate about such "women's work" and its "skills" being unrecognized is extensive; see, for example, Phillips and Taylor 1986 and, more recently, Bolton 2005).

The physical demands of the job, however, can be strenuous and damaging, involving bending, stretching, and carrying heavy loads such as beds and vacuum cleaners. So, although likened to housework, cleaning hotel rooms is heavy-duty housework: "Don't get me wrong. You think when you come in it's just like housework, but it's not. It's a lot more than housework because you are not pulling out units every day in your house," said one room attendant. Back injuries and pains are not uncommon among room attendants, more so than in many manufacturing jobs (UniteHere 2006). The job also involves regular use of cleaning products, many of which contain hazardous chemicals that can be serious pollutants (see Wynhausen 2005) or physical irritants (Malik 2006). As a consequence, health problems can develop, as one room attendant explained:

> I would say personal health would be a risk, like doing a lot of damage to your back because you are doing the beds and you are bending, you are doing the toilet, constantly down and up, and your legs as well, and some of the chemicals are quite strong I find. . . . It's just like commonsense sort of thing, but I would say, for your body, it's a high risk.

Although management set targets for the cleaning of rooms, this cleaning could be affected by a number of factors. In some older hotels, idiosyncrasies in the physical layout of the rooms and some of their features—for example, cornicing—made them difficult to clean. In two of the hotels, recent refurbishments had not eliminated these problems, either because of room redesign limitations or because the problems were compounded by the addition of new materials, such as chrome bathroom fittings that required heavy cleaning. Significantly, rooms in upper market hotels required more work, both because they contained considerably more amenities and because cleaners were held to higher standards so as to achieve a more standardized, exacting presentation. Such rooms might include a separate lounge, kitchen, and dining area and could be filled with over one hundred complimentary products. One housekeeper stated, "It's not just physically, it's mentally [tiring] as well because you need to remember everything."

There are fewer amenities in midmarket hotels, and the room layouts are more basic. Consequently, work in these hotels can be easier in that there are fewer tasks to be completed and less detail to be remembered by the room attendants. The difference in working in the two market segments is experienced most by TWA room attendants, who are hired to work in both types of hotel. The housekeeping supervisor in H1, a five-star hotel, stated that TWA staff often left soon after being hired because work in that hotel was too difficult, owing to the high standards expected, and alternative work in budget hotels was easily available. Moreover, even though budget hotel work was generally easier, agency pay rates were the same for all hotels. As one former agency worker said, "[They go to] different hotels, you know, maybe three or four stars, because in five stars it's really hard work." Given that wage rates are relatively similar for all hotels see later in the chapter), it can therefore be better for TWA workers to work in midmarket, cost-led hotels because there room attendants do less "involved" work for the same pay as workers in the upper market, quality-led hotels, in which more in-room amenities require more work but not necessarily a type of work that is qualitatively different.

## TRAINING AND DEVELOPMENT

Interviewees acknowledged that room attendant jobs could be learned relatively quickly. On-the-job training and the shadowing of existing workers was common. Workers would then work alone, initially cleaning fewer rooms with supervision before being deemed competent. To be able to work to an acceptable standard and speed could take up to six weeks in the midmarket hotels. With more extensive amenities, this period rose to six months, the executive housekeeper in the five-star hotel H1 claimed.

However, beyond receiving statutory occupational health and safety training, there were other differences between the upper and midmarket hotels. Upper market hotel employers were more committed to formalized, initial training and to regular ongoing training thereafter. Training could involve the development of room attendants' technical and behavioral skills and aspects of customer service. Rigorous training in brand standards was also evident: rooms had to be identical in terms of layout, right down to the requirement that teacups be pointed in the same direction. A trainer would observe and assess new room attendants. H1 provided its own training for agency workers because it felt that the training provided by the agency was insufficient. In the midmarket hotels, training beyond statutory occupational health and safety tended to be limited. Training was typically on-the-job and often unmonitored because supervisors might themselves be cleaning rooms. One room attendant noted that she received no training at all when she first started and had to immediately start cleaning rooms. Only in one midmarket hotel was additional training available—for example, in customer care—but the extent to which room attendants could take up these additional opportunities was unclear.

Opportunities for progression within housekeeping departments (for example, to supervisory or managerial positions) were limited in all of the hotels owing to the flat structure and smaller size of these departments. Some of the hotels provided opportunities for room attendants to work in other departments, such as food and beverage, where they could work as bar or wait staff. In some cases, there were opportunities to move to jobs in other hotels within the chain or group. As the general manager from H4 recognized, "If you've got absolutely no qualifications, you probably come in as a room attendant, and then most people, if you are personable enough and have the skills to be front-facing, then you can easily transfer to front of house and progress from there." This possibility is important. The hotel industry is one of the few industries in which internal job mobility (and into middle and senior management) is possible without formal qualifications. However, the bottom rung of the ladder of this mobility typically starts with front-of-house jobs such as reception rather than with back-of-house housekeeping. Moving into more customer-facing positions could also be a problem for women with domestic responsibilities, since they typically would have to transfer from working relatively fixed hours during the day to working shifts and unsocial hours.

Significantly, there were again differences between the progression opportunities available in the upper and midmarket hotels. In the midmarket hotels, progression to other departments or hotels was possible, but training to enable that progression was limited. In the upper market hotels, the training and development opportunities were more formally structured, and the wider number of facilities in the hotel and the higher staffing levels provided a wider range of jobs and more supervisory positions. Three upper market hotels provided some form of "career ladder" for room attendants. One offered a jobs escalator of different roles through which room attendants could progress, accompanied by formal training; with high labor turnover in this hotel, graduation along this escalator was feasible. Moreover, a number of contract staff were often made permanent. In another case, the hotel provided scheduled training opportunities accompanied by information days and staff had access, through a hotel learning resource center, to the company "university." In this case, staff were allocated one hour per week during working hours for learning.

Nevertheless, in practice, opportunities to take advantage of this learning were constrained by operational difficulties, even in upper market hotels. As one room attendant explained: "You don't get much time during the day here. The head of housekeeping did say that if you are going to do that [learning], she would try and give you less rooms, but that's not guaranteed, you know, that goes by how the business is." Even in the case of an upper market hotel that provided English-language training for its migrant staff, work pressures limited these workers' capacity to participate in the on-site classes. As typical nontraditional learners, other room attendants' fear of learning could also be a problem: "We are a bit scared as soon as you say [the chain's] 'university courses'. I mean, I did too, I really freaked out when I was told you had to do this, but I think they are great now, and I have been trying to encourage the girls," said the hotel's head housekeeper. Some room attendants were unable to take advantage of promotion opportunities that entailed a move to another hotel within the chain in a different location because of their domestic responsibilities. The women felt anchored to a particular locality and unable to extend their travel-to-work times. Domestic relocation with the severing of support networks can be a problem for such women, as can receiving low pay and not being able to afford the necessary additional travel costs (Dutton et al. 2005).

## Pay and Benefits

Pay rates were similar across all the hotels and driven by the United Kingdom's national minimum wage (NMW). The majority of the hotels paid at a rate equivalent to the NMW of £5.05 (US$10.19), including those hotels in the upper market segment (see table 3.4). The most striking variation is by type of payment based on location. In Glasgow, all hotels paid an hourly rate at the NMW and used only directly employed workers. However, in London, pay at the two mid-market budget hotels was based on a rate per room cleaned—that is, on piecework, with one hotel using a contract cleaning company. In the two upper market London hotels, room attendants were paid a salary and had the highest hourly equivalent, while some use was made of temporary agency workers paid at the NMW.

Two hotels that were owned by the same parent company, H1 and H2, had a policy of paying above the NMW. The company maintained this policy, the general manager of H1 argued, because these pay levels attracted staff of high quality who were less likely to leave. At H2, room attendants were employed through contract cleaners and were

Table 3.4 Pay, Hours, and Contracts in the Case Study Hotels

| | London | | | | Scotland | | | |
|---|---|---|---|---|---|---|---|---|
| | H1 | H8 | H2 | H3 | H4 | H6 | H5 | H7 |
| Star rating | Upper market, five-star | Upper market, five-star | Midmarket, budget | Midmarket, budget | Upper market, four-star, deluxe | Upper market, four-star, deluxe | Midmarket, two- to three-star | Midmarket, two- to three-star |
| Pay | £6.20 per hour (equivalent) | £5.71 per hour (equivalent) | £1.77 per room (with variations, maximum £5.66 per hour) | £2.47 per room (with variations, a range of £3.29 and £6.18 per hour) | £5.05 per hour | £5.05 per hour | £5.05 per hour | £5.05 per hour |
| Hours per day | 8 | 8 | 5 | 6 | 8 | 8 | 4 to 5 | 4 to 5 |
| Contracts | Direct and TWA | Direct, casual and TWA | Subcontract, direct and TWA | Direct, variable hours | Direct and casual | Direct | Direct, variable hours | Direct, variable hours |

*Source:* Authors' compilation.

paid on a piece rate—£1.77 (US$3.57) per room, with an expected sixteen rooms to be cleaned per five-hour shift. With this maximum target, the equivalent hourly pay rate was £5.66 ($US11.42). At H3, the other hotel using piecework, room attendants were employed directly by the hotel. Payment was £2.47 (US$4.98) per room, and room attendants were expected to clean an average of twelve rooms per shift, but with occupancy rates fluctuating significantly, so too did the number of rooms to be cleaned. Consequently, the hourly equivalent also varied widely. Such piecework was intended to reduce costs: "We want to pay by the room. . . . We can't afford not to, it's as simple as that, because it doesn't take a rocket scientist to work out if the hotel's full we're going to make money, if the hotel is empty we're going to struggle, and that's one of the issues that we have," explained the operations director of a cleaning company. In hotels in which piece rates were tight, this arrangement could result in workers being paid less than the NMW if the time needed to clean rooms was longer than that prescribed by management—an outcome that is illegal in the United Kingdom, but a real possibility if rooms are messy and take longer to clean, as room attendants noted.[3]

Room attendants, even in the upper market hotels, were blunt about the pay rates: "For the work you do, the rate of pay is unbelievable," said one. Another, who also worked at an upper market hotel, said bluntly, "The pay is crap." Head housekeepers acknowledged the problem, linking low pay, poor work, and alternative job opportunities. A head housekeeper at an upper market hotel said:

> I think it's difficult to get the right people now. . . . People don't want to come into the hotel industry. . . . I think it is all down to pay. . . . If you can sit in Tesco's for £4.85 [the NMW in 2004–2005] on your bum putting food through a scan, then people are going to do that rather than physically bending down and moving beds and washing floors and stuff like that.

To earn more in one budget hotel, room attendants were paid extra for cleaning particularly messy rooms, but only at management's discretion. In two other cases, room attendants who took longer to clean messy rooms sometimes did so as unpaid working time. In addition to not receiving overtime premiums, there were also no additional payments for working weekends. For employees who were paid by piece rates, the only way to earn more money would be to clean more rooms, and those attendants paid by the hour would have to work additional hours, over which they had no control. One room attendant explained that, "if you want a good wage, you really need to work for it, you need to work these departs [customers checking out], you need to stay for these hours."

For the majority of room attendants, including contract cleaners and TWA staff, the nonwage benefits were minimal, mainly consisting of statutory holidays and sick pay. This situation was most evident in the middle market, where hotels had budgetary constraints. Furthermore, it was sometimes difficult to disentangle holiday pay and sick pay: room attendants would use holiday entitlements instead of sickness benefits because, under United Kingdom statutory sick pay arrangements, no payments are received for the first three days of illness: "I don't need to go on the sick because I've got my holidays," explained one room attendant. "You get more money for a holiday than you do sick pay, because [another room attendant] was on the sick and she said, 'I can't live on these wages.' She said the sick pay was terrible, so she had to come back."

The upper market hotels tended to offer more, although still limited, financial and nonfinancial fringe benefits, including participation in the corporate membership scheme that entitled members to various discounts on accommodation, facilities, and food and beverage in any hotel within the group or chain, even worldwide. Many employees regarded these benefits as good but questioned their capacity to take advantage of them; some were even ignorant of their existence. One upper market hotel introduced a yearly bonus of £1,000 to all permanent staff as a way of tackling recruitment and retention difficulties; another had a long service bonus of £500 and also offered improved holiday entitlement and sick pay linked to length of service. The majority of hotels had a policy of awarding an "employee of the month" with either a gift or a monetary bonus. Room attendants could also receive tips and gifts from guests; however, these gratuities were minimal and infrequent. Nonfinancial benefits from the company could include a uniform, free food, and staff parties; only one hotel, and in greater London, provided staff accommodation. Some head housekeepers used the benefits as informal incentives to recognize room attendants' work and maintain morale. For example, the head housekeeper at H6 would reward room attendants if they had to clean extra rooms: "[Head housekeeper]'s quite good with us right enough," one room attendant explained. "We'll get a bottle of wine . . . or a dinner for two in the restaurant kind of thing."

## MOVING BEYOND LOW WAGES AND IMPROVING JOB QUALITY

This research has confirmed that room attendants' jobs are typically taken by so-called marginal workers—such as women returning to work and migrant laborers—and that they are often employed either part-time or on temporary contracts for work that is physically hard, routine, and repetitive. Training and development are available, but the feasibility of take-up is constrained. Pay and remuneration is at or only marginally above the NMW. Indeed, it seems that the NMW has become the going rate for room attendant pay. However, although the NMW has failed to raise relative wage levels for room attendants, pay in many hotels would undoubtedly be lower without it. Nevertheless, there are differences in the jobs of room attendants that seem to be a consequence of hotel market segment, as table 3.5 illustrates.

The key difference is that room attendants in the upper market segment have slightly better terms of employment, greater access to training and progression, and more stable working hours, although they are also subject to greater monitoring and must pay more attention to detail. Nonetheless, these differences should not mask the commonalities in room attendant jobs across the hotel market segments. Low pay and work low in accredited skill prevail across all hotels, regardless of market segment. This finding is echoed by the United Kingdom-based living wage campaign: "We're finding that whether it's the top end or the bottom end of the hotel value chain, they're paying at or slightly above the minimum wage," said one campaigner. Low wages are not just a structural feature of cost-driven hotels but also a feature of those profitable hotels pursuing high-quality product strategies: "[They're] very profitable. They're doing fantastically well because they are getting a lot from customers for this quality product and paying the same to staff as their low-cost, cheaper competitors," the campaigner added. These findings question the presumption that the provision of high-value-added products is necessarily accompanied by better-quality jobs with higher skills and pay (Finegold and Soskice 1988). Instead, it suggests that, in the hotel industry at least, the link between business strategy and job quality is weak, as it is in several other parts of the United Kingdom's service sector (Lloyd 2005).

Debate about the relationship between job quality and the attrac-

Table 3.5  Room Attendants Jobs Across Hotel Market Segments

| | Upper Market Hotels | Midmarket Hotels |
|---|---|---|
| Type of worker | Women returners and migrants. Migrants concentrated in London, returners in Glasgow. Returners typically unqualified, some migrants overqualified. | Women returners and migrants. Migrants concentrated in London, returners in Glasgow. Returners typically unqualified, some migrants overqualified. |
| Working patterns | Guaranteed working hours, tending to be full-time and permanent, though supplemented by part-time casuals and agency labor in London. | Variable part-time hours. Some outsourcing and agency labor in London. |
| Work organization | Hard, repetitive, and routine work. Cleaning targets set. Lower room targets, but task complexity higher. Greater monitoring. | Hard, repetitive, and routine work. Cleaning targets set. Higher room targets, but task complexity lower. Greater monitoring in branded hotels, less in independents. |
| Training and development | Statutory, with basic on-the-job training. Tighter monitoring of standards. Development opportunities available, with formalized progression. Constraints on take-up. | Statutory, with basic on-the-job training. Loose monitoring of standards. Development opportunities available but informal. Constraints on take-up. |
| Pay and benefits | Basic pay at or above NMW. Some additional benefits and bonuses available. Gratuities minimal and infrequent. Some structured nonfinancial benefits available, but issue of take-up. | Basic pay at or close to the NMW. Gratuities minimal and infrequent. Few structured nonfinancial benefits available. |

*Source:* Authors' compilation.

tiveness of these jobs is being sidestepped currently. With an abundant supply of workers willing to work on minimum wages, there is little pressure on employers, even in a city with a high cost of living such as London, to improve wage rates, work organization, or terms of employment. Migrant workers in the Southeast of England are filling these jobs at wages that do not provide an adequate living and at market rates below those which the indigenous population are willing to accept. In Glasgow, local workers—particularly women who are "captives of love" (SCER 2006) in that their employment opportunities are constrained by domestic responsibilities—accept these pay levels but express deep dissatisfaction. There is also evidence that Scottish hotels, too, are beginning to look toward migrant workers as a solution to recruitment difficulties.[4]

This situation compounds the perception among employers that workers rather than jobs are the problem. The best that workers can do in these circumstances is exit—creating high labor turnover—or remain, biting the lip of dissatisfaction, even if occasional band-aids are applied by management in the form of fringe benefits that try to hold morale together.

The Labour government recognizes that low pay can be a problem. The intention when it introduced the NMW was to tackle what the then Secretary of State called the "scandal of poverty pay" (quoted in CIPD 2006, 1) by providing a "living wage" (Howarth and Kenway 2004). Although the NMW has raised wages for workers at the bottom end of the United Kingdom labor market generally (see chapters 1 and 2), it has had considerably less effect in the hotel industry. However, that low pay persists in the United Kingdom hotel industry despite the NMW should not be surprising. Earlier wage regulation in the industry similarly had limited impact, as Wood (1995) points out. Until the early 1990s, the United Kingdom had a number of wages councils that set pay across industries covering nearly 2.5 million workers. Thirty-nine percent of these workers were covered by hospitality wages councils. Supported by employers' organizations, the then Conservative government abolished these councils. Evidence indicates that they did provide a wages floor and that post-abolition relative pay fell in a significant proportion of hotels (see, for example, Radiven and Lucas 1997). Wages councils had very little impact on low pay, however, because, as Wood states, individual employers used the councils' minimum pay rates as the going rate for pay and employers' organizations used the boards to check wage rises. Similarly today, Incomes Data Services (2005, 12) reports that pay rises in the United Kingdom hotel industry are "largely driven by the increase in the NMW." Only two of its sample of twenty large hotels raised pay rates marginally above the NMW. Significantly, the British Hospitality Association opposed the introduction of the NMW, but later applauded what it considered to be the setting of a "realistic" rate that had minimum impact because, as surveys of the industry at the time indicated, many employers were already paying at or slightly over that rate (IDS 2000). In addition, underpayment occurred in the 1990s, Wood states, as employers denied employees the higher overtime rates to which they were entitled. All of these points resonate with the findings of our research on current low pay in the hotel industry—that wages are driven largely by the NMW benchmark and that, coupled with a particular form of employment, some wages being paid skirt the line of legality. The lesson, suggests Wood (1995, 80), is that "the history of the industry tells us . . . that—even with (albeit limited) wages regulation and monitoring—hospitality sector employers are skilled at either ignoring the law or finding ways around it." Employers can do so because of the vulnerability of employees in the industry, who are "unorganised, transient and often [accept] hotel and catering jobs as a last resort" (80).

Although seemingly beneficial to employers, this is an approach that also creates problems for these employers. Persistent high labor turnover creates recruitment and retention difficulties, raises indirect labor costs through persistent recruitment and induction efforts and basic training provision, and also threatens to undermine hotels' attempts to improve the level of service quality they offer to customers. However, employers can address these problems through improved job quality. Bernhardt and her colleagues (2003b) have outlined initiatives that in the United States deliver "win-win" solutions for employers and employees. These initiatives acknowledge employer needs (more functional and numerical labor flexibility and increased retention) and employee needs (career development opportunities, reasonable workloads, and more stable employment) and identify solutions that respond to both—better training opportunities and structured cross-utilization of room attendants in other hotel departments. However, if this evidence is indicative, such initiatives require regional consortiums of employers, trade unions, government, and community groups.

Echoing this need and anticipating the operation of the NMW, Wood (1995) argued that better protection of low-paid workers in the United Kingdom would be possible if government regulation was supplemented by better monitoring and enforcement through trade unions—and a raft of studies have demonstrated that unionized workplaces have higher pay and better conditions (Group of 150 Australian Industrial Relations, Labor Market, and Legal Academic

2005).[5] The general lesson, Wood (1995, 79) concludes, is that "wages protection systems are not an adequate substitution for collective action and organization." He suggests that this role—the outcomes of which would be improvements to job quality, including pay—is one that unions would willingly undertake. Unfortunately, the United Kingdom hotel industry is not currently unionized. However, unions are not antithetical to the hotel industry; union density is higher in the industry in other countries, and this union presence can positively affect job quality, as Bernhardt and her colleagues (2003a, 2003b) and Angie Knox and Dennis Nickson (2007) have indicated for the United States and Australia, respectively. Nevertheless, it should be noted that in the United States it is only in "unique cases" (Bernhardt et al. 2003a, 65) that hotel management works in partnership with unions to deliver better jobs.

As a living wage campaigner stated, "Low-paid people have very little political voice, and they're not, for the main part, in trade unions." Thus, in the United Kingdom at least, other strategies are required if room attendants' pay is to be improved. Most obviously, a political movement is required to force the issue onto the government's policy agenda.[6] To this end, the living wage campaign group, which is an alliance of faith and community groups, charities, and trade unions, is spearheading a "name and shame" campaign, targeting industries that systematically pay low wages. The campaign has had a number of successes with employers in London in financial services, hospitals, and local government and, with funding from American trade unions, is now turning its attention to the hotel industry. The campaign recognizes three points: first, that the organization of hotel workers has not been a priority for unions in the United Kingdom; second, that in the United States unionization makes a positive difference to hotel workers' pay and conditions; and third, that ownership within the industry is increasingly consolidated and internationalized—hence, American unions' willingness to support a United Kingdom campaign. This internationalization offers an opportunity for national unions to work in concert.[7] As the campaign organizer explained:

> The hotel sector is a tough sector, but one that's ultimately very promising because you can't export the jobs, it's a growth industry, and it's a profitable industry. . . . There's very widespread anti-union practices by employers. Nevertheless, the fundamental

should be such that if you can't organize in that industry, you're never going to get unions that do anything in the global economy.

Low-paid hotel workers cannot be unionized immediately because of the lack of an organizing tradition among these workers by the relevant United Kingdom unions and because many of these workers, particularly migrant workers, also lack a culture of unionism (Wills 2005). As a consequence, what is required as a stepping-stone into trade unionism is intermediate organization that provides support services and in so doing collectivizes workers' interests and actions. This strategy is one worth pursuing since, as this research has revealed, firm business strategy alone in the hotel industry is insufficient to deliver better jobs, nor has government intervention through the NMW had a dramatic positive impact upon room attendants' pay. Without the addition of a living wage type of campaign, room attendant jobs in the United Kingdom will remain hard work, with restricted opportunities and low pay.

## NOTES

1. Barbara Ehrenreich (2001) and Elisabeth Wynhausen (2005) both worked in restaurants attached to hotels, and much is already known of such jobs (see, for example, Fine 1996; Kelliher and Perrett 2001). Polly Toynbee (2003) was employed as a cleaner, but in a hospital.
2. The LPT was £5.77 (US$11.64) in 2005, using the Labour Force Survey. The data are derived from a source different from that used for the ASHE figures provided in most of the other chapters. As a result, the LPT is calculated at a lower rate. Using ASHE data, we calculated that nearly 90 percent of hotel cleaners were paid below the LPT of £6.59 (US$13.30) in 2006.
3. NMW legislation recognizes that some workers can be paid for "output work"—for example, by commission or piecework—but stipulates that pay for this work should not be lower than the rate of the NMW and that overtime must be included as part of hours worked (CIPD 2006).
4. The fieldwork in Glasgow was completed just prior to the influx into Scotland of migrant labor from the accession countries (see Baum et al., forthcoming).
5. Although it should be noted that the wage premium for union mem-

bership appears now to be disappearing in the United Kingdom (see chapter 2).

6. The living wage for London in 2005 was calculated at £6.70 (US$13.52) per hour (Living Wage Unit 2006). This living wage is premised on enabling full-time workers and their families to live free of poverty, taking into account state benefits and tax credits.

7. There can be significant practical problems for international union organization, however, as John Gennard and his colleagues (2003) outline.

## REFERENCES

Aslan, Arsène H., and Roy C. Wood. 1993. "Trade Unions in the Hotel and Catering Industry: The Views of Hotel Managers." *Employee Relations* 15(2): 61–70.

Avila, Oscar. 2005. "Amenity Creep Making It Almost Impossible for House-keepers to Clean a Hotel Room in 30 Minutes, the Pace Required to Clean 15 Rooms per Shift." *Chicago Tribune*, August 23, 2005: 13.

Baum, Tom, Frances Devine, Eli Dutton, Niamh Hearns, Shamim Karimi, and Jithendren Kokkranikal. Forthcoming. "Cultural Diversity in Hospitality Work." *Cross Cultural Management*.

Bernhardt, Annette, Laura Dresser, and Erin Hatton. 2003a. "The Coffee Pot Wars: Unions and Firm Restructuring in the Hotel Industry." In *Low-Wage America*, edited by Eileen Appelbaum, Annette Bernhardt, and Richard J. Murnane. New York: Russell Sage Foundation.

———. 2003b. "Moving Hotels to the High Road: Strategies That Help Workers and Firms Succeed." Madison, Wisc.: University of Wisconsin, Center on Wisconsin Strategy.

Bolton, Sharon C. 2005. *Emotion Management in the Workplace*. London: Palgrave.

British Hospitality Association (BHA). 2005. *Trends and Statistics*. London: BHA.

*Caterer and Hotelkeeper*. 2005. "Market Snapshot: Budget Hotels." *Caterer and Hotelkeeper*, April 26. Accessed May 4, 2006, at http://www.caterer search.com/Articles/2005/04/26/57622/Market+snapshot+Budget+hotels .htm.

———. 2006. "Market Snapshot: Hotels." *Caterer and Hotelkeeper*, April 26. Accessed August 2, 2006, at http://www.caterersearch.com/Articles/ 2006/04/24/ 57630/ Market+snapshot+Hotels.htm.

Chartered Institute of Personnel and Development (CIPD). 2006. *National Minimum Wage*. Accessed at www.cipd.co.uk/subjects/pay/minimwage/ nmw,htm?IsSrchRes=1.

Department of Trade and Industry (DTI). 2006. *Trade Union Membership 2005*. London: DTI.

Dutton, Eli, Chris Warhurst, Dennis Nickson, and Cliff Lockyer. 2005. "Lone Parents, the New Deal, and the Opportunities and Barriers to Retail Employment." *Policy Studies* 26(1): 85–101.

Ehrenreich, Barbara. 2001. *Nickel and Dimed*. New York: Metropolitan Books.

Fine, Gary Alan. 1996. *Kitchens: The Culture of Restaurant Work*. Berkeley, Calif.: University of California Press.

Finegold, David, and David Soskice. 1988. "The Failure of Training in Britain: Analysis and Prescription." *Oxford Review of Economic Policy* 4(3): 21–53.

Gennard, John, Harvie Ramsay, Chris Baldry, and Kirsty Newsome. 2003. "Barriers to Cross-Border Trade Union Cooperation in Europe: The Case of Graphical Workers." In *Emerging Human Resource Practices*, edited by Csaba Mako, Christopher Warhurst, and John Gennard. Budapest: Akademiai Kiado.

Group of 150 Australian Industrial Relations, Labor Market, and Legal Academic. 2005. "Research Evidence About the Effects of the 'Work Choices' Bill: A Submission to the Inquiry into the Workplace Relations Amendment (Work Choices) Bill 2005." Canberra, Australia.

Grugulis, Irena, Chris Warhurst, and Ewart Keep. 2004. "What's Happening to Skill?" In *The Skills That Matter*, edited by Chris Warhurst, Ewart Keep, and Irena Grugulis. London: Palgrave.

Home Office. 2006. *A Points-Based System: Making Migration Work for Britain*. Norwich, U.K.: Her Majesty's Stationery Office. Accessed September 19, 2007, at http://www.homeoffice.gov.uk/documents/command-points-based-migration?view=Binary.

Howarth, Catherine, and Peter Kenway. 2004. *Why Worry Anymore About the Low-Paid?* London: New Policy Institute.

Hunter-Powell, Patricia. 2005. "The Unseen Department." *Hospitality* (September): 14–16.

Hunter-Powell, Patricia, and Diane Watson. 2006. "Service Unseen: The Hotel Room Attendant at Work." *International Journal of Hospitality Management* 25(2): 297–312.

Incomes Data Services (IDS). 1999. "Pay in Hotels." *IDS Report* 795(October): 11–18.

———. 2000. "The Impact of the National Minimum Wage in 1999." *IDS Report* 802(February): 14–17.

———. 2005. "Pay in Hotels." *IDS Pay Report* 943(December): 11–15.

Kelliher, Clare, and Gilly Perrett. 2001. "Business Strategy and Approaches to HRM: A Case Study of New Developments in the United Kingdom Restaurant Industry." *Personnel Review* 30(4): 421–37.

Key Note. 2003. *Market Report Plus—Hotels*. Middlesex, U.K.: Key Note Ltd.

———. 2005. *Market Report Plus—Hotels*. Middlesex, U.K.: Key Note Ltd.

Knox, Angie, and Dennis Nickson. 2007. "Regulation in Australian Hotels: Is There a Lesson for the U.K.?" *Employee Relations* 29(1): 50–67.

Labour Market Trends. 2006. April. Office for National Statistics. London: Palgrave Macmillan. Accessed at http://www.statistics.gov.uk/downloads/theme_labour/LMT_Apr06.pdf.

\Lennon, John, and Roy Wood. 1989. "The Sociological Analysis of Hospitality Labor and the Neglect of Accommodation Workers." *International Journal of Hospitality Management* 8(3): 227–35.

Living Wage Unit. 2006. *A Fairer London: The Living Wage in London*. London: Greater London Authority (GLA).

Lloyd, Caroline. 2005. "Competitive Strategy and Skills: Working Out the Fit in the Fitness Industry." *Human Resource Management* 15(2): 15–34.

Lucas, Rosemary. 2004. *Employment Relations in the Hospitality and Tourism Industries*. London: Routledge.

Malik, Zaiba. 2006. "A Dirty Business." *The Guardian*, December 9, 2006: 45–47.

McCauley, Ian, and Roy Wood. 1992. "Hotel and Catering Industry Employees' Attributes Towards Trade Unions." *Employee Relations* 14(2): 20–28.

Meiklem, Peter John. 2004. "Highland Hospitality . . . Courtesy of Eastern Europeans." *Sunday Herald*, November 14, 2004: 9.

Mintel. 2004. *Hotels*. London: Mintel.

———. 2005. *Budget Hotels U.K.* London: Mintel.

Nickson, Dennis, Tom Baum, Erwin Losekoot, Alison Morrison, and Isabelle Frochot. 2002. *Skills, Organizational Performance, and Economic Activity in the Hospitality Industry: A Literature Review*. SKOPE Research Monograph 5. Oxford: Universities of Oxford and Warwick.

Office of National Statistics (ONS). 2004. *Annual Business Inquiry*. London: ONS.

———. 2006. "Local Area Labor Markets: Statistical Indicators." Accessed at www.statistics.gov.uk.

People1st. 2004. *Market Assessment for the Hospitality, Leisure, Travel, and Tourism Sector*, London: People 1st.

———. 2005. *Market Assessment for the Hospitality, Leisure, Travel, and Tourism Sector*. London: People1st.

———. 2006. *Hotels Industry Report*. London: People1st.

Phillips, Anne, and Barbara Taylor. 1986. "Sex and Skill." *Feminist Review* 6(1980): 79–88. Reprinted in *Waged Work: A Reader*, edited by *Feminist Review*. London: Virago.

Radiven, Nicholas, and Rosemary Lucas. 1997. "Abolition of Wages Councils and the Introduction of a National Minimum Wage with Particular Reference to British Hotels." *International Journal of Hospitality Management* 16(4): 345–59.

Salt, John, and Jane Millar. 2006. "Foreign Labor in the United Kingdom: Current Patterns and Trends." *Labor Market Trends* 114(10): 335–55.

Scottish Center for Employment Research (SCER). 2006. *Valuable Assets: A General Formal Investigation into the Role and Status of Classroom Assistants in Scotland's Primary School*. SCER Report 11. Study for the Equal Opportunities Commission (Scotland). Glasgow: University of Strathclyde (July). Accessed at http://www.eoc.org.uk/PDF/DoE_research_report.pdf.

Toynbee, Polly. 2003. *Hard Work*. London: Bloomsbury.

UniteHere. 2006. *Creating Luxury, Enduring Pain: How Hotel Work Is Hurting Housekeepers*. Accessed at http://www.hotelworkersrising.org/pdf/Injury_Paper.pdf.

Wills, Jane. 2005. "The Geography of Union Organizing in Low-Paid Service Industries in the U.K.: Lessons from the T&G's Campaign to Unionize the Dorchester Hotel, London." *Antipode* 37(1): 139–59.

Wood, Roy. 1995. "Wages Council Abolition: Doing Labor a Favor?" *Renewal* 3(1): 72–81.

———. 1997. *Working in Hotels and Catering*. London: Routledge.

Wynhausen, Elisabeth. 2005. *Dirty Work*. Sydney: Pan Macmillan.

# CHAPTER 4

# Business Strategies, Work Organization, and Low Pay in United Kingdom Retailing

*Geoff Mason and Matthew Osborne*

In 2005 the retail sector in the United Kingdom employed about 3 million workers, representing around 11 percent of all workers in the economy. As many as 49 percent of retail employees were low-paid, by the definition established in chapter 1, and thus the retail industry accounted for a sizable proportion (26 percent) of all low-paid workers in the United Kingdom. This proportion far outweighed other sectors employing large shares of low-paid workers, such as health services and hotels, which employed 13 percent and 12 percent, respectively, of all low-paid workers in Britain.[1]

Retail workers in the United Kingdom are the visible face of a highly concentrated industry in which the largest firms are noted for relatively high levels of profitability (Howard and Reynolds 2004), while productivity levels in the industry as a whole compare unfavorably to those in many other countries, in part because of relatively low average levels of physical capital per worker (O'Mahony and de Boer 2002).

According to Elizabeth Howard and Jonathan Reynolds (2004), this disparity between profitability and labor productivity performance reflects the fact that large retailers in the United Kingdom are generally less likely than their American or continental European counterparts to compete solely on low prices and are more likely to seek to compete on labor-intensive customer service features as well (for example, greater availability of staff to answer questions, relatively short waits for customers at cash registers, and provision of bag-packing services). This perspective is consistent with estimates that in large retail companies the number of employees per 1,000 square feet of net selling space is roughly 70 percent greater in the United Kingdom than in the United States or France (Howard and Reynolds 2004).

The prevailing business strategies of large retailers in the United Kingdom can be readily linked to the high incidence of low pay in the industry. For example, the most likely explanation for retailers' greater emphasis on labor-intensive services compared to their rivals in continental Europe is that labor costs are relatively low in the United Kingdom (Competition Commission 2000).[2] At the same time, compared to retailers operating in the much larger American market, there is less scope for retailers in the United Kingdom to compete on a low-cost, low-service model through economies of scale in purchasing and store operation (Howard and Reynolds 2004).

In this chapter, we explore the links between employers' business strategies and low pay in retailing by focusing in detail on employment, work organization, and pay in eight case study firms, which are evenly divided between food retailing and electrical and electronic goods retailing. The next section provides an overview of employment and pay for selected occupations (sales assistants and checkout operators) in the United Kingdom retail industry as a whole. Then we describe our research methodology and case selection criteria. After we outline the business and labor resourcing strategies pursued in the case study firms, we go on to focus on work organization and pay in sales assistant and checkout operator jobs and assess the impact of the national minimum wage (NMW) on pay-setting in the case study firms. The following section examines other aspects of job quality and job satisfaction and considers the role of trade unions and other labor market institutions in protecting the terms and conditions of retail workers' jobs. Finally, we summarize our findings.

## INDUSTRIAL STRUCTURE, EMPLOYMENT, AND PAY IN UNITED KINGDOM RETAILING

Just over one-third of retail employees in the United Kingdom are involved in the sale of food, drink, and related products (SIC 52.11), a sector that is henceforth referred to as food retailing. Electrical goods retailing (SIC 52.45) accounts for about 3 percent of all retail employees (Office for National Statistics 2004). The great majority of retail enterprises employ fewer than five people and in total account for less than 10 percent of total employment in the industry. Around 70 percent of all retail employees work in enterprises with 250 or more employees. In food retailing, this proportion rises to 88 percent; in electrical goods retailing, it is 62 percent (ONS 2003).

Food retailing is dominated by a number of large enterprises, the top four of which now account for almost two-thirds of sales (Mintel 2004). Over the last four decades, there have been sharp changes in the relative positions of these four companies. In common with large retailers in other countries, these firms and their nearest rivals have sought with varying success to source products on a global scale and to increase the share of own-label products in total sales. They have also invested heavily in IT systems for product scanning and stock management, but without the same emphasis on labor savings as is common among their French and German counterparts. In recent years, these large retailers have undertaken numerous takeovers and rebrandings of formerly independent chains of convenience stores, along with moves in some cases into nonfood products for which recent margins and sales growth have been higher than for food.

Electrical goods retailing principally refers to retail sales of electrical household appliances and radio and television goods. However, in terms of business ownership and strategy, the sale of these items is closely associated with computers, mobile phones, and related electronic products. "White goods" retailing in the United Kingdom is increasingly dominated by two large chains, while a number of smaller competitors have gone out of business in recent years. This shift reflects partly the market power of the two main players and partly the downward pressure on retail prices resulting from cheap imports. The main competition for the two dominant chains now tends to come from general merchandise stores and from food supermarket chains that have diversified into nonfood areas. In addition, there are some independent electrical/electronic goods retailers that depend on the membership of a buying group or support from a branded supplier to gain access to purchasing power and marketing campaigns (Burt and Sparks 2003).

In both food and electrical goods retailing, the emphasis placed by the market leaders on developing customer loyalty and enhancing service quality while simultaneously minimizing labor and associated costs gives human resource managers two key sets of labor resourcing issues to resolve:

1. Matching labor requirements to customer flows that fluctuate sharply between different hours of each day, different days of each week, and different periods during each year

2.  Securing relatively low levels of labor turnover so as to maximize the proportion of employees who have the experience needed to keep store operations running smoothly and to meet service quality objectives

One obvious strategy to secure a workforce that is flexible enough to fit in with fluctuating hours requirements and yet is also likely to be more interested in stable patterns of employment than in high pay is to focus on groups of people who are available to work part-time and are not wholly dependent on their part-time salaries in order to live. Examples include married women who have primary responsibilities for child care and housework in their homes, school and university students, and older retired people who are already receiving pensions.

Analysis of Labour Force Survey (LFS) data shows that female part-timers constitute the bulk of employees in sales assistant and checkout operator jobs. Taken together, these occupations represent about 45 percent of all retail employment. Almost three-quarters of sales assistants are female, as are 81 percent of checkout operators (table 4.1).[3] Both occupations include a high proportion of part-timers (defined as working less than thirty hours per week): 64 percent of sales assistants and 73 percent of checkout operators. According to the Annual Survey of Hours and Earnings (ASHE), women account for 80 to 81 percent of part-time employees in both occupations. Even among part-timers, there is a wide variation in hours worked. For example, the median time worked per week for sales assistants is twenty-one hours, but 25 percent of them work an average of fifteen hours or less, while for checkout operators the median and lower quartile hours figures are twenty and fourteen hours, respectively (table 4.1). The heavy use of part-timers contrasts with a limited reliance on temporary staff to cover fluctuations in staffing requirements—for example, seasonal peaks in demand.[4]

Young workers (sixteen to twenty-four year olds) accounted for 46 percent of sales assistants in 2005 and 42 percent of checkout operators. The remainder of the workforce was spread fairly evenly across the twenty-five-to-fifty-nine age range. Those age sixty or older accounted for only 4 percent of sales assistants and 7 percent of checkout operators (table 4.1). Students constituted a larger share of part-time employees than the over-sixty group, but their importance varied greatly from company to company. For example, in a 1999 sur-

Table 4.1  Sales Assistants and Checkout Operators in
United Kingdom Retailing, Analyzed by Gender,
Working Hours, Contractual Basis, Age Group,
Ethnicity, and Qualifications, 2005

|  | Sales Assistants | Checkout Operators |
|---|---|---|
| Gender |  |  |
| Male | 27% | 19% |
| Female | 73 | 81 |
| Usual hours per week, ex-cluding overtime |  |  |
| Thirty plus hours | 36 | 27 |
| Less than thirty hours | 64 | 73 |
| Type of employment contract |  |  |
| Permanent | 94 | 96 |
| Temporary | 6 | 4 |
| Age group |  |  |
| Sixteen to twenty-four | 46 | 42 |
| Twenty-five to twenty-nine | 8 | 6 |
| Thirty to thirty-nine | 13 | 16 |
| Forty to forty-nine | 15 | 14 |
| Fifty to fifty-nine | 13 | 16 |
| Sixty to sixty-four | 3 | 5 |
| Sixty-five or older | 1 | 2 |
| Migrants |  |  |
| United Kingdom national | 92 | 91 |
| Not United Kingdom national | 8 | 9 |
| Highest qualification category[a] |  |  |
| Graduate | 5 | 3 |
| Other NVQ4 or equivalent | 4 | 5 |
| NVQ3 | 27 | 22 |
| NVQ2 | 35 | 36 |
| Below NVQ2; other qualifications or no qualifications | 29 | 34 |
| Ethnic background |  |  |
| White | 91 | 88 |
| Black Caribbean | 1 | 2 |
| Black African | 1 | 1 |

Table 4.1 (*Continued*)

|  | Sales Assistants | Checkout Operators |
|---|---|---|
| Indian | 2 | 3 |
| Pakistani | 1 | 1 |
| Bangladeshi | 1 | 1 |
| Other Asian | 2 | 3 |
| Other ethnic | 1 | 2 |
| Usual hours worked per week, excluding overtime (number of hours) | | |
| Lower decile | 8 | 10 |
| Lower quartile | 15 | 14 |
| Median | 21 | 20 |
| Upper quartile | 36 | 30 |
| Upper decile | 40 | 39 |
| Number of observations | 8,949 | 1,981 |

*Source:* Labour Force Survey (LFS).
*Notes:* Retailing is defined as 1992 SIC codes 521 to 526 inclusive.
[a] "Other NVQ4" includes BTEC higher national and teaching and nursing qualifications or equivalent; NVQ3 includes A levels and trade apprenticeships or equivalent; NVQ2 includes GCSE Grades A to C, city and guilds craft, GNVQ intermediate, or equivalent.

vey of the big food retailers the student share of employment ranged from 5 to 10 percent in some firms to 35 to 40 percent in others (IDS 1999).

Employees in retail occupations are generally less well qualified than the average employee in the United Kingdom, with disproportionate numbers either holding no qualifications above GCSE or equivalent or possessing no qualifications at all. A very small proportion of retail employees have degrees or other higher education qualifications (table 4.1).

Over 90 percent of sales assistants and checkout operators are classified as white in the Labour Force Survey, and a similar proportion are U.K. nationals (table 4.1). The 5 percent share of Asian and Asian British employees and 2 percent share of black and black British employees in each group are broadly in line with the proportions of those ethnic groups in the United Kingdom's workforce as a whole.

Data from the Annual Survey of Hours and Earnings show that in

Figure 4.1    Gross Hourly Earnings of Sales Assistants, by Gender and Full-Time or Part-Time Status, 2005

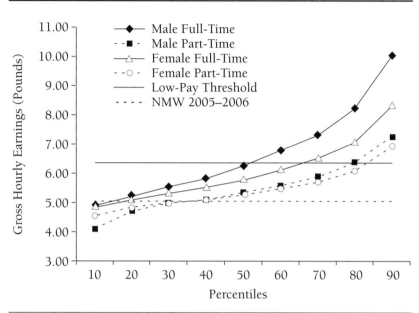

*Source:* Annual Survey of Hours and Earnings (ASHE), Office for National Statistics (ONS).

2005 as many as 75 percent of retail sales assistants earned below the low pay threshold as defined in chapter 1. However, there was considerable variation between male and female employees and between full-timers and part-timers. Male full-time staff earned more than female full-timers at all points in the wage distribution: 50 percent of male full-timers were above the low pay threshold, whereas the same was true of only 30 to 35 percent of female full-timers (figure 4.1). Among part-timers, the differences between males and females were relatively small at each point on the wage distribution, with as many as 80 to 85 percent of all part-timers earning below the low pay threshold.

By comparison with sales assistants, there was much less pay dispersion among checkout operators, and male/female and full-time/part-time earnings were fairly close together at each point on the wage distribution (figure 4.2). In all these different groups of

Figure 4.2　Gross Hourly Earnings of Checkout Operators, by Gender and Full-Time or Part-Time Status, 2005

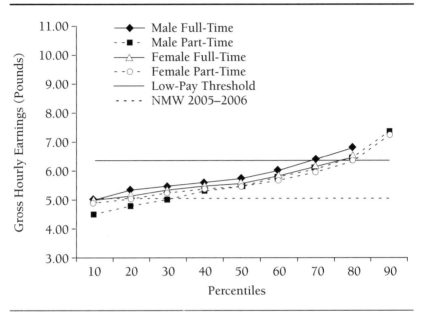

*Source:* Annual Survey of Hours and Earnings (ASHE), Office for National Statistics (ONS).

checkout employees, only about one-fifth earned more than the low pay threshold.

The relatively high earnings of full-time sales assistants at the upper decile level presumably reflect the inclusion of sales staff paid on commission as well as supervisors and team leaders.[5] The extent of pay dispersion in this occupation also reflects retail companies' responses to regional differences in labor market conditions. For example, Incomes Data Services (IDS) (2003) notes that some retailers have a structured system of regional pay zones designed to allow higher rates of pay in response to regional variations in recruitment and retention difficulties. Other companies permit local managers to raise pay rates for certain employees above the spot rate for their grade.

## METHODOLOGY AND SAMPLE SELECTION

Our eight case study retail firms were evenly divided between food retailers and firms selling electrical and electronic goods. The firms were chosen from those listed in the FAME company accounts dataset.[6] Our main aims in selecting the firms were to achieve a mix of company sizes, a mix of national and regional chains, and a mix of business strategies in terms of market positioning. In particular, we wished to compare firms selling predominantly high-quality products with those selling mainly low-priced products in order to assess any effects of different business strategies on pay and job quality. Just over 40 percent of the firms that were formally requested to participate agreed to do so. In the descriptions that follow, the activities of these firms are described only in general terms in order to ensure their confidentiality.

As shown in table 4.2, the four food retail firms consisted of three national chains and one regional chain. Two of these firms targeted the "high end" of the market by offering a wide range of premium-priced products, while the other two sought to compete primarily through discount pricing. Of the four electrical retail firms, two were national chains and two were regional, but the latter firms were expanding their national sales through the Internet. It was harder to distinguish market positioning in electrical retailing since all four firms were seeking to compete heavily on price. However, in terms of average sales per employee (a rough indicator of the average unit value of products sold), two of the case study firms were in the upper quartile for electrical retail, another was at the median level, and the fourth firm was in the lower quartile (table 4.2, column 3).[7]

In each organization, we conducted two sets of semistructured interviews: first, with managers in headquarters, and then with store managers, junior store managers and supervisors, and sales assistants at a selected store.[8] The store locations were chosen to cover a wide mix of differing local labor market conditions (table 4.2, columns 4 to 6). Across the eight firms, interviews were carried out with a total of twelve headquarters managers, fifteen store managers, and thirty-one sales assistants and checkout operators (in a mixture of individual and group interview formats). The interviews ranged in length from one to two hours with managers, ten to twenty minutes with individual employees, and thirty to forty-five minutes in group interviews with employees. The employees interviewed were chosen by managers, raising the possibility of selection bias. Nonetheless, these interviews yielded a range of opinions and responses and provided useful insights into employee perspectives to balance those provided by managers.

Table 4.2 The Case Study Retail Firms, Analyzed by Sector, Employment Size Range, Market Positioning, and Local Labor Market Conditions for Store Visits

| | | | | Case Study Retail Stores | | |
| Code | Sector | Employment | Market Positioning | Local Unemployment Rate (TTWA)— Men and Women[a] | Local Unemployment Rate (LAD)— Men and Women[b] | Local Unemployment Rate (LAD)— Women Only[b] |
| --- | --- | --- | --- | --- | --- | --- |
| R1 | Food | 20,000-plus | National chain, mainly premium-priced products | 4.3% (store 1); 2.1 (store 2) | 3.2% (store 1); 2.5 (store 2) | 1.4% (store 1); 1.9 (store 2) |
| R2 | Food | 20,000-plus | National chain, predominantly discount pricing | 4.2 | 3.1 | 3.1 |
| R3 | Food | 20,000-plus | National chain, mainly premium-priced products | 6.1 | 5.2 | 3.3 |
| R4 | Food | Under 1,000 | Regional chain, discount pricing | 3.0 | 3.0 | 2.9 |

| | | | | | | |
|---|---|---|---|---|---|---|
| R5 | Electrical | Under 1,000 | Regional stores, national Internet business; relatively high average sales per employee | 4.1 | 3.9 | 3.0 |
| R6 | Electrical | Under 1,000 | Regional chain, middle ranking on average sales per employee | 4.7 | 3.1 | 3.2 |
| R7 | Electrical | Under 1,000 | National chain, relatively high average sales per employee | 6.4 | 2.4 | 1.6 |
| R8 | Electrical | 1,000 to 5,000 | National chain, relatively low average sales per employee | 5.4 | 4.5 | 3.3 |

*Source:* Columns 1 to 4: authors' compilation; columns 5 to 7: Office for National Statistics (ONS), Annual Population Survey, Job Centre Plus Administrative System, Annual Business Inquiry (2005); all else—authors' compilation.
[a] Refers to the travel-to-work area (TTWA) in which each case study retail store was located. The current criteria for defining TTWAs are that at least 75 percent of the area's resident workforce must work in the area and at least 75 percent of the people who work in the area must also live in the area.
[b] Refers to the local area district (LAD) in which each case study retail store was located.

## BUSINESS AND LABOR RESOURCING STRATEGIES IN THE CASE STUDY RETAIL FIRMS

In both food and electrical retailing, the labor resourcing strategies adopted by firms were closely linked to their competitive market strategies.

### Food Retailing

Business strategy in the food retailing sector tends to be differentiated on three main dimensions:

1.  *Target markets*: Some firms adopt a "high-quality" approach, targeting more affluent consumers with a wide range of relatively elaborate and expensive products. At the other end of the scale, some firms compete primarily on price and tend to locate their outlets in lower-income neighborhoods. A third category of retailer adopts an intermediate position (Burt and Sparks 2003).

2.  *Formats*: Some smaller companies tend to rely on formats such as "neighborhood stores" rather than on superstores, but as just noted, the larger chains have started to develop store portfolios that include a wide range of different formats.

3.  *Pricing*: A contrast is sometimes drawn between "every day low pricing" (EDLP) and selective low price "promotions" (Roe 2002).

In practice, however, many retail firms adopt a hybrid EDLP/promotional approach. Furthermore, in the context of the United Kingdom, low price strategies do not necessarily equate with low service quality in the same way as is exemplified by German-owned discounters such as Aldi and Lidl, whose entrance into the United Kingdom retail market during the 1990s met with only limited success (Mintel 2004). On the contrary, the United Kingdom's market leaders, who have built up their positions by developing customer loyalty, place great public emphasis on service quality as experienced by customers (for example, by offering a wide range of products, by making staff available to answer inquiries, and so on).

This emphasis was reflected in our case study firms. Two of

them—R3 and R1—specialized in food made with high-quality in-gredients that it sold at prices reflecting this quality (although they tried nonetheless to avoid being seen as "expensive"). Both offered an extensive range of services to customers (including assistance with packing bags and carrying goods to cars), and their training pro-grams emphasized the development of customer-facing skills. The other two firms—R2 and R4—competed more directly on price, but their emphasis on the quality of customer service (for example, by keeping checkout lines to a minimum, providing bag-packing ser-vices, and having staff available to answer queries) was just as strong as in the chains selling premium-priced products (see table 4.3, col-umn 3).

The primary consideration for labor resourcing strategy in all four chains was the need for flexible staffing to cover nonstandard work-ing hours such as evenings, weekends, and public holidays and also to adjust to seasonal fluctuations. With the exception of R3, the cen-tral approach among our cases was to rely heavily on part-time em-ployees, particularly women who were seeking to combine employ-ment with child care responsibilities (and were thus more amenable to working evening and weekend shifts when their partners were at home). This was supplemented in varying degrees by employment of students and older persons in their late fifties and early sixties.

Thus, at R1 approximately 69 percent of staff were part-time, and females represented 77 percent of checkout operators and 52 percent of sales assistants. At R2, particular emphasis was placed on offering "family-friendly hours," and some 72 percent of employees were part-timers, 69 percent of them female. At R4—a small regional chain of convenience stores—all sales assistants worked part-time, and vir-tually all of them were female. R3 had a large proportion of female staff in sales positions but was distinctively different in using a core team of mostly female full-timers to cover weekday shifts and part-time students, both university and secondary, to staff the evenings and weekends. The full-timers worked a four-week rotation that was announced well in advance, and the students worked set shifts to which they could be allocated at short notice. In total, 77 percent of sales staff at R3 were female, but the 16 percent share of part-timers was small compared to the other food retailers.

In three of the four firms, therefore, management's requirements for numerical flexibility were met in the main by fragmentation of the permanent labor force into a large pool of part-time employees

Table 4.3 The Case Study Retail Firms, Analyzed by Market Positioning and Labor Resourcing Strategies

| | Sector and Market Focus | Business Strategy (Market Positioning) | Female | Part-Time | Other Aspects of Labor Resourcing Strategy |
|---|---|---|---|---|---|
| R1 | Food, national chain | Sells high-quality, expensive foods; targets affluent areas; offers high-quality service with many extra services for customers. | 61% | 69% | "Mature ladies and mothers" work weekday shifts, and students work evenings and weekends. Covers fluctuations in demand by using temporary staff. |
| R2 | Food, national chain | Discount retailer; uses parent company buying power to achieve low prices and "will not be beaten on price"; emphasizes good customer service and offers many additional services. | 69 | 72 | Uses high proportion of part-timers because of need for flexibility in small departments; covers fluctuations in demand by using overtime plus "seasonal part-timers" who are often retired people. |
| R3 | Food, national chain | Premium brand; sells high-quality food at expensive prices, but prices are lower than "premium ranges" of other chains. | 77 | 84 | Covers fluctuations in demand by recruiting a fresh batch of temporary employees each Christmas and in the summer; also uses overtime. |
| R4 | Food, regional chain | Price-competitive; emphasizes good quality and fresh foods; competes on service. | Close to 100 | Close to 100 | Covers fluctuations in demand by using overtime. |

| | | | | | |
|---|---|---|---|---|---|
| R5 | Electrical, regional chain, national Internet business | Rebranding introduced "Internet price matching," reducing prices to 20 to 30% cheaper than the competition; being small, can react quickly; Internet/phone division is 65 to 70% of sales. | 30 | 11 | Uses temporary staff and overtime to cover fluctuations. |
| R6 | Electrical, regional chain | Good relations with manufacturers allow it to negotiate good deals on certain lines; tries to be "people-friendly." | 23 | 11 | Covers fluctuations in demand by using overtime. |
| R7 | Electrical, national chain | Price-competitive; changes product range to suit demand; focuses on customer service and product knowledge. | 2 | 12 | Part-timers are mostly young. Covers fluctuations in demand by using overtime plus bank of casual staff. |
| R8 | Electrical, national chain | Focuses on specialized products (e.g., components) and product knowledge of staff; competes in a market with rapidly falling prices. | Mostly male | Some part-time | Many staff are students. Part-timers used for evenings and weekends. Uses overtime to cover fluctuations in demand. |

*Source:* Authors' compilation.

(working widely varied numbers of hours per week) rather than by recruitment of temporary staff. These employers used fixed-term employment on a relatively small scale, primarily during seasonal peak periods. R4 took on temporary employees—many of them students who came back each year—in order to cope with increases in demand at Christmas and in the summer. R3 took on a large number of staff each Christmas on temporary (fixed-term) contracts, with a view to taking some of them on permanently after their contract was over. At both R1 and R2, the main response to seasonal fluctuations was to develop banks of "seasonal part-timers"—often students or retired people—who remained permanently "on the books" but came in to work only when required. This helped ensure that temporary staff were familiar with store procedures and did not require repeated initial training.

Perhaps because of the English-language skills required to serve customers, there were many fewer examples of recently arrived immigrants working in the retail cases than in some of the other industries covered in this book (for example, food processing and hotel cleaning). However, in both food and electrical retail cases, the recruitment of black British or Asian British staff typically reflected the ethnic mix in local areas, sometimes as the result of a store's explicit policy in order to allow it to be seen as part of the local community. For example, at R2, managers regularly compared the ethnic backgrounds of the store staff against demographic data for the area.

## Electrical Retailing

In terms of resourcing labor requirements, the electrical retail firms were markedly different from the food retailers in their greater reliance on male full-time staff. This reflected a strong desire for sales staff to have preexisting knowledge of electrical and electronic products in order to interact with customers. That knowledge is believed to be more commonly found among men than among women and thus cannot readily be acquired by recruiting among women who are willing to work part-time for long periods of time. A female assistant store manager at R7 tried to explain why such a low proportion of sales assistants in the company were female:

> Only this morning did a man ring up, I answered the phone, and he said, "A woman working in a hi-fi shop!" and then he laughed,

and then he said, "Well, don't worry, it's only an easy question that you should be able to answer." . . . I think the lack of knowledge that women tend to think they have . . . women just don't have the confidence to give it a shot.

The dominance of male staff is illustrated by R5: male sales staff tended to work in sections of the store such as plasma TVs and hi-fi equipment, where commission rates were relatively high, while female colleagues would tend to sell white goods such as washing machines and dryers, which had a lower commission yield. "Some of us have better areas than others," admitted a male assistant manager, though he added that "the girls are more happy to sell the white goods, like fridge freezers and washing machines rather than plasmas and LCDs." A female sales assistant seemed to concur: "A lot of people do go for the commission, but I'm not bothered. . . . One of my colleagues will hover around the plasma TVs because he thinks he can get more that way."

The emphasis on product knowledge was common to all four electrical retail firms in spite of significant differences between them in market positioning. One of the two firms with a comparatively high value of sales per employee was R7, a relatively large chain by electrical retail standards that used to focus on hi-fi equipment but now stocked other home entertainment items such as LCD/plasma TVs and DVD players. The other high-end electrical retailer, R5, was a smaller, regionally based firm, but a growing proportion of its sales came from its Internet division, which drew sales from across the United Kingdom. R5 managers saw their small size as an advantage that allowed them to adapt quickly to new trends. Both firms placed high priority on customer service skills and required a high degree of product knowledge from sales staff. R7 looked for product knowledge at the time of recruitment, but at R5 this was more an issue for training (for example, training courses provided by equipment manufacturers).

R6 was another regional company, with sales per employee close to the industry median. It sold a wide range of electrical products and did not specialize in any particular area. R6 had an Internet division but had not yet achieved the same degree of market penetration as R7. Its perceived strength lay in flexibility and good relations with suppliers, which allowed it to negotiate favorable terms when prices were changing rapidly. R6 also tried to maintain a reputation as a local business, encouraging staff to be "people-friendly." It made use of the product training supplied by manufacturers, but not to the same extent as R5 or R7.

R8 was by far the largest of the four electrical chains and had been protected to a large extent from the sector's fierce price competition in white goods by the fact that it occupied a niche market selling electrical components. Like other electrical retailers, it required sales staff to have a high level of product knowledge, but its low pay rates had made it difficult to attract workers of the required quality.

In three of the four cases—R5, R6, and R7—the central labor resourcing strategy was to use full-time staff to cover all shifts, including evenings and weekends, with rotations provided well in advance. In these three firms, roughly 11 to 12 percent of staff were part-time, and the vast majority were male (table 4.3, columns 2 and 3). In R5, for example, it was made clear to job applicants that they were expected to work weekends; this was usually not a deterrent, however, since applicants were attracted by the higher levels of sales at weekends and therefore the higher commissions they could earn. The exception was R8, where full-time staff worked the core weekday hours and part-time staff, often students, were used to cover evenings and weekends.

At R7, overtime was used to manage fluctuations in demand, both on a day-to-day basis and seasonally. It also drew on a bank of casual staff to work in back-office roles when extra support was needed, and occasionally it also used temporary employees. At R5 and R8, overtime was used to raise staffing levels over the Christmas period. R5 also took on a large number of extra employees in the Internet division at this time. At R6, overtime was used to cover fluctuations in demand throughout the year, but seasonal fluctuations were dealt with by taking on temporary employees. R8 responded to seasonal fluctuations by asking employees to work overtime.

## WORK ORGANIZATION AND PAY

Food and electrical retailers also differed greatly in their organization of work for sales assistants, with knock-on effects on recruitment criteria, training provision and pay.

## Recruitment, Initial Training, and Work Organization

The recruitment criteria pursued by food and electrical retail firms showed that they were looking for very different types of employees. The food retail firms tended to look for attributes such as "a positive attitude," friendliness, communication skills, and basic numeracy and literacy skills. These qualities were often described in terms of "customer service skills," but the food retailers typically did not look for prior customer service experience, nor did they require that sales assistants have any prior knowledge of the products or of retail operations (table 4.4, column 1). None of the food retailers had specific requirements in terms of educational qualifications, which goes some way to explaining the low qualification levels in retail occupations (table 4.1). In R3, a new recruitment process involved lengthy group interviews during which applicants took part in team exercises and role-plays under the scrutiny of managers in order to assess their communication and customer service skills. Managers thought that this process had resulted in a "higher caliber of new starters." In R1, a manager at headquarters said the firm put a lot of emphasis on communication skills during the recruitment process, looking out for those with a "passion for delivering the service" and an ability to work well without supervision, as well as "reasonable literacy and numeracy."

By contrast, as noted earlier, the electrical firms placed great emphasis on product knowledge. As in food retail, very little emphasis was placed on the qualifications of applicants, although one exception was R5, where new employees were expected to have GCSE math and English. In R6 and R7, recruitment managers looked for some level of prior knowledge of electrical products, and in R8 job applicants were asked to identify electrical components. At R5, a headquarters manager commented that:

> [Job applicants] might have sold a lot, but they know nothing about electrical items, that's something we can train. . . . We've run campaigns in the past where we have clearly asked for people with electrical experience, and to be honest, it's extremely difficult to find that people have [electrical experience].

Table 4.4 Recruitment Criteria, Initial Training, Starting Pay Rates, and Median Gross Hourly Pay for Sales Assistants in the Case Study Firms

| | Recruitment Criteria | Initial Training | Starting Gross Pay per Hour—Adults[a] | Median Gross, Pay per Hour—All Employees[a] |
|---|---|---|---|---|
| Food | | | | |
| R1 | Communication skills plus "reasonable numeracy and literacy" | Two to five days of induction training, then work through a checklist for the next three months | £ 5.10 | £ 6.40 |
| R2 | Attitude, customer service skills, literacy and numeracy | Twenty-five hours of induction training followed by up to twelve weeks further development, leading to a NVQ2, partly funded by Learning and Skills Council | 5.10 | 5.50 |
| R3 | Customer service skills | Two days off-the-job training, including cash register training and health and safety | 5.50 | 6.00 |
| R4 | No specific criteria | Twelve-hour induction split between headquarters and store, then thirteen-week trial period | 5.10 | 5.10 |

**Electrical**

| | | | |
|---|---|---|---|
| R5 | Retail experience, communication and presentation skills, electrical experience | Internet: two-day induction training plus three weeks shadowing others. Stores: varies according to individual experience or knowledge | 7.80 | 9.20 |
| R6 | Product knowledge and customer service skills | A three-month probationary period acts as a screening method; training required for "difficult to use" computer system | 5.80 | 7.70 |
| R7 | Product knowledge, tested on trial day in workplace before recruitment decision is made | Four-day seminar training covering rules, procedures, company history, company service, career opportunities, and technical training | 5.80 | 8.20 |
| R8 | Product knowledge and/or retail experience | Induction training lasting half a day, followed by job-specific training, in which new hires work through workbooks on specific knowledge and tasks for each role | 5.10 | 5.40 |

*Source:* Authors' compilation.

*Note:* "Sales assistants" here include checkout operators, since in many firms the two occupations are not separately identified.

[a] The estimated median pay rate is here defined such that half of all sales assistants earn above that rate and half below it. Where applicable, estimated pay levels include performance-related sales commissions and bonuses and annual company bonuses.

It was taken for granted that these selection criteria would lead to a predominantly male workforce as a result of prevailing social attitudes toward electrical and electronic products.

The differences in recruitment criteria between food and electrical retail firms were mirrored by differences in the extent of interaction with customers and in the division of labor between sales assistants and checkout operators. For example, as a matter of policy, food retail sales assistants typically did not approach customers; their interaction with customers was limited to answering queries about the whereabouts of products, serving at the checkouts, and offering help where it was needed—for example, with bag-packing. Staff were expected to gain detailed knowledge about products only if they were serving on specialized counters such as meat or fish, in which case they needed to be able to prepare products and give advice about which products were most suitable for customers' requirements. These skills were particularly important in one of the high-end stores, R1, where employees were given detailed training on how to cook meat and fish and which wines were most suitable to drink with them. However, these counters typically accounted for only a small proportion (about one-fifth) of all sales assistants in the national food retail chains; the smaller regional chain R4 had no specialist staff at all. Therefore, for a large majority of food retail employees, product knowledge played a very minor role in their jobs. Much more emphasis was placed on the ability of sales assistants to operate the checkouts if they were called on to do so at short notice.

In the electrical retail firms, interaction with customers was a core part of the sales process. Sales assistants were expected to greet customers and, if the customer wished, to offer detailed advice and information about specific products. This kind of customer interaction was strongly motivated by the commission that sales assistants received from each sale. In two cases, R5 and R7, sales assistants took care of the whole transaction, operating the cash register and then taking "ownership" of the customer's after-sales service arrangements. The same overall responsibility for the complete sales process also arose for sales assistants responding to Internet inquiries. In R6 and R8, there were specialist cashiers who operated the registers without engaging in the sales process, but in R6 even this part of the transaction was overseen by sales assistants who needed to log the sales in order to record their commissions.

In general, sales assistants in food retail operated with a great deal less personal autonomy than those in electrical retail. Typically, they were organized in teams under a section manager (or under the store manager or a supervisor in the smaller retailer R4). After managers at R3 had tried to increase the autonomy of teams and reduce the number of section managers, they reported that the teams had become "dysfunctional" without sufficient direction, and so the number of section managers was increased again. In R2, sales assistants gave the impression that they simply followed orders on a daily basis:

> We go where we are needed, it could be on provisions [for example, dairy or produce], or it could be queue-busting on the checkout, or we could be doing replenishment.

> We do anything that needs to be done if we're called on by the managers.

> The guidelines are all laid out so we follow them.

A lack of autonomy was also evident in many store processes. At R1, teams were used as a means to give daily instructions to sales assistants, and at R4 sales assistants routinely worked on the cash registers unless they were asked to do other tasks by the manager or supervisors. At R2, sales assistants simply had to use a handheld console to scan items when dealing with reordering. This information was then transferred to a computer system, which calculated orders automatically according to a product range determined at headquarters.

In spite of these differences between food and electrical retailers in recruitment criteria and work organization, there were few differences between them with respect to initial training (table 4.4, column 2). Across all eight case studies, new recruits typically received two to five days of specific induction training to introduce them to the company and the job they would be doing, followed by a varied mixture of on-the-job training using workbooks, computer-based training courses, and coaching. R2 was unusual in that it worked with a government-funded training program to offer national vocational qualification, level 2 (NVQ2) to all employees on completion of the initial training process. R2 had made changes to its induction training so that it could be recognized in this way—for example, by adding modules about disability and by increasing assessment of on-the-job training. Managers reported that the NVQs not only helped employees' self-esteem but also allowed the company to get funding from the government-financed Learning and Skills Council. The real differences in training provision between food and electrical retailers emerged with respect to continuing training (discussed later in the chapter) because of the prevalence of new product training in the electrical cases.

## PAY RATES FOR SALES ASSISTANTS AND CHECKOUT OPERATORS

Pay data show marked differences between food and electrical retail employees, reflecting the different levels of product knowledge and individual autonomy in each type of job and the greater opportunities to earn sales commissions in the electrical jobs (table 4.4). In two of the three national food chains, starting pay for adult sales assistants (including checkout operators) was just above the national minimum wage level of £5.05 (US$10.31) per hour in 2005; in the third national food chain, it was 45 pence above the NMW.[9] Across all three of these firms the median gross hourly wage ranged between £5.50 and £6.40 (US$11.23 and US$13.06)—that is, it was no higher than the low pay threshold, but there were substantial variations in wage rates within each company, reflecting different regional labor market conditions. The highest median pay rate among the food retailers, at R1, reflected the effects of a company-wide annual bonus system, which supplemented basic pay rates by roughly 15 percent. In the smaller regional chain R4, the median gross hourly wage at £5.10 (US$10.41) was only just above the NMW, and according to employees, this low pay rate contributed to relatively high labor turnover. However, this point was not conceded by a headquarters manager, who preferred to blame the company's high turnover on staff having "personal reasons" for moving on.

By contrast, in three of the electrical firms median gross hourly pay was well above both the NMW and the low pay threshold, ranging from £7.70 (US$15.72) in R6 to £9.20 (US$18.78) in R5; this range reflected the scope for earning sales commissions on top of basic hourly pay. However, R8 was an outlier among the electrical firms, with a median pay rate of only £5.40 (US$11.02) per hour in spite of its requirement that newly recruited staff demonstrate preexisting product knowledge. As with the lowest-paying food retail firm, R4, R8's pay rate contributed to high turnover rates, which management preferred to live with rather than accept a significantly higher pay bill.

In the national food chains, the NMW had initially been seen as too low to affect their pay-setting arrangements, but in recent years it has started to impinge on these firms' pay rates. For example, in R2 a headquarters manager told us that when the NMW was first introduced, the company's pay rates were "well above" the minimum, but subsequent up-ratings had eroded the gap and now the company's policy was to stay five pence above the minimum. An R3 store manager described the effects of recent increases in the NMW: "There was a big leap up to £5.70 an hour base rate. . . . It was partly the result of the minimum wage, where that was expected to head in the next year or so, and also to reflect the job we are asking our sales assistants to do." And a headquarters manager at R4 explained that "we pay just a tad over the minimum wage. . . . We used to be higher than that, but you know how it's hiked up. . . . We would probably have been around fifteen to twenty pence above it."

In a common response to the growing impact of the NMW, all three national food retail chains had introduced new contracts for sales assistants that increased the basic hourly rate, in order to comply with the NMW, but reduced the opportunities to earn additional payments such as bonuses and premium rates for working unsocial hours. At R2, a new contract of this kind had been made compulsory for new recruits and optional for existing workers, but it was made clear that employees who refused to change would be given fewer opportunities to earn premium rates and thus would probably end up being worse off on the old contract. In the case of R3, an annual bonus that had been worth as much as 5 percent of sales assistants' annual salary was abolished in spite of some resistance from employee consultative groups.

## JOB QUALITY AND JOB SATISFACTION

In this section, we first consider the opportunities at case study firms for sales assistants and checkout operators to progress to more skilled or better-paid employment within the firm. We then examine qualitative evidence on the degree of job satisfaction or dissatisfaction experienced by these workers.

## CONTINUING TRAINING AND CAREER PROGRESSION

There were sharp differences between food and electrical retailers in the content of the continuing training they offered (table 4.5, column 1). In the electrical cases, ongoing training included substantial elements of product knowledge training, often provided by the manufacturers of the products. In R6, training sessions took place on Saturday mornings, before the store opened. These training courses were popular with sales assistants, despite the fact that they were outside paid hours, because they provided knowledge that helped sales and therefore increased commission earnings. In R5 and R7, employees had at least four days of off-the-job training per year, mainly consisting of product knowledge training. In R8, sales staff got thirty to sixty minutes of training each week, mostly concerning product familiarization and often provided by manufacturers.

By contrast, in the food retail cases, ongoing training was mainly focused on customer service skills and store systems. In R1, computer-based learning was used to teach sales staff about store processes, such as ordering, and customer service training was provided for key employees, who then went back to their sections and sought to influence others. In R2, computer-based learning was used to develop product knowledge and customer handling skills. In both of these stores, extra training was also available for specialist staff who worked on counters such as fresh fish, meat, or baked products. In R3, ongoing training was limited to occasional short courses—for example, a course on health and safety and a one-day customer service training event.

In principle, all eight firms offered sales assistants some prospect of career progression. In the electrical firms, there was scope for internal promotion to managerial positions through management training or by temporarily filling in for team leaders. However, sales assistants were often unwilling to take up promotion opportunities because, if they were successful at selling, their commission earnings could take their salaries close to those of team leaders or even managers. For those who were willing and able to move between stores, opportunities were available for employees with some length of service. In food retail, there were some career progression opportunities through management training schemes, but these opportunities were generally limited to full-time employees and to those who were prepared to move between stores. For example, in R1 management training was not open at all to part-timers, and there was a feeling among the store employees that full-timers tended to be more appreciated than part-timers. In general, managers were reluctant to consider options that would offer better promotion prospects for part-time female staff, such as job-sharing, and justified their approach in terms of availability and mobility. "Sections of thirty people can't run with a part-time manager," said a store manager at R1. A regional headquarters manager at R3 explained that "what we would require of anyone who wants to be a section manager is that they must be mobile to at least five stores. . . . I would say that that is the most difficult aspect of management within [R3], the requirement to have mobility."

However, in group interviews with sales assistants, there were few signs of concern at the lack of progression opportunities for part-time female workers because most of them deemed their careers secondary to their family commitments. Indeed, many of the female interviewees were keener to emphasize the extent to which they enjoyed their work and their friendships with fellow employees than they were to criticize any aspect of their employment: Sales assistants at R2 and R3 had this to say:

> The positive side is the people you work with. It's very family-oriented—most people have relatives working here, and relationships are formed here.

> I know everyone, we get along very well. . . . I don't think there's anything [I dislike], I'm very happy here.

The question arises as to whether this apparent job satisfaction should be taken at face value or whether it reflects the ability of many workers to remain positive in the face of limited options.

## JOB SATISFACTION AND DISCONTENTS

In the light of the apparent acceptance of the terms and conditions of their employment by many low-paid women part-timers working in industries, such as retail, that have large concentrations of female employees, Catherine Hakim (2000, 2004) has argued that many of them are simply expressing their "preferences" in choosing flexible forms of employment that, albeit low-paid, enable them to meet do-

Table 4.5 Continuing Training and Career Progression Opportunities for Sales Assistants in the Case Study Retail Firms

| | Continuing Training | Career Progression |
|---|---|---|
| **Food** | | |
| R1 | Mostly on-the-job training, although there are some off-the-job customer service courses, plus computer-based skills courses. Employees can request training at reviews. | Scope for promotion as new branches are opened, although opportunities are limited for part-time workers and those who are not mobile. |
| R2 | Computer-based learning includes product knowledge and customer handling. | Management training available for four sales staff per store each year (0.5 to 1%). Generally demands for progression are met—there is little pent-up demand. |
| R3 | At least one day of off-the-job training per employee in last twelve months, focused on customer service skills. There has also been training for coaches and section coordinators. | Opportunities for part-time staff, but mobility is required. A new "career path" has laid down the requirements for progression to each level, but many sales staff are not interested in progressing to management jobs, which are seen as "stressful." |
| R4 | Courses on newspapers and magazines, chilled products, food and hygiene, and so on, are optional for part-time staff. Supervisors encouraged to take NVQs and SVQs. | Progression to supervisor available only if they can work full-time; most are not interested because of family commitments. |

| | Training | Progression |
|---|---|---|
| **Electrical** | | |
| R5 | Customer service training and product training, often with manufacturers, usually once a week. Also ongoing individual coaching. | Opportunities for internal progression, but with commission earnings, sales staff are often happy to stay where they are. |
| R6 | Frequent product training, often with manufacturers, is popular because it helps make sales and earn commissions; there is also a subsidized retail NVQ program. | Scope for progression via team leader role, but some employees do not want to progress, either because they have family commitments or because they can earn more money in sales (through commissions). |
| R7 | Average of four days of off-the-job training per year, mainly technical training dealing with new products and technology; also feedback on company performance. Manufacturers come in to provide training on their own products. | Management development courses and emphasis on internal promotion, although promotion usually requires mobility between stores. |
| R8 | Ongoing training includes weekly training sessions, usually product training with manufacturers, lasting thirty to sixty minutes per employee per week. "Workbook" training enables promotion to new roles. | Internal promotion is common, and employees feel that the company rewards loyalty. It is harder for part-time staff to progress. |

*Source:* Authors' compilation.

mestic commitments. However, Rosemary Crompton and Clare Lyonette (2005) present evidence that female workers' choices regarding jobs and working hours are influenced more by "structural" factors (such as the availability of child care) and individual characteristics (such as education level) than by individual preferences.

Indeed, in the course of our group interviews, some of the issues that emerged suggested that many female sales assistants were dissatisfied with certain aspects of their job, even though it suited their personal circumstances to remain in it. These discontents had typically more to do with problems over working hours and contractual issues than with pay and career advancement.

For example, R4 sales staff complained that the hours (which were restricted to part-time contracts) were shorter than they wanted, and R1 employees complained that the allocation of hours was inflexible. At R2, we heard that employees did not like having to work unsocial hours such as evenings and weekends. In some cases, managers apparently resorted to allocating hours at short notice. In this context, Eli Dutton and her colleagues (2005) argue that there is often a "clash of flexibilities" in retail in the United Kingdom: a small number of hours makes the job attractive to women who have child care responsibilities, but the requirement that employees be available to work at short notice and during unsocial periods can cause problems in the absence of someone to look after the children.

Among other job quality issues that were mentioned by employees, two concerns were particularly prominent: the physical demands of the work done by sales assistants (R5, R7, R2, R3, R1, and R4) and problems with abusive customers (R8, R1, R2, R7, and R5). Electrical firm employees mentioned that the physical demands involved moving heavy items of equipment around the store; in food retail employees complained about moving heavy boxes around and unpacking them onto the shelves, while checkout operators were concerned about repetitive strain injuries. In several cases, management had tried to lessen the physical burden of the work. In R7, the manager was careful to make sure sales staff were complying with guidelines about how many people were required to carry certain items. R1 had had problems with checkout staff taking sick leave due to stress, and employees speculated that this was a key reason for the reliance on part-time work. Managers had introduced training for the staff to help them shift heavy loads. In R3, the issue of physically demanding jobs was bound up with concerns about management's lack of responsiveness, since employees' requests for safety clothing, such as special boots, had been ignored. According to one sales assistant,

> there's no let-up for older staff, and we had one old lady leave because it was just too heavy for her. . . . To get an idea of just how hard it is, you should come here at six o'clock in the morning and see the work we have to hack out.

Encounters with angry or demanding customers were also identified as a negative aspect of job quality in a number of the cases. For example, when there were problems fulfilling a customer's requirements, such as when items were out of stock, sales assistants often found themselves taking the blame from the customer. This was true in both electrical and food retail firms, although the problems that occurred were slightly different in nature, since in electrical retail negative reactions were sometimes the result of sales staff making unrealistic promises to customers.

## EMPLOYEE REPRESENTATION

An aspect of the debate about whether part-time female workers are freely choosing whether to fit in with employers' flexibility requirements concerns the limited extent to which such employees are able to unite to defend or seek improvements in the terms and conditions of their employment.

For example, unions had a very limited impact on working conditions and pay for the sales assistants and checkout operators in our sample. A union was recognized in only one case (R2), and even there it had little influence at the store level and did not negotiate over pay for sales assistants: "We let them [the union] know things," commented a headquarters manager, "but they don't have any rights." At R7, in discussion about trade unions, a manager said: "We try to avoid employing that sort of person."

In other cases, there was either no union presence or unions with only a few members. The limited union involvement in our case study firms reflects the fact that in the combined wholesale and retail sector in the United Kingdom in 2003, only 12 percent of employees are union members—well below the 18 percent average for all private sector employees. In the United Kingdom's private sector as a whole, 29 percent of employees are working in workplaces where a trade union is recognized and 18 percent in establishments where pay is affected by collective agreements of one kind or another. However, both of these two indicators of union influence are also lower in retailing (DTI 2004).

The two main unions involved with retailing are the USDAW (Union of Shop, Distributive, and Allied Workers) and the GMB (Britain's General Union), a large cross-industry union. In recent years, their retail membership figures have increased slightly, and their ability to negotiate with some retail employers has improved, largely as a result of the Employment Relations Act of 1999, which set out new procedures requiring that unions be recognized by employers if at least 10 percent of employees in the bargaining unit are union members and if a number of other conditions are met. However, as our cases indicate, many retailers do not enter into substantive pay negotiations with any union, even when a particular union has been formally "recognized" for negotiation purposes (for example, when there are disputes involving union members). Moreover, it is still for management to decide what issues it is willing to bargain about.

Apart from the weak presence of unions, another factor helping retail firms to maintain their strategy of recruiting low-paid flexible employees in the last few years has been the introduction of tax credits. For example, R4 managers reported that a high proportion of employees were receiving the Working Tax Credit, and although it was regarded as a burden for the employer, it was also seen as helping with the retention of staff.

Even where elaborate arrangements had been made for non-union forms of employee representation and consultation, pay was generally a matter of management prerogative, and indeed, there were signs in some firms that recent changes in employment contracts (for example, abolishing premium payments for working unsociable hours) had been pushed through consultative committees against resistance from some employees. At R1, consultative committees have been established to discuss "bread-and-butter" issues such as whether or not sales assistants work on bank holidays and the consequences of age discrimination legislation. Some employees whom we interviewed expressed concerns that some issues had not been the object of real consultation; for example, the issue of working on bank holidays "got snuck in," reported an R1 sales assistant, "even though it was an attraction of the job not to have to do it."

On the other hand, there were also some examples of issues that had been productively discussed in non-union consultative committees. For example, at R1 employees expressed positive views about the role of such committees in deciding changes in sickness policy. And at R3 managers told us that similar consultative groups had been strengthened so that they were "not just lip-service groups." However, following the consolidation of the annual bonus into a higher hourly rate (described earlier), the groups became an outlet for staff frustration. An R3 team leader remembered one such incident:

> There was some serious negative feedback at the time, as I recall. . . . I know of some guys who were invited to go on coaching courses, and they said, "No way," and that was their way of protesting.

## SUMMARY AND ASSESSMENT

The retail industry accounts for a sizable proportion (26 percent) of all low-paid workers in the United Kingdom. Many of them are female part-timers. Compared to continental Europe, labor costs in the United Kingdom are relatively low, and this enables many British retailers to compete effectively through labor-intensive service strategies and to achieve high levels of profit by international standards in so doing.

To develop a stable workforce that is both low-paid and flexible enough to fit in with their fluctuating labor requirements, British food retailers have tended to recruit heavily among groups of people who are available to work part-time and who are not wholly dependent on their salaries in order to live. Examples include married women with primary responsibility for child care and housework in their homes and school and university students. By contrast, electrical retailers tend to recruit heavily among male full-time workers, who are expected to possess or acquire sufficient product knowledge to engage in intensive discussions with customers.

Sales assistants in our case study firms in electrical retailing typically had greater personal autonomy in their daily work than their counterparts in food retail and, because of opportunities to earn commissions on sales, the majority of them were paid well above the low pay threshold. In our food retail cases, most assistants engaged in low-skilled work, following orders on a daily basis, and median pay rates fell below or were just on the low pay threshold. It was notable

that work organization and pay rates were much the same in food retail firms selling premium-priced products as they were in firms that
targeted the discount-price sector of the market.

Retail workers' pay has only just started to be affected by the
NMW, which in its early years was too low to affect pay-setting
arrangements in the larger firms in this sector. Following recent up-
ratings in the NMW, a common response by retail employers has
been to introduce new contracts for sales assistants that increase the
basic hourly rate in order to comply with the NMW but reduce the
opportunities to earn additional payments such as bonuses and premium rates for working unsocial hours.

Career prospects in retail are especially limited for part-time workers (most of whom are female) because promotion tends to be restricted to full-timers who are willing and able to move between
stores. Interviews with female sales assistants suggested that many of
them are unconcerned about this problem because they give greater
priority to their domestic responsibilities than to paid employment.
Such findings have led some researchers to argue that many women
are simply expressing their "preferences" in choosing flexible forms
of employment that, even if low-paid, enable them to meet domestic
commitments. However, there is other evidence that female workers'
choices regarding jobs and working hours are influenced more by
"structural" factors such as the availability of child care and by low
levels of education and human capital.

In fact, our interviews with female sales assistants suggested that
many of them were dissatisfied with aspects of their employment,
even though it suited their personal circumstances to remain in their
current jobs and they felt very positive about their relationships with
coworkers. These discontents typically had more to do with problems over inconvenient working hours and contractual issues than
with pay and career advancement. Both male and female sales assistants also expressed concerns about the physically demanding nature
of their work.

More generally, the question of whether female sales assistants are
freely choosing to fit in with their employers' flexibility requirements
hardly arises because of the marked reduction in influence in recent
years of trade unions and other organizations that in the past have
sought to defend or improve the terms and conditions of retail employment. In several of the case study firms, managers held negative

opinions about unions and strongly preferred to work through in-house consultative committees or similar mechanisms. However, none of these committees were involved in negotiations over pay rates, and in some cases workers felt that the committees had been unable to protect them against recent changes in contracts (such as the abolition of premium payments for working unsocial hours).

The marked contrast in pay and job quality between food and electrical retail firms raises the question of whether the two sets of firms exemplify, respectively, "low road" and "high road" employment practices of the kind that Annette Bernhardt (1999) has identified in American retailing. In some ways, the differences between the two sectors in product knowledge requirements, customer interactions, and scope for payment by commission on sales are so marked that there seems to be little scope for food retailers in the United Kingdom to make strategic choices to pursue the kinds of employment practices found in electrical retail. However, the relatively high-skill, high-personal-autonomy approach to work organization in German food retail firms shows that alternative approaches are feasible so long as they are supported by national labor market institutions, such as the long-standing retail apprentice training system in Germany (Mason, Osborne, and Voss-Dahm 2006).

In the context of the United Kingdom, electrical retail firms represent one small, specialized sector of retailing, and there is little hope that their employment practices will spread to the much larger food retail sector. In the absence of training institutions of the German kind, and given not only the continued availability of prospective employees seeking part-time work to supplement household incomes but also the weakness of trade unions in the industry, food retail employers in the United Kingdom will continue to face strong labor market and other institutional incentives to base their employment and customer service strategies on the deployment of low-skilled, low-paid workers. What turns out to be distinctive about the United Kingdom's food retail industry is the combination of low-paid workers with relatively high levels of customer service on dimensions such as having staff readily available to cut down on checkout lines, answer customer queries, and provide personal services if requested. This contrasts not just with the predominant business strategies in German food retailing but also with the "low-pay, low-service" model pursued by large retail discount firms in the United States.

## NOTES

1. These figures are based on Labour Force Survey estimates.
2. Estimates for 1999 prepared by London Economics and cited by the U.K. Competition Commission report on retailing suggest that average hourly labor costs in the United Kingdom (including employers' social security or national insurance contributions) were roughly 41 percent below Germany, 13 percent below the United States, and 11 percent below France (Competition Commission 2000, appendix 10.3).
3. Angela Canny (2002) reports increased employment of male part-time students on checkouts in recent years.
4. This may reflect reluctance by many retail employers to go through a new recruitment and initial training process each time peaks in demand arise.
5. Supervisors and team leaders are not defined separately from others in their occupation groups in the U.K. standard occupational classification.
6. FAME (Financial Analysis Made Easy), published by Bureau van Dijk Electronic Publishing, is a database of publicly available financial information on 1.9 million companies in the United Kingdom and Ireland. It covers all PLCs and a large number of private limited companies in the United Kingdom.
7. This assessment is based on calculations of average sales per employee in 2002 for 77 electrical retail firms listed in FAME. In food retailing, average sales per employee among the 104 firms listed in FAME are highly correlated with firm size (reflecting economies of scale) and therefore do not serve as an indicator of the average unit value of products sold. However, in electrical retailing there is no such correlation between firm size and average sales per employee.
8. In one case (R1), interviews were carried out at two stores.
9. Sales assistants and checkout operators are grouped together here because in nearly all the case study stores available pay data did not distinguish between the two occupations.

## REFERENCES

Bernhardt, Annette. 1999. "The Future of Low-Wage Jobs: Case Studies in the Retail Industry." Working paper 10. New York: Institute on Education and the Economy.

Burt, Steve, and Leigh Sparks. 2003. "Competitive Analysis of the Retail Sector in the U.K." Report prepared for the Department of Trade and Industry. Stirling, U.K.: Institute for Retail Studies, University of Stirling.

Canny, Angela. 2002. "Flexible Labor? The Growth of Student Employment in the U.K." *Journal of Education and Work* 15(3): 277–301.

Competition Commission. 2000. "Supermarkets: A Report on the Supply of Groceries from Multiple Stores in the United Kingdom." Accessed at http://www.competition-commission.org.uk/rep_pub/reports/2000/446 super.htm.

Crompton, Rosemary, and Clare Lyonette. 2005. "The New Gender Essentialism: Domestic and Family 'Choices' and Their Relation to Attitudes." *British Journal of Sociology* 56(4): 601.

Department of Trade and Industry (DTI). 2004. *Trade Union Membership 2003, Employment Market Analysis and Research*. London: DTI.

Dutton, Eli, Chris Warhurst, Dennis Nickson, and Cliff Lockyer. 2005. "Lone Parents, the New Deal, and the Opportunities and Barriers to Retail Employment." *Policy Studies* 26(1): 86–101.

Hakim, Catherine. 2000. *Work-Lifestyle Choices in the Twentieth Century*. Oxford: Oxford University Press.

————. 2004. *Key Issues in Women's Work*. London: GlassHouse Press.

Howard, Elizabeth, and Jonathan Reynolds. 2004. "Assessing the Productivity of the U.K. Retail Sector." Oxford: Oxford Institute of Retail Management, Templeton College, University of Oxford.

Incomes Data Services (IDS). 1999. "Students in Employment." Report 776. London: IDS.

————. 2003. "Pay in the Retail Sector 2003." Report 889. London: IDS.

Mason, Geoff, Matthew Osborne, and Dorothea Voss-Dahm. 2006. "Labor Market Outcomes in Different National Settings: U.K.-German Comparisons in Retailing." Paper presented to the annual conference of the Society for the Advancement of Socioeconomics. June 30-July 2, 2006, Trier, Germany.

Mintel. 2004. *Food Retailing—U.K.* London: Mintel (November).

Office for National Statistics (ONS). 2003. "Size Analysis of United Kingdom Businesses: Data for 2003, Commerce, Energy, and Industry." PA1003. London: HMSO.

————. 2004. "Annual Business Inquiry." Accessed at http://www.statistics.gov.uk/abi/.

O'Mahony, Mary, and Willem de Boer. 2002. "Britain's Relative Productivity Performance: Updates to 1999." London: National Institute of Economic and Social Research.

Roe, Jolyon (consultant, AC Nielsen Consulting Group). 2002. "Positioning a Pricing Strategy in the Hierarchy of Service, Convenience, and New Product Development." Prepared by AC Nielsen Consulting Group (December 20). Accessed at http://www.kamcity.com/library/articles/ACN pricinging.htm.

# CHAPTER 5

## Improving the Position of Low-Wage Workers Through New Coordinating Institutions: The Case of Public Hospitals

*Damian Grimshaw and Marilyn Carroll*

This chapter explores the characteristics of low-wage work in the United Kingdom's public hospital sector (the National Health Service), which is the United Kingdom's largest employer, with a workforce of some 1.3 million. We focus on two target occupations, assistant nurses and cleaners. One in five assistant nurses and three in five cleaners are estimated to be paid below the low pay threshold. The quality of jobs for these workers is necessarily shaped by the changing financial and labor market pressures faced by hospital managers, much like the other private sector occupations addressed in this book. However, unlike the other examples of low-wage work, in this chapter we show how new "coordinating institutions" negotiated by the social partners (employers, unions, and government) to cover the entire public hospital sector also play a major role.

The context for the new institutions is complex. The overriding impression is one of conflicting political agendas, pilot initiatives, stalled and delayed policy reforms, and challenging (if not chaotic) demands for micromanagement coupled with strict national-level performance targets in everything from hospital finance to cleanliness. But as well as being at the center of a fast-changing political agenda of welfare services reform, the public hospital sector has also been at the vanguard of a raft of new policies and initiatives to reform pay, employment relations, and work organization. These reforms constitute an important change in the institutional architecture—improving basic pay, providing new career paths, reducing job insecurity, and extending terms and conditions to outsourced workers. From the perspective of labor market theory, these new institutions are illustrative of institutions that provide the social partners with the

capacity for cooperative engagement in collective discussion and negotiation (Elster 1998). Compared to other sectors characterized by
a weak role for the social partners, the presence of coordinating institutions may improve information sharing, long-term trust, and the
shared capacity to respond to future unanticipated challenges (Hall
and Soskice 2001, 11–12).

The most notable of the coordinating institutions are a new harmonized and coordinated national pay structure, a newly established,
national, not-for-profit organization that supplies nursing temps, and
a new governmental code that requires private subcontractors to establish terms and conditions equivalent to the national pay agreement. Our data suggest that the new institutions have established the
basis for positive prospects for low-wage workers, reflecting the coordinated initiatives of trade unions (to improve the status of the
very low-paid), government (to increase expenditures), and employers (to address skill development). Nevertheless, several notable tensions and obstacles remain. We begin with a review of the organization of the public hospital sector and its size, performance, and
workforce composition.

## THE UNITED KINGDOM PUBLIC HOSPITAL SECTOR

The publicly funded and publicly provided hospital sector, the National
Health Service (NHS), dominates health care provision within the
United Kingdom, accounting for around 85 percent of total health care
spending. It is organized according to the principle of universal health
services that are free at the point of use to the patient and funded
through taxation.[1] This means that spending on hospitals is highly
politicized and scrutinized and that it must meet a range of competing
demands, including increasing patient expectations and the politics of
public sector expenditure. As such, politics, bureaucracy, transparency,
and the United Kingdom-specific welfare state model all play important
roles in shaping the context for patterns of work and employment.

During the late 1980s and the 1990s, under successive Conservative governments, the public hospital sector experienced tight restrictions on spending coupled with market reforms (compulsory
competitive tendering and the establishment of NHS "trusts" in place
of hospitals). Data from the OECD show that while health care
spending as a share of GDP in the United Kingdom already lagged

behind Germany and the United States in 1970 (3.9 percent, 4.8 percent, and 5.1 percent, respectively), by 1999 a far larger gap had opened up (7.3 percent, 10.6 percent, and 13.0 percent).[2]

Politics matters with regard to health care spending, and the election of the Labour government in 1997 made a significant impact (Peston 2005). After an initial two-year freeze on public spending, the first three-year Comprehensive Spending Review for 1999 to 2002 included real growth in total public spending of 2.25 percent per annum (with faster rises in health and education), and the second review for 2002 to 2004 included higher rises, especially for the health sector, funded from a special 1 percent levy on National Insurance contributions. A comparison of the five-year periods before and after 1999 shows that real growth in public health expenditures averaged just 1.56 percent per year between 1993–94 and 1998–99 and then jumped to 8.18 percent between 1999–2000 and 2004–2005 (HM Treasury 2006, table 3.3).

Increased spending responded to a growing demand for services and a political ambition to reduce waiting lists. In the ten-year period up to 1997–98, the number of inpatients had grown by around 40 percent (DoH 2005). This upward trend continued in many other areas of hospital activity: for example, accident and emergency (A&E) attendances increased by 35 percent in the five years up to 2006–2007.[3] Nevertheless, increased expenditures, coupled with strict performance targets, have enabled hospitals to reduce waiting lists; for example, the number of patients waiting more than six months for an operation was cut by around 70 percent between 1997 and 2004 (HM Treasury 2004). While there is controversy about the hospital practices of work intensification and opportunistic shifting of resources to achieve these targets, it is clear that a substantial increase in the numbers employed has played a strong role. Table 5.1 illustrates the massive expansion in the NHS workforce since 1999, from just over 1 million to 1.4 million employees by 2005 (data for England only).

The pattern of job growth varies by occupation. The number of doctors and qualified scientific, therapeutic, and technical staff has grown slightly above the average for the NHS, while nurses have witnessed average growth. Support workers, such as porters, are the only group to have witnessed a persistent downward trend, reflecting outsourcing practices and rationalization. And while the numbers employed in hotel, property, and estates jobs have declined significantly over the ten-year period (again, owing to outsourcing), recent

Table 5.1 Employment in the National Health Service, England, 1995 to 2005 (in Thousands)

| | 1995 | 1997 | 1999 | 2001 | 2003 | 2005 | Percent Change 1995 to 2000 | Percent Change 2000 to 2005 |
|---|---|---|---|---|---|---|---|---|
| Total employed staff | 1,052 | 1,059 | 1,097 | 1,166 | 1,283 | 1,365 | 6% | 22% |
| Doctors | 84 | 90 | 94 | 99 | 109 | 122 | 14 | 27 |
| Qualified nurses (and midwives) | 317 | 319 | 330 | 350 | 386 | 404 | 6 | 20 |
| Qualified scientific, therapeutic, and technical staff | 91 | 96 | 102 | 110 | 122 | 135 | 16 | 27 |
| Qualified ambulance staff | 15 | 15 | 15 | 15 | 16 | 18 | 2 | 23 |
| Support to clinical staff | 279 | 284 | 297 | 326 | 361 | 376 | 10 | 22 |
| Assistant nurses[a,b] | 125 | 133 | 140 | 153 | 167 | 168 | 16 | 16 |
| Support workers (porters)[a] | 44 | 38 | 36 | 35 | 33 | 33 | -22 | -5 |
| Clerical and administrative[a] | 61 | 64 | 68 | 78 | 90 | 100 | 19 | 38 |
| NHS infrastructure support | 181 | 171 | 171 | 180 | 200 | 220 | -4 | 27 |
| Central functions (finance, HR, IT) | 72 | 71 | 74 | 81 | 92 | 106 | 7 | 36 |
| Hotel, property, and estates (laundry, catering, builders, electricians) | 88 | 78 | 73 | 71 | 72 | 75 | -19 | 6 |
| Managers and senior managers | 21 | 22 | 24 | 27 | 35 | 39 | 21 | 56 |

*Source:* Department of Health, *NHS Bulletin* (2004, tables 1b, 2a).
[a] Owing to data availability problems, these figures refer only to persons in these occupations providing support to doctors and nursing staff; other staff also provide support to scientific and technical staff and to ambulance staff, but data for detailed occupational groups are not available.
[b] Numbers include health care assistants.

years have seen a small rise. Finally, there have been substantial increases in the number of managers employed (a near doubling over the period), as well as significant investment in posts in the central management functions of finance, IT, and human resource management, during the period 2000 to 2005 (from 78,000 to 106,000).

## PRESSURES ON PUBLIC SECTOR HOSPITALS

Changes to systems of finance and governance present radical challenges to the way public sector hospitals manage health care.[4] While decisions on spending are highly centralized, responsibility for its execution and accountability for balancing the budget are placed on local hospital management. Groups of hospitals in local areas were formed into self-governing "trusts" in the 1990s, redefined as public corporations and required to make a 6 percent return on the value of their assets in addition to a target to improve productivity by 2 percent per annum (DoH 2002). In July 2003, the policy changed, and trusts were once again defined as falling within central government (HM Treasury 2004). The legacy of these profit targets, however, was the need to use much of the increased health spending since 1999 not only to hire more employees but to clear deficits.

Among the most controversial changes in financing is the Private Finance Initiative (PFI). This is a form of public-private partnership in which a consortium of private sector firms provides the capital investment for a new hospital (or the refurbishment of existing buildings) and recoups the money through a charge on the services provided by the hospital (Grimshaw et al. 2002). Crucially, each PFI agreement transfers large groups of workers employed in the NHS hospital (in cleaning, catering, portering, estates, and maintenance) to the private sector firm. These "ancillary" services are then sold by the private sector consortium back to the client NHS hospital. The practice of transferring low-paid groups of staff to a private sector firm has proved controversial in light of evidence that the workers receive less generous pensions and work alongside other employees paid at lower rates. There have been significant campaigns on this issue, leading to new policy reforms, which we consider later in the chapter.

A further challenge is a change in the nature of hospital funding. Since 2006, hospitals have faced increased uncertainty in funding since patients referred to them have been entitled to choose from between five alternative health providers (including a private sector, or voluntary-sector, hospital). Also, the government is in the process of establishing a new model of funding hospital activities (to be fully implemented by 2008–2009) in which a fixed rate will be paid for each procedure, based on the average national cost. The rationale for these changes is "to support patient choice and encourage trusts to respond to patient preferences" and "to impose a sharper budget discipline on hospitals" (Audit Commission 2004, 2). However, the independent Audit Commission has warned of "significant transitional and longer-term risks" (3), including the difficulties of coding the required data, perverse incentives that may encourage unnecessary patient admissions, false upcoding of activities, and withdrawal of services provision for activities with above-average costs.

Finally, important changes to governance systems have been introduced for high-performing public hospitals that successfully apply for "foundation trust" status. Foundation trusts remain under public ownership and primarily treat NHS patients free at the point of use. However, they are meant to operate in "a middle ground between the public and private sector." Unlike other trusts, they can make independent investment decisions by raising funds outside Treasury limits, are free to opt out of national pay deals, and are not subject to performance management by regional strategic health authorities; foundation trusts have to deliver on national targets and standards but are free to choose how.[5] Again, the policy is controversial. There are concerns that a two-tier health care system will emerge, with the foundation trusts that perform best investing more and attracting the best staff through local pay and conditions.[6]

These radical changes in governance appear to have worsened budgetary pressures on public sector hospitals, despite the record increases in health spending (Shaoul 2005). During 2005–2006, the NHS accumulated an estimated £700 million deficit (around 1 percent of the total NHS budget), and many hospitals were forced to take unprecedented measures to cut jobs. The government response has been to blame poor hospital financial management. Trade unions organized mass protest rallies, and the general secretary of the Royal College of Nursing said, "The government has to give trusts more time and flexibility to balance their books so that this scorched earth policy of cutting patient services and jobs is stopped" (*The Guardian*, April 19, 2006).

## LOW-WAGE WORKERS IN HOSPITALS

Two low-wage groups, assistant nurses and cleaners, were the focus of our research. Various job titles describe the position of assistant nurse, including health care assistant, assistant nurse, nurse auxiliary, and clinical support worker. The assistant nurse provides basic care to the patient, records and monitors health indicators, and may undertake certain nursing tasks such as venepuncture or electrocardiograms (ECGs). All types of assistant nurses work under the supervision of a qualified nurse. Cleaners (or domestic assistants) clean and maintain patient wards, bathrooms, and common dining areas, as well as corridors, operating theaters, and other work areas.

Wages are low for both groups, especially for cleaners. In 2005 the median gross hourly pay for assistant nurses was £7.28 (US$14.87), and for hospital cleaners it was £5.60 (US$11.44) (Labour Force Survey data). For cleaners, this rate was only slightly higher than the national minimum wage (NMW) of £4.85 (US$9.90), which applied during most of 2005, but it compared favorably to cleaners in all sectors, for whom the median was £5.34 (US$10.90). Both groups earn significantly less than the median gross hourly pay for all employees of £8.65 (US$17.66). And compared to the low pay threshold of £5.77 (US$11.78) (two-thirds of the median for all employees), 21 percent of assistant nurses are low-paid and 55 percent of hospital cleaners. The pay distribution is especially flat for cleaners: the first and ninth deciles are compressed between pay of £4.66 (US$9.52) and £7.43 (US$15.17) (figure 5.1).

However, like other public sector employees, these workers benefit from relatively generous entitlement to holidays, sick pay, maternity leave, and pensions. Compared to the national legal minimum of twenty days of annual leave, cleaners and assistant nurses are entitled to twenty-seven days plus eight public holidays, and after ten years' service, thirty-three days plus eight public holidays. They receive supplements to statutory sick pay—up to six months of half pay and up to six months of full pay after five years' service. Maternity leave is paid at full pay minus the statutory pay for the first eight weeks and at half pay plus the statutory pay up to the total of full pay for the next eighteen weeks. Finally, assistant nurses and hospital cleaners join a final salary pension scheme.

Both groups of workers are predominantly female, with an especially high share of part-time women working among the cleaners. In

Figure 5.1  Distribution of Hourly Pay for Hospital
Cleaners and Assistant Nurses, 2005

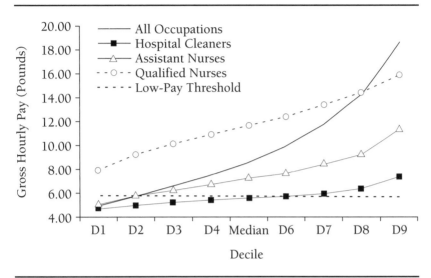

*Source:* Labour Force Survey (LFS) (2005). Data kindly provided by Matt Osborne at the National Institute for Economic and Social Research (NIESR).
*Note:* Sample sizes are 516 (assistant nurses), 1,316 (qualified nurses), and 116 (hospital cleaners). Because the sample size for hospital cleaners is small, we ran a check with pooled 2004 and 2005 data, and this confirmed a similar interdecile distribution.

2005 nine out of ten assistant nurses were women, and nearly one in two (46 percent) of these women worked in part-time jobs. For cleaners, data are available only for the whole economy: they show that 80 percent are women and 82 percent of women work part-time. Most staff are employed on permanent contracts, but employers of assistant nurses rely heavily on temporary agencies to manage staffing cover. Assistant nurses may work solely for a temporary work agency or for an internal "bank" organized by the hospital, either because they cannot find suitable permanent work or because they prefer shorter, more flexible hours. Also, many assistant nurses employed by the NHS work additional hours with an agency, or bank, but do not earn overtime premiums and receive a lower pay rate than their normal basic rate.

Formal educational qualifications are not a requirement for entry into either of these two occupations. For assistant nurses, there is no statutory requirement to be trained to a particular level. However, all hospitals are obliged to offer training—national vocational qualifications, level 2 (NVQ2)—and to provide NVQ3 training to satisfy the entry requirements for assistant nurses to move into nurse training. Also, hospitals provide mandatory training in moving and handling, fire safety and hygiene. A new policy initiative, the "skills escalator," promises to open up opportunities for people at relatively low skill levels. It also encourages hospitals to engage with local communities to tackle problems of unemployment and social exclusion by attracting a wider range of people to join the NHS.

Trade unions play a strong role in jointly regulating the employment conditions of low-wage workers in public sector hospitals. Like other areas of the public sector, the estimated union density of 44 percent in 2005 for health care is high.[7] This is significantly higher than other areas of service work, such as hotels and restaurants, which have only a 4 percent union density (Grainger 2006). Cleaners and assistant nurses are faced with a wide choice of representative bodies to defend their interests at work. The main trade unions are Unison (the largest trade union), Amicus, Britain's General Union (GMB), the Union of Shop, Distributive, and Allied Workers (USDAW), and the Transport and General Workers' Union (TGWU).[8] Since 2001, assistant nurses with NVQ qualifications have also been able to join the nursing professional association, the Royal College of Nursing.

Finally, the outsourcing of ancillary services has had a major adverse impact on employment conditions for cleaners in public sector hospitals. Until late 2005, all public sector hospitals undertaking new private sector–financed hospital building programs under a public-private partnership were required to outsource ancillary services. Transferring cleaners have their terms and conditions (except pensions) protected through adapted European legislation (the Transfer of Undertakings Protection of Employment). However, there is no legal protection against subsequent changes to terms and conditions following transfer or against the setting of worse conditions for new recruits (leading to the problem of a two-tier workforce in private subcontracting firms).[9]

## THE RESEARCH METHOD

The research involved case studies of seven public sector hospitals in two geographical areas—four in the Northwest of England and three in the Midlands. We originally aimed to choose two regions to contrast tight and loose labor markets. With relatively low rates of unemployment overall, however, there were only small differences across regions, and these did not have an impact on the results. Each hospital is properly described as an "acute hospital trust" as part of the National Health Service. Table 5.2 outlines the characteristics of the case study hospitals.

At each hospital, we interviewed managers from finance, human resources, nursing, domestic services, and temporary work agencies (or in-house "banks"). We also aimed to interview two staff members from each of the target occupational groups, assistant nurses and cleaners. However, we were unable to gain permission to speak to cleaners at three hospitals where they were employed by a private firm. All interviews were tape-recorded and fully transcribed. Documentary evidence and workforce statistics were also provided by the hospitals.

## THE CHALLENGES FACING THE ORGANIZATION OF LOW-WAGE WORK

All seven hospitals faced a similar set of challenges to the management of assistant nurses and cleaners, albeit varying in scale and form. Here we review the implications for costs, patient care, and general service quality of the following interrelated issues:

- Financial pressures

- Tight labor markets

- Outsourcing of cleaning

- High use of agency temps

### FINANCIAL PRESSURES

Three hospitals recorded a deficit in 2004–2005, and a fourth anticipated a deficit of £6.4 million (US$13.07 million) for 2005–2006 (see table 5.2). Financial problems can no longer be obscured within the aggregate national balance of accounts since they have a direct impact on each hospital's performance rating. In two cases, the rating was downgraded because of the financial deficit, from three-star to two-star at hospital 3 and from three-star to one-star at hospital 5.[10]

Table 5.2 The Case Study Hospitals

| | 1—Small-Town Hospital | 2—Large PFI Hospital | 3—City Hospital | 4—City PFI Hospital | 5—One-Star Hospital | 6—City Suburb Hospital | 7—Rural PFI Hospital |
|---|---|---|---|---|---|---|---|
| Location | Greater Manchester | West Midlands | Greater Manchester | Greater Manchester | Northwest Midlands | Greater Manchester | Southwest Midlands |
| Local rate of unemployment[a] | 4.6% | 5.1% | 4.5% | 4.5% | 2.6% | 4.5% | 3.8% |
| Number of staff | 4,339 | 6,663 | 5,400 | 5,500 | 2,227 | 4,281 | 1,600 |
| Number of beds | 831 | 1,417 | n.a. | 855 | n.a. | 800 | n.a. |
| National performance rating | Three-star | Three-star | Two-star | Three-star | One-star | Three-star | Two-star |
| Management of cleaning | In-house | Mixed: supervisors outsourced; non-supervisory staff in-house | Mixed: four sites in-house; two sites outsourced | Outsourced | In-house | Outsourced (in-house from April 2006) | Outsourced |
| Privately financed building program | No | Yes | No (yes from 2008) | Yes | No | No | Yes |
| Private cleaning firm | n.a. | ISS Mediclean | ISS Mediclean | Sodexho | n.a. | ISS Mediclean | Sodexho |
| Financial balance (2004–2005) | Deficit £743,000 | Forecast deficit £6.4 million (2005–2006) | Deficit £7.7 million | Surplus £59,000 | Deficit £2.5 million | Surplus £450,000 | Surplus £20,000 |

*Source:* Authors' compilation using information supplied by case-study managers.
[a] "Rate of unemployment" refers to local travel to work area.

Reflecting the national situation, finance managers described conditions as very difficult. The head of finance at hospital 2 remarked: "I think the NHS is going through the hardest time that I can remember—ever since I've been involved in finance. I think this financial year is going to be significantly worse." And hospital 5's annual report for 2004–2005 noted: "We as a trust are experiencing our toughest year since our creation in 1993."

Managers recognized the apparent contradiction between record increases in public spending on health care and the financial problems many hospitals were experiencing. In four hospitals, finance managers argued that the new contract for consultants and the new national pay system, labeled "Agenda for Change," exceeded budgeted costs and were a drain on new monies. The head of finance at hospital 2 estimated a shortfall for Agenda for Change of around £4 million (US$8.17 million), and for the consultant contract at least £3 million (US$6.13 million). Nevertheless, the general impression was that these additional costs were inevitable to correct past inequities among staff; as the hospital 1 finance director put it, "It has cost a significant amount of money, but it has righted some of the wrongs in terms of people being underpaid before." Other common pressures, such as the new payment-by-results scheme and the extension of patient choice (discussed earlier), had yet to make a significant impact at the time of fieldwork. And some pressures were specific to the hospital. For example, hospital 5 had limited capacity in orthopedics and was forced to run clinics during the evenings at premium rates while awaiting the completion of a new facility.

The three hospitals with deficits over £2 million (US$4.08 million) each had a cost recovery plan involving job cuts and/or redeployment of staff. At hospital 2, each clinical division had been instructed to cut forty jobs, primarily through offering voluntary redundancies, but with "no holds barred on which job," according to the head of finance. Hospital 5 had so far managed by redeploying staff. But the most radical plan was at hospital 4, which had successfully turned around a budget deficit of £17 million (US$34.72 million) to a surplus in 2004–2005 and improved its star rating from zero stars to three. The hospital had sacked the former executive management team and made new appointments to the posts of director of finance, human resources, operations, and estates, each with the mission of reducing costs. Within human resources, costs were reduced by cutting sickness and absence levels, reducing the nursing skill mix, reducing agency use for temporary staff cover, and reducing the total pay packet for junior doctors; the last measure alone generated savings of around £2 million.

## TIGHT LABOR MARKETS

In the context of a national pay structure that offers very limited scope for altering rates of pay, tight labor markets presented a serious challenge to the seven case study hospitals. During 2005, the national rate of unemployment was 4.7 percent.[11] And unemployment was low in each of the travel-to-work areas of the seven case studies, varying from 5.1 percent (hospital 2) to 2.6 percent (hospital 5) (see table 5.2). We used two measures to provide further corroboration of the relative tightness of local labor markets: the human resource manager's qualitative assessment of recruitment difficulties, and the level of staff turnover (table 5.3).

In all seven hospitals, managers said they experienced few difficulties in recruiting assistant nurses. However, extensive use of temporary agencies to fill nursing vacancies casts a rather different light on this result. Most hospitals experienced significant problems recruiting and retaining cleaners. For example, the estates manager at the city hospital (number 3), where turnover among ancillary staff was 22 percent, told us that she experienced "great difficulties" recruiting cleaners and carried between forty and seventy vacant cleaner posts during 2005 out of a total of 350. Common issues were that pay was too low to attract sufficient applicants and that, once hired, many cleaners quit because of the level of hard work required or because of discomfort with working in a hospital environment. The following comments are illustrative. According to the human resource manager hired from a private firm by hospital 2:

> We are continually turning over domestics. . . . Some people do find it off-putting, especially where they are working on some wards, say, like a stroke ward, where the smell can be overpowering. . . . And some people don't realize how hard a job it is, because this isn't just like an office cleaner where you just come in with a vacuum and just do the bits you can see, flick the duster around, and empty a bin.

## Table 5.3  Evidence of Tight Local Labor Markets

|  | Recruitment Problems? | | Staff Turnover | |
|---|---|---|---|---|
|  | Assistant Nurses | Cleaners | Assistant Nurses | Cleaners[b] |
| 1. Small-town hospital | No | No | 5.2% | 9.6% |
| 2. Large PFI hospital | No | Yes | 6 | 18 |
| 3. City hospital | No | Yes | — | 22 |
| 4. City PFI hospital | No | Yes | — | "High" |
| 5. One-star hospital | No | Yes | 12%[a] | 26% |
| 6. City suburb hospital | No | No | "Very footloose" | "Not high" |
| 7. Rural PFI hospital | No | Yes | "Not high" | Conflicting opinions |

*Source:* Authors' compilation using information supplied by case-study hospital managers.

[a] This figure refers to "clinical support staff."

[b] All staff turnover figures for cleaners refer to the entire ancillary workforce (including cleaners, caterers, and porters).

The domestic manager at hospital 3 said:

> The wages are not good for the amount of hours and the amount of responsibility [domestics] have on the wards.

At hospital 7, we could not obtain hard data on turnover among domestics and received conflicting views from managers. The manager from the private cleaning firm claimed that "retention is very good for domestic staff," yet the human resource manager at the hospital argued that "[Sodexho] has a high turnover because we do their Criminal Records Bureau checking, and I know that there is a constant throughput." Recruitment difficulties were primarily experienced for the evening shift (5:00 PM to 8:00 PM).

Staff turnover among assistant nurses tended to be relatively low, with the exceptions of hospital 5, where local unemployment was the lowest among the seven case studies, and hospital 6 (see table 5.3). At "One-star Hospital" (number 5), the human resource director argued that the problem was caused by high turnover among younger recruits. At hospital 6, the human resource director identified competition with a new shopping center as a factor, along with an underappreciation among some staff of the value of the public sector pension scheme.

## Outsourcing of Cleaning

Three hospitals were contractually obliged to outsource staff to meet the conditions of a privately financed building program, a fourth outsourced to cut costs, and a fifth outsourced cleaners at four of six sites only (table 5.2). For hospital managers, the challenge was establishing a common approach to services delivery and management of staff with the private sector firm in order to maximize teamwork and meet service quality standards. In two case studies, the conflict in human resource approach proved a significant obstacle. The human resource director at "City PFI Hospital," hospital 4, identified "ineffective personnel management" in the private firm as threatening the overall quality of services provision. "If they don't recruit and retain, if they don't have an appropriate skill mix [and] don't pay the going rate, it affects our quality of services," said this human resource professional. At hospital 2, the human resource manager perceived the management capabilities of the private sector partner to be weak:

> I just think some of [the private firm's] techniques and . . . the speed at which they manage things—it's slow. . . . There were some attendance issues, and I said, "Well, why has it taken you this long to get to this stage?". . . For me, they haven't brought any [expertise].

An additional obstacle involved the planning of new building space and closure of old space and the associated uncertainty in estimating the staffing volumes required. This was most evident at "Large PFI Hospital" (number 2), where the second-largest privately financed building program in the country was under way. To manage the uncertainty, ISS Mediclean offered fixed-term contracts to new recruits during 2004–2005. The obvious consequence was increased staff turnover: "they just walk," said ISS Mediclean's human resource manager. Workforce data confirm this view and show a skewed age profile among ancillary workers, with 42 percent age fifty and over, compared to 27 percent for assistant nurses employed by the hospital.

Among the three hospitals that had retained cleaning services in-house, this strategy was defended as the best way to ensure quality standards. The human resource director at "One-star Hospital" (number 5) argued:

We have a duty to look [at outsourcing]. But there's a real issue that you should never compromise quality for what would be relatively marginal financial gain. . . . Our chief executive is passionate about keeping [cleaning] in-house, and that's because there have been so many horror stories from different organizations.

## HIGH USE OF AGENCY TEMPS

All seven hospitals faced high costs from the use of agency temps. National statistics suggest that the costs of in-house (known as "bank") and external agency staff increased by 30 percent per annum from 2001 to 2005 (Griffiths 2005). The pressures driving high usage are threefold. First, in common with American trends (Houseman, Kalleberg, and Erickcek 2003), hospital managers used agency temps to relieve pressure in tight labor markets to raise wages. Second, hospital managers argued that using agency staff was preferable to paying overtime. And third, uncertainty about the volume of health services to be purchased from one year to the next necessitated a flexible staffing approach. The human resource director at hospital 5 strongly advocated a three-year commissioning cycle in place of the present annual round to facilitate workforce planning.

Agency temps were mostly used to fill qualified nurse and assistant nurse positions. For example, at hospital 4 half the temps used covered assistant nurse posts, and at hospital 5 four in five agency shifts filled were by assistant nurses. In fact, high agency use generated a bias toward reducing the skill mix in staffing the ward, since an available assistant nurse would normally be accepted when a shift for a qualified nurse could not be met.

There was an important difference in the type of agency used (see table 5.4). The three inner-city hospitals (numbers 3, 4, and 6) contracted with the national agency operated by the NHS, NHS Professionals (NHSP). The other four hospitals managed an in-house list of available staff. The number of those who signed on with banks was surprisingly large in some cases, with around 1,000 at hospital 1, 500 at hospital 2, and 220 at hospital 5. Use of the national NHS organization thus seemed more appropriate for the large city hospitals, where nurses would sign on with the national agency and then work at a range of nearby hospitals. By contrast, the smaller hospitals may have had an incentive to retain control over their in-house bank,

## Table 5.4 Use of Agency Temps to Fill Assistant Nurse Posts

| | National NHS Agency (NHSP) | In-House Bank | Private-Sector Agency | Other Details |
|---|---|---|---|---|
| 1. Small-town hospital | No | Yes | Only as backup | Problems with the quality of staff supplied from external agency |
| 2. Large PFI hospital | No | Yes | No | — |
| 3. City hospital | Yes | No | Only as backup and for some specialist posts | Problems with the quality of staff supplied from external agency |
| 4. City PFI hospital | Yes | No | No | — |
| 5. One-star hospital | No | Yes | Only as backup | — |
| 6. City surplus hospital | Yes | No | No | — |
| 7. Rural PFI hospital | No | Yes | Yes | Gradual shift to primary reliance on in-house bank at time of fieldwork |

*Source:* Authors' compilation using information provided by case-study hospital managers.

since, "by opening our bank up to NHS Professionals, that opens it up to other hospitals," as the hospital 4 human resource director explained. Four hospitals used private temp agencies, but mainly only as a backup. At hospital 5, managers preferred to pay incumbent nurses overtime rates before approaching an external agency. The reasons largely reflected negative experiences with quality. The deputy chief nurse at hospital 3 remarked that "some of the quality of the people you get through agencies is very poor, and I don't know what a lot of those agencies do in terms of their selection procedures, but I don't think they're at a level that we would like them to be." The hospital 6 human resource director said, "We only use agencies if we can't recruit from NHSP, because they're expensive, and also they're much more unknown, and we know that the quality of care reduces with agency staff."

Because managers typically used agency nurses rather than pay overtime, many nurses who had signed with the agency (or bank) also had permanent contracts with the hospital. This varied from 30 percent of agency staff at hospital 5 up to shares of 60 percent and 65 percent at hospitals 4 and 1, respectively. The agency also offered some employees the opportunity to provide temporary cover in a department of the hospital where they sought to gain experience. However, we uncovered no evidence that using agency temps was cheaper than paying overtime, and some managers were skeptical. For example, the assistant director of nursing at hospital 4 told us, "With the breakdown of costs and everything, it actually, in the longer term, does look like it would be slightly cheaper to pay them [nurses] overtime than [use] NHSP."

Finally, we note that the use of agency workers to cover cleaner posts was negligible in all seven hospitals—a surprising finding given the difficulties in filling those vacancies. There were several reasons. First, incumbent workers could be asked to work overtime without incurring premium rates since they were part-time workers. Second, some managers, like the domestic manager at hospital 3, claimed that agency cleaners were more expensive than permanent workers and that this caused tensions with permanent cleaners. And third, some managers had experienced problems with the quality of agency staff.

## THE NEW COORDINATING INSTITUTIONS TO IMPROVE PAY AND JOB QUALITY

The years 2004 and 2005 witnessed the negotiation and implementation of three major innovations in national institutions for the public hospitals workforce. In different ways, these represented the culmination of long-running trade union campaigns, shifting priorities in the government's political agenda for public sector reform, and evident problems (as highlighted earlier) for employers regarding human resource management. Each new set of rules emerged out of long-standing conflict among the social partners and offered the prospect of a new institutional space for unions, employers, and government to engage in cooperative negotiation and deliberation, forging strong trust relations and building a shared capacity to direct future strategy in the sector. The result has been that the main drivers shaping pay and job quality for cleaners and assistant nurses have not been market conditions but coordinating institutions, albeit operating within the complex context of the challenges already discussed.

A first institutional innovation involved a radical change in the system of wage-setting with a new national agreement in 2004, the "Agenda for Change," replacing the old "Whitley" system of wage-setting, which involved more than a dozen different sets of terms and conditions for different occupations. Following union-employer negotiations—established as a model of industrial relations partnership—this established three new pay spines: one for staff covered by the Doctors and Dentists Pay Review Body; a second for staff covered by the Nurses and Other Health Professionals Pay Review Body; and a third for other NHS staff, with the exception of senior managers (DoH 2004). Under the new structure, the pay for assistant nurses is recommended by the Nursing and Other Health Professionals Pay Review Body. It balances evidence taken from NHS employer bodies, government, unions, and professional associations representing staff groups within its remit. The review body then makes a recommendation to government. A new Pay Negotiating Council sets the pay awards for cleaners, along with other groups not covered by the pay review bodies. Importantly, unlike the previous system of fragmented pay settlements for different groups of workers (Seifert 1992), there is a new direct linkage between basic pay awards for staff on the second pay spine and staff on the third pay spine. This means that cleaners now benefit, in principle, from a coordinated approach to pay rises and the stronger bargaining power of the professional nurses' association. Indeed, an additional reform in 2007 has extended the Pay Review Body to include staff groups covered by the Pay Negotiating Council.

The input of trade unions influenced the choice of three particular objectives of this agreement: to harmonize terms and conditions across occupational groups in the public hospital sector; to improve the relative position of the very lowest-paid workers; and to ensure that as many staff as possible moved to a pay band that increased the potential maximum rate of pay over what they had enjoyed previously. Early press releases from both unions and NHS managers emphasized the improvements in basic rates of pay. For example, a grade B cleaner with a basic hourly rate of £4.92 (US$10.05) on the old pay scale transferred to a new band 1 rate of £5.89 (US$12.03), an increase of 20 percent. Similarly, newly recruited assistant nurses saw a rise from £5.69 (US$11.62) to a band 2 rate of £6.09 (US$12.44), an increase of 7 percent (table 5.5). The rise is greater for cleaners since they also benefited from a reduction in the working week from thirty-

Table 5.5  Comparison of Basic Hourly Pay Rates Between Old and New National Pay Scales (April 2005)

| | Old Pay Scale for Ancillary Staff (Whitney) | | | New Harmonized Pay Scale (Agenda for Change) |
|---|---|---|---|---|
| | Grade B | Grade C | Grade D | Band 1 |
| Cleaners | | | | |
| | | | | £6.43 |
| | | | | £6.26 |
| | | | | £6.09 |
| | | | | £5.89 |
| | | | £5.31 | |
| | | £5.13 | £5.13 | |
| | £5.09 | | | |
| | £5.00 | £5.00 | | |
| | £4.92 | | | |

| | Old Pay Scale for Nursing Staff (Whitney) | | New Harmonized Pay Scale (Agenda for Change) | |
|---|---|---|---|---|
| | Grade A | Grade B | Band 2 | Band 3 |
| Assistant nurses | | | | |
| | | | | £8.40 |
| | | | | £8.21 |
| | | | | £7.95 |
| | | | | £7.73 |
| | | £7.61[a] | £7.56 | £7.56 |
| | | £7.36 | £7.28 | £7.28 |
| | | £7.12 | £7.02 | £7.02 |
| | £6.89[a] | £6.89 | £6.83 | |
| | £6.68 | £6.68 | £6.63 | £6.74[b] |
| | £6.46 | | £6.43 | £6.43[b] |
| | £6.27 | | £6.26 | £6.18[b] |
| | £6.07 | | £6.09 | |
| | £5.88 | | £5.89[b] | |
| | £5.69 | | | |

*Source:* Authors' compilation using information provided by case-study hospital managers.
[a] Additional increment for staff with NVQ2 in care (grade A) and NVQ3 (grade B).
[b] Special transitional pay rate.

nine to thirty-seven and a half hours; the change in hours accounted for approximately 25 percent of the increase in the basic rate.

Implementation of the new pay structure was decentralized to the hospital, allowing for the adaptation of idiosyncratic job descriptions to appropriate pay banding through local job evaluation. This was a costly exercise, involving a great deal of managerial time reviewing jobs and negotiating individual appeals. Indeed, some managers would have preferred a national matching of all jobs to the national pay scale to avoid repetition of administrative work and to prevent hospitals placing similar jobs in different bands. Nevertheless, all human resource managers in the seven hospitals welcomed the general spirit of the new national agreement, especially its capacity to improve partnership relations with unions ("Agenda for Change has been an absolute godsend as far as partnership working goes," said hospital 4's assistant human resource director) and the opportunity it presented to advance the position of low-wage workers ("I think it's an opportunity to grasp and pay people or reward people for developing and taking on additional duties," said the assistant director of human resources at hospital 2).

A second coordinating institution is the new national organization to provide temporary cover for nursing positions. Largely in response to "failing" in-house banks at particular hospitals, as well as escalating costs of external agencies, the Department of Health created NHS Professionals (NHSP) in 2004 (operational since 2005). NHS spending on temporary staffing in 2002–2003 was estimated at £3 billion (US$6.13 billion), and it had grown by an average of 16 percent each year since 1996–97. In addition, as outlined in the NHSP strategic plan, the government sought to address other problems, including the high dependence of public hospitals on for-profit agencies, inefficient management of in-house nursing banks, and inconsistent pay policies. NHSP grew rapidly during its first years of operation, and by March 2006 it had captured 20 to 25 percent of the NHS market for agency temps.

Its overriding goal is to reduce spending on temporary cover—in stark contrast to the ambition of for-profit agencies to expand the market. The NHSP strategic plan document also reveals that it achieved this goal in its first year of operation, reducing agency spending on nursing temps by 15 percent (reversing the upward trend of previous years). This result was underpinned by NHSP research (a survey of three thousand nurses) that sought to identify the share of agency workers who wanted to work flexibly or gain experience in new areas, on the one hand, and the share of temp use that reflected poor management, on the other.

When a hospital signs up to NHSP, it transfers the management of its internal bank. NHSP undertakes a six-month program of research in cooperation with local hospital managers to collect and analyze data from different wards. It then feeds back advice to hospital managers about how to reduce their use of temps, as described by an NHSP senior manager:

> But the real nub of it is that for hospitals we provide effective management information. . . . We know absolutely every day what shifts have been booked, why they have been booked, who they've been booked by, and when and who they've been filled by. So we can tell, over time, what the value for money for each of these shifts are. . . . Typically, within the first year of operation for an average hospital with, say, an average expenditure of about £4 million (US$8.17 million), we can probably save them half a million pounds straight away just by managing their need more effectively.

Also, NHSP charges lower fees. In 2005–2006 it charged a flat 7.5 percent service fee as opposed to the average 15 percent commission charged by private agencies. The fee covers training and support for workers as well as management of payroll. In addition, NHSP provides full pay and nonpay benefits to temporary staff as members of the public hospital sector. This includes the NHS final salary pension scheme and access to training provision. And perhaps the most innovative function of NHSP is its policy to identify new recruits from the socially excluded and long-term unemployed.[12] At hospital 4, for example, NHSP recruited cohorts of twelve people to a two-week training program. Instead of a wage, each participant continued to claim full welfare benefits in order to avoid the high financial penalties of switching from welfare to work.

The third new institution is a national framework that strengthens protection of the terms and conditions for privately employed workers who provide outsourced services to hospitals. A long trade union campaign during the 1990s and early 2000s successfully brought to the public's attention the inequities of a "two-tier workforce" among the private sector workers who provide ancillary services to the country's public hospitals. The Department of Health finally acted in October 2005 and ordered that most workers, including cleaners, would be entitled to "terms and conditions no less favourable" than the collectively bargained national pay structure for public sector workers (that is, the Agenda for Change).[13] This response forms part of a broader policy approach to public services, the "two-tier code," and represents something like a new national wage extension agreement. Our interviews suggest that hospital managers welcomed this new policy. At hospital 4, the human resource director was concerned about the "ethics" of the private sector cleaning firm offering worse terms and conditions to its new recruits and argued, "We want Sodexho to pay reasonable rates for their people." Her opinion was mirrored in the comments of her counterpart at hospital 6, who said, prior to the announcement of the new policy:

> We would want our contracted-out staff to have the same terms and conditions as other staff, because in essence we want them to be fully part of the team and for there to be a seamless join between our [contracted-out] domestic staff and [public sector] staff.

As such, the new framework agreement facilitates improved cooperation between public and private sector managers as well as constructive input from trade unions.

At hospital 2, a new kind of agreement had been reached reflecting a second strand of the government's new approach to outsourcing. During 2005, the government also removed the obligation for hospitals to transfer nonsupervisory ancillary staff as part of PFI contracts. A major goal of this policy was to protect workers' relatively generous public sector pensions, a condition of employment that is still excluded from the employment protection legislation known as Transfer of Undertakings (Protection of Employment) (TUPE). The policy is called the "retention of employment" model, and hospital 2, after three-way negotiations between unions, the private contractor, and hospital management, happens to be one of the first examples in the United Kingdom of its implementation. The model required the transfer of all staff who deliver "hard" ancillary services (estate services), along with supervisory staff of "soft" services (cleaning, portering, security, and linen), but all nonsupervisory soft services workers were retained as employees of the public sector. In total, 800 staff were retained, and 125 estate staff plus 70 to 80 supervisory staff were transferred. Our interviews with cleaners revealed their satisfaction with having retained their public sector employment conditions. A domestic at hospital 2 said:

> I'd rather stay with the [public sector] because at least you've got something substantial there. Because these contract people, they're not very good. Because some of our women have worked for ISS Mediclean before, like in Asda, and they're a terrible firm. They are not very nice.

## IMPROVEMENTS IN JOB QUALITY?

In this section, we assess the extent to which the three new coordinating institutions have helped to improve job quality by promoting better pay, a matching of worker skill with job needs, a carefully negotiated division of labor, and opportunities for skill development and pay progression. We show that the potential for improvements is tempered by the need for hospital managers to respond to the financial and labor market pressures described in section 6, generating new tensions and contradictions in the organization of low-wage work.

### ARE PAY RATES SHELTERED FROM THE EXTERNAL MARKET?

Comparison of pay rates between the old and new national pay structures for public sector hospital workers demonstrates that the new pay agreement did secure a significant pay rise, especially for the lower-paid (see table 5.5). Most cleaners and assistant nurses we interviewed believed that the pay was fair compared to other job opportunities. One cleaner had previously worked as a fully qualified nursery nurse but then quit and started as a full-time cleaner because the pay was better. Others compared their pay favorably with that of similarly skilled workers in the care sector.

> *Cleaner at hospital 3:* I could go and do care work, but it's less. It's like £4.85 an hour. I'm not going to do that for that. I used to do it before I came here.

> *Cleaner at hospital* 2: I think that [public sector hospitals] pay a
> lot more than domestics in other jobs, definitely. And I mean,
> you've got sickness pay as well. I was off for fourteen months and
> still got paid, which was wonderful.

> *Assistant nurse at hospital* 2: If I'm having a bad day, I think, "Oh,
> I'm going back to work in residential [care]." And then I reflect
> back to the pay on that, and I think, "No, you're all right where
> you are. Leave that newspaper alone!"

Thus, pay rates did appear to be positively sheltered from external "market rates." However, there was dissatisfaction with regard to the level of pay in relation to level of education, skill, experience, and age.

> *Assistant nurse at hospital* 1: A lot of people have gained from [the
> new pay agreement], but I don't feel that we have, for what we're
> expected to know and expected to do in this job.

> *Cleaner at hospital* 5: Now we've got our NVQ . . . but we don't get
> any more money. . . . We get more qualifications, but we don't get
> any extra pay.

Some of the dissatisfaction with the new pay rates reflected the problem that higher *basic* rates of pay did not always amount to higher *total* pay. There were two reasons for this. First, under the previous national pay structure, hospitals could include performance supplements for some workers. Among the seven case study hospitals, we found evidence of long-standing agreements with ancillary workers, including bonus payments, higher consolidated basic rates, attendance allowances, and special premiums for working in accident and emergency. All such supplements have subsequently been abolished. Second, at the time of our fieldwork (2005), hospital workers also expected to lose out from proposed changes in enhancements for working overtime and unsocial hours. For example, unsocial hours premiums of 33 percent for night work, 50 percent for Saturdays, and 100 percent for Sundays were expected to be replaced by a less generous sliding scale of between 9 and 25 percent, depending on the average number of unsocial hours worked per week. Estimates by the main trade union, Unison, suggested that most workers would not be worse off under the new rates because the enhancements would be applied to *all* hours worked.[14] However, in interviews workers were strongly opposed to the idea of abolishing the long-standing custom and practice of paying time and a half and double time. As a domestic at hospital 1 explained:

> But the thing that is bothering me at present . . . when I do my weekends, I get time and a half for Saturday and double time for Sunday, which helps to boost up our low pay an enormous amount. Now, under Agenda for Change . . . they want us to work weekends for the same rate of pay as we do in the week. And it will not work.

Our evidence reflected a national pattern of worker dissatisfaction, such that during 2005–2006 unions won an agreement with employers to retain the old unsocial hours payments until a revised set of conditions could be agreed upon. Proposals that circulated in February 2007 (to be implemented in April 2008) suggest that employers might concede a U-turn and reintroduce standard premium rates of time and a half and double time for the lowest-paid staff (band 1) and the same principle, albeit at incrementally less generous rates, would apply to wages for staff at higher bands. The new pay framework thus appears to have demonstrated its capacity to engage the social partners in constructive negotiation in responding to a matter of considerable concern, as revealed by our interviews with low-wage workers.

A final issue concerns the impact of the new institutional arrangements on conditions for cleaners in the five hospitals where some or all were employed by a private firm. With the new "two-tier code," cleaners with protected terms and conditions following staff transfer experienced the same change in pay as other cleaners employed in-house. Moreover, cleaners who had been newly recruited by the private sector firm enjoyed a considerable improvement, not only in the basic rate of pay but also in holiday entitlement, unsocial hours premiums, and sick pay. For example, cleaners employed by Sodexho at hospital 7 were all paid a flat rate of £5.09 (US$10.40) per hour and were looking forward to an increase to rates varying from £5.89 to £6.43 (US$12.03 to US$13.13).

At hospital 2, where a "retention of employment" model had been agreed upon, cleaners employed by the hospital were paid higher rates than their supervisors who were employed by the private cleaning firm, ISS Mediclean. Supervisors were paid an annual salary of £11,000 to £12,000 (US$22,469 to US$24,512), compared to a range of £11,486 to £12,539 (US$23,463 to US$25,614) for cleaners on the new public sector pay scale. In the words of the associate human resource director, "The supervisors have been saying, 'Get on with it. What are you going to do about it ISS [Mediclean]? Come on, pull your finger out.'" The human resource manager at ISS Mediclean recognized that this was a problem but argued that the issue was "Who's going to pay for the five days' extra holiday? Who's going to pay for the increase in rates of pay?" Since our fieldwork, the government agreed to fund the bulk of the costs associated with raising the terms and conditions of private sector cleaners to the level of the public hospital pay agreement.

## Do Workers' Skills Match Job Requirements?

A second issue we explored is the degree to which worker skills and qualifications broadly fit with those required for the job. A challenging work environment demands continuous improvements in skills and qualifications, whereas the opposite situation applies where workers are employed "below their potential" (Grant, Yeandle, and Buckner 2005). We consider progress along job ladders in the next section. Here we simply present a snapshot of skills for the employees interviewed.

Table 5.6 shows a profile of the twelve assistant nurses and six cleaners interviewed in the seven hospitals. Reflecting the aggregate composition of these two groups, most of the interviewees were women. Also, they mostly belonged to the older age groups. Most were in their forties and fifties, the eldest being fifty-five. Length of service with the current employer varied between three and twenty-seven years but tended to be relatively long, with thirteen interviewees having five or more years' service.

Entry into both cleaning and assistant nursing jobs requires no specific educational qualifications. Human resource managers informed us that it was desirable for cleaners to have a "reasonable standard" of literacy and numeracy and for assistant nurses to have "GCSE standard" in math and English. Also, past experience in care work was desirable for entry into assistant nursing. However, the data we collected for the eighteen employees interviewed displayed a remarkable diversity of education and past work experience, and many of them were considerably overeducated or had higher-than-expected skills from previous jobs. Table 5.6 separates interviewees into four groups according to their level of education (standard and above-standard) and prior work experience (standard and above-standard).

The majority of our interviewees (eleven out of eighteen) had qualifications or work experience above that required for their job. Some assistant nurses had very high levels of education, up to nine O levels or GCSEs in two cases. When quizzed about their choice of employment, one of these assistant nurses, employed at hospital 5, told us, "I never thought I'd actually be clever enough to be a nurse, so I thought I'd go for the next thing." Past work experience was also above what one would expect for three cleaners and five assistant nurses, including a cleaner who had been an NVQ3 qualified nursery nurse. Our interviewees also included three who had formerly run their own business.

This small sample of data thus suggests that there is a great deal of untapped potential among cleaners and assistant nurses. One of the major reasons our interviewees offered for their occupational down-grading was the decision to fit flexible (and typically part-time) working hours around their family commitments, given the con-straints of making adjustments in their former higher-paid job. All sixteen women interviewed had families and had either withdrawn from the labor market or worked part-time when their children were young. A cleaner at hospital 4 argued that she had no alternative but to accept her low-wage job because of her family life, and another who had swapped a lucrative career in cable TV sales when her son was young saw her income cut from £2,000 a month to £200 (US$408.56).

## IS THE DIVISION OF LABOR CAREFULLY NEGOTIATED?

Work on a hospital ward is a team effort. Qualified nurses, assistant nurses, housekeepers, and cleaners each have their designated tasks, their notion of job territory, but they also work together to get the job done, often to meet the urgent needs of the patient. We heard many examples of teamwork in which individuals crossed the

# Table 5.6 Levels of Education and Past Work Experience Among Cleaners and Assistant Nurses

| | Sex | Age | Years Worked in Public Hospitals | School Qualifications | Work Experience |
|---|---|---|---|---|---|
| **Standard education; standard work experience** | | | | | |
| Assistant nurse | M | 25 | 5 | None | Care assistant in private nursing home |
| Assistant nurse | F | 35 | 5 | Three O levels | Catering; ward housekeeper |
| Assistant nurse | M | 40 | 10 | None | Hospital porter; care assistant |
| Assistant nurse | F | 43 | 3 | Four GCSEs | Child welfare |
| Cleaner | F | 48 | 4 | Two GCSEs | Airline catering |
| Cleaner | F | 55 | 27 | Two O levels | Factory work |
| Cleaner | F | 53 | 15 | None | Office, shop, and factory work |
| **Above standard education; standard work experience** | | | | | |
| Assistant nurse | F | 27 | 3 | Nine GCSEs | Care assistant in private nursing home |
| Assistant nurse | F | 46 | 10 | Six CSEs | Hairdressing; factory and shop work |
| Assistant nurse | F | 43 | 3 | Seven CSEs | Home care |

## Standard education; above-standard work experience

| | | | | | |
|---|---|---|---|---|---|
| Assistant nurse | F | 54 | 9 | Two O levels | Office, factory, and shop work; dairy farm manager (own business); bus driver; radio operator |
| Assistant nurse | F | 40 | 9 | CSEs | Shop manager; marketing (own business); cable TV sales; cleaner |
| Cleaner | F | 54 | 7 | None | Accounts/bookkeeping; child-minding |
| Cleaner | F | 51 | 16 | None | Tailor; retail supervisor |
| Cleaner | F | 42 | 7 | CSEs | qualified nursery nurse |

## Above-standard education; above-standard work experience

| | | | | | |
|---|---|---|---|---|---|
| Assistant nurse | F | 47 | 4 | Five CSEs and Two GCSEs | Aerobics teacher |
| Assistant nurse | F | 48 | 9 | Seven O levels | Owner of hair salon |
| Assistant nurse | F | 46 | 8 | Nine O levels | Accounts clerk; cleaner |

*Source:* Authors' compilation using information provided by cleaners and assistant nurses during interviews.

*Note:* Up until 1988, there was a two-tier exam system for sixteen-year-olds. Academically able pupils took General Certificate of Education Ordinary Level (O level) examinations in a number of subjects. Those less academically gifted took the Certificate of Secondary Education (CSE) examinations. In 1988 these were combined into a single system of GCSEs (General Certificate of Secondary Education).

boundaries of their job to facilitate the delivery of a particular service:

> *Assistant nurse at hospital 3*: If it's quiet on the ward and the cleaner hasn't arrived, we don the appropriate colored aprons and stuff and go and help. Obviously if the meal is hot it needs to be served.

> *Cleaner at hospital 5*: Yes, I do it [respond to buzzers]. It's not my job, don't get me wrong. But . . . especially if I know the patient . . . and I can tell going to their bed in the morning, if their breathing is a bit off or if there's just something that's not quite right. I'll go and say to a member of staff, "Could you go and see John."

But the willingness of staff to work as a team did not obscure a relatively strict division of labor between cleaners and assistant nurses. We asked the employees questions about the types and frequencies of the tasks they undertook, and we present the results in figure 5.2. This shows the wider range of job duties typically undertaken by the assistant nurse compared to the relatively narrow focus of cleaners on general cleaning and patient area cleaning. In addition to making beds and cleaning around the patient area, the assistant nurse typically provided basic care to the patient, recorded and monitored health indicators, and might undertake certain nursing tasks such as venepuncture or ECGs. All assistant nurses worked under the supervision of a qualified nurse. By contrast, cleaners were very aware that physical assistance or physical care for patients was obviously outside their job description. As a cleaner at hospital 1 put it: "It's a definite no-no that you would not help a patient out of a chair, out of bed, you know, anything like that . . . because we're not covered if we have an accident with them." Figure 5.2 shows that the cleaners we interviewed did not provide physical patient care, make beds, or assist with administration (taking phone calls or making appointments).

Nevertheless, there are areas of overlap. Similar to the results of research in American hospitals, the differences across our case studies largely reflected different approaches to integrating cleaners and assistant nurses into the patient care team (Appelbaum et al. 2003). Attending to patients' needs falls outside a cleaner's job description yet was considered by some to be an inevitable part of their job. The

## Figure 5.2 The Division of Labor Between Cleaners and Assistant Nurses

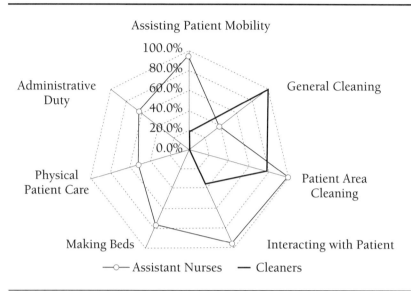

Source: Authors' compilation using information provided by cleaners and assistant nurses during interviews.

Note: Based on our very small sample of twelve assistant nurses and six cleaners. Answers to questions were scored as 1 ("always"), 2/3 ("often"), 1/3 ("sometimes") and 0 ("never"). Some questions involved aggregated responses to individual questions: "assisting patient mobility" involved separate questions on helping patients to move and taking them to the toilet; "interacting with the patient" combined questions on giving emotional support, responding to the patient buzzer, and reporting information; "administrative duties" combined responses to taking phone calls and making appointments.

score for "interacting with patient" was 96 percent for assistant nurses and 37 percent for cleaners; while cleaners would rarely respond to a buzzer or report information about a patient, five of the six interviewed said that they would offer emotional support to a patient on a daily or weekly basis. The strongest overlap was for "patient area cleaning." All assistant nurses said that they cleaned around the patient area every day (a score of 100 percent), and all except one of the cleaners did this daily or weekly.[15] Assistant nurses were responsible for cleaning spills of bodily fluids and in some wards also for regular cleaning bathroom facilities. In addition, assistant nurses undertook other cleaning when no cleaners were on duty.

*Assistant nurse at hospital 6:* It's our responsibility to clean the baths and the sinks when the patients have used them. If there's any spillage on the ward—if the patient has been sick or whatever—that's our responsibility to clean up spillages and just tidy round after ourselves.

*Assistant nurse at hospital 7:* Sometimes at night when a room needs deep cleaning, we have to do that because there are no domestic staff on.

One issue is the extent to which the pay bands for cleaners and assistant nurses adequately reflect the difference in the range of their tasks. In 2005–2006 cleaners were paid on band 1, a range of £5.89 to £6.43 (US$12.03 to US$13.13), and assistant nurses on band 2, a range of £6.09 to £7.56 (US$12.44 to US$15.44), with the possibility of progression to band 3 should a more skilled post become available, paid on a range of £7.02 to £8.40 (US$14.34 to US$17.16). This means that an experienced assistant nurse in a band 2 post (which accounts for the majority of assistant nurses in hospitals) earns just 18 percent more than an experienced cleaner. Moreover, when quizzed about overlaps of tasks, assistant nurses were more likely to talk about the need to coordinate their work with qualified nurses and to cover for their job duties when they were busy. But here the pay differential is very wide—a newly qualified nurse earns 57 percent more than a newly recruited assistant nurse. While assistant nurses understood that nurses' higher pay reflected their degree qualification and technical knowledge, it nevertheless caused some frustration. An assistant nurse at hospital 1 complained:

They say "nurse assistant," but I mean, when I was on the ward at [hospital name], you did everything the same as a nurse, bar give medication. And that's really frustrating when you're on maybe a third of their wages. And you work really, really hard. . . . And it annoys me when you see frilly jobs in, like, shops and supermarkets, and they are on more money than me.

This issue reflects a long-standing dilemma in the organization of nursing work in United Kingdom hospitals. Since at least 1905, the need for a "second-tier nurse" has been advocated (Abel-Smith 1960). However, the regulated approach to the second-tier posi-

tion—the "state-enrolled nurse" with a two-year program of training—was abolished and the less regulated "third-tier nurse" is what
we now know as the assistant nurse. Current efforts to improve the
skill and status of the assistant nurse must confront a long history of
underinvestment. During the 1980s, under pressure to reduce expenditures, managers used less expensive nursing assistants to carry
out tasks traditionally undertaken by qualified or enrolled nurses
(Dingwall, Rafferty, and Webster 1988, 225). Then, in the 1990s, hospitals used the new post of "health care assistant" to cut costs and
whittle down the skill-mix ratio between qualified and unqualified
nursing staff (Grimshaw 1999; Lloyd and Seifert 1995; Thornley
1996). The new pay structure may offer a positive development if
hospital managers can redesign sufficient numbers of jobs to fit the
characteristics of a band 3 post. This would shift the overall positioning of the nurse assistant toward the middle between cleaning
and qualified nursing. However, the nature of the job tasks is not the
only determinant of pay: skills and qualifications are also essential ingredients.

## DO INCREMENTAL JOB LADDERS LEAD TO SKILL
## DEVELOPMENT AND PAY PROGRESSION?

A final test of enhanced employment prospects is the opportunity for
skill development and pay advancement along carefully designed
vertical job ladders within an organization (Doeringer and Piore
1971). The new national pay structure extends the possible pay scale
for assistant nurses from a minimum-maximum range of 100 to 134
percent to 100 to 138 percent (from £5.69 to £7.61 (US$11.62 to
US$15.54) per hour to £6.09 to £8.40 (US$12.44 to US$17.15); see
table 5.5), and considerable effort has been invested in extending the
possibilities of advancement into new, higher-skilled posts. For
cleaners, however, the pay scale was not significantly expanded from
what was already a very narrow band: the previous pay scale of £4.92
to £5.31 (US$10.05 to US$10.84) per hour represented an 8 percent
maximum progression, and the new pay scale of £5.89 to £6.43
(US$12.03 to US$13.13) represents a 9 percent progression. We consider opportunities and obstacles for each group separately.

At all seven hospitals, the majority of assistant nurses were paid at
the band 2 level and were encouraged to take the NVQ2 qualification
in care. There were also several examples of new band 3 posts that re-

quired NVQ3 skills, and these were offered as possible paths of progression for band 2 assistant nurses. For example, two hospitals had introduced the new role of junior doctor's assistant. This is an assistant nurse who is on call and trained to assist junior doctors by carrying out routine procedures such as cannulation and phlebotomy. Also, four hospitals had introduced the new post of assistant practitioner for assistant nurses who wished to further their career but without taking the academic route into nursing. This post involved completing an NVQ3 plus a two-year foundation degree, which would qualify the employee to carry out procedures such as venepuncture and ECG recording and to be paid at band 4 rates. Interestingly, this post was described by managers as similar to that of the old state-enrolled nurse, the so-called second-tier nurse. Finally, all seven hospitals offered temporary transfers to nurse training on 80 percent of salary for assistant nurses who wished to become qualified nurses.

Despite these opportunities, there were also obstacles to progression. First, several interviewees had completed the NVQ3 qualification but had not been promoted to a band 3 post because promotion occurred only when a post became available, not when the skill had been acquired. As the assistant director of nursing at hospital 4 put it, "What wasn't explained to people is that qualifications don't necessarily match role progression." Unsurprisingly, therefore, we found evidence of dissatisfaction among those assistant nurses who had been funded, and encouraged, to complete a level 3 qualification but were still paid at the same rate as those with a level 2 or with no qualification. Managers recognized this was an issue.

A second obstacle to progression was in part a response to this issue, combined with cost pressures on the funding for training provision and on the payroll. In some hospitals, we discovered, managers had changed their strategy toward skill development and during 2005 had limited the chance to complete a level 3 qualification to those who were either defined as occupying a role that required level 3 skills or earmarked for a forthcoming band 3 post vacancy. The deputy chief nurse at hospital 3 explained:

> We don't automatically go, "Oh, that's it, you can have this now then." Otherwise, you'd have no control over your pay, and it also may be that actually whilst it's nice for the individual to go and do their NVQ3, you don't actually require that level of skills and

knowledge on your ward. But you're quite happy to support them to go and get the qualification so they can apply for other jobs.

A third obstacle was that in some situations, even where a level 3 post had been created, there was a mismatch with the pay rate. For example, in the renal unit at hospital 3, two assistant nurses who were training as assistant practitioners were still paid a band 2 salary despite working in a post that required extra qualifications. One of them commented:

> I've got NVQ level 2 and level 3 in care, NVQ level 3 in hemodialysis, and, as I say, I'm now working for this foundation degree. . . . We've been told that we are going to be a band 2, as we currently are, which we are going to object to. Because we think that, as an ordinary [assistant nurse] is a band 2, we should be slightly higher because of our extra involvement.

A fourth obstacle was that while the temporary transfer route was open to experienced assistant nurses who wished to become qualified nurses, the number of places offered was very limited (around ten to sixteen annually), and those places were "always oversubscribed," as the deputy chief nurse at hospital 3 noted.

Cleaners who were directly employed by the hospital were placed on band 1 in the new pay structure. The expectation was that cleaners employed by a private firm (at hospitals 2, 4, 6, and 7) would be transitioned to similar rates during 2006. Unlike assistant nurses, cleaners were not required to undertake formal qualifications, although training provision for NVQ1 and in some cases NVQ2 was available. However, there was little incentive for cleaners to acquire qualifications since there was no pay increment. As one cleaner from hospital 2 complained: "We have to have all these training things, right, but it doesn't do anything at all for our job, because we're still staying in band 1. . . . The nurses and things like that, when they do all these training things, they go higher up."

Furthermore, we found evidence at one of the hospitals that training resources for the NVQ program were directed at assistant nurses, for whom there was a clearer developmental path. The human resource director at hospital 5 believed that managers had to consider, "What will be the return for the trust?" Consequently, while cleaners at hospital 5 could complete NVQ1, this was not compulsory, nor

was it actively encouraged by managers in view of the limited resources.

Three of the seven hospitals had introduced the new post of ward
housekeeper, and the private firms supplying cleaners to hospitals 4,
6, and 7 had introduced a similar new role, the patient services assistant or ward steward. These new roles were introduced nationally
with the aim of improving the patient environment and lowering rates
of hospital-acquired infections. Their duties involve serving drinks,
arranging flowers, and generally keeping the patient area tidy. They
are defined as band 2 posts and thus potentially provide a new career
path for cleaners, in addition to the more conventional route to the
post of cleaner supervisor or the larger step to assistant nurse. However, while cleaners welcomed the opportunity to earn higher pay,
they did not believe that the housekeeper role was of a higher value in
terms of the duties required. A cleaner at hospital 1 remarked:

> She makes tea for them. She will change the flowers, generally
> tidy up round where they are. She will assist to feed the patients.
> So it's sort of a step up from a cleaner. . . . I feel we're worth more
> than what we get. And I feel . . . we're doing the heavy slogging
> stuff for less.

A final issue for cleaners concerns the complications introduced
by outsourcing. In particular, outsourcing can rupture the job ladder
connecting skilled cleaners to the post of assistant nurse. Managers at
hospitals 4 and 7 expressed concern that fewer cleaners were applying for assistant nurse posts than previously when cleaning was managed in-house. Part of the problem was a lack of information sharing
between the hospital and the private firm, as well as the unwillingness of the private cleaning firm to lose its more able staff. Hospital
managers were aware of these tensions and wary about undermining
partnership relations with the private cleaning firms by poaching
cleaners. The hospital 2 human resources director said:

> When we go over to the [contractor's] induction program, we
> quite often get asked, "What are the opportunities to come and
> work in the NHS?". . . We're sitting there with their manager say-
> ing, "We're not here to poach you!" But clearly we would wel-
> come them if they take an interest in a particular area. So it's a lit-
> tle bit sensitive really, because clearly [Sodexho] want to keep
> their best workers.

A second complication was introduced by the new retention of employment model implemented at hospital 2. This model ruptures the internal job ladder between cleaner and supervisor because progression to supervisor requires a change of employer from the public hospital sector to the private firm, ISS Mediclean. And while the new coordinating institution represented by the two-tier code means that pay rates are as favorable, those staff who transfer still lose other benefits, such as the generous public sector pension scheme.

## SUMMARY AND ASSESSMENT

Our analysis of low-wage work in public sector hospitals in the United Kingdom suggests that the negotiation of what we call "coordinating institutions," involving deliberation by the social partners (unions, employers, and government), can establish a positive framework within which to advance the position of low-wage workers. The new pay agreement establishes a harmonized set of terms and conditions, improves basic rates at the bottom of the pay structure, and for the first time links the two national pay settlements of the Nursing and Other Health Professionals Review Body, which covers assistant nurses, and the Pay Negotiating Council, which covers cleaners. By 2007, the logic of the new arrangement was taken a step further with the creation of the NHS Pay Review Body, which will cover all staff paid under the national pay agreement beginning in 2008–09. Also, the innovative creation of a national organization to manage the supply of nursing temps extends national terms and conditions (including pensions) to agency workers and appears to have already reversed a five-year trend of increasing hospital reliance on costly temporary work agencies. A third coordinating institution is the long-awaited two-tier code, which extends employment conditions agreed to under the national collective agreement to cleaners (and other workers) who provide hospital services and are employed by a private sector firm. Thus, rather than an investigation of diverse employment policies and practices and different forms of work organization in the seven case study hospitals, this chapter demonstrates how reforms to the institutional architecture, inspired by trade union campaigns and a government willing to act (albeit with a long delay), can provide a real impetus for improved conditions for low-wage work.

But the organization of work and the careful design of employment policy at the level of the hospital still matter. So too do the constantly shifting pressures on hospital spending and business strategy, as well as the conflicting demands on hospital managers to respond to strengthened forms of quasi-market competition. As a result, our case study data reveal evidence of new opportunities, but also obstacles and tensions surrounding the implementation of new employment policies. Drawing on qualitative interview data, we examined four potential dimensions of improved job quality for assistant nurses and cleaners. First, we found that new pay rates were generally perceived to be fair relative to comparable jobs in alternative organizations, but largely unfair as a reflection of the employee's level of education, skill, age, and experience. This finding was reinforced by evidence of a mismatch between workers' capabilities and job requirements—in particular, we found a surprising level of over-education and over-experience among interviewed workers, suggesting a considerable source of untapped productive potential (see also Grant, Yeandle, and Buckner 2005). Third, we found a relatively harmonious blurring of teamwork and detailed division of labor among cleaners and assistant nurses, with a great deal of cooperation in those tasks that maximized patient welfare within the hospital. However, our evidence suggests that as a wide range of nursing, administrative, and ancillary tasks have been increasingly delegated to the assistant nurse, this has not been accompanied by a substantial shift in the relative level of assistant nurses' pay, which remains very close to that of cleaners. Finally, while hospitals have introduced new posts that extend the job ladder for assistant nurses, there has been insufficient attention to job redesign to increase opportunities for pay progression, and it is unclear that future public spending rounds will provide the needed resources for managers to invest in more high-skilled posts. In addition, outsourcing of cleaning services has disrupted job ladders by requiring a change of employer, both from cleaner to assistant nurse and, in the special case of the retention of employment model, from cleaner to supervisor.

## NOTES

1. Michael Moran (1999) suggests that, given the wider United Kingdom context of a liberal welfare state regime, a more appropriate definition is a service that meets citizen needs to the best of its ability with given resources (cited in Bach 2004, 25).

2.   It is also notable that United Kingdom health care spending failed to keep up with Spain, which increased its health care spending from 1.5 percent to 7.7 percent as a share of GDP from 1970 to 1999.

3.   Department of Health, "Hospital Activity Statistics: Data Requests," accessed April 2007 at http://www.performance.doh.gov.uk/hospital activity/data_requests/index.htm.

4.   Current reforms follow a shift in policy in 1989 (marked by the government white paper "Working for Patients") that introduced the internal quasi-market in the National Health Service. This redefined hospitals as "trusts" that compete as providers against private hospitals for a bundle of health care services purchased by "primary care trusts" (including general practitioners).

5.   See "Background to NHS Foundation Trusts," Department of Health, accessed March 2005 at http://www.dh.gov.uk/en/Policyandguid ance/Organizationpolicy/Secondarycare/NHSfoundationtrust/DH_406 2852.

6.   The Select Committee in 2003 called for new provisions to limit local pay flexibility: "We understand that in time it is the government's intention to ensure a 'level playing field' within the NHS, with high performing NHS Foundation trusts being the norm rather than an elite. However, if these reforms are implemented in their present form . . . stronger safeguards will need to be put in place to ensure that aggressive poaching of scarce staff does not take place. These should include an obligation on Foundation trusts to consult local NHS employers before altering staff terms and conditions" (paragraph 147, cited in DoH 2003).

7.   In 2005 union density in the public sector was 59 percent, compared to just 17 percent in the private sector (Grainger 2006).

8.   Since the fieldwork in May 2007, two of these unions—Amicus and the TGWU—combined to form the United Kingdom's largest union, Unite.

9.   Research has identified the increased job insecurity and work intensification that are associated with post-transfer job cuts, mishandling of the redundancy process, and new pressures to work to performance contracts (Grimshaw and Hebson 2004). Also, the market-based principles of outsourcing have weakened the traditional norms underpinning a "public sector ethos": notions of public service have been replaced by private gain, the collegial process by personal accountability and uniform, and transparent pay and promotions structures by discretionary individual remuneration (Hebson, Grimshaw, and Marchington 2003).

10.  The Healthcare Commission (the independent inspection body for both the NHS and independent health care providers) annually

awarded each provider a rating of between no stars and three stars, based on a range of performance indicators. This has now been replaced by a new system, the "Annual Healthcheck."

11. Moreover, unemployment data disaggregated at the local level reveal very limited variation; during 2004–2005, just 12 out of 297 travel-to-work areas scored an unemployment rate of 7 percent or more, and 17 areas scored a rate of 2 percent or less.

12. This is undertaken as part of the new "skills escalator" policy, designed to broaden access to employment and develop job ladders within the public hospital sector (McBride et al. 2006).

13. Among the workers covered are so-called soft facilities management staff—cleaners, catering assistants, laundry staff, and porters. Excluded groups are the "hard" groups—estate and maintenance workers (largely men).

14. However, those working a large share of unsocial hours would lose. For example, an experienced grade A assistant nurse on night shifts (three nights per week, 9:00 PM to 7:30 AM, including weekends) earned £8.35 (US$17.05) per hour on Whitley rates, but just £7.96 (US$16.25) on the new rates, despite receiving the maximum 25 percent enhancement (Unison 2004).

15. When this was not part of a cleaner's duty, it was because the ward employed "housekeepers," a new grade of cleaning staff specifically charged to clean patient areas.

## REFERENCES

Abel-Smith, Brian. 1960. *A History of the Nursing Profession*. London: Heinemann.

Appelbaum, Eileen, Peter Berg, Ann Frost, and Gil Preuss. 2003. "The Effects of Work Restructuring on Low-Wage, Low-Skilled Workers in U.S. Hospitals." In *Low-Wage America: How Employers Are Reshaping Opportunity in the Workplace*, edited by Eileen Appelbaum, Annette Bernhardt, and Richard J. Murnane. New York: Russell Sage Foundation.

Audit Commission. 2004. "Introducing Payment by Results: Getting the Balance Right for the NHS and Taxpayers." London: Audit Commission.

Bach, Stephen. 2004. *Employment Relations and the Health Service: The Management of Reforms*. London: Routledge.

Department of Health (DoH). 2002. "HR in the NHS Plan: More Staff Working Differently." London: DoH.

———. 2003. "The Government's Response to the Health Committee's Second Report of Session 2002–2003 into NHS Foundation Trusts." London: HMSO (July).

———. 2004. *Agenda for Change: Final Agreement*. London: DoH (Decem-

ber). Accessed at http://www.dh.gov.uk/en/Publicationsandstatistics/Pub
lications/PublicationsPolicyAndGuidance/DH_4095943.

———. 2005. *Health and Personal Social Services*. London: DoH. Accessed
March 11, 2005, at www.performance.doh.gov.uk/HPSSS.

Dingwall, Robert, Anne Marie Rafferty, and Charles Webster. 1988. *An Introduction to the Social History of Nursing*. London: Routledge.

Doeringer, Peter B., and Michael J. Piore. 1971. *Internal Labor Markets and
Manpower Analysis*. Lexington, Mass.: D. C. Heath.

Elster, Jon, editor. 1998. *Deliberative Democracy*. New York: Cambridge University Press.

Grainger, Heidi. 2006. *Trade Union Membership 2005: Employment Market
Analysis and Research*. London: Department for Trade and Industry.

Grant, Linda, Sue Yeandle, and Lisa Buckner. 2005. "Working Below Potential: Women and Part-time Work." Working paper 40. Manchester, U.K.:
Equal Opportunities Commission.

Griffiths, Julie. 2005. "The Talent Agency." *People Management* 11(11): 16–
17.

Grimshaw, Damian. 1999. "Changes in Skills-Mix and Pay Determination
Among the Nursing Workforce in the U.K." *Work, Employment, and Society* 13(2): 293–326.

Grimshaw, Damian, and Gail Hebson. 2004. "Public-private Partnerships in
the U.K.: The Limits to Contracting and the Prospects for Employment."
*Economia and Lavoro* 38(1): 139–63.

Grimshaw, Damian, Steve Vincent, and Hugh Willmott. 2002. "Going Privately: Partnership and Outsourcing of Public Sector Services." *Public Administration* 80(3): 475–502.

Hall, Peter A., and David Soskice. 2001. "An Introduction to Varieties of
Capitalism." In *Varieties of Capitalism: The Institutional Foundations of
Comparative Advantage*, edited by Peter A. Hall and David Soskice. Ox-
ford: Oxford University Press.

Hebson, Gail, Damian Grimshaw, and Mick Marchington. 2003. "PPPs and
the Changing Public Sector Ethos: Case Study Evidence from the Health
and Local Authority Sectors." *Work, Employment, and Society* 17(3): 481–
501.

HM Treasury. 2004. *2004 Spending Review*. London: HMSO. Accessed at
http://www.hm-treasury.gov.uk/spending_review/spend_sr04/spend_sr04
_index.cfm.

———. 2006. *Public Expenditure Statistical Analyses 2006*. Cm 6811. London: HMSO.

Houseman, Susan N., Arne L. Kalleberg, and George A. Erickcek. 2003.
"The Role of Temporary Agency Employment in Tight Labor Markets."
*Industrial and Labor Relations Review* 57(1): 105–27.

Lloyd, Caroline, and Roger Seifert. 1995. "Restructuring the NHS: The Impact of the 1990 Reforms on the Management of Labor." *Work, Employment, and Society* 9(2): 359–78.

McBride, Anne, Annette Cox, Stephen Mustchin, Marilyn Carroll, Paula Hyde, Elena Antonacopoulou, Kieran Walshe, and Helen Woolnough. 2006. *Developing Skills in the NHS.* Report for the Department of Health Policy Research Program. Mimeo. University of Manchester.

Moran, Michael. 1999. *Governing the Health Care State: A Comparative Study of the United Kingdom, the United States, and Germany.* Manchester, U.K.: Manchester University Press.

Peston, Robert. 2005. *Brown's Britain: How Gordon Runs the Show.* London: Short Books.

Seifert, Roger. 1992. *Industrial Relations in the NHS.* London: Chapman and Hall.

Shaoul, Jean. 2005. "Accounting for Public Money After Privatization: An Information Deficit." Unpublished paper. Manchester Business School, University of Manchester.

Thornley, Carole. 1996. "Segmentation and Inequality in the Nursing Workforce." In *Changing Forms of Employment: Organizations, Skills, and Gender*, edited by Rosemary Crompton, Duncan Gallie, and Kate Purcell. London: Routledge.

Unison. 2004. "Agenda for Change Briefing." October. Accessed March 18, 2005 at http://www.unison.org.uk/resources/does_list.asp?k=health%20Care.

# CHAPTER 6

## Supply Chain Pressures and Migrant Workers: Deteriorating Job Quality in the United Kingdom Food-Processing Industry

*Susan James and Caroline Lloyd*

The food-processing industry is one of the largest manufacturing sectors in the United Kingdom, employing approximately 413,000 workers, representing just under 13 percent of manufacturing employment (ABI 2006). Despite its size and importance, it is in slow decline as consumer expenditure on food stagnates, prices are squeezed, and imports grow. Large supermarket chains increasingly dominate the sale of food products and exert considerable power over large parts of the processing sector. The changing patterns of consumer demand, intensified pressure from retailers, an oversupply in some sectors, and increased levels of regulation, particularly in relation to food hygiene, have led some commentators to describe the environment as "fiercely competitive" (see Dench et al. 2000; IDS 2004; Wilson and Hogarth 2003).

Automated, continuous production processes, using a predominantly low-skilled workforce, are prevalent within much of the industry, and a high proportion of companies produce relatively simple, standardized products for the mass market (Mason, Van Ark, and Wagner 1996; Wilson and Hogarth 2003). The work of food-processing operatives is often low-paid and routine, sometimes physically unpleasant, and prone to high levels of accidents. Recent data indicate that around one-third of jobs fell below the low-pay threshold (LPT) in 2006, with that figure rising to over half for women workers (ASHE 2006). Reflecting the position of many companies as "bottom-end" employers, migrant workers have been an important source of labor for a number of years, a trend that has intensified with the expansion of the European Union and the growth in temporary agencies. However, not all jobs are the same: a few high-profile companies offer better wages than others, and a range of considerable additional benefits, including pensions.

This chapter examines the extent to which changing competitive conditions within food manufacturing are affecting the quality of process operatives' jobs. The first section sets the context for the research by identifying the key features of the UK food-processing industry and the main characteristics of operative jobs. The next section outlines the research methodology, which is based on six case studies undertaken within the meat and confectionary subsectors. The main part of the chapter draws on these cases to explore the ways in which management has sought to improve competitiveness and its implications for the quality of employment. In this investigation we emphasize work organization, health and safety, pay and benefits, and opportunities for progression. The final section considers how far the regulatory and institutional environment has shaped elements of job quality. The evidence from this chapter indicates that in the absence of a tightly regulated labor market, the increasing power of the supermarkets, alongside the widespread availability of cheap migrant labor, has placed downward pressure on terms and conditions of employment.

## THE UNITED KINGDOM FOOD-PROCESSING INDUSTRY

The food-processing sector has traditionally been regarded as one of the more successful parts of manufacturing in the United Kingdom. In the early 1980s, it was second to the United States in terms of output and in ownership of the world's largest multinational companies (MNCs) (Smith, Child, and Rowlinson 1990). Although it still remains an important part of the manufacturing sector, with a turnover of £66 billion (US$135 billion) in 2005 (ABI 2006), and does reasonably well in comparative productivity measures, it has nevertheless slipped behind Germany and France to become the third-largest food manufacturer in Europe. As with many other advanced industrialized economies, consumer expenditure on food in the United Kingdom has failed to keep pace with the growth in national income, and real food prices have been in decline. The combination of these trends, alongside a growing penetration of the UK market by imports, has seen the value of turnover fall by 10 percent over the last decade. Despite concerns about foreign competition, the sector is far less open than many others, with imports accounting for only 26 percent of the market in 2004 (ONS 2006a). The perishable nature of many products, the existence of specific national tastes, and the bulkiness of certain foods that makes transport costs prohibitive help maintain home production advantages (Dench et al. 2000).

Over 15,000 enterprises are involved in the manufacture of food products in the United Kingdom. Around 90 percent of these are small companies of less than 20 people (SBSAU 2006), which tend to offer a narrow range of products or to serve predominantly local markets. However, in terms of turnover and employment, it is the larger organizations that dominate in the form of MNCs, subsidiaries of foreign-owned enterprises, and large, homegrown manufacturers. Companies with more than 250 employees in the United Kingdom account for over 70 percent of the workforce and three-quarters of industry output. Despite the gradual trend toward consolidation within the sector, firms tend to specialize in particular market segments—for example, Cadbury Schweppes in confectionary and soft drinks and United Biscuits in cookies and snacks. A further key distinction, also reflected in profit levels, is between companies that mainly or exclusively manufacture their own brands and those that produce retailers' "own labels." For the largest 150 food manufacturers, branded producers made average profit margins of 13 percent, compared to 5.4 percent for own-label producers (Davis 2006).

Exports account for only 15 percent of sales in the United Kingdom (ONS 2006b), similar to levels found in France and Germany but well below the international orientation of the industry in the Netherlands and Denmark, where over one-half and two-thirds of production, respectively, is exported. As a result, the structure and organization of the increasingly concentrated domestic retail markets in these three large economies is extremely important for manufacturers. The United Kingdom has one of the most concentrated retail sectors in Europe (DEFRA 2006a), ensuring that the balance of power is firmly set in favor of the largest food retailers. The "Big Four" supermarkets—Tesco, Sainsbury's, ASDA (acquired by Wal-Mart in 2003), and Morrisons—account for 62 percent of all grocery sales (DEFRA 2006a). The intense competition between these supermarkets features a significant emphasis on price, particularly for more basic products, and extensive use of their own labels. At the same time, there has been a rapid expansion in the convenience food market, predominantly in prepreparedmeals and snacks, as well as in the higher-priced specialist and luxury food markets. Although the latter may attract a higher margin for manufacturers, supermarkets have increasingly moved to compete in these "premium" sectors with their own labels, thereby threatening to undermine the position of the branded companies. Within Europe, the United Kingdom is now second only to Switzerland in shares of own-label products, at close to 40 percent of the grocery market (DEFRA 2006a).

The Big Four's centralized buying policies ensure that the supermarkets have little or no direct contact with either the grower or the farmer, while being able to dictate prices and terms to manufacturers and suppliers (Duffy, Fearne, and Hornibrook 2003). Suppliers are subject to intensive audits and accreditation, particularly in relation to hygiene and quality procedures, which adds to the costs and duplicates the increasing levels of European statutory regulation (DEFRA 2006b; Newsome and Thompson 2006). Sally Dench and her colleagues (2000) found that the greatest pressures were exerted on those manufacturers that supply supermarket own-label products. Strong and well-known brands in this environment are in a better negotiating position, given that customers will expect to see these products on the shelves, but they can also be threatened with "delisting" (removal from shelves) and may be expected to pay for promotional discounts (Duffy, Fearne, and Hornibrook 2003). These pressures on brands, alongside relatively stagnant markets, have led a number of large MNCs to rationalize their manufacturing facilities across Europe. Mars, Nestlé, Unilever, Heinz, and Kraft, for example, have all closed plants (some in the United Kingdom), divested lower-margin businesses, and either threatened or actually shifted some production to low-cost sites in Eastern Europe, Russia, and China.

Since the early 1980s, concern about retailer practices and the general concentration of the sector have led to the referral of the grocery sector on a number of occasions to the Monopolies and Mergers Commission (MMC). However, it was not until 2001, following a recommendation from the Competition Commission (the body that replaced the MMC), that a statutory "Code of Practice" was introduced, detailing how the big supermarket retailers should deal with their suppliers. The commission had found widespread examples of "requiring or requesting . . . non-cost related payments or discounts, sometimes retrospectively; imposing charges and making changes to contractual arrangements without adequate notice; and unreasonably transferring risks from the main party to the supplier" (CC

2000, 6). Attempts to assess the effectiveness of the code (and its use) have been hindered by fears among suppliers about the repercussions of complaining (OFT 2004, 2006). In 2006 the sector was again referred to the MMC, with a requirement to include an evaluation of supply chain effects. Initial findings reported that although there were no "widespread problems in the supply chain, there are still concerns" (CC 2007). However, there continues to be a problem of individual suppliers being unwilling to provide specific evidence on the activities and power of the supermarkets.

## FOOD-PROCESSING WORK

Employment has been in a slow decline over the past twenty years, with an estimated 300,000 jobs lost in the food and drinks sector (DEFRA 2006b). Most of this decline has been attributed to the gradual concentration and automation of production. Men, who account for nearly two-thirds of the workforce, predominantly work as machine operatives or in off-line jobs, while women have tended to be concentrated in the most unskilled areas, particularly packing (Flecker, Meil, and Pollert 1998; Smith, Child, and Rowlinson 1990). Over the last six years, the proportion of part-time women has declined significantly (see table 6.1). Full-time work is the main organization of working time, with only around one-tenth of the workforce now on part-time contracts. In addition, unlike in most other European economies, overtime is a common feature of the sector, with 20 percent of full-time men working in excess of forty-eight hours per week (ASHE 2006). The proportion of ethnic minorities working in the sector and the age profile reflect the distribution within the United Kingdom's population as a whole (Improve 2006).

The manufacturing process within the food industry, as well as the job of process operative, varies considerably—from continuous production with high levels of automation right down to handmade, individual, or small-batch products (Dench et al. 2000; DfES 2001). Automating the production process is believed to have led to a reduction in the demand both for traditional (higher-level) technical skills and for unskilled workers carrying out routine manual operations (DfES 2001). Research on the sector indicates that, with the exception of the small craft producers, skill requirements in food processing are generally fairly basic and are often related to manual dexterity or simply the ability to undertake routine and repetitive

Table 6.1 Employment Levels in Food Manufacturing: Great Britain (Thousands), June 2000, 2004, and 2006

| | Male Full-Time | Percentage of Total | Male Part-Time | Percentage of Total | Female Full-Time | Percentage of Total | Female Part-Time | Percentage of Total | Total |
|---|---|---|---|---|---|---|---|---|---|
| 2000 | 253.7 | 60.3 | 10.5 | 2.5 | 109.9 | 26.1 | 46.6 | 11.1 | 420.6 |
| 2004 | 236.8 | 62.8 | 9.8 | 2.6 | 97.7 | 25.9 | 32.5 | 8.6 | 376.8 |
| 2006 | 225.5 | 62.1 | 9.3 | 2.6 | 98.5 | 27.1 | 30.0 | 8.3 | 363.2 |

*Source:* Office for National Statistics (ONS) (2001, 2005, 2006c). Figures for Northern Ireland are not available. The data are derived from a different survey from that used to estimate the U.K. employment figure.

Figure 6.1  Gross Hourly Wages of Food, Drink, and
         Tobacco Process Operatives, by Gender, 2006

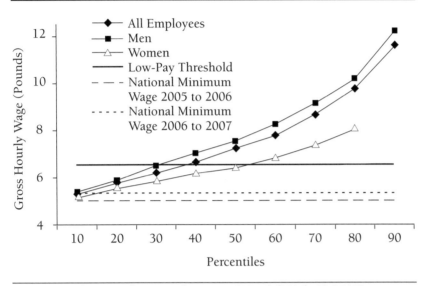

Source: Annual Survey of Hours and Earnings (ASHE) (2006), SOC 8111.

tasks (Dench et al. 2000; Wilson and Hogarth 2003). Many jobs can
be learned in a short space of time, often less than a week, with training predominantly driven by health and safety and hygiene regulations (Dench et al. 2000). It is not surprising, therefore, that over half
of all employees in the sector do not have a qualification (level 2) that
reaches even basic school-leaving expectations (at sixteen years of
age in the United Kingdom), compared to one-third for the population as a whole (Improve 2006; Leitch 2005).

Pay rates for most process operators are low: around one-third of
all workers, and over half of women, are paid below the LPT in 2006
(figure 6.1). This rate is similar to that found in Germany but contrasts significantly with Denmark, France, and the Netherlands,
where only a relatively small proportion of workers in this sector are
low-paid. Women earn on average 84 percent of the male wage, while
part-timers suffer the lowest wages regardless of gender (figure 6.2).
Reflecting the different market segments, as well as premiums on
shift patterns such as nights and weekends, pay rates vary significantly, with the top fifth of operatives earning over £10 (US$20.45)

Figure 6.2 Gross Hourly Wages of Food, Drink, and Tobacco Process Operatives, by Full-Time and Part-Time Work

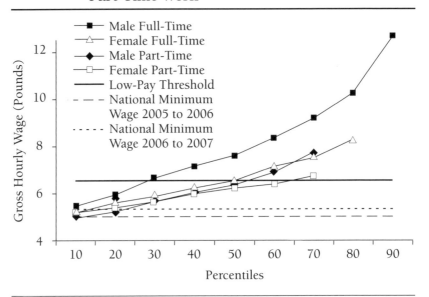

*Source:* Annual Survey of Hours and Earnings (ASHE) (2006), SOC 8111.

per hour and the bottom quarter paid less than £6 (US$12.27). Typical of the United Kingdom's industrial relations system, there are no sectoral collective bargaining agreements in this sector, as are found in many other European countries. Nevertheless, trade unions are recognized in many of the larger companies, where they negotiate over pay and conditions.

Food processing is accepted, even by employers, as having a poor reputation, with low pay, generally repetitive and boring work, unpopular shift arrangements, and a poor health and safety record (Dench et al. 2000; HSE 1999; Scott 1994; Wilson and Hogarth 2003). One indication of the low quality of many jobs in the sector is the high labor turnover rate, which is estimated at between 20 and 30 percent over the last four years, compared to a manufacturing median of 15 to 18 percent (CIPD 2003, 2004, 2005, 2006). However, turnover varies considerably depending on the employer. According to Dench and her colleagues (2000), those employers that have a relatively high status within the local community, including paying higher salaries, have significantly lower levels of turnover and fewer problems in recruiting new employees.

Migrant labor (sometimes illegal) has been a feature of the food industry for many years, particularly for lower-paying organizations and those requiring seasonal workers. Companies in the East Midlands, for example, have relied heavily on workers from Europe (particularly Portugal) and from the Indian subcontinent (Wilson and Hogarth 2003). Labour Force Survey estimates indicate that 13,000 foreign-born workers were employed in the food, drink, and tobacco sector in 2000 (Dobson et al. 2001). More recently, the government has sought to encourage migrants in a bid to meet reported shortages at the bottom end of the labor market. In 2002 a work permit scheme was introduced that enabled the recruitment of individuals from outside the European Union, specifically for jobs in fish and meat processing; as a result of this scheme, 4,355 workers entered the United Kingdom in 2005 (Salt and Millar 2006). However, it was the opening up of jobs to workers from the accession countries (the Czech Republic, Estonia, Hungary, Latvia, Lithuania, Poland, Slovakia, and Slovenia) in 2004 that has brought a large influx of migrants. A recent survey (Precision Prospecting 2005) on the use of temporary workers in the food sector estimated that there were 150,000 workers filling an average of 40,000 jobs as they move in and out of the sector and the country. Ninety percent of those workers were migrants, and 64 percent came from the accession countries.

Major concerns have been raised about the treatment of migrant workers and, more recently, their impact on local communities. The death of twenty-one Chinese cockle pickers (working illegally) in 2004 in Morecombe Bay provided the impetus for the regulation of "gangmasters" (organizations or individuals that provide people to undertake work in the agriculture and food industry). Since August 2006, all agencies and employers providing labor to the food-processing industry must have a license, although the requirements are limited mainly to proof of adherence to employment law. The movement of many migrant workers into rural areas, where much of the food-processing sector is located, has raised concerns about the ability of local services to cope amid sometimes hostile reactions from the incumbent populations (see, for example, CAB 2005).

It is perhaps surprising, given its size and importance to the United Kingdom's economy, that the food-processing industry has rarely been a focus of academic study or policy interest. It is one of the few parts of the manufacturing sector that employs significant proportions of low-wage workers, yet we know very little about what happens to them within the firm. This research therefore provides a unique opportunity to explore some fundamental questions at the heart of current government policymaking. How positive an impact are new employment regulations having on the quality of working life? We know that retailers are squeezing costs out of suppliers, but what effect is this having on their employment strategies? Crucially, is the growth in the employment of migrant workers having a detrimental influence on the quality of process operative jobs?

## THE MEAT-PROCESSING AND CONFECTIONARY INDUSTRIES

The case studies in this chapter were drawn from the confectionary and meat-processing industries. These two sectors provide significant contrasts in terms of their relationships with retailers and the general competitive environments that they face. Meat processing is the largest sector in food manufacturing, representing 20 percent (£13.8 billion (US$28.23 billion)) of total output and employing 112,000 people (ABI 2006). This sector has been in a long-term decline that has been fueled by the reduction in consumption of joints of meat and exacerbated by more recent downturns following the BSE (mad cow disease) crisis and the foot-and-mouth outbreak. Meat is a prime example of where the supermarkets wield considerable power: because of their extensive use of discounting and tight controls over prices, manufacturers struggle to make a profit. It is estimated that over two-thirds of all meat sales are through the four largest supermarket chains (Fenn 2005), with the vast majority being sold as own-label. In the context of retailers rationalizing their suppliers, more stringent quality standards, and the rising costs of raw materials, a series of mergers have taken place in the United Kingdom and across Europe. Despite greater concentration within the sector, it nevertheless remains relatively fragmented and highly competitive. Gross value added (GVA) per employee at £30,500 (US$62,384) is well below the average in food processing (£42,200 (US$86,314)), while labor costs as a proportion of value-added is significantly higher—63 percent compared to the industry average of 49 percent (ABI 2006).

The confectionary sector accounts for 7.9 percent of food manufacturing; with a total output of £5.2 (US$10.63) billion, it employs 26,000 workers (ABI 2006). In contrast to meat processing, supermarkets have far less influence on confectionary companies. There are a greater variety of distribution outlets—for example, gas stations and convenience shops—and a very small percentage of own-label products (5 percent) (Tambe 2003, 29). Furthermore, the sector is dominated by three big MNCs—Cadbury Schweppes, Masterfoods, and Nestlé Rowntree—which together account for over two-thirds of the market. GVA per employee is very high, at over £91,000 (US$186.113), with labor costs representing only 31 percent of total value added. The importance of brands has ensured that some companies have been able to achieve high profit margins, often at levels of over 10 percent. In addition, the influence of the Quaker family roots of some of these companies, such as Cadbury and Rowntree, has traditionally led to relatively good terms and conditions of employment, alongside a significant role for trade unions. However, stagnating markets have led to rationalization of production facilities and job losses across Europe and within the United Kingdom.

In selecting cases for the research, it was decided that only larger workplaces (with over one hundred employees) would be included in order to capture those companies that employ significant numbers of operatives and thus have the potential to offer some sort of progression opportunities. The aim was also to provide examples of different product markets and union/non-union presence in order to see whether these factors affected the quality of employment. We approached fifty-three companies over a fifteen-month period; only five agreed to give us access. One more meat case was included on the basis of interviews with union representatives only.

The extreme difficulties encountered in securing access can partly be explained by the intense pressure that companies faced; these pressures left them with little space for what were perceived as nonessential activities. It may also be that a number of companies were simply unwilling to reveal what happens within their plants, whether legal or illegal. While the best employers are probably excluded from our case studies—given that the major MNCs operating in the confectionary industry declined to take part—it would be fair to assume, given that they agreed to give us access, that the companies in this study exemplify the better-than-average employer in the food-processing sector.[1]

The six case study companies were in the mid to upper end of their

Table 6.2 The Case Study Food-Processing Companies

| | Confectionary | | | Meat | | |
|---|---|---|---|---|---|---|
| | Chocs | SweetCo | Novelty | Clucks | PoultryCo | BaconCo |
| Ownership | Midsized Europe | Single-Site United Kingdom | Single Business United Kingdom | Midsized United States | Large United States | Midsized United Kingdom |
| Workplace size[a] | | | | | | |
| Employees | 100 to 150 | 100 to 150 | 500 to 750 | 500 to 750 | 500 to 750 | 100 to150 |
| Agency | Up to 100 | Up to 50 | Up to 300 | Up to 100 | Up to 150 | Up to 70 |
| Unionized | Yes | Yes | No | Yes | Yes | Yes |
| Female | 55% | 60% | 45% | 37%[d] | 33% | 10% |
| Part-Time | 4% | 40% | 5% | 8%[d] | 2% | 0% |
| Total interviewees[b] | 17 | 8 | 11 | 18 | 14 | 2 |
| Management | 3 | 2 | 4 | 6 | 4 | 0 |
| Team leaders/supervisors | 4 | 1 | 3 | 2 | 1 | 0 |
| Operatives/related workers | 10 | 4 | 4 | 10 | 8 | 1 |
| Union/employee representatives | 1 | 1[c] | 3 | 2 | 1 | 2[c] |
| Temporary work agency interview | Yes | Yes | Yes | Yes | No | No |
| Factory tour | Yes | No | Yes | Yes | Yes | No |

Source: Authors' compilation.
Note: All companies were guaranteed anonymity; therefore, pseudonyms have been provided.
[a] Details have been left vague to avoid identification of the companies.
[b] Numbers do not necessarily add up, since union representatives are also included under their job role.
[c] Includes a full-time officer.
[d] Figures also cover another factory on a nearby site.

product markets and, with one exception, were unionized (see table 6.2). We conducted semistructured face-to-face interviews with a range of managers, team leaders, production operatives, and trade union and employee representatives, and we were given guided tours in four of the factories. In addition, we undertook telephone interviews with managers of three temporary work agencies that served four of the companies. In total, seventy-three interviews took place, ranging in length from thirty minutes for operatives to between one and two hours for managers. All but four interviews were recorded and transcribed. Because management put forward individuals for interviews, the issue of selection bias was raised, but in all cases it was possible to talk to union or employee representatives.

## COMPETITIVE CONDITIONS

The three meat-processing case studies appear to be characteristic of their sector in terms of their reliance on own-label production for supermarkets and their low margins (see table 6.3). Clucks and PoultryCo were very similar in that they both processed chickens that were mainly sourced in-house, they were both owned by a private company based in the United States, and they both supplied own-label products to two major supermarkets. While PoultryCo produced fresh meat cuts and processed ready-meals, Clucks was purely a further processing plant that undertook the marinating and cooking of chicken. BaconCo slaughtered, butchered, and packed fresh pork and further processed the meat into one bacon product. Eighty percent was sold as own-label to one large supermarket chain; the remainder was used as ingredients for products at the company's other plants. Having been a loss-making business that changed hands a number of times, BaconCo had recently started to make a small profit.

Management at the two chicken companies cited the rising cost of raw materials and price squeezes by the retailers as the key factors behind their low profit margins. As a result, they were under constant pressure to reduce costs while also having to respond to the supermarkets' stricter guidelines and regulations on quality control. A Clucks general manager explained:

> My job, as well as the rest of the guys' jobs, is how do we do it better in the factory to then compensate for the fact that the retailers continue to put the thumbscrews on, to drive the prices . . . down.

Table 6.3 Market Characteristics of the Case Study Food-Processing Companies

| | Chocs | SweetCo | Novelty | Clucks | PoultryCo | BaconCo |
|---|---|---|---|---|---|---|
| Product | Chocolates | Sweets and chocolate products | Sweets and chocolate products | Cooked chicken products | Fresh/prepared chicken, ready-meals | Fresh pork and bacon |
| Main market | Upper end/adult, seasonal | Adult/mid-market | Niche/children/seasonal | Midmarket | Low- to upper-end market | Midmarket |
| Production process | Large-batch | Mass production | Batch/mass production | Large-batch | Large-batch 8 | Mass production |
| Percentage branded | 66 | 100 | 25[a] | 0 | 5 | 20[b] |
| Percentage retailer own-label | 33 | 0 | 50 | 100 | 95 | 80 |
| Ownership changes last six years | — | Management buyout | Family firm sold to PLC | Family firm sold to MNC | — | Sold to larger company |
| Change in profit levels last six years | Improved 5 to 10% | Loss-making before MBO; now 3 to 5%; insufficient to pay off debts | Varied; 2005–2006 a good year; 5 to 10% | Margins of around 1% | Margins of less than 3% | Loss-making to very small profit |

Source: Authors' compilation.
[a] Plus 25 percent for other confectionery companies.
[b] To other plants.

Although costs were a key issue, the biggest problem for management was dealing with the supermarkets' constantly changing demands, which made it impossible to plan even on a daily basis. Examples were given of orders being doubled or tripled at 8:30 in the morning, with delivery required by 7:00 in the evening, which is particularly difficult to do when dealing with a perishable product. The previous year Clucks had nearly lost its business with one supermarket (which accounted for around half of the factory's output) because of an inability to meet these types of short-term orders. As one manager explained, relatively long-term relationships based on trust had been replaced with short-term contracts undertaken on the Internet, where a supplier could be dropped at any time. Not all of the Big Four supermarkets behaved in the same way; two of the companies (BaconCo and PoultryCo) commended one supermarket in particular for providing relatively stable orders.

The three confectionary companies manufactured their own brands and had a more diversified range of outlets for their products. Chocs had a long history of making a traditional type of chocolate but had recently diversified into a more modern, youthful market. It also undertook significant own-label production for two retailers. SweetCo, a recent management buyout (MBO) of a loss-making business, had originally been owned by one of the main confectionary MNCs in the United Kingdom. It mass-produced a small range of strong brands that, with the exception of one product, were consumed year-round. Novelty was a niche manufacturer of a large number of different confectionary products, predominantly aimed at children. It had a smaller share of branded products, with the majority produced under contract to other confectionary companies and as own-label for retailers. In contrast to the meat processors, these three companies were making reasonable operating profits, although SweetCo's profit margin was not sufficient to cover interest payments on the debt acquired from the buyout.

Although the supermarkets did not wield power to the same extent over the confectionary manufacturers, the supermarkets remained a key outlet for their products. A major source of frustration was the difficulty in gaining access to shelf space over the whole year, as retailers considered many of the three companies' products to be seasonal. In addition, cost pressures manifested in the form of demands for cheaper prices and discounts, while uncertainty and changing orders had led to sudden peaks or slumps in production.

Nevertheless, as producers of nonperishable and branded goods, they had a certain amount of leeway in their ability to manufacture for stock. Both Chocs and Novelty worked largely with nonsupermarket retailers for their own-label products, and they saw these relationships as more partnership-based and longer-term. Consequently, these two companies did not experience the same pricing and very short-term order fluctuations as those dealing with some of the supermarkets. However, a significant proportion of Novelty's market was based on its ability to respond rapidly to contractors' demands, which inevitably led to uncertainty and variability in production schedules.

## Keeping Up with the Competition

All six companies had made changes to their operations in the last five years in order to be successful—or simply to survive—in the context of a relatively difficult competitive environment. Four of the companies had responded by making substantial investments in the development of new products (see table 6.4), and most had been successful. For example, Novelty had introduced a range of year-round products, while PoultryCo had moved into the more lucrative area of ready-meals and was involved in developing a range of products in partnership with a supermarket. Nevertheless, of central importance to all of the case study companies were the steps that had been taken to remove costs from the business.

All but BaconCo had purchased new pieces of equipment designed to increase levels of automation. SweetCo was furthest along in this process: it had just installed a robotic system to replace the one remaining area of hand-packing. In general, technology tends to be introduced in a piecemeal fashion: a new machine may be fed by one that is fifty years old. As a result, the machines often have to be "patched together" by the intervention of simple manual operations. Clucks had invested in a continuous cooker and automated packing machine, but the meat still had to be individually hand-placed on the conveyor belt to enter the cooker. Typically, recent technological change had reduced quality variability, increased output, and removed some of the most labor-intensive and least-skilled manual operations. Other "process improvements" were also being made, such as removing blockages between lines and reorganizing work flows, ensuring that workers had less downtime. There were also examples

Table 6.4 Innovation and Cost-Saving Measures in the Last Five Years

| | Chocs | SweetCo | Novelty | Clucks | PoultryCo | BaconCo |
|---|---|---|---|---|---|---|
| New products | Yes | Yes | Yes | No | Yes | No |
| Technological and process changes | Some | Major | Major | Major | Some | None |
| Work intensification | No | Yes | Yes | Yes | Yes | Yes |
| Agency workers | Increased; sole recruitment source | Increased; occasional recruitment source | Increased; main recruitment source | Increased; sole recruitment source | Increased; main recruitment source | Increased; recruit direct from overseas |
| Wages | Relative decline | Relative decline | — | Relative decline | Relative decline | — |
| Labor turnover (estimates) | 10% | 4% | 32% | 34% | 15% | n.a. |
| Main reductions in benefits | Closed final salary pension scheme | Loss of canteen; cuts in sick pay, pensions, maternity leave, etc. | — | Closed pension scheme | Closed pension scheme to new recruits; cut sick pay | — |

*Source:* Authors' compilation.

in five of the companies of straightforward work intensification through having fewer workers on a line, speeding up lines, or increasing targets.

Another way of reducing costs, pursued by all the companies, involved suppressing wage increases below inflation and reducing operatives' benefits. This relatively slow process, however, might cut labor costs by only a percentage point or two each year. In contrast, replacing direct employees with agency workers can deliver much faster results, particularly in workplaces with high labor turnover. All the companies had been using agency workers over a number of years, predominantly to deal with seasonal fluctuations in demand—prior to Christmas and Easter for the confectionary companies and during the barbecue season and at Christmas for the meat processing companies. More recently, all the companies had increased the number of agency workers and were using them for more varied reasons.

The main benefit of agency workers they cited was being able to match workers more closely to fluctuating orders; this flexibility allowed lower levels of overtime and a reduction in the number of core staff who had to be paid even if there was no work available. As one production manager at PoultryCo explained, "It's just an easy turn-on of the tap." The ease with which the "tap" could also be turned off ensured that job losses as a result of new technology or the removal of a product could be made without the negative consequences of redundancies. Crucially, agency workers were cheaper than employees; because they were paid lower wage rates and lacked rights to company benefits, making them cost-effective even for those companies (SweetCo and BaconCo) that experienced minimal variations in orders. A Chocs section leader was blunt:

> From a financial level, let's be brutal about it—we have no commitment to them other than during the time they are here. . . .
> From a cost point of view, although we are paying for their hourly rate, the pensions, holiday, sickness, etc., again, that's gone. . . .
> [It's] harsh, but the reality is, if there is somebody who is really difficult, just doesn't really fit in, we can get rid of them.

With the opening up of the UK labor market to the accession countries, all but SweetCo had shifted to mainly using Polish workers, as it had been generally found to be easier to deal with foreign nationals from only one country. A number of managers explained the difficulties of dealing with several different languages; tensions between some national groups could also be a problem. With only one foreign language, each factory needed only a couple of Polish workers with fluent English who could translate for the non-English-speaking majority. Company managers expressed extreme satisfaction with most of the new workers, whom they described as "more willing" and "able" than local people. One section leader at PoultryCo explained:

> I would say each year . . . it's got better and better, so that the caliber of people that come to us are extremely good. . . . Of course, if they are coming from, say, Eastern Europe, wages are so poor there that the attraction of what is a considerable wage, not for living standards here but what can be taken home, means that they want to work, and that's incredible, people who are coming here who are intelligent, who really want to work even though the job may be repetitive and boring.

An additional advantage was that agency workers could be used as a pool from which to draw any permanent employees required, thereby avoiding the constraints of recruiting in local labor markets.

## THE QUALITY OF EMPLOYMENT

### WORK ORGANIZATION

The majority of workers in the case study companies were classified as food operatives, a broad job category that covered a variety of roles within the manufacturing process. The lowest-paid jobs were those that involved routine manual operations where the only machinery was a moving conveyor belt. In confectionary, these workers were predominantly female hand-packers who, for example, put chocolates into a box. In meat processing, simple manual tasks also took place in production, such as placing chicken onto a conveyor belt prior to cooking. These jobs were highly repetitive, with very short cycle times, and in confectionary they often required considerable dexterity. For example, at Chocs a packer was expected to count and place ten sweets into a box seventeen times in one minute. Normally taking only around a week or so to become proficient, those who filled these jobs were often temporary agency workers.

In the more automated areas, the tasks tended to involve fewer small hand movements and had slightly more variety. Operatives were involved in supplying and moving products—for example, feeding cartons into a packing machine or removing bags of sweets that were not the correct weight. Some jobs required the use of machines that, for example, stapled bags, wrapped sweets, or inserted ingredients. Since these jobs, and those of hand-packers, involved repetitive movements, most of the companies had introduced some form of job rotation so that workers moved around a line undertaking a range of similar tasks.

The more complex operative jobs, and those that normally received additional payments, usually entailed responsibility for a specific area or piece of machinery within the production process. For example, a tumbler operator prepared and mixed ingredients, while a labeler ran the labeling machine for a line, making frequent adjustments and sorting out minor problems. In confectionary, the operatives' roles were more complex because manufacturing the product—chocolates and sweets—involved using a wider range of ingredients, heating, cooling, molding, and enrobing. The process was also subject to variation as a result of external temperatures and ingredients, making it necessary for operatives to intervene even in automated processes. In some areas, small teams of operatives shared the tasks required for a section of production, such as adding ingredients, setting up, and monitoring temperatures, consistencies, and cooking times or adjusting the line for different products and in some cases minor repairs. Some of these jobs could take several months to learn.

Job segregation by gender was apparent within the factories, although there was some evidence that this division was not as strict as it had been in the past. In all cases, with the exception of BaconCo, where 90 percent of workers were men, women disproportionately worked in the lowest grades, particularly in packing. The small number of part-time and fixed-hour contracts, designed to suit women with young children, were used mainly to fill the packing lines. In production areas, the lowest grades were normally full-time positions that were often worked on a rotating two-shift system (a week of 6:00 AM to 2:00 PM shifts followed by a week of 2:00 PM to 10:00 PM). These workers were also mainly women. However, increasing numbers of men were filling these jobs; for the most part, they were agency workers, but they also included older men, age fifty and over, many of whom had lost jobs in other industries. Women were working in the higher-skilled operative grades and supervisory positions in greater numbers, yet men still took the large majority of these jobs. Although most operatives had left school at sixteen with few, if any, qualifications, there were some workers with qualifications and experience in other areas of work—for example, as an apprenticed baker and butcher, a chef, a mechanic, and a hairdresser.

Operatives on the basic grades found their work to be boring and highly repetitive. Job rotation had been introduced, but this simply meant undertaking three or four equally dull tasks rather than just one. One agency worker operative at Chocs complained, "You stay in packing room, and your job is to pack, to pack, to pack, to pack . . . is very boring for myself . . . to be just packer, I feel very stupid." A BaconCo operative described his job:

> My job is doing this: I have to bend down—I have five or six hundred pieces to do, have to bend down six hundred times, pick it up six hundred times, put it in the machine six hundred times. All six hundred times, take it out, pick it up, turn it round, clip it six hundred times. Pick it up, put it in another container six hundred times.

The ability of line operatives to talk together as they worked was considered by many to be essential to making these very repetitive jobs bearable and for a few even enjoyable. However, workers at some companies (Chocs, Novelty, and PoultryCo) complained that this social aspect of factory life was being undermined by their inability to communicate with agency workers, many of whom spoke little English. Those with higher-graded jobs expressed less dissatisfaction with the actual content of the work. Although these jobs were not considered particularly challenging or interesting, they did provide a less routine and repetitive range of tasks.

Most workers were said to "work in teams," although team meetings took place only at Chocs. This was also the only company where senior managers were considered to have a reasonable relationship with shop-floor workers. In the other cases, managers appeared to do little to actively engage employees; in particular, workers felt that communication was virtually nonexistent, and they were rarely consulted over changes affecting their work. A positive dislike or distrust of meetings was apparent among a number of the factory managers (BaconCo, SweetCo, Clucks), leading to a vacuum of information. "I think personally there is no communication whatsoever, unless it's a bollocking," said one operative at SweetCo. Another at PoultryCo noted: "We are not stupid. You know, we still got a brain, although we tend to leave it at home when we come to work because you don't need to use it. But we have an opinion, and we think we should have more input." The trade unions within the companies seemed unable to push for greater openness or for effective consultation. Although consultative bodies existed (except at BaconCo), they had fallen into disuse at SweetCo, PoultryCo, and Clucks because management viewed them as an optional extra that they could ill afford.

## Health and Safety

Food processing has one of the worst health and safety records in manufacturing, with most problems being linked to manual handling and slippages. Conditions in the confectionary factories were generally fairly good, and, although relatively noisy, most areas were clean and kept at a reasonable temperature. In contrast, the meat-processing factories were wet, cold, and noisy, with some areas (such as slaughtering) being particularly unpleasant. In both sectors, workers had to wear hairnets, often ear plugs, and rubber boots and were required constantly to wash hands and take off protective clothing with each break.

Trade unions and employee representatives felt that health and safety was the area where they were probably most effective, largely owing to the legislative backing they received. In most cases, local reps undertook regular safety audits and dealt with compensation claims. The main issues in packing and line operative jobs were injuries relating to repetitive work routines, which can lead to repetitive strain injury (RSI), back, shoulder, and neck problems. In these companies, job rotation was the most frequent response, although its use was by no means systematic. At Clucks and PoultryCo, health and safety was given a high profile; as a result, these companies had very few accidents. Job rotation (normally every thirty minutes at each company) took place in all areas with short cycle times. Nevertheless, at Clucks there were regular problems with extremely low temperatures, and less attention seemed to have been given to reducing the physically heavy tasks. Some jobs were identified as "male only" because of the weights involved. One male operative at Clucks said: "We shift sort of ten tons plus a day, the five of us on that line, so lifting and throwing it on the line and moving it about. You do a lot of lifting, and it is now starting to play my back up." Chocs was also considered to be "strict" in terms of health and safety, although job rotation took place in most areas only once per shift. The non-unionized Novelty was the worst example in confectionary: minor accidents and injuries were common, and job rotation was implemented only in certain areas. A female team leader at Novelty explained, "On cellotape, you cut your hands to pieces, you get blisters, and the [machines], your neck goes. . . .they are horrific, they are horrible lines, and I am too tall to do them. So we have to pick on little people, and then the backs of their legs go and their necks go, and it's just . . . the lines are cruel." However, the recent introduction of an employee consultative committee had led to some improvements.

The company with the poorest health and safety approach was BaconCo. Work there involved a lot of lifting, and despite the highly repetitive nature of the jobs, in most areas job rotation was not used. Management also frequently failed to deal with potentially hazardous practices and machinery. The workplace union representative claimed that the company had paid out £200,000 (US$409,040) in compensation for injuries related to health and safety issues over the previous seven years, giving recent examples of a finger chopped off, scalds, and shoulder strains. The local union official claimed, "It seems to me that's a price they are willing to pay to get that extra product. . . . Health and safety has been sacrificed for the need to actually produce more."

Long working hours were also a feature of most of the factories (except SweetCo). At Chocs, the introduction of an annualized hours system meant that, for several months a year, all operatives had to work regular ten-hour shifts, five days a week. Some workers found this schedule particularly grueling. "I don't like the ten hours," said one female operative. "This is our fourth month. It's too long. . . . By the time you leave in the morning and then you get home, you go to bed really. I'm quite lucky actually, because my daughters cook my dinner for me."

At four of the companies (Novelty, Clucks, PoultryCo, and BaconCo), overtime work was common for both men and women, and many operatives had signed the "opt-out" of the maximum forty-eight-hour week stipulated in the European Working Time Directive. In the three meat plants, workers reported that in the past they had often worked eighty hours or more per week. Concerns about health and safety had led management at Clucks and PoultryCo to impose a sixty-hour maximum working week, although production demands could, and did, override this. At BaconCo there was no such maximum, and little heed was paid to the rest periods specified in the Working Time Directive. There was no evidence of operatives being coerced to sign the opt-out; instead, they were keen to work extra hours in order to receive additional payments (normally one and a half times their normal rate). A number insisted that, without overtime, take-home pay would be so low that they would be forced to leave.

## Pay and Benefits

Low pay was endemic across the companies: four of the case study plants employed a significant proportion of operatives at rates below the LPT, and all agency staff were paid close to, or at, the NMW (see table 6.5). Pay rates in the five unionized companies were negotiated with the relevant trade unions at the workplace level. The company with the lowest median rates of pay, Chocs, utilized large numbers of hand-packers, while many of those running machines were on the lowest grade. The use of annualized hours was also a factor, in that, despite the scheduling of both shift work and ten-hour days for significant parts of the year, no additional payments were made. BaconCo had the highest median rate, possibly owing to the virtually all-male workforce, as well as the fact that the factory had slaughtering jobs, which are typically higher-paid. Pay rates, however, varied far more *within* each workplace, reflecting the different nature of the operative role. As a result, the highest levels of pay for operatives were found in the confectionary companies, where some jobs required higher levels of skill.

Across the cases, the lowest-paid employees were the small number of packers or line operatives working on fixed shifts, mainly women part-timers, who were paid close to or at the NMW (Novelty, Clucks, and PoultryCo). Pay for agency workers was generally well below that of most direct employees, and only at two confectionary companies were some paid above the minimum wage for shift work and/or higher-level skills. Agency workers were often used at weekends and during unsocial hours (including nights) and were paid at the same or only a little above the standard hourly rate.

In four of the cases, the pay rates for basic operative grades were toward the bottom end of the local labor market, although they were

Table 6.5  Pay Rates for Operatives in Food-Processing Companies

| | Chocs | SweetCo | Novelty | Clucks | PoultryCo[a] | BaconCo |
|---|---|---|---|---|---|---|
| Date | 1.1.05 | 1.4.05 | 1.7.05 | 1.10.05 | 25.2.06 | 1.4.06 |
| Trainee | £5.64 | £6.28 | £5.50[b] | £5.71[b] | £6.22[b] | £5.39 |
| Lowest-paid operative | £5.64 | £7.22 | £5.05 | £5.37 | £5.41 | £6.26 |
| Median pay | £5.64 | £7.22 | £6.45[b] | £6.03[b] | £6.71[b] | £7.61 (mean) |
| Highest grade (percentage of operatives) | £7.61 (3%) | £9.10[b] (33%) | £10.19[b] (0.5%) | £7.11[b] (10%) | £7.77[b] (1%) | £8.24 (n.a.) |
| Percentage below LPT | 83 | 0 | 41 | 63 | 29 | Below 10 |
| Agency pay | £5.05 to £5.52 | £5.05 | 5.05 to £5.60 | £5.05 | £5.05 | £5.05 |
| Highest grade open to operatives (with training) | £9.58 | £9.10[b] | £10.19[b] | £7.38[b] | £8.27[b] | £8.24 |
| Team leader pay (highest) | £8.45 | £12.00 or more[b] | £7.61[b] | £7.38[b] | £8.27[b] | n.a. |

Source: Authors' compilation.
Notes: All rows refer to direct employees except for row 7 (agency pay). LPT = £6.32 per hour.
[a] Pay rates include another factory. Pay in the factory case study was toward the lower end.
[b] Alternating two shifts.

not considered to be out of line with similar jobs available to those with few qualifications. However, pay was felt to have deteriorated at three of these companies (Chocs, Clucks, and PoultryCo), having previously been somewhat higher in relative terms (see table 6.4). The other two companies paid above the norm: BaconCo was located in a low-paying rural area where most other jobs were at the minimum wage, and SweetCo maintained its superior position despite the deterioration in relative pay over the past five years. Even for those in higher-paying jobs, salaries were not considered to be adequate to support a family. The only way to live on the pay was to share accommodation costs, be part of a dual-income family, or undertake substantial levels of overtime. "I have to do overtime," said one female operative at Clucks. "My son works in this factory anyway. . . . My husband, he's disabled, so he can't work. . . . So I do the overtime so that I can pay the mortgage." Nevertheless, relying on overtime to provide a living wage was problematic, since hours could suddenly be reduced, as had happened at Novelty, Clucks, and PoultryCo.

Operatives in the companies also received some benefits that were above the statutory minimum—for example, paid breaks, additional holidays, and sick pay (see table 6.6). Sick pay was one of the most important benefits, and the generosity of the company schemes varied considerably. At SweetCo, workers received 80 percent of salary for six months followed by 50 percent for six months, while at BaconCo the only entitlement was six weeks of full pay for a worker undergoing an operation. All but one company (Clucks) contributed to some sort of pension scheme, although the take-up varied. Cost pressures within the sector, as outlined earlier (see table 6.4), had led many of these companies to reduce benefits; in particular, closing final salary pension schemes, no longer offering pensions, threatening to close existing schemes, and reducing sick pay. The only company moving in the opposite direction was BaconCo, where the union had succeeded in pressing management to introduce very limited sick pay and to raise overtime rates for agency workers and direct employees.

## Progression

The food-processing sector has traditionally offered local people (often in rural areas) employment without any requirements for qualifications, as had been the situation in the six case study plants. Although labor turnover was often high, all of the companies had some

Table 6.6 Hours and Benefits for Food-Processing Operatives (Directly Employed Only)

| | Chocs | SweetCo | Novelty | Clucks | PoultryCo | BaconCo |
|---|---|---|---|---|---|---|
| Main shift pattern | Annualized hours: 8 hours (two rotating shifts) and 10 hours (two to five days per week) | Part-time, fixed, and 8 hours (two rotating shifts) | 8 hours (two rotating shifts) | 8 hours (two rotating shifts) | 8 hours (two rotating shifts) | Fixed, 7:00 AM to 3:30 PM |
| Hours | 39 | 40 | 37.5 | 40 | 40 | 40 |
| Breaks (minutes) | 60, paid | 45, paid | 15, paid; 30, unpaid | 45, paid | 40, paid | 30, paid; 30, unpaid |
| Holidays (days)[a] | 22 to 26, plus 8 bank holidays | 25, plus 8 bank holidays/in lieu | 20 to 25, plus 8 bank holiday/in lieu | 24 to 26, plus 8 bank holidays/in lieu | 20 to 25, plus 8 bank holidays/in lieu | 25 to 26, plus 8 bank holidays |
| Pension | Defined benefit | Company | Stakeholder | None | Company and stakeholder | Money purchase |
| Sick pay (per year)[a] | 6 to 12 weeks at full pay | 12 days at full pay, 6 months at 80%, 6 months at 50% | 5 to 10 days at full pay (not paid first week) | 3 to 26 weeks (not paid first week) | 4 to 16 weeks at full pay (not paid first week) | 6 weeks at full pay for hospital operations only |
| Other | Annual profit-related bonus of up to £500; attendance bonus of up to £250 per year; canteen | (Recently closed canteen) | Annual £250 to £500 bonus for low individual absence; canteen | Canteen | Canteen | None |

Source: Authors' compilation.
[a] Benefits increase with length of service.

workers with long service who had remained more or less on the same basic job or who had progressed to higher-graded positions. Whether this will continue to be possible is open to question. One of the key issues that arose within three of the companies (Chocs, Clucks, and BaconCo) was the claim that the companies no longer recruited local workers, preferring the cheaper and "hardworking" migrant workers from Eastern Europe. At two of the other companies (PoultryCo and Novelty), the majority of new recruits were also taken not from the local labor market but from overseas. At Clucks, this was considered a major issue because of the relatively high levels of local unemployment. A twenty-four-year-old team leader at Clucks commented:

> I am one of the youngest here. . . . People locally do want to work here, because I know people who have applied at the gate, and they have been told there is no positions. And then the next minute I see another person, another agency coming in. So it's not like people don't want to work here.

For a small minority of agency workers, these companies did provide opportunities to move into permanent employment. However, this transition could take considerable time—for some, over two years. Meanwhile, they experienced high levels of job insecurity and no guarantees about a permanent position.

Once workers were established on a basic grade within the companies, their opportunities to move into a machine operative position, quality control, coach, or team leader role were generally considered to be widespread. The exception was BaconCo, where workers could acquire different skills (and more money) but remained routine line operatives. The only progression was to a small number of supervisor positions, and these posts were never openly advertised. At the other two meat companies, although the higher-graded jobs were less routine and repetitive, the extra skills and pay gained were relatively limited, even for positions with more responsibility, such as senior team leader (see table 6.5). In addition, higher-graded jobs were open only to those working full-time at PoultryCo and only to those prepared to work regular overtime at Clucks.

At two of the confectionary companies (Chocs and Novelty), the more complex and varied production processes presented more opportunities, not only within the operative role but also by moving to the position of technician. This new job involved responsibility for setting up the machinery, doing minor maintenance, and undertaking various technical tasks, and it was open to operatives prepared to undertake both on- and off-the-job training. One of the technicians explained that she had started at Chocs as a line operative, was promoted to supervisor, and then moved to her current role. She had completed an NVQ2 in engineering with the company and was undertaking her level 3. In contrast to these two confectionary companies, the third one, SweetCo, no longer provided progression opportunities for those who had reached the position of operative. The gap between operative and team leader was now considered by management to be too great for internal promotion, and all the recent appointments—some of them graduates—had been external. One operative believed that this lack of progression had nothing to do with any lack of capability among the operatives. "I think they [the new management] have a very low opinion of workers," she said, "but there are some very clever people here."

Across the six case study companies, a number of middle and senior managers had worked their way up from the shop floor. Over recent years, however, the widespread cost-cutting practice of removing managerial layers was felt to have curtailed this route, so that once an individual became a team leader, there was little prospect of further advancement.

## A REGULATORY FLOOR VERSUS LABOR MARKET OPENNESS

Within the case study companies, it was clear that pressures to reduce costs and the flexibility requirements of retailers had led managers to pursue a variety of approaches to lowering their labor costs. This section draws out the ways in which employer response has been shaped by the United Kingdom's regulatory and institutional environment. The issues of greatest relevance were found to be the NMW, health and safety legislation, including the Working Time Directive, the regulation of agency work and migrant workers, and trade union activity.

With the growth in the use of low-paid agency workers, the NMW is playing an increasingly important role in regulating pay within the sector. Given the lack of difficulty in recruiting agency workers, it was clear that the minimum wage was acting as a floor to prevent these companies from paying less. Above-inflation rises in the NMW had also seen the bottom grades in some companies converging with the minimum rate. At one company (Novelty), the least-skilled operative grade was paid at the NMW, while at two others (Clucks and PoultryCo) pay was set at only a few pence above the October 2006 rate. However, only a small proportion of employees were paid at the NMW, since most operatives worked shifts and received additional percentage payments on top of these lowest grades. Shift premiums have ensured that differentials are maintained; as long as the NMW is upgraded in line with average earnings, further deterioration in relative pay should be restricted.

The tightening of health and safety legislation over a number of years, much of which has emanated from the European Union, does seem to have led to improvements in the working environment, particularly with regard to long working hours, repetitive movements, and accidents. Nevertheless, there was still considerable variation in managerial approaches and the extent to which companies actively sought to provide a safe working environment. This variation seemed to be influenced by a number of factors, including cost pressures, the broader corporate philosophy, the activities of trade unions and employee representatives, and the specific approach of the factory manager. Only at SweetCo was there seen to be a reversal of past trends: health and safety conditions had recently been undermined as a result of a change of ownership, the drive for output, and the marginalization of trade unions.

One of the main difficulties in health and safety is dealing with issues of repetitive strain and muscular injuries brought about by the very nature of the work. None of the companies had made any attempt to redesign jobs in ways that might remove or improve the routine tasks they entailed. Instead, they hoped that simply introducing job rotation around a set of repetitive actions would alleviate any problems.

A further key aspect of health and safety is specific to the United Kingdom because of the limited regulation of working time in comparison with much of the rest of the European Union: the potential dangers of working long hours in a manufacturing environment with moving machines and cutting equipment. The European Working Time Directive appeared to have led to a reduction in overtime, despite many operatives having signed the forty-eight-hour opt-out. Management attempts to reduce excessive overtime (more than twenty hours per week) derived not just from concerns about the company's liability in the event of a health and safety incident but also from the desire to shift toward the use of cheaper agency workers. However, the continued uncertainty in orders from supermarkets in some companies meant that regulations were still being broken and that longer working hours were permitted for higher-skilled operatives who could not be replaced with agency workers. Cutting working time may be one way of improving the working environment, yet it can have a significant impact on workers' income. Overtime was the main way in which both men and women had sought to ensure a reasonable income, and the reduction in hours had simply cut take-home pay, with no compensatory increases in hourly wage levels.

The lack of equal treatment regulations for agency workers, coupled with the opening up of the labor market to workers from the accession countries, has led to significant increases in the numbers of agency workers. Once used principally for seasonal peaks and troughs, they are now also providing a cheap year-round source of labor. Although companies have to pay agencies a fee, they save financially on holidays, sick pay, pensions, and additional shift and bonus payments. In addition, the companies' lack of commitment to these workers enabled managers to consider them an instantly disposable workforce and to avoid problematical terminations or layoffs among permanent employees.

In the context of the United Kingdom's relatively low levels of unemployment, the availability of large numbers of agency workers had removed any pressure that might have emanated from the labor market. Only one company, SweetCo, had no difficulty in recruiting locally, thanks to its relatively high pay levels. In the other cases, wages and conditions were rarely good enough to attract a sufficient number of the "right quality" of local workers into these jobs. Nevertheless, these recruitment difficulties and, in some cases, high turnover levels, such as at Novelty and Clucks (32 to 34 percent), were not considered major problems because of the constant supply of migrant workers who were keen to be made permanent. At SweetCo, this had become so apparent that the managing director refused to listen to any complaints about low workforce morale, arguing that if anyone did not like working there, ten people were waiting to take their job. Although this was an extreme view, none of the other companies placed any emphasis on the need to improve employee retention or paid much attention to issues such as consultation and communication.

The high density of agency workers in each of the factories had not helped the trade unions in terms of their organizational ability and strength. Only at BaconCo had the union exerted efforts both to recruit agency workers and to improve their conditions through discussions with company management and the agency. In the case study companies, there was evidence of some union influence over pay levels (Clucks and BaconCo), in the development of new grading structures (Clucks, PoultryCo), and on disciplinary and health and safety issues. Union organization, however, tended to be fragile because of declining membership and a lack of effective local stewards, who had no recourse to arguments about recruitment and retention. Their general inability to exert much influence within the case study companies no doubt also reflected the reality that management (with the exception of PoultryCo) had provided few facilities and little time off and, in the past, had resisted or attempted to undermine union organization. Two of the companies (Chocs and BaconCo) recognized the unions only because of legislation. There was no evidence to suggest that conditions in the one non-unionized plant (Novelty) were any better or worse than in the others, although the grading structure (currently under review) was recognized as being discriminatory and arbitrary and health and safety was inferior to the other two confectionary companies.

To sum up, the companies have faced employment and health and safety legislation and active, although weak, trade unions that have constrained their ability to cut labor costs. Nevertheless, the relatively limited nature of the regulations in the labor market and the lack of powerful institutional bodies, in the context of the widespread availability of migrant workers, have muted many of the labor market pressures that these companies might have expected to face.

## SUMMARY AND ASSESSMENT

The quality of operatives' jobs in the six food-processing companies appears to be on a downward trend. Wages are in relative decline, benefits are being cut back, and there is evidence of work intensification. In addition, a growing proportion of the workforce are now agency workers who are offered only the legal minimum in wages and conditions and who suffer from an extremely high level of job insecurity. The one area where conditions are improving is in health and safety; this improvement is largely driven by a combination of union activity and tightening legislation. Most of these jobs are not only badly paid but extremely dull and monotonous. Little attempt has been made to improve functional flexibility or extend basic operative skills through job redesign, as was found in companies in France, Germany, and Denmark. There are opportunities to progress in these companies, but very few operatives manage to move into jobs where the pay rate is high enough to ensure a reasonable standard of living without undertaking significant amounts of overtime.

One of the main factors driving down job quality in meat processing is the relative power of the supermarket retailers. Their ability to squeeze prices and make unreasonable delivery demands forces manufacturers to search continually for ways to reduce costs and increase numerical flexibility. It is rather harder to make the same case for confectionary companies, given that they produce branded goods with a wide variety of outlets. Competition is largely national and based around a relatively stagnant market that requires companies to seek ways to cut costs and increase market share. In both sectors, workers and their trade unions have generally been unable to resist manufacturers that seek competitive advantage by undermining wages and conditions. Even where companies have improved profit margins by moving into higher value-added markets—for example, ready-meals or quality chocolates—there have been no corresponding improvements in pay levels.

The United Kingdom's flexible, low-waged labor market ensures that these companies are able to pursue this "low road," with few, if any, incentives to consider alternative approaches. The availability of migrants who are willing to fill positions as agency workers for rates of pay significantly below the going rate is key. Contrary to the views outlined in a recent House of Lords (2005) report, it is difficult to conclude that the opening up of the labor market to the accession countries is not having a depressive effect on wage levels. Employment regulations introduced under the New Labour government (such as the NMW), the right to union recognition, and the Working Time Directive have failed to improve the quality of working life in these companies. Instead, they are acting largely as buffers to limit the deterioration in conditions and provide a minimum standard for new workers. While industry pressures look very similar across Europe, companies in Denmark, France, and the Netherlands have been less able to compete by reducing wage costs, partly owing to strong sectoral collective bargaining that ensures higher rates of pay and better working conditions. In contrast, the United Kingdom resembles more closely developments in the German meat sector, where pay rates have plummeted owing to high levels of migrant workers and fragmented bargaining. With hourly pay in some areas dropping to between €3 and €5 (US$4.28 to US$7.13), it indicates the importance of the NMW in the United Kingdom in avoiding the worst possibilities for (legal) low pay.

In an industry in which the United Kingdom proudly describes its manufacturers as "world-class innovators" (FFB 2006), it is a stark prospect that all but one of these "better-than-average" companies are paying wages that are so poor that they can fill all their vacancies only by seeking workers from overseas. The prospects for those who are destined to work in jobs at the lower end of the sector, therefore, can only be described as extremely grim. Despite the new regulations on gangmasters, there is little doubt that a section of the workforce will continue to be subject to unscrupulous employers and agencies that are unwilling to meet even the basic legal requirements. Without an NMW that is significantly higher than its current level and rigorously enforced, many jobs across the food-processing industry will remain extremely low-paid and badly designed, providing an inadequate income, a threat to health, and a poor work-life balance.

## NOTES

1. All companies were guaranteed anonymity; therefore, pseudonyms have been provided.

## REFERENCES

Annual Business Inquiry (ABI). 2006. *Annual Business Inquiry 2005*. London: Office of National Statistics.

Annual Survey of Hours and Earnings (ASHE). 2006. *Annual Survey of Hours and Earnings*. London: Office of National Statistics.

Certified Institute of Personnel Development (CIPD). 2003. *Labour Turnover 2003: A Survey of Ireland and the U.K.* London: CIPD.

———. 2004. *Recruitment, Retention, and Turnover 2004: A Survey of the U.K. and Ireland*. London: CIPD.

———. 2005. *Recruitment, Retention, and Turnover: Annual Survey Report 2005*. London: CIPD.

————. 2006. *Recruitment, Retention, and Turnover: Annual Survey Report 2006*. London: CIPD.

Citizens Advice Bureau (CAB). 2005. *Home from Home: Experiences of Migrant Workers in Rural Parts of the U.K. and the Impact on Local Service Providers*. London: CAB.

Competition Commission (CC). 2000. *Supermarkets: A Report on the Supply of Groceries from Multiple Stores in the U.K.*, Volume 1. London: CC.

————. 2007. "Grocery Inquiry Goes Local" (press release). January 23, London.

Davis, Glynn. 2006. "Rising to the Challenge." *The Grocer* (July 1): 32–36.

Dench, Sally, Jim Hillage, Peter Reilly, and Jenny Kodz. 2000. *Employers Skill Survey: Case Study—Food Manufacturing Sector*. Sheffield, U.K.: Department for Education and Employment.

Department for Education and Skills (DfES). 2001. *An Assessment of Skills Needs in Food and Drink Manufacturing*. Sheffield, U.K.: DfES.

Department for Environment, Food, and Rural Affairs (DEFRA). 2006a. *Economic Note on U.K. Grocery Retailing*. London: DEFRA.

————. 2006b. *U.K. Food and Drink Manufacturing: An Economic Analysis*. London: DEFRA.

Dobson, Janet, Khalid Koser, Gail Mclaughlan, and John Salt. 2001. *International Migration and the U.K.: Recent Patterns and Trends*. Occasional paper 75. London: Home Office, Research, Development, and Statistics Directorate.

Duffy, Rachel, Andrew Fearne, and Susan Hornibrook. 2003. "Measuring Distributive and Procedural Justice: An Exploratory Investigation of the Fairness of Retailer-Supplier Relationships in the U.K. Food Industry." *British Food Journal* 105(10): 682–94.

Fenn, Dominic, editor. 2005. *Meat and Meat Products: Market Report 2005*. Middlesex, U.K.: Key Note Ltd.

Flecker, Jörg, Pamela Meil, and Anna Pollert. 1998. "The Sexual Division of Labour in Process Manufacturing: Economic Restructuring, Training, and 'Women's Work.'" *European Journal of Industrial Relations* 4(1): 7–34.

Food From Britain (FFB). 2006. "British Food and Drink Exports Enter Decade of Growth Predicts FFB." Press release, April 18. London: FFB.

Health and Safety Executive (HSE). 1999. *A Recipe for Safety: Health and Safety in the Food and Drink Industries*. Suffolk, U.K.: HSE Books.

House of Lords. 2005. *Economic Migration to the EU*. London: HMSO, European Union Committee.

Improve. 2006. *Demand for Skills in the U.K. Food and Drinks Manufacturing Sector: Stage 1 of the Sector Skills Agreement: Demand Drivers*. York, U.K.: Improve Ltd.

Incomes Data Services (IDS). 2004. *Pay Report: Food and Drink Manufacturing*. London: IDS (August).

Leitch, Sandy. 2005. *Leitch Review of Skills: Skills in the U.K.: The Long-Term Challenge: Interim Report*. London: HM Treasury.

Mason, Geoff, Bart Van Ark, and Karin Wagner. 1996. "Workforce Skills, Product Quality, and Economic Performance." In *Acquiring Skills*, edited by Alison Booth and Dennis Snower. Cambridge: Cambridge University Press.

Newsome, Kirsty, and Paul Thompson. 2006. "Supermarkets, Systematic Rationalisation, and Labour Process Change in the Scottish Food Supply Chain." Paper presented to the International Labour Process Conference, Birkbeck Conference. April 10-12, 2006, London.

Office of Fair Trading (OFT). 2004. *The Supermarkets Code of Practice*. London: OFT.

———. 2006. *The Grocery Market: The OFT's Reasons for Making a Reference to the Competition Commission*. London: OFT.

Office for National Statistics (ONS). 2001. *Labour Market Trends*. London: ONS (October).

———. 2005. *Labour Market Trends*. London: ONS (October).

———. 2006a. "Food Sector 1992–2004." In *U.K. Input-Output Analyses*. London: ONS.

———. 2006b. *Annual Abstract of Statistics*, 142. Basingstoke, U.K.: Palgrave Macmillan.

———. 2006c. *Labour Market Trends*. London: ONS (October).

Precision Prospecting. 2005. *Secondary Processing of Food Manufacture and the Use of Gang Labour: The Gangmasters (Licensing) Act 2004*. Report for DEFRA. Woodbridge, U.K.: Precision Prospecting.

Salt, John, and Jane Millar. 2006. "Foreign Labour in the United Kingdom: Current Patterns and Trends." *Labour Market Trends* (October): 335–55.

Scott, Andrew. 1994. *Willing Slaves? British Workers Under Human Resource Management*. Cambridge: Cambridge University Press.

Small Business Service Analytical Unit (SBSAU). 2006. *SME Statistics 2005*. London: SBSAU.

Smith, Chris, John Child, and Michael Rowlinson. 1990. *Reshaping Work: The Cadbury Experience*. Cambridge: Cambridge University Press.

Tambe, Rozmeen, editor. 2003. *Confectionery: Market Report Plus 2003*. Middlesex, U.K.: Key Note Ltd.

Wilson, Rob, and Terence Hogarth. 2003. *Tackling the Low Skills Equilibrium*. London: Department of Trade and Industry.

# CHAPTER 7

# "It's Just the Nature of the Job at the End of the Day": Pay and Job Quality in United Kingdom Mass-Market Call Centers

*Caroline Lloyd, Geoff Mason, Matthew Osborne, and Jonathan Payne*

After rapidly expanding in the 1980s and 1990s, call centers now figure prominently in most national economies, employing 1 to 3 percent of the working population in the European Union, the United States, and Australia (Holman 2005, 111). The United Kingdom has been described as the "the call centre capital of Europe" (Poynter 2000, 151), with employment representing just under 3 percent of the workforce (Key Note 2006). The development of the call center industry is partly a reflection of the large cost savings to be obtained from the concentration of selling and customer service functions in dedicated locations.

Early media and academic coverage depicted call centers as "electronic sweatshops" (Garson 1988), "twentieth century panopticons" (Fernie and Metcalf 1998), and mass battery phone farms. Employees were thought to be subject to "total" managerial surveillance and control and to occupy highly routinized, stressful, low-wage, and "dead-end" jobs. Although these images continue to live on in the public imagination, they have largely given way to a more nuanced academic discussion and a greater appreciation of call center diversity. Most contemporary studies acknowledge that call centers vary considerably in terms of size, the nature of operations, market segment, management approach, job complexity, and skill requirements and that they are also sites of worker resistance (Batt 2000; Beirne, Riach, and Wilson 2004; Deery and Kinnie 2004; Frenkel et al. 1998, 1999; Glucksmann 2004; Holman 2005; Kinnie, Hutchinson, and Purcell 2000; Taylor and Bain 1999, 2001).

While the burgeoning literature on call centers, often written from a labor process perspective, has placed issues of managerial control and job quality center stage, there has been relatively little discussion of pay. This is somewhat surprising given that this is a highly labor-intensive sector where agent salaries represent around 58 percent of costs (ContactBabel 2005) and the specter of offshoring to low-wage developing economies, such as India, Malaysia, and South Africa, is seen as a real threat to job security. Although they are among the better paid of the jobs studied in this book, 30 percent of call center agents in the United Kingdom fell below the low pay threshold in 2006, a figure that rose to 40 percent for part-timers. The levels of low pay are significantly higher than in Denmark, France, and the Netherlands.

This chapter explores the quality of call center agents' jobs within the context of changing competitive conditions and the United Kingdom's institutional environment. The case studies are mass-market call centers drawn from the finance and utilities sectors. We consider five aspects of call center work: work organization, pay, the use of temporary agency workers, working time, and career progression. The first section provides background information on the development of the UK call center industry and an overview of employment, pay, and job quality in the industry. We then explain the methodology of the project. The following sections present the findings from eight call center case studies, describing the competitive conditions in which firms are operating and variations in the quality of call center employment. The chapter then explores some of the factors shaping the nature of call center work within the cases. In some instances, employers have responded to the need to meet service quality standards by upgrading terms and conditions of employment, as well as improving employees' experience of work. However, they fail to address the lack of employee discretion and the routine and repetitive nature of the job itself.

## CALL CENTER EMPLOYMENT IN THE UNITED KINGDOM

The rise of the call center industry in the United Kingdom as a major form of employment dates back to the late 1980s, when larger firms, particularly in the finance and utilities sectors, began to use call centers as a new cost-efficient means of delivering customer service (DTI 2004). Many organizations subsequently responded to widespread criticisms of the poor quality of service—and to their own realization that call centers could be used for more than simple transactions—by paying closer attention to the quality of calls, delivering "customer satisfaction," and adding value, for example, through cross-selling (Mintel 2005).

There are currently around 5,800 call centers in the United Kingdom, comprising 540,000 agent positions and employing 742,000 call center agents (Key Note 2006).[1] Although employment continues to rise, the rate of growth has slowed to about 3 percent per year, a far cry from the 20 percent rates seen in the late 1990s. The majority of call centers in the United Kingdom are small, with less than 50 workstations. However, more than half of all employees work in large call centers with over 250 workstations (DTI 2004). Most call centers are in-house operations and can be found across a wide range of industries, including finance (25 percent of agent positions), utilities (6 percent), telecoms (7 percent), and retail companies (13 percent) (DTI 2004). Around 10 percent of all call center employees are estimated to work for outsourcers, that is, third-party suppliers of call-based customer service activities.

During the last five years, there has been significant media and industry attention on the phenomenon of offshoring, as a number of high-profile companies—for example, British Telecom, HSBC, and Prudential—have relocated part of their in-house operations to call centers overseas, particularly India, in order to take advantage of low-cost, English-speaking labor. However, there is little reliable information on the number of jobs that have been moved abroad. There are reports that 12 percent of companies surveyed have undertaken some offshoring (ContactBabel 2005), and that only around 5,000 agent positions in India are serving the UK market (CCA 2003). The apparently limited extent of offshoring, despite the proclaimed cost benefits, may indicate the importance that many organizations attach to customer satisfaction and maintaining service quality.

Table 7.1 provides data from the Labour Force Survey on the characteristics of call center employment in the United Kingdom.[2] Call center agents are disproportionately female compared to the workforce as a whole and more likely to be younger, with over half under the age of thirty (see also IDS 2001; Merchants Limited 2000). Agents are fairly representative in terms of ethnic distribution, notwithstanding a slightly higher proportion of Asian and Asian British per-

Table 7.1  Key Characteristics of Call Center Agents in the
United Kingdom Compared to the Total
Workforce (Employees Plus Self-Employed),
2005

|  | Call Center Agents | Total Workforce |
|---|---|---|
| Gender | | |
| Male | 39% | 54% |
| Female | 61 | 46 |
| Age | | |
| Under twenty-five | 41 | 14 |
| Twenty-five to twenty-nine | 15 | 10 |
| Thirty to thirty-nine | 20 | 24 |
| Forty to forty-nine | 15 | 25 |
| Fifty to fifty-nine | 8 | 20 |
| Sixty and older | 1 | 7 |
| Working hours | | |
| Part-time (less than thirty hours) | 26 | 23 |
| Full-time (thirty hours or more) | 74 | 77 |
| Ethnic group | | |
| White | 91 | 92 |
| South Asian | 5 | 3 |
| Black | 2 | 2 |
| Other ethnic group | 2 | 2 |
| Nationality | | |
| United Kingdom national | 92 | 92 |
| Not United Kingdom national | 8 | 8 |
| Highest qualification[a] | | |
| Graduate | 9 | 21 |
| Other NVQ4 or equivalent | 8 | 10 |
| NVQ3 | 31 | 25 |
| NVQ2 | 38 | 23 |
| Below NVQ2; other qualifications or no qualifications | 15 | 22 |
| Number of observations | 748 | 225,248 |

Source: Labour Force Survey (LFS) (2005).
[a] Other NVQ4 includes BTEC Higher National and teaching and nursing qualifications or equivalent; NVQ3 includes A levels and trade apprenticeships or equivalent; NVQ2 includes GCSE grades A through C, City and Guilds craft, GNVQ intermediate, or equivalent.

Figure 7.1  Gross Hourly Wage Distribution for Call Center
             Agents, by Full-Time and Part-Time Status, 2006

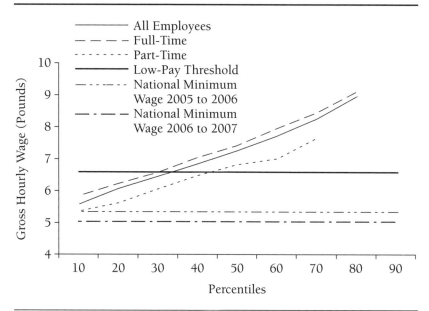

Source: Annual Survey of Hours and Earnings (ASHE) (2006), SOC 7211.

sons. Other research has found that in large cities or close to universities, students and new graduates often constitute a significant part of the workforce (DTI 2004). As one might expect, however, there are far fewer graduates among call center agents compared to the workforce as a whole. Nevertheless, agents are not typically unqualified: a higher proportion hold qualifications at GCSE/A level or their equivalent relative to the United Kingdom's labor force (see also Holman and Wood 2002).[3]

As noted earlier, about 30 percent of agents are paid below the low pay threshold, which is defined here as two-thirds of the median gross hourly wage for all employees (figure 7.1). Full-time agents receive at least 50 pence per hour more than part-time agents at every point on the wage distribution. Other data from the Labour Force Survey suggest that there is very little difference in pay levels according to gender, but as chapter 2 notes (see table 2.7), those on temporary contracts and with lower-level qualifications (below NVQ3) are more likely to experience low pay. Although there are no detailed statistics on call center salaries across different sectors, surveys indicate that the public sector, financial services, and utilities pay above-average rates, the outsourcing sector pays below average, and that this gap continues to widen (DTI 2004; IDS 2005).

Apart from concerns about low pay in some parts of the industry, call center work also suffers from an image of monotony and boredom. Many call center agents find themselves exposed to an endless succession of calls, often lasting only a matter of a few minutes, while being subject to high levels of managerial control, including extensive performance monitoring, call measurement, and target setting (see Bain et al. 2002). Not surprisingly, some commentators have argued that call centers are indicative of the "Taylorisation of white collar work" (Taylor and Bain 1999, 109). However, it is widely recognized that such methods are not applied uniformly either across or within call centers.

Research has highlighted how call center managers are faced with the challenge of reconciling two potentially competing and contradictory "logics" (see Deery and Kinnie 2004). The first logic—the drive to secure efficiency and achieve cost reductions by maintaining call volumes and throughput—is *quantitative*. The second—the need to secure adequate levels of service quality—is *qualitative* (Houlihan 2002; Hutchinson, Purcell, and Kinnie 2000; Korczynski 2002; Taylor and Bain 1999, 2001). As Phil Taylor and Peter Bain (1999, 111) note, "It is difficult to overstate the extent to which this quantity/ quality dilemma preoccupies call centre managers." The nature of call center work depends in large part on the balance that is struck between these two competing logics, and that balance may vary both across and within call centers. It is also affected by a range of contextual factors, such as the nature of the product or service, local labor market conditions, management priorities, and the effectiveness of collective institutions such as trade unions (Batt 2000; Batt, Hunter, and Wilk 2003; Kinnie, Hutchinson, and Purcell 2000; Taylor and Bain 2001).

Call center jobs range along a spectrum from the repetitive and routine, where the emphasis is on high-volume call handling and cost minimization, to those requiring more extensive product knowledge, a higher degree of relationship building, and relatively sophisticated communication and interpersonal skills (see Holman 2005). This variation, however, does not mean that there is an even spread or distribution of jobs along this spectrum. According to David Holman (2005, 126, 116), the majority of call centers are more akin to mass-service call centers: most jobs fall "towards the lower/middle end of the Taylorist-Empowered job design continuum and are characterised by low control" (see also Bain et al. 2002; Batt and Moynihan 2002). This is consistent with research in the United Kingdom indicating that employment remains concentrated in large, high-volume, and outsourced operations (Callaghan and Thompson 2002), with an average call length for the industry as a whole of less than four minutes (ContactBabel 2005). Levels of job discretion have also been found to be considerably lower compared with Denmark, France, and Germany (Holman, Batt, and Holtgrewe 2006).

Also indicative of both low pay and poor job quality are high average levels of labor turnover, which are widely seen as a key problem by both academic observers and those within the industry. Over the past four years, studies have reported average labor turnover rates of between 15 and 25 percent (see ContactBabel 2005; DTI 2004; IDS 2003), with attrition most marked among outsourcing specialists (35.7 percent) and in regions with the greatest numbers of outbound telemarketing centers (see DTI 2004). By contrast, call centers in the finance and utilities sectors are found to have average attrition rates of around 12 percent and 10 percent, respectively (DTI 2004). Most studies agree that the main drivers of high turnover are low pay, lack of career advancement, and the desire to escape work that is often highly pressurized, stressful, unhealthy, and monotonous (see DTI 2004; Halford and Cohen 2003; Holman 2005; Taylor et al. 2003). Indeed, recent studies suggest that more than half of agents leaving a call center quit the industry altogether (ContactBabel 2005).

For those who do remain within the industry, there is some evidence that there are only limited progression opportunities and very short career ladders available in many call centers (Belt 2002; Lockyer et al. 2002). Graduates are disproportionately represented at management level, while team leader positions are dominated by those qualified to A level or above (Holman and Wood 2002). Lack of progression, particularly for those with minimal qualifications, may also be compounded by a relatively weak training and skills infrastructure in which opportunities for training to recognized industry standards, such as NVQs in call handling, are at best patchy and lack commitment from many employers (E-skills UK 2003).

Most studies on call centers have focused on management controls and work organization. The evidence around issues of pay and broader aspects of job quality, including progression, has received only limited attention. The case study evidence presented in this chapter addresses these underresearched areas in the context of the industry's competitive and regulatory environment. The next section presents a brief outline of the research methodology and provides some background information on the case study companies.

## METHODOLOGY AND CASE STUDY SELECTION

In selecting the case studies, we focused on larger call centers (over one hundred operators) in mass consumer markets in the finance and utilities sectors. These sectors led the development of the call center industry and continue to represent a sizable proportion of the market. It was felt that they provided the opportunity to explore the varying impact of deregulation across Europe, which is particularly prominent in the utilities. They are also sectors with relatively high levels of unionization, which was important given that one aim of this study was to examine the influence of trade unions on job quality. The objective was to secure a mix of in-house and outsourcing firms as well as union and non-union workplaces. In addition, we chose firms with a view to achieving a mix of regional locations and some variation in job design. As shown in table 7.2, the sample consists of six in-house call centers (three in financial services and three in utilities), along with two outsourcers operating in these sectors. Five of the workplaces recognized at least one union. The growing internationalization of the sector is reflected in the ownership profile: half of the call centers were foreign-owned. The workplaces cannot be seen as representative of the call center industry as a whole because these companies were within the higher-paying and more unionized sectors of utilities and finance. In addition, the firms that agreed to participate are also likely to be self-selecting from the "better" companies.

The fieldwork was conducted between March 2005 and April 2006. In each organization, we conducted semistructured face-to-face interviews with call center managers, human resource managers, team leaders, individual customer service agents, and union representatives.[4] Further interviews were carried out with managers of five temporary work agencies that were supplying personnel to the case study firms. We conducted a total of 129 individual interviews across the eight call centers and five temporary work agencies. The interviews were recorded and ranged in length from one to two hours with

Table 7.2 Case Study Call Centers: Main Characteristics and Number of Interviews

| Call Center | Main Business | Ownership | Employment in Call Center | Union Presence | Number of Interviewees | | | |
|---|---|---|---|---|---|---|---|---|
| | | | | | Managers | Team Leaders | Agents, Union Reps | Temp Agency Managers |
| F1 | Mass, customer finance | United Kingdom | 100 to 200 | Yes | 3 | 2 | 10 | 2 |
| F2 | Outsourcer, contracts in finance and utilities | United States | 200 to 500 | No | 3 | 6 | 10 | 1 |
| F3 | Mass, customer insurance | United Kingdom | 500 to 1,000 | No | 4 | 4 | 9 | — |
| F4 | Mass, customer finance | European | 100 to 200 | No | 3 | 4 | 17 | — |
| U1 | Monopoly, energy emergency service | United Kingdom | Site 1: 100 to 200 Site 2: 200 to 500 | Yes | 8 | 2 | 7 | 2 |
| U2 | Outsourcer, contracts in utilities | United Kingdom | 100 to 200 | Yes | 6 | 2 | 4 | 2 |
| U3 | Mass, residential and business energy supplier | European | 500 to 1,000 | Yes | 2 | 2 | 4 | 1 |
| U4 | Monopoly, mass, residential and business water supplier | European | 100 to 200 | Yes | 2 | 2 | 5 | — |

*Source:* Authors' compilation.

call center managers to between fifteen and forty-five minutes with individual agents. All companies provided a tour of the workplace, and at three of the call centers about one hour was spent listening to calls. Management put forward individuals for interview, raising the possibility of selection bias. Notwithstanding these caveats, the range of responses and managerial approaches across the cases provides substantial data with which to explore variations in the nature of call center work and the factors that shape workers' experience.

## COMPETITIVE CONDITIONS, REGULATORY PRESSURES, AND EMPLOYER STRATEGIES

In this section, we first review the market conditions in the financial services and utilities sectors, as well as the outsourcing sector, which provide the main context for the business strategies pursued by the call center case study firms. We then go on to differentiate between the call centers with respect to their market position and exposure to regulatory pressure.

The United Kingdom is one of the world's leading international financial services centers, employing over one million people and accounting for 5 percent of gross value added (GVA) in 2003 (ONS 2004). Major changes have taken place in market conditions over the last twenty years, in particular the liberalization of financial services in the mid-1980s, which expanded the number of operators and intensified competition. The subsequent slowdown in the economy in the early 1990s saw large-scale job losses, mergers, branch closures, and the move toward call centers as a means to reduce costs (see Bain and Taylor 2002; Marshall and Richardson 1996; Poynter 2000). Against the backdrop of new market entrants and slow revenue growth, companies were acutely aware that increased profitability depended not just on cutting costs but on the ability to "cross-sell" a range of financial products to existing customers. With limited regulation of the sector, "mis-selling" of financial products was rife. As a result, the Financial Services Authority (FSA) was established in 2000 as the single regulatory body for the financial services sector. The new regulations require that those offering financial advice or selling financial products have specified levels of knowledge and competence. These regulations have affected many of the call centers in terms of the training requirements for operators and the information they are required to provide to callers.

The nationalized utility sector of electricity, gas, and water was privatized in stages during the late 1980s and early 1990s. Established state monopolies became private companies, and regulators were set up to oversee aspects of their operations, such as pricing policy. The opening up of the sector to competition from 1998 intensified competitive pressures as a wave of companies entered the marketplace. Although some subsectors comprise regulated (private) regional monopolies (such as water), in electricity and gas numerous consumer providers have sprung up, often acting as "multi-utility" suppliers of energy products. However, firms in this industry remain subject to detailed regulation in order to control access to networks, promote competition, and ensure compliance with safety standards. As in the financial services sector, many utility firms were also early developers of call centers to handle contacts with their large customer bases.

Outsourcers still represent only around 10 percent of all call centers in the United Kingdom, although they doubled in size between 2001 and 2005 and now account for approximately 60,000 agent positions (Mintel 2005). These companies tend to be either former mail-order and utility businesses that have moved into competing for a wider range of contracts (DTI 2004) or foreign-owned firms, the majority being American-headquartered, pan-European multinationals. Originally used primarily for one-off campaigns, out-of-hours activity, telesales, and excess capacity calls from in-house centers, they are increasingly obtaining longer-term contracts with firms in the utilities and telecommunications industries as well as contracts to carry out central and local government activities. Competition has intensified in the outsourced market, particularly as a result of American service providers expanding into the United Kingdom (Mintel 2005).

## MARKET POSITIONING AND BUSINESS STRATEGIES

In terms of business strategy and exposure to regulatory pressure, the eight case study firms have been divided into three broad categories:

1.  In-house call centers exposed to competition for customers, predominantly through their parent companies' products (F1, F3, F4, and U3)

2. In-house call centers for firms operating as monopolies but subject to significantly higher levels of regulation than the other call centers (U1 and U4)

3. Call centers that are directly exposed to competition through bidding for contracts (the two outsourcers, F2 and U2)

Of the financial services cases in the first category, F1 dealt with savings and investment transactions and sales for the mass retail banking market. F4 provided a direct (via telephone or Internet) banking service around one simple savings account. F3 sold a range of insurance products for domestic customers, including coverage for cars and homes. Both F1 and F3 had recently been taken over by large and highly profitable United Kingdom-based financial institutions, while F4 was a foreign-owned operation that had recently entered the UK market with considerable success.

These three call centers belonged to highly profitable financial institutions and were performing well; as a result, they were under less pressure than others in the sample to reduce labor costs. Instead, they placed greater priority on providing a quality service (a quick response and a polite and accurate interaction), keeping within the regulatory rules, and increasing the number and variety of products sold. Their approach to managing their employees also partly reflected company values and a desire to be seen as a "good" local employer or an "employer of choice." U3 also fits into the first category, since it competed with other energy suppliers to attract and retain household and business customers on the basis of price and service quality. It was one of the largest and most profitable companies operating in that sector.

Both U1 and U4 may be described as "natural monopolies" subject to regulatory authorities that determined the terms and conditions under which they operated. U1 was responsible for the safety, development, and maintenance of an energy supply network, while U4 was a water supplier. Managers in both companies reported sharp downward pressure on costs because their regulators could restrict annual price increases if they were deemed to be inefficient on a variety of quality standards. For example, a senior manager at U4 said that the company had found itself to be low-ranking on key measures such as how fast it responded to billing and payment inquiries. Nevertheless, the lack of competition and the nature of regulation within the utilities sector had enabled both companies to achieve substantial and, in the case of U4, expanding profits.

By contrast, both the outsourcer firms operated in the market for call center service contracts, which is notably insecure since large portions of business can come and go over relatively short time periods. F2 was an American-owned outsourcing call center that had a range of short- and long-term contracts, including simple transaction handling for a retail bank during busy periods. U2 was a subsidiary of a large utility company and so had some features in common with the other utilities cases, most notably a union presence and a similar benefits package. Both outsourcers saw themselves as "quality operators" rather than competing solely on price, and both had developed long-term contracts with some clients. However, a significant proportion of their business relied on winning short-term and excess capacity contracts in the context of an increasingly difficult market. An operations manager at F2 explained:

> The market place has changed enormously in the last couple of years because of the offshore pressures. . . . There is a huge amount of capacity. There is a lot of competition around, lots of outsourcers, lots of in-house operations.

Although F2 was itself profitable, it was part of a larger business unit that was making an overall loss. It found itself being squeezed by competitors cutting prices and by a lack of investment in computer systems, which was placing considerable pressure on the call center to hold down labor costs, particularly wages. By contrast, both U2 and its parent company were profitable, but the firm experienced continuing difficulties in balancing the provision of client-specific services with relatively short-term contracts. Their efforts to hold down labor costs had led to a sizable proportion of agents retained on temporary agency contracts rather than being offered permanent positions, as well as the periodic switching of jobs within the firm to cheaper locations in the United Kingdom.

## THE QUALITY OF CALL CENTER WORK

In all of the case study firms, agents were dealing with mass-market products and answering inbound calls from customers. Agents were assigned a workstation with a computer and telephone headset and were grouped in teams of about ten members. Normally agents spent the vast majority of the shift receiving calls fed to them by an automatic call distribution system. With each call, the relevant package and/or personal details of the caller were brought up from the computer. The amount of clerical work undertaken after the call was finished was generally minimal, with more complex or lengthy operations passed to other workers.

## WORK ORGANIZATION

There were differences in terms of the actual content of the calls and the knowledge required of employees. Using managerial estimates of the average time taken for new agents to reach full proficiency (including the time needed for initial off-the-job training), the case study centers were allocated to one of two categories of job complexity: "low-complexity" jobs required less than two months to become proficient, and "medium-complexity" jobs required between two and six months (see table 7.3).[5]

Jobs of the lowest complexity were found at F4, where calls were scripted and agents performed routine transactions in relation to one bank account. This work typically involved opening and closing accounts, making deposits and transfers, changing customer details, setting up a regular savings plan, and dealing with customer complaints. With calls typically lasting only three to four minutes, one agent described the work as "so tedious, it was like watching paint dry." Another spoke of being "chained to your desk and having to listen to the same kind of people . . . for ten or eleven hours a day." A call center manager considered that boredom was "the biggest challenge" because the agents' role was so limited.

By contrast, the most complex jobs were found at U3, where one agent described the work as "skilled and complex," and a manager said it took up to six months for agents to learn the job. Agents were expected to be able to use twelve internal systems, including handling financial transactions and setting up meter readings, and they were required to have a detailed knowledge of a number of different products and contractual arrangements. With scripting generally limited to the beginning and end of the call, agents could exercise some discretion in their interaction with customers.

Despite some variations in tasks and call complexity, a major source of dissatisfaction across all the call centers was the nature of

## Table 7.3 Job Complexity, Tasks, and Knowledge Requirements in Case Study Firms

| | Job Complexity for Majority of Employees[a] | Job Tasks and Knowledge Requirements | Typical Call Length |
|---|---|---|---|
| **In-house centers operating in competitive markets** | | | |
| F1 | Medium | Transactions, advice, and selling on twenty-five accounts. Some product knowledge required. No scripting, but some use of standard phrases. | 5 minutes |
| F3 | Medium | Quote and sell up to four insurance products. Some product knowledge required. Use of scripts. | 3 to 4 minutes |
| F4 | Low | Transactions on one simple account. Use of scripts. | 3 to 4 minutes |
| U3 | Medium | Registration of new customers, dealing with changes of supplier, cross-selling of products. Detailed product knowledge required. Limited use of scripts. | 6 minutes |
| **In-house centers subject to tight regulation** | | | |
| U1 | Medium | Taking emergency calls, providing safety advice, and answering customer queries. Safety knowledge is critical. Use of scripts. | 2.5 minutes |
| U4 | Medium | Debt collection, assistance with range of supply problems. Some product knowledge required. Limited use of scripts. | 5 minutes |
| **Outsourcers** | | | |
| F2 | Low | Simple transactions and giving/receiving information. Use of scripts. | 2 to 3 minutes |
| U2 | Medium | Responding to customer queries and assistance with range of problems. Some product knowledge required. Use of scripts varies between contracts. | No data available |

*Source:* Authors' compilation.
[a] Estimated time to reach full proficiency: low = less than two months, medium = between two and six months.

the job itself—the monotony and repetition involved in taking calls of a similar type. An F3 agent remarked: "I think it's just the nature of the job at the end of the day . . . the fact that you're in a call center and you're taking nonstop calls. . . . It's just some people can do that for a long period of time and others can't." "It can get a bit tedious," said a U1 agent. "To be honest . . . every now and again you'd turn around and someone would be gone . . . maybe they just found the job too boring."

The regulatory aspects of work in the financial services and utilities sectors often led managers to introduce lengthy phrases that agents had to read verbatim, thereby further increasing the repetitiveness of the interaction and limiting the scope for employee discretion. All of these jobs demanded considerable stamina: agents were required to deliver consistent levels of service quality for long periods in the context of high call volumes and extensive monitoring.

In all eight call centers, agents were subject to a varied bundle of individual targets encompassing both quantitative and qualitative dimensions that typically included call quality and accuracy, call length, "wrap-up times" (after the call work), timekeeping, and attendance. Some team leaders and agents described their work as "complicated" and "pressured" because, in addition to meeting sales targets, they were also asked to deliver on targets for average calls per hour and a maximum wrap-up time when they were "not ready" to take new calls. Overall, the pressures associated with targets were not felt to be extreme. Nevertheless, failure to achieve targets on a consistent basis was linked in all of the organizations to a "performance management system" that was used to both reward and discipline employees and could eventually result in dismissal. Contrary to expectations, less complex jobs did not necessarily equate with more aggressive monitoring or pressurized targets, while more complex jobs were not always less target-driven.

All the utility cases had targets for either the number or length of calls. As management sought to respond to pressures to cut costs while also meeting service quality standards, the targets clearly illustrated the "quantity/quality" dilemma they faced. Thus, one agent at U3 spoke of how the pressures to meet call volume targets could damage service quality:

> Nine calls an hour would be fine if you were only just taking information, but if you are trying to offer advice, you can hardly do

that within three minutes. . . . When there are complexities to do with other departments, then it's not at all attainable.

Similarly, the call center at the outsourcer firm U2 had an interest in keeping call times short but was subject to pressure from clients to focus on "first opportunity resolution," that is, to minimize the number of customers who needed to call back about problems within a week of their original call. One agent commented: "We don't know where we stand. We want to give the best customer service, but we are under pressure to get the talk time down."

By contrast, none of the four finance cases generally employed targets on call time or calls per hour, and there was a low incidence of abusive customers outside the departments that specifically dealt with customer retention. In F3 and F4, nearly all operators considered their individual targets achievable and realistic. Dissatisfaction with targets was higher at F1 and F2, but for different reasons. At F1, the range and level of targets, particularly in relation to sales and wrap-up times, made promotion hard to achieve, while more senior agents found it difficult to earn commissions. Agents at the outsourcer F2 focused on the impact of a more punitive approach to targets and the direct link to pay: a good performer who achieved only a satisfactory ("on-target") rating for one measure, such as call quality or absenteeism, could end up losing £30 (US$61.36) per week for three months.

## Pay and Benefits

Of the eight cases, four undertook collective bargaining with trade unions over the pay and conditions of call center agents. Since there are no industry-wide agreements, pay systems and rates are determined at either the workplace or business level. The only standardized form of pay regulation, therefore, is through the NMW, and given that fewer than one in ten of all call center agents were paid close to this, we would not expect it to have a significant impact on the cases. Individualized performance-related pay (linked to individual targets) and/or commission-based pay were important features of all the call centers regardless of whether there was a collective agreement or management determined pay unilaterally.

The lowest median rates of pay for agents (combining direct employees and temporary agency staff) were found at the two outsourcer call centers, F2 and U2, which faced the most challenging and volatile market conditions (see table 7.4). U2's median rate of pay for direct employees was comparable to that in some in-house call centers, but overall pay rates were brought down by the use of a very high proportion (64 percent) of agency workers. Among the in-house call centers operating in competitive markets, F1 was toward the lower end, particularly for direct employees, while F3, F4, and U3 were at the top of the distribution. The two call centers subject to tight regulation (U1 and U4) offered middle- to lower-ranking pay rates. For the most part, agents were paid above the low pay threshold for 2005 (£6.32 [US$12.93] per hour), except for those at F2 (direct employees and agency staff) and agency workers at U2 and F1. Across the eight call centers, most agents were earning significantly above the NMW. The exception was F2, where the training and agency rates were set at the minimum wage due to be implemented in October 2006. Under the F2 pay system, those who "underperformed" in their first year could find their pay reduced to £5.10 (US$10.43) per hour—only five pence above the NMW in place at the time. In this case, the NMW would appear to have provided a floor to wages and a degree of protection against the cost-cutting strategies of the organization.

It was clear from interviews with agents that earning above the LPT still did not ensure adequate means to support a family or enter the housing market unless the agent was part of a multi-income household. As one agent at F3 commented, "For a single person trying to buy a house on this salary, you've got no chance." Many young people made the salary work by living with their family or renting accommodation with friends and partners. Other workers were part of a household in which there was another wage earner, or they received child tax credits. Some older workers supplemented their income with a pension from previous employment.

Employee perceptions of pay depended greatly on their personal circumstances as well as the alternative employment options available to them locally. Although many agents considered their pay to be poor, it was mostly regarded as average for call center work in the local area and as reasonable given the demands of the job and the qualification requirements. One agent at F3 remarked, "For a job where you don't have to actually have qualifications as such, like a degree, I think it's a very good rate of pay." Even at F2, which offered the lowest pay, there was a recognition that the pay was still better than what

## Table 7.4 Agents' Pay and Benefits

| | Starting Gross Hourly Pay for Direct Employees | Median Gross Hourly Pay for Direct Employees[a,b] | Median Gross Hourly Pay for Agency Staff[a] | Median Gross Hourly Pay for All Staff[a] | Other Major Benefits for Direct Employees[c] | Agency Staff as Percentage of Total Call Center Agents |
|---|---|---|---|---|---|---|
| In-house centers operating in competitive markets | | | | | | |
| F1 | £6.45 | £7.10 | £6.00 | £7.10 | Company pension; free shares | 26 |
| F3 | £6.90 | £9.30 | — | 9.30 | Company pension | 0 |
| F4 | £7.70 | £9.20 | — | 9.20 | Company pension; BUPA | 0 |
| U3 | £7.00 | £12.30 | 7.00 | 11.70 | Company pension | 11 |
| In-house centers subject to tight regulation | | | | | | |
| U1 | £6.50 | £8.00 | 7.10 | 7.20 | Company pension | 86 |
| U4 | £7.80 | £8.50 | — | 8.50 | Company pension | 0 |
| Outsourcers | | | | | | |
| F2 | £5.35 | £5.80 | 5.35 | 5.80 | None | 11 |
| U2 | £5.60 | £7.30 | 6.80 | 7.00 | Company pension | 64 |

*Source:* Authors' compilation.

[a] The estimated median pay rate (including commissions) is here defined such that half of all call center agents earn above that rate and half below it.

[b] Estimated pay levels for permanent staff include performance-related bonuses and annual company bonuses.

[c] These are in addition to holidays and sick pay above statutory levels.

was offered by many of the alternative employers available to those with limited qualifications. One agent said, "I think it's quite good, to be honest, because I've worked at Tesco's and Woolworth's in [name of town], and it's nowhere near that. It's under a fiver—well, it was, I am talking a couple of years ago. . . . So I think the money is quite good."

Call center employees received significant additional benefits (with the exception of the outsourcer F2). These consisted of a range of benefit packages that included a company pension scheme, sick pay (ranging from twenty days to eight months fully paid), and higher-than-statutory levels of paid holiday entitlement. Even so, it was evident that a number of employees had opted not to join their company pension scheme. The financial call centers also provided a range of financial products at discounted rates, from free shares to cheap mortgages and loans. These seven call centers had relatively good physical environments—subsidized canteens, space for breaks, and so on—that were seen as positive factors in agents' experience of work. Although offering similar levels of paid holiday, F2 provided few additional benefits other than death in service and a stakeholder pension, and it limited sick pay to ten days per year. It was also the only call center where there were widespread complaints about the physical environment—in particular, the inadequacies of the air-conditioning system and the dirtiness inside the building—and about the limited facilities, such as the lack of a canteen.

## THE USE OF TEMPORARY WORK AGENCIES

There was considerable variation in the utilization of temporary agency workers across the case studies. Of the four financial call centers, two (F1 and F2) used agency workers on a regular basis, the vast majority of them being part of a "temp-to-perm" recruitment process. This practice enabled the companies to reduce the costs of recruitment, while also providing a "filter" whereby they could assess new workers' capabilities and then either offer them permanent positions or remove them quickly and easily. In both cases, new agents were recruited via the agency, and after thirteen weeks of employment they were moved onto permanent contracts if they met company performance requirements. Pay rates were set at or below the entry rate for direct employees. At both F3 and F4, agency workers were generally not used because of the difficulty in recruiting suitable people; in the context of competition for labor, F3 and F4 found that direct hiring was necessary to obtain the right caliber of staff. By contrast, a readier supply of local workers enabled F1 and F2 to use agencies as a recruitment channel.

Two of the four utility call centers made extensive use of agency workers (86 percent and 64 percent) primarily for reasons of numerical flexibility but also to help cover seasonal peaks in demand (U1) and to vary staff numbers at short notice as contracts began and ended (the outsourcer U2). Previously, the other two utility call centers had also made heavy use of agency staff, but concerns about labor turnover and work quality had led U3 to reduce its share to 11 percent of total agents and U4 to eliminate agency workers entirely. At peak times of the year, U4 now preferred to subcontract work to an outsourcing call center.

Numerical flexibility was not the only reason agency workers were utilized to such an extent. As outlined in the previous section, the gaps in pay and conditions between direct employees and agency staff provided substantial cost savings. In the five call centers where agency workers were used, their median gross hourly pay rates fell well below the equivalent rates for direct employees, being some 7 to 15 percent lower at F1, F2, U1, and U2 and as much as 43 percent lower at U3. The absence of pension benefits and limited entitlements to holiday and sickness pay for agency staff increased the cost gap between them and direct employees. While the temp-to-perm recruitment process raised few concerns for new agents at F1 and F2, the many temps working at U1 and U2 were in insecure positions for much longer and had far fewer opportunities to obtain permanent employment. The interviews revealed that the difference in benefits was a prime reason for pent-up demand for promotion to full employee status.

There was much dissatisfaction among agency staff at both U1 and U2 with this type of employment practice, leading to problems with service quality and high labor turnover. At U1, the relationship with the temporary staffing agency had been put under strain as a result of the agency's difficulties in meeting recruitment targets without relaxing selection criteria. According to one manager, as many as one-third of recent new recruits selected by the agency had failed to complete their initial training and probation period. As a result of these types of problems, both call centers were beginning to reduce their reliance on agency workers.

## Working Time

All of the call centers operated from at least 8:00 AM until 8:00 PM, Monday to Saturday, with only one closed on a Sunday. Two utility call centers were open twenty-four hours a day, seven days a week. In addition, call numbers varied throughout the day and week, presenting management with the problem of matching staff levels to short-term changes in call volumes. The ways in which the call centers chose to deal with long opening hours and fluctuating labor requirements had major implications for the quality of agents' jobs.

The most common approach was to use rolling shift patterns in which agents alternated between shifts—for example, working early shifts one week and late shifts the next week, including a certain number of weekends. There were many different variants on this shift pattern, however, dictated in part by opening hours and call volume flows but also by labor supply factors and management approaches. Full-time agents worked on average between thirty-five and thirty-seven and a half hours per week, with the majority on standard eight-hour shifts, although some companies, such as F3 and F4, also offered either eleven- or twelve-hour shifts. Only the two call centers that opened twenty-four hours a day paid a premium for working unsocial hours. Part-time workers typically accounted for 30 to 40 percent of all employees in the centers, and female employees represented a majority share of agents in all eight centers.[6] In some cases, management specifically targeted women with domestic responsibilities to fill part-time shifts during peak hours or when positions were harder to fill (such as early evenings). Students were also considered ideal candidates for working unsociable hours. In two call centers, agents had signed "opt-outs" from the European Working Time Directive and thus could work more than the stipulated forty-eight-hour week, although there was no evidence that employees were being put under direct pressure to do so.[7]

In half of the call centers (F1, F2, U2, and U3), shift allocations were a major source of dissatisfaction for agents, particularly those that involved rotation over one week or over several weeks and offered agents little or no choice. The issues they raised included being unable to undertake regular weekly activities, such as evening classes or sporting activities, alongside the disruption of sleep patterns and routines associated with rotating from early to late starts. By contrast, shift preference schemes had been introduced at F3 and F4 in response to dissatisfaction with shift allocation and problems with recruitment and retention; these schemes, which gave 95 percent of agents their first choice of shifts (normally regular fixed hours), had been very successful and popular with employees. Similar schemes had been introduced at U1 and U4, although at the latter agents and team leaders still encountered difficulties changing shift allocations. An alternative option was pursued by the outsourcer F2, whose management preferred employees to be on fully flexible shifts but retained 60 percent of agents on fixed-hours or school-time-only contracts. Despite the company's low pay, these fixed hours enabled it to recruit women with young children as well as those who wanted to combine work with other activities, especially since there were few employment alternatives for this group in the local area.

## TRAINING AND CAREER PROGRESSION

A key element of job quality is whether call center work is a "dead-end" job or whether it offers opportunities for training and career progression. Reflecting the national picture, employees entered the call centers with a variety of educational backgrounds—some with few or no qualifications, others with degrees. Although managers typically stated that they preferred to recruit agents with GCSE math and English at grades A* to C, in practice they were usually prepared to take on anyone who could satisfy their company's tests and who displayed the appropriate personality for the job.[8] The call centers provided initial off-the-job training, ranging from as little as one week to as much as six weeks. Subsequent opportunities for training arose to varying extents across the cases because of the need to bring agents up to speed with new products or issues that customers might be raising.

All eight call centers provided possibilities for some permanent staff to progress to the team leader level (table 7.5). A number of companies had development programs that trained agents to become team leaders or allowed them to progress via intermediate roles such as coach and senior call handler. However, the flat organizational structure inhibited further progression because the number of vacancies available was finite. Several current managers had worked their way up as the industry underwent rapid expansion in the 1990s, but such opportunities appear to be shrinking now that the industry has stabilized.

Table 7.5 Training and Career Progression in Case Study Call Centers

| | Average Initial Off-the-Job Training Times | Continuing Training | Career Progression (Permanent Staff Only) |
|---|---|---|---|
| In-house centers operating in competitive markets | | | |
| F1 | Four weeks (pass accreditation exams) | Limited ongoing training—linked to products | Grading structure within agent job; team leader; limited moves to other functions |
| F3 | Six weeks | Various training options in learning resource center, including team leader training | Grading structure within the job; team leader |
| F4 | Two weeks | Various training options—intranet site with training packages, language courses, NVQs in call handling | Limited to team leader role |
| U3 | Five weeks | Refresher training and training for progression to coach or team leader | Limited number of coach and team leader positions |

| | | | |
|---|---|---|---|
| In-house centers subject to tight regulation | | | |
| U1 | Two weeks | Opportunities for training for permanent staff for coach and team leader roles | Some limited positions as coach and team leader |
| U4 | Three weeks | Team leader development scheme | Limited number of team leader roles; large volume of administrative job opportunities in the wider company |
| Outsourcers | | | |
| F2 | Three to five days | Ongoing training restricted to new contract training | Team leader; limited moves to other functions |
| U2 | Five weeks | Training usually linked to progression via floor-walker role to team leader; refresher skills and new product training | Limited number of team leader positions |

*Source:* Authors' compilation.

In principle, being part of a larger organization should provide the possibility of moving across to other functions, but the numbers of employees doing this appeared to be small. As the human resource manager for F1 explained, "We do get quite a lot of people who look to move out of the processing or contact center areas and into support functions, but again, we don't have too many vacancies in those areas." At F4, management claimed that many of those initially recruited had been attracted by the prospect of advancing within a large multinational financial institution. In reality, the only operations in the United Kingdom were two call centers and a small head office, leading the call center manager to admit that there had been a tendency for progression opportunities to be "oversold" in the past. For some agents, this had become a source of frustration. As one commented, "I am doing absolutely fine in my job, I meet all my requirements, but there haven't been the opportunities to progress, which sort of leaves me feeling constrained in my job and frustrated that I can't move further."

The single exception was U4, which offered significant opportunities for agents to move to other parts of the wider organization, a prospect that proved attractive to new recruits and was made possible by the colocation of the call center with other administrative departments. One agent described the situation at U4:

> One of the reasons why I came to work [here] was because I knew that there was scope to move to other areas. . . . Even in the first week of training, the trainer said, "You know, when jobs come up, just apply for them.". . . Five months is a long time to work in a call center for me. If the right thing comes up at the moment, I'll apply for it.

A senior manager explained that there was a positive side to agents treating the call center as an entry-level job to the wider company, provided they did not move on too quickly. There was now "an unwritten rule which says that people can't move jobs within twelve months."

The lack of progression opportunities was clearly a source of dissatisfaction for a number of call center agents. At the same time, several interviewees spoke of "drifting into" call center work, and many stated that they had no wish to develop a call center career or remain within the industry. Because call centers are usually willing to take on employees with limited formal qualifications, they can provide many people with a stepping-stone into the world of work. For some graduates, call center work also offers the chance to gain valuable work experience as well as the chance to pay off student debt before deciding on what kind of career to pursue.

## SOURCES OF VARIATION IN JOB QUALITY

What factors were significant in shaping employees' job quality and experience of work across the eight case studies? Product market regulation is clearly relevant here. For example, in the financial services sector, the FSA requires that all staff, whether involved in giving advice or not, be compliant with the relevant regulations and codes of practice. In many cases, this has led to the more extensive use of scripts to ensure that agents remain within the letter of the law. Similarly, in the utilities, regulations dictate that calls in some centers be handled within a certain time if there is a threat to safety, and there are also restrictions on what sales staff can do and say—for example, in terms of persuading customers to switch suppliers.

A further factor that appeared to be important in terms of the actual complexity of the job, and therefore employees' knowledge and skill requirements, was the nature of the product or service. Thus, at F1, agents were required to have knowledge of over twenty different types of bank accounts and to engage in cross-selling. By contrast, the job of F4 agents was rendered much simpler and more monotonous by the decision of the organization to focus on marketing a single type of account. However, it is difficult to establish a clear link between pay and job complexity across the eight case studies. It is certainly the case that the top payer (U3) also had the highest level of job complexity and that the lowest payer (F2) was one of the two centers where the typical agent's job ranked as low-complexity. Yet the other low-complexity center (F4) was among the top payers, illustrating that other elements were at play in determining pay levels.

In some cases, companies were paying higher rates and had improved their overall employment package primarily in order to attract and retain employees of the caliber required to meet service quality standards in the context of local labor market conditions. Because F3 was located in the heart of a city widely regarded as the "call center capital of the North" its employees had a range of alternative employment options available locally, such that labor turnover stood at over 50 percent in 2003. As one manager explained, "The biggest problem we've got here is that we are central and there's lots more call centers out there that can be offering different, better packages." Management had introduced a number of measures to address recruitment and retention problems, such as improving initial training, introducing a shift preference scheme, and developing a new five-grade pay matrix both to increase pay and to offer a greater sense of progression in the role. A range of employee involvement initiatives had been introduced, such as regular "vibe checks," "workouts," and question-and-answer sessions designed to provide time for management and employees to discuss particular issues as well as improve commitment and morale. Turnover had fallen to below 20 percent in two years.

At F4, a tight local labor market, coupled with the need to maintain employee motivation and service quality in the face of a highly repetitive job, led management to provide opportunities for individuals to "get off the phones" and work in other departments or on various projects. Such opportunities were highly prized—the more so because the pressure to staff the phones made these projects available only to a small minority. Efforts had also been made to improve the social atmosphere at work by putting on family fun days, charity events, and social activities outside working hours. While these initiatives were often welcomed by employees, their impact tended to be relatively marginal; many employees' experience of work continued to be shaped primarily by the restricted nature of the call center job itself. As one agent at F4 remarked, "It's not quite the worst job I've had, but it's very close. It's a shame, because it's a nice place to work, it's good people, but it's the job which I don't enjoy."

U3 had also increased pay levels in order not to be outdone by rival employers, especially in the competition for agents with one or more years' experience, who were regarded as critical in meeting the quality standards imposed by the regulator. The outsourcer U2, despite facing intense competitive pressures, was unable to keep labor costs down because of the tight local labor market in which it operated.[9] By contrast, F1 and F2 had experienced few problems when it came to recruiting new staff in local or neighboring labor markets and were therefore not under the same pressures to either increase wages or improve general working conditions.

Consideration should also be given to factors pertaining to the United Kingdom's institutional environment. The substantial use of temporary agencies in a number of our cases may reflect the relatively low level of regulation governing the use of agency workers in the United Kingdom compared to many continental European countries. New regulations introduced in 2003 tightened the rules relating to the payment of temp-to-perm fees and imposed new obligations on agencies to state whether or not temps were on employment contracts. Nevertheless, agencies do not have to offer employment contracts to their temps, and there is no requirement that agency workers be paid the same as other employees doing the same job. This enables companies to realize considerable cost savings by engaging agency workers at lower rates of pay and excluding them from company benefits. It also provides management with the flexibility to match staffing levels much more closely to fluctuations in call volumes. Even so, heavy reliance on agency workers does not always represent a viable or sustainable management strategy. Thus, all of the utility companies had either increased the proportion of permanent positions, with a view to securing higher customer service standards and better staff retention, or were in the process of doing so. The use of agency workers may therefore be viewed as another facet of management's perennial dilemma: how to reconcile pressures to cut costs while maintaining sufficient levels of service quality.

A recent study in the United States has emphasized the role of trade unions in shaping call center job quality and helping to maintain relatively high wages, benefits, and job security in some firms (see Batt, Hunter, and Wilk 2003). Unions were recognized in five of our cases, with four undertaking collective bargaining with trade unions over the pay and conditions of call center agents. The exact proportion of employees who were union members could not be identified in all the call centers. Where management estimates were available, they ranged from 30 percent at F1 to 50 percent at one of the U1 centers. There was no clear link between pay levels and collective bargaining in our call centers. Two of the four highest-paying call centers in our sample (U3 and U4) were covered by collective bargaining agreements, but the other two (F3 and F4) were not. However, such a comparison, based as it is on a relatively small sample of firms located in very different labor markets, does not provide conclusive evidence either way about union impact.

In the non-union call centers, those employees selected for interview by management were divided as to the need for trade union representation, with some questioning their relevance and others insisting that employees had much to gain from the support of a trade union. Within the unionized call centers, unions typically became involved with issues such as disciplinary procedures and working time. However, we found little evidence of any strategic attempt on the part of unions to engage with a broader bargaining agenda around issues such as breaks, targets, or work organization. In several cases, the union was felt to have a fairly limited impact, and many agents and team leaders were unaware of any day-to-day activities of the union. Union membership was largely concentrated among permanent employees, and apparently little effort had been made to recruit agency workers, despite the efforts of several large unions in designing methods to attract agency staff, including signing collective bargaining agreements with leading temporary work agencies (Heery 2004). The exception was U1, where attempts had been made to recruit agency workers but with limited success.

## SUMMARY AND ASSESSMENT

The literature on call centers has moved on from an early monolithic narrative of sweated labor and "total" managerial control and now acknowledges that call centers are far from homogeneous and generate different and varied outcomes for employees. While many studies have drawn attention to the role played by commercial pressures, technical and bureaucratic forms of control and business, and human resource approaches in shaping workers' experience, relatively little attention has been devoted to the issue of pay or to the way in which distinctive features of the UK's labor market and institutional environment may shape employer strategies.

Across the eight case studies, the majority of agents were paid above the low pay threshold, and average pay levels were, in all but two companies, in the top half of the call center pay distribution. In focusing our research on the higher-paying sectors of utilities and finance, we found that regulatory factors emanating from employment law played a limited role in shaping conditions for most of the call center workers in our study. Regulation of services and standards in both sectors has nevertheless increased the importance attached to call accuracy. Unlike some of the other occupational groups covered in this book, most directly employed call center agents are eligible for a range of nonpay benefits, such as a company pension and sick pay. Pay levels for call center agents, however, despite being generally higher, are still not adequate to support a family or to enable an individual to enter the housing market. Furthermore, many employees did not take advantage of company pension schemes, an essential way to help avoid poverty in old age.

Because our findings on pay differences across the eight case studies failed to support a clear link between pay and job complexity in mass-market call centers, we suspect that other influences are at work. Important here are pressures resulting from a tight local labor market—or perhaps more typically, the concentration within a given locality of many call centers that are all "pulling on" the same finite labor supply. These factors are significant in exerting pressure on employers to upgrade terms and conditions of work in an industry where culture and language play an important role and customer expectations regarding service quality limit the extent to which even relatively routinized service functions can be automated or offshored. Furthermore, in contrast to other low-wage industries covered in this book, such as hotels and food processing, call center employers cannot simply circumvent the problem of tight labor markets by using migrant workers, many of whom do not speak English as a first language.

A distinctive feature of the United Kingdom's flexible labor market is the extent to which employers can use temporary agency workers. Agency workers are in a position of relative disadvantage that is often compounded by the absence of the pension benefits and limited holiday and sick pay entitlements that may be on offer to direct employees in the same call center. They provide management with opportunities for cost-cutting, the flexibility to match the labor supply with demand, and the possibility of screening prospective employees through "temp-to-perm" transitions. However, the use of agency workers is far from problem-free. Despite the competitive and regulatory pressures to drive down costs, high levels of temporary agency staff can have detrimental consequences in terms of labor turnover, absenteeism, and service quality. Even employers that want to use the temp-to-perm route may find that the local labor market conditions, along with the requirements of the job, simply do not permit such an approach.

Although management in some call centers, faced with high labor turnover and the need to ensure sufficient levels of service quality, had introduced various measures to build morale and commitment, these responses rarely extended to the actual design of the call center job. For the most part, the focus was on providing employees with more choice over shift arrangements, creating a few opportunities to "get off the phones," introducing formal employee involvement mechanisms aimed at promoting better communication between management and the workforce, building progression opportunities within the current job role as a means of managing development expectations, or arranging social activities to improve the working atmosphere. While such initiatives were nontrivial in the sense that they were often welcomed by many of the call center workers we interviewed and went some way toward improving their overall experience of working life, these initiatives had little or no impact on the restricted nature of the job itself, which was designed so as to limit employees' discretion or control over their work. This picture of relatively low discretionary job design across the eight case studies is consistent with the literature on call centers in the United Kingdom as well as with recent cross-national studies that suggest that call center agents in Britain tend to exercise lower levels of discretion compared to their counterparts in a number of other European economies (Holman, Batt, and Holtgrewe 2006).

Some call center workers clearly enjoy their work, and many more aspire to give good customer service and derive satisfaction from being able to do so. Where the "system" gets in the way—through, for example, the use of contradictory targets—it can be a source of frustration for employees as much as for customers on the other end of the line. At the same time, call center work is often hard and stressful, although in our cases the main source of strain derived not so much from performance management systems and the pressure of targets (though they clearly play a part) as from the constant requirement to interact with customers (some of whom may be abusive) in the context of a job that is often highly repetitive and monotonous and calls upon huge resources of stamina. For most agents, the job of working in a mass-market call center quickly becomes something to be endured—and therefore something that can be tolerated only for so long.

Flat organizational structures tend to limit vertical progression opportunities, and while some employees clearly do manage to progress—mainly to the team leader level—many find that even this relatively short career ladder is unavailable to them. Others may take a call center job hoping that it will lead to a better job elsewhere in the company. While one of our case studies in the utilities sector was able to treat its call center as an entry point into the wider organization, there are inevitably constraints on management's ability to operate such a system, which depends on companies locating their call centers close to these wider functions and then having sufficient opportunities available to meet demand. Research from the other countries in this project indicates that call center jobs do not have to be like this. In Germany and Denmark, levels of autonomy, discretion, and functional flexibility were found to be much higher, while call centers in France and Denmark were more likely to provide a career path into the wider organization. The United Kingdom thus appears to resemble more closely American and Dutch call centers in having relatively low levels of discretion and limited progression opportunities.

Not surprisingly, many call center workers in the United Kingdom end up voting with their feet, some in search of alternative call center work and better pay and conditions where it is available locally; a significant number, however, vow never to return to the industry. It is unclear what happens to them, where they go in the labor market, or what kind of future beckons for them. In some firms, management appeared to be able to operate relatively comfortably with labor turnover levels in the region of 20 to 30 percent. Given the problem of maintaining employee motivation and service quality in what is often a dull yet demanding job, it might be argued that management actually benefits from relatively high, but manageable, levels of churn. In firms subject to regulation with associated service quality obligations, however, turnover problems have pushed management to improve job quality, whether through increasing pay, reducing the proportion of agency staff, or bringing shift arrangements more into line with staff preferences.

## NOTES

1. "Agent position" refers to a single workstation. Agent positions do not necessarily equate with the number of agents, since there may be more than one agent per workstation.
2. These data have to be treated with caution, since a large part of the workforce is not captured owing to definitional issues over job classification.
3. "GCSE level" refers to five General Certificates of Secondary Education, grades A* through C, which are normally taken at the end of compul-

280 LOW-WAGE WORK IN THE UNITED KINGDOM

sory schooling at age sixteen. "A levels" are academic qualifications normally taken at age eighteen.

4. In one case (U1), interviews were carried out at two different call centers.

5. Job complexity categories are relative measures in relation to call center work and do not reflect how these jobs can be classified in terms of other occupations. This measure of complexity is not unproblematic, particularly for cross-country comparisons. Comparative data from Denmark, France, Germany, and the Netherlands indicate that on average call center agents in the United Kingdom take significantly longer to become competent, yet their jobs have lower levels of discretion (see Holman, Batt, and Holtgrewe 2006).

6. Note that the proportions of female and part-time agents in the case study call centers are broadly consistent with those found in the LFS analysis relating to the wider industry (see figure 7.1).

7. For further discussion of the opt-out procedure in relation to the European Working Time Directive, see chapter 2.

8. GCSEs math and English grades A* to C are academic qualifications normally taken at the end of compulsory schooling at age sixteen. Around half of school-leavers do not achieve this standard in both math and English.

9. Some other call centers operated by U2 paid less per hour than the case study center we visited precisely because of different local labor market conditions.

## REFERENCES

Bain, Peter, and Phil Taylor. 2002. "Ringing the Changes? Union Recognition and Organisation in Call Centres in the U.K. Finance Sector." *Industrial Relations Journal* 33(3): 246–61.

Bain, Peter, Aileen Watson, Gareth Mulvey, Phil Taylor, and Gregor Gall. 2002. "Taylorism, Targets, and the Pursuit of Quantity and Quality by Call Centre Management." *New Technology, Work, and Employment* 17(3): 170–85.

Batt, Rosemary. 2000. "Strategic Segmentation in Frontline Services: Matching Customers, Employees, and Human Resources." *International Journal of Human Resource Management* 11(3): 540–61.

Batt, Rosemary, and Lisa Moynihan. 2002. "The Viability of Alternative Call Centre Production Models." *Human Resource Management Journal* 12(4): 14–34.

Batt, Rosemary, Larry Hunter, and Steffanie Wilk. 2003. "How and When Does Management Matter? Job Quality and Career Opportunities for Call Center Workers." In *Low-Wage America*, edited by Eileen Appelbaum,

Annette Bernhardt, and Richard J. Murnane. New York: Russell Sage Foundation.

Beirne, Martin, Kathleen Riach, and Fiona Wilson. 2004. "Controlling Business? Agency and Constraint in Call Centre Working." *New Technology, Work, and Employment* 19(2): 96–109.

Belt, Vicki. 2002. "A Female Ghetto? Women's Careers in Call Centres." *Human Resource Management Journal* 12(4): 51–67.

Callaghan, George, and Paul Thompson. 2002. "'We Recruit Attitude': The Selection and Shaping of Routine Call Centre Labour." *Journal of Management Studies* 39(2): 233–54.

ContactBabel. 2005. *The U.K. Contact Centre Operational Review 2005.* Sedgefield, U.K.: ContactBabel.

Customer Contact Association (CCA). 2003. "Research and Information: Frequently Asked Questions." Accessed at http://www.cca.org.uk/research/FAQs.asp.

Deery, Stephen, and Nick Kinnie. 2004. "Introduction: The Nature and Management of Call Centre Work." In *Call Centres and Human Resource Management: A Cross-national Perspective*, edited by Stephen Deery and Nick Kinnie. Basingstoke, U.K.: Palgrave.

Department of Trade and Industry. (DTI). 2004. *The U.K. Contact Centre Industry: A Study.* London: DTI.

E-skills UK. 2003. *The E-skills U.K. Contact Centre Survey.* London: E-skills.

Fernie, Sue, and David Metcalf. 1998. "(Not) Hanging on the Telephone: Payment Systems in the New Sweatshops." Discussion paper 390. London: London School of Economics, Centre for Economic Performance.

Frenkel, Stephen J., Marek Korczynski, Karen Shire, and May Tam. 1999. *On the Front Line: Organization of Work in the Information Society.* Ithaca, N.Y.: Cornell University Press.

Frenkel, Stephen J., May Tam, Marek Korczynski, and Karen Shire. 1998. "Beyond Bureaucracy? Work Organization in Call Centres." *International Journal of Human Resource Management* 9(6): 957–79.

Garson, Barbara. 1988. *The Electronic Sweatshop: How Computers Are Transforming the Office of the Future into the Factory of the Past.* Ithaca, N.Y.: Cornell University Press.

Glucksmann, Miriam A. 2004. "Call Configurations: Varieties of Call Centre and Divisions of Labour." *Work, Employment, and Society* 18(4): 795–811.

Halford, Victoria, and Harvey Cohen. 2003. "Technology Use and Psychosocial Factors in the Self-reporting of Musculoskeletal Disorder Symptoms in Call Centre Workers." *Journal of Safety Research* 34(2): 167–73.

Heery, Edmund. 2004. "The Trade Union Response to Agency Labour in Britain." *Industrial Relations Journal* 35(5): 434–50.

Holman, David. 2005. "Call Centres." In *The New Workplace: A Guide to the Human Impact of Modern Working Practices*, edited by David Holman,

Toby D. Wall, Chris W. Clegg, Paul Sparrow, and Ann Howard. Chichester, U.K.: Wiley.

Holman, David, and Stephen Wood. 2002. *Human Resource Management in Call Centres.* Sheffield, U.K.: University of Sheffield, Institute of Work Psychology, in association with Customer Contact Association Research Institute U.K.

Holman, David, Rosemary Batt, and Ursula Holtgrewe. 2006. *Global Call Center Report.* Ithaca, N.Y.: International Perspectives on Management and Employment.

Houlihan, Maeve. 2002. "Tensions and Variations in Call Centre Management Strategies." *Human Resource Management Journal* 12(4): 67–86.

Hutchinson, Sue, John Purcell, and Nick Kinnie. 2000. "Evolving High Commitment Management and the Experience of the RAC Call Centre." *Human Resource Management Journal* 10(1): 63–78.

Incomes Data Services (IDS). 2001. *Pay and Conditions in Call Centres 2001.* London: IDS.

———. 2003. *Pay and Conditions in Call Centres 2003.* London: IDS.

———. 2005. "Pay and Conditions in Call Centres 2005." *Pay Report* 937: 7–14.

Key Note. 2006. *Call Centres.* Hampton, Middlesex, U.K.: Key Note Ltd.

Kinnie, Nick, Sue Hutchinson, and John Purcell. 2000. "Fun and Surveillance: The Paradox of High Commitment Management in Call Centres." *International Journal of Human Resource Management* 11(5): 967–85.

Korczynski, Marek. 2002. *Human Resource Management in Service Work.* Basingstoke, U.K.: Palgrave.

Lockyer, Cliff, Dora Scholarios, Aileen Watson, and Dirk Bunsel. 2002. "Career and Commitment in Call Centres." Working paper 19. Leeds, U.K.: Economic and Social Research Council (ESRC) Future of Work Program.

Marshall, J. Neill, and Ranald Richardson. 1996. "The Impact of 'Telemediated' Services on Corporate Structures: The Example of 'Branchless' Retail Banking in Britain." *Environment and Planning* 28(10): 1843–58.

Merchants Limited. 2000. *1999/2000 The International Call/Contact Centre Benchmarking Report.* Milton Keynes, Merchants Limited.

Mintel. 2005. *Call Centres Industrial Report, U.K., December 2005.* London: Mintel International Group Ltd.

Office for National Statistics (ONS). 2004. *UK 2005: The Official Yearbook of the United Kingdom of Great Britain and Northern Ireland.* London: The Stationary Office.

Poynter, Gavin. 2000. *Restructuring in the Service Industries: Management and Reform of Workplace Relations in the U.K. Service Sector.* London: Mansell.

Taylor, Phil, and Peter Bain. 1999. "An Assembly Line in the Head: Work and Employment Relations in the Call Centre." *Industrial Relations Journal* 30(2): 101–17.

———. 2001. "Trade Unions, Workers' Rights and the Frontier of Control in U.K. Call Centres." *Economic and Industrial Democracy* 22(1): 39–66.

Taylor, Phil, Chris Baldry, Peter Bain, and Vaughan Ellis. 2003. "'A Unique Working Environment': Health, Sickness, and Absence Management in U.K. Call Centres." *Work, Employment, and Society* 17(3): 435–58.

# CHAPTER 8

# Low-Wage Work in the United Kingdom: Employment Practices, Institutional Effects, and Policy Responses

*Damian Grimshaw, Caroline Lloyd,*
*and Chris Warhurst*

Prompted by a previous study in the United States, and as part of a wider European study also looking at Germany, Denmark, France, and the Netherlands, the research presented in this volume has explored low-wage work in the United Kingdom. For all but a few of the thirty-seven organizations included in the five-industry United Kingdom study, the targeted occupations were low-wage, and in almost all cases they were more likely to be so than in the other European countries. These case studies highlight many of the issues that prevail in the British economy, where more than one in five employees is engaged in low-wage work. What the research demonstrates is that a detailed interrogation of the inner workings of organizations helps both to disentangle the many conditions that shape low-wage work and to identify the factors that might encourage employers to adopt business approaches that ameliorate low-wage jobs.

An important feature of the research design for all five case study chapters was the collection of qualitative data, supported by statistics on earnings and employment at the industry, sector, and organizational levels. Interviews with various managers in the organizations and employees working in the targeted low-wage jobs enabled the research to encompass a range of views, capture unanticipated issues, and unravel the complex context in which existing business approaches are adopted. This research approach not only complemented but supplemented the quantitative data presented in chapter 2, enabling more detailed analysis and understanding of the nature of the work and the characteristics of the workers in the selected jobs. It thus revealed the peculiar and often contradictory mechanics of the low-wage labor market—features that are best investigated through detailed case study research (see Grimshaw 2005).

The case studies shed light on the role of economic, institutional, and social conditions in shaping low-wage work. In some cases, access to new pools of labor (the previously inactive or new migrant workers) shifted the balance of supply and demand. In others, workers were trapped in a vicious cycle of low levels of education and training and low pay that offered few obvious incentives for the employer or the employee to invest in human capital. But in many cases, low pay was not simply the result of economic factors narrowly interpreted. Institutional influences—such as the lack of workplace- or industry-level collective bargaining and the weakness of both labor market and product market regulations—as well as social, political, and gender relations played prominent roles. Examples of how institutional and social forces dampened pay levels were varied and included the failure by employers to recognize and reward particular skills; the unwillingness of employers to pay more despite healthy profits; the inability of trade unions to bargain effectively for members segmented by gender or employment status; the political agenda that subjects low-wage, public sector workers to intense cost competition with private sector firms; and the persistent discriminatory belief among some employers that women in part-time employment earn "pin money." A critical lesson from these findings is that academic and policy discussions about low-wage work must extend beyond narrow economic issues to address more seriously the institutional and social constitution of the low-wage labor market in the United Kingdom economy.

In the final section of this chapter, we argue that there are many ways, particularly through state intervention, in which the proportion of low-wage workers in the United Kingdom could be reduced to resemble more closely our European neighbors while minimizing any adverse effects on employment levels. Since unemployment is currently relatively low and reducing poverty is a key target of United Kingdom government social policy (see Smith 2007), now would seem an appropriate time to begin this process. Policies are required that not only focus on mechanisms to shift more firms away from the predominant competitive strategy of low-skill, low-cost, and low-value-added (see chapter 2) but also provide a significantly higher floor for wages and conditions than is currently the case.

The chapter is organized as follows. The next section analyzes the varied responses of the thirty-seven case study organizations to particular competitive pressures and details the impact on the target occupational groups. The following section argues that, despite the fragmented and largely uncoordinated nature of the United Kingdom labor market, there are six key institutional features that have an important effect on conditions and prospects for low-wage workers. Given this institutional context, the next section explores policy responses, outlining a possible new deal for low-wage earners in the United Kingdom. A short section with concluding remarks ends the chapter.

## HOW ARE COMPANIES RESPONDING TO COMPETITIVE PRESSURES?

Each of the case study chapters has detailed the ways in which the competitive environment has affected the quality of jobs for specified groups of workers. Table 8.1 highlights the key pressures and market conditions confronting the case study organizations. All were tackling the challenge of having to keep costs down while maintaining or improving the quality of their products or services. Nevertheless, the extent of the pressures and the balance between them varied substantially across firms and industries. It is notable that the growing presence of international competition through trade, offshoring, and relocation of firms was not a major factor in the organizations investigated. Competition was predominantly national, regional, or even locally based in character. The call center industry has been subject to the offshoring of operations to lower-cost countries, particularly India (see Taylor and Bain 2005), but so far this process has been relatively limited. While food processing is in part shaped by international competition—imports grew from 19 to 26 percent of domestic consumption between 1992 and 2004 (ONS 2006)—competition with foreign-based firms was not reported as a major factor in the firms selected for this study.

Comparing the five industries, cost pressures were particularly intense within food processing, midrange hotels, and retailers. Food processing is the only manufacturing industry we studied; although the level of international trade is relatively low, imports are gradually rising, while consumer expenditure on food is growing steadily, albeit less than other items of exportation. In the context of intense cost and delivery demands from the major supermarkets, food processors have predominantly focused on cost reduction, rationalization, and mergers and acquisitions rather than on innovation and R&D. In the hotel industry, there has been significant ownership consolidation combined with new entrants and a major focus on cost-cutting whilst maintaining service quality. The industry is characterized by volatile markets with periods of rapid expansion linked to upswings in the business cycle and large drops in occupancy rates during downturns. Overexpansion during the last economic boom has subsequently seen midmarket hotels squeezed between the new "budget" entrants and the upper-market hotels setting higher service standards and offering discounted room rates. In contrast, the retail industry has enjoyed a relatively long period of growth in consumer expenditure. However, the majority of companies remain very cost-focused as the large chains attempt to win greater market share from both their key competitors and small independents. Cost reduction is being achieved partly by squeezing suppliers (such as food processors) and tight control of wage bills.

The other two industries, call centers and hospitals, have been restricted in their ability to pursue similar cost-cutting strategies for various reasons. The call center case studies were drawn from finance and utility companies, many of which have been very profitable in recent years. Tightening service regulations and/or efforts to increase market share led a number of the case study companies to focus on improving service quality. However, these efforts have been hampered by high labor turnover and extensive reliance on agency workers, in response to which some improvements have been made to elements of job quality. By contrast, other call centers engaged in outsourcing are in a different position in that they face a greater threat from overseas relocation, moves by some contracting organizations to bring operations back in-house, and considerable overcapacity following the years of rapid expansion. For these companies, cost reduction remains a priority.

Hospitals operate in a very different environment, being located within the public sector and subject to direct government intervention in their financial and employment practices. They are also a target of high-profile political campaigning from trade unions and the general public in terms of resources and employment conditions. The national pay framework in the National Health Service (NHS) and the apparent end of the two-tier system—whereby staff working for private contractors could be on terms and conditions inferior to those of workers directly employed—have raised costs significantly.

Table 8.1 Market Position and Competitive Pressures in the Case Study Organizations

| Industry | Market | Key Competitive Pressures[a] | Other Factors in the Sector |
|---|---|---|---|
| Call centers | | | |
| Competitive markets | Profitable and expanding | Quality of service, regulatory rules (costs) | Fluctuations in call volumes; recruitment difficulties in some areas- |
| Monopolies | Profitable | Regulatory requirements (costs) | |
| Outsourcers | Overcapacity | Costs, short-term response (quality of service) | |
| Food processing | | | |
| Meat | Supermarket label, very low margins | Retailer power, cost, delivery (quality) | Seasonal fluctuations in demand |
| Confectionery | Most own-brand, higher margins, but competitive | Marketing, retailer power, cost, delivery | |

| | Product market conditions | Principal competitive pressures | Secondary pressures[a] |
|---|---|---|---|
| **Hotels** | | | |
| Upper end | Volatile markets | Cost, expanding facilities and amenities, quality service | Frequent fluctuations in demand |
| Midmarket | Volatile markets and intensified competition | Cost, expanding amenities | |
| **Hospitals** | | | |
| In-house | Public-sector, budgetary constraints | Cost, service quality | National pay system, end of two-tier pay and conditions; recruitment difficulties in some areas |
| Outsourced | Contracted, budgetary constraints | Cost, service quality | |
| **Retail** | | | |
| Food | Highly concentrated | High end: quality of product, service (costs) Low end: costs, service | Fluctuations in customer flows; electrical: rapid changes in products |
| Electrical | Downward pressure on prices | Costs, product knowledge, response to demand | |

*Source:* Authors' compilation based on data described in chapters 3 through 7.
[a] Secondary pressures in parentheses.

Although there was a substantial 40 percent increase in funding by the Labour government between 1999 and 2004, the combination of a new financial management system, ambitious performance targets (for example, concerning waiting lists), and an expanded workforce left some hospitals facing severe financial problems during 2005 and 2006. With labor costs making up the largest part of their budgets, a number of hospitals were beginning to cut both posts and "soft" expenditures, such as training.

To what extent, then, were the case study organizations attempting to remain competitive or stay within budget by cutting labor costs, either in absolute terms or relative to total turnover? There are a variety of methods through which this aim might be achieved: introducing technological change, working "smarter," working "harder," cutting wages and conditions of current and/or new workers, and matching the number of workers more tightly to business demands. The ability to pursue particular approaches depends on the nature of the product or service, alongside the constraints imposed by regulations, trade unions, recruitment and retention issues, and the employees themselves.

Within the case study organizations, it is fair to say that limited attention had been given to investing in technology or to working "smarter." Automated scanners in retailing have been around for a number of years and have already speeded up checkout operations and been applied to the reordering of products. In call centers, systems are constantly being updated, and there is some use of automated responses and the Internet, but these technical changes have yet to produce a dramatic impact on the number of operatives and the nature of their jobs. In food processing, new equipment has been installed, albeit at a slow pace, primarily for the purpose of cutting labor costs and increasing capacity. There remains much manual work involving repetitive actions or requiring considerable stamina but little skill. In hotels, scant attention has been paid to technological applications that could reduce the physical demands of the cleaner's job—for example, in relation to bed lifting. Moreover, when refurbishing rooms, hotel management fails to consider designs that would reduce cleaning demands. Working smarter, such as by increasing levels of training or redesigning jobs to extend the skills utilized, is largely restricted to hospitals. However, even here the positive changes are being threatened by recent budgetary constraints.

A more common method used by the case study firms to reduce labor costs was downward pressure on wages and benefits. In a number of industries, employees experienced declining relative wages (hotels, food retailing, and food processing), the loss of bonuses and payments for working unsocial hours (food retailing), and reductions in overtime and benefits (food processing). More dramatic cuts in the payroll have been made through the employment of agency workers on inferior terms and conditions compared to direct employees (hotels, food processing, and call centers). However, problems with high staff turnover, recruitment difficulties, and quality issues in call centers and in one of the food processing companies had led to a partial reversal of this approach.

Many organizations also sought to reduce costs by matching staffing arrangements more directly to fluctuating business needs—that is, the number of shoppers or telephone calls, the occupancy rate in hotels, and the daily orders from supermarkets. All of the industries, with the exception of hospitals, face substantial fluctuations in customer demand over the day, week, or year. Shift work, annualized hours, overtime, part-time hours, variable hours, temporary workers, agency workers, and piecework were all used to varying degrees within the case study organizations. These different types of contractual arrangements allow a very high degree of numerical flexibility that is not usually possible in most other European countries where labor market regulations are tighter.

## The Impact on Low-Wage Workers

A high proportion of workers in each of the occupations in our research earn low wages (that is, they earn below the low pay threshold; see table 8.2). Indeed, they account for a majority among hotel room attendants, hospital cleaners, retail sales assistants, and checkout operators. It is in these occupations that the rates of female participation and the levels of part-time work are particularly high. In addition, substantial numbers of assistant nurses, process operatives, and call center agents are paid just above the low pay threshold. Living on these wages is difficult, and low-wage workers frequently opt to obtain more income through overtime or second jobs or attempt to make ends meet by sharing or renting accommodations or by living with parents. Nevertheless, reflecting the national pattern presented in chapter 1, many of these low-paid workers do not live in house-

Table 8.2 Characteristics of the Target Low-Wage Occupations, 2006

| Industry | Occupation | Female | Part-time[a] | Below LPT: Defined in Terms of All Employees' Earnings[b] | Below LPT: Defined in Terms of Full-Time Employees' Earnings[c] |
|---|---|---|---|---|---|
| Hotels | Cleaner | 85% | 56% | 89% | 94% |
| Retail | Sales and retail assistant | 71 | 65 | 72 | 83 |
| Retail | Retail assistant and check-out operator | 75 | 75 | 69 | 87 |
| Hospitals | Nursing auxiliary | 86 | 44 | 17 | 38 |
| Hospitals | Cleaner | 90 | 66 | 56 | 74 |
| Food, drink, and tobacco processing | Process operative | 29 | 13 | 31 | 47 |
| Various | Call center agent | 71 | 24 | 31 | 51 |
| All United Kingdom industries | All occupations | 46 | 25 | 22 | 30 |

*Source:* Annual Survey of Hours and Earnings (ASHE) (2006). We thank Matt Osborne at the National Institute for Economic and Social Research (NIESR) for providing the analysis of the ASHE data.
[a] Less than thirty hours per week.
[b] The low-pay threshold defined on the basis of all employees' earnings (including part-timers) was £6.59 in 2006.
[c] The low-pay threshold defined on the basis of full-time employees' earnings was £7.41 in 2006.

holds below the income poverty line since they form part of dual-income (or triple-income) households.

Just as pay varies across the industries and organizations, so too do the additional benefits on offer (see table 8.3). All workers in the United Kingdom have access to the (largely) free-of-charge national health care system, while statutory rights include twenty days of paid holiday, sick pay (£70.05 (US$142.98) in 2006 from the fourth day of absence), maternity leave (six weeks at 90 percent of earnings; twenty weeks at £108.85 (US$222.18) per week), and paternity leave (two weeks at £108.85 per week). Traditionally, it has been left to collective bargaining or unilateral management decision as to whether to offer additional provisions above these basic minimums. In our case study organizations, the most generous benefits were available to those working in the public sector hospitals, where all employees were entitled to a package that included extra holidays, sick pay, maternity leave, and pensions. Some of the private sector employers, particularly in call centers and to a more limited extent in food processing, also offered employees some of these benefits. In retail, with the exception of one company, benefits were more basic, focusing mainly on pensions, and hotels offered workers no more than the statutory minimum, which left them severely disadvantaged when sick and without any occupational pension.

The additional benefits offered to directly employed workers are not available to the many agency staff who work alongside them—with the exception of agency workers in hospitals who have signed up with the new national not-for-profit agency (see chapter 5). Agency workers experience the ultimate "hire-and-fire" regime, have significantly lower rates of pay, and often lack the security of a guaranteed number of weekly working hours. With the accession countries joining the European Union and the migration of workers from Eastern Europe and the Baltic states, many companies in the food and hotel industries have expanded their use of agency workers. The evidence suggests that these workers are often prepared to accept jobs with wage levels significantly below that deemed acceptable within local labor markets in the United Kingdom. In food processing, this possibility has enabled employers to continue to recruit while, at the same time, restricting wage increases and cutting benefits and pensions. Hotels have also experienced a major shift toward agency work, particularly in London. Direct employees are usually paid the national minimum wage (NMW) and receive few additional

Table 8.3 Main Indicators of Job Quality and Direction of Change in the Case Study Sectors

| Industry | Pay per Hour (Median Case) | Benefits (Above Statutory)[a] | Agency Use | Numerical Flexibility | Career Progression | Direction of Change in Job Quality[b] |
|---|---|---|---|---|---|---|
| Hotels | £5.05 | None | Very high in London | Very high | Some: supervisor, other departments | – Flexibility<br>– Agency<br>– Pay<br>– Work effort |
| Retail | | | | | | |
| Food | £5.75 | Limited: some pensions | No | Moderate | Limited: supervisor, management | – Pay<br>– Flexibility |
| Electrical | £7.95 | Limited: some pensions | No | Moderate | Some: supervisor, management | No change |
| Food processing | £6.71 | Varied: sick pay, holidays, some pensions | High | High | Fair: higher-skilled, supervisor | + Health and safety<br>+ Pay and benefits<br>– Pay and benefits<br>– Agency<br>– Flexibility<br>– Work effort |

| | Pay | Benefits | | | Progression | Direction of change |
|---|---|---|---|---|---|---|
| Hospital Cleaner | £5.60[c] | Significant: sick pay, maternity, holidays, pensions | No | Moderate | Limited: supervisor, nursing assistant | + Pay and benefits<br>+ Progression<br>− Work effort |
| Assistant nurse | £7.28[c] | | Some | Low | Good: intermediate grades, nursing | + Pay<br>+ Progression |
| Call centers | £8.25 | Significant: sick pay, maternity, holidays, pensions | High | High | Some: supervisor | + Pay<br>+ Flexibility<br>+ Agency |

*Source:* Authors' compilation based on data described in chapters 3 through 7.

[a] The main benefits considered are holidays, sick pay, maternity pay, and pensions. Many organizations provided other fringe benefits, such as share options, subsidized canteens, and discounted products.

[b] The direction of job quality change, as indicated by key aspects of the job, is assessed either as largely positive (+), and so improving, or as largely negative (−), and so deteriorating. Where there is no clear direction of change, the specific aspect of job quality is excluded from the table.

[c] Median gross hourly pay derived from Labour Force Survey data.

benefits, so that agency workers can often be more expensive (per hour). However, agency workers offer managers the flexibility to vary the number of workers according to the rooms occupied on a daily basis, as well as providing a lengthy probationary period for screening prior to direct recruitment.

Managers in the case study organizations imposed strong demands for working-time flexibility in many of the target occupations. Rotating and variable shift patterns were common across all the industries. These could disrupt routines and sleep patterns and sometimes limited possibilities for workers to pursue nonwork activities. In retail, hotels, and most call centers, workers often received no premium for shift work. Overtime was also common in hospitals, food processing, and call centers. Because of the United Kingdom's opt-out arrangements in relation to the forty-eight-hour working week under the European "Working Time Directive" (see chapter 2), many food processing operatives were working up to, and even more than, sixty hours per week. Although there was no evidence of managerial coercion to work these long hours, it was often a necessity for these workers if they were to achieve adequate levels of pay. However, while workers relied on this additional income, it was unpredictable, and in a number of companies the opportunity to work overtime was increasingly unavailable. In other industries (predominantly hotels but also food retailing), some workers had to accept contracts with variable hours or part-time hours and could only hope to use overtime (on standard pay rates) to make up the longer hours that they required.

Many workers had few qualifications and low job expectations. Most of their jobs were narrowly defined, with low levels of discretion and little movement between tasks or departments. Work was a means to obtain an income, and the opportunity to mix socially with good colleagues was a bonus (if employees in food processing, retail, and call centers are indicative). Such interaction made working time pass more quickly and less laboriously. A further potential source of job satisfaction was the presence of a listening and communicative management, although this was a much rarer phenomenon. Both are points long noted by studies from Mayo (1946) onward. There were a significant number of workers, particularly in call centers and hospitals and among migrant workers, who could be said to be overqualified for their jobs. Some of these workers hoped that their entry-level jobs would lead to something better. However, limited competency in the English language was a clear barrier to gaining higher-paid work for many migrant workers. For workers who wanted part-time work, who were reentering the labor market after breaks for raising children, or, in the case of older workers, who were seeking work after being made redundant elsewhere, there seemed few alternatives in the labor market despite their qualifications and prior experience.

There were opportunities for career progression for some workers. However, although such options may have led to jobs that were intrinsically more interesting (for example, quality control) or that involved more responsibility (supervisor or team leader), with the exception of those working in call centers, these jobs too were rarely paid at rates much above the low pay threshold. Moreover, the chances for further promotion were often extremely restricted owing to flat organizational structures and a common preference for recruiting externally for skills rather than providing extensive training within the organization. For the large number of part-time workers in these industries, prospects were limited. The evidence suggests that supervisory posts were often open only to full-time workers, while management development programs required not just that an applicant be a full-time worker but that the individual be able to move between different locations (for example, different supermarkets or hotels); such freedom of movement frequently was not a feasible option for workers with domestic responsibilities. As a result, part-time workers were concentrated in the lowest-skilled jobs and excluded from shift premiums and unsocial hours payments (outside of public hospitals), although they were still expected by employers in some industries (retailing, hotels) to be very flexible in terms of working time.

The final column in table 8.3 makes a judgment about the predominant trends found within the case study organizations in terms of the changing quality of employment. Food processing has probably experienced the greatest deterioration in conditions of work, followed by the hotel industry (which is lowest in absolute terms). Both of these industries have seen high levels of market competition and widespread use of foreign agency workers. The main trends in call centers and hospitals have been toward general improvements, fueled largely by labor market and trade union pressures, respectively. However, jobs remain highly routinized and fragmented within call centers, while work intensification is a prominent feature of hospitals. Retail workers face more limited changes, although the loss of unsocial hours premiums and employer demands for more flexible working times are becoming increasingly common.

## INSTITUTIONAL EFFECTS ON LOW-WAGE WORK IN THE UNITED KINGDOM

The analysis thus far demonstrates that the prospects of low-wage workers are shaped to a large extent by employers' responses to a range of competitive pressures and changing labor market conditions. The case studies show that such responses, in the form of changing pay and employment practices, vary both by industry and with respect to the dominant labor force group employed. But while employers typically responded individually (with the notable exception of public sector hospitals), they did not do so in a vacuum. A raft of labor market institutions, albeit weak relative to those in other European countries, have enabled or constrained particular employment practices; these include legislation on employment protection and working time, trade unions and collective bargaining arrangements, and regulations on low wages. Thus, while employers undoubtedly enjoy a relatively strong role as architects of the labor market structure (reflecting the liberal market economy status of the United Kingdom model), institutions do matter—especially since they provide a means of exploring the potential for further policy interventions to improve conditions for the low-wage workforce. This section examines the ramifications of the United Kingdom's weak and uncoordinated institutions in perpetuating the disproportionately large share of people in low-wage work compared to continental Europe.

An additional purpose of our analysis is to highlight, where appropriate, those characteristics of the United Kingdom labor market that differ from those found in the United States. On the one hand, the United Kingdom shares many features of the American labor market (for further details, see table 1.1). It has a high proportion of low-wage workers, buoyant job growth in most low-wage industries (such as hairdressing, social care, retail, hotels and restaurants, and security), relatively weak employment protection, a low and declining ratio of unemployment benefits to earnings, high wage inequality with a large wage penalty for working in low-status jobs, relatively weak unions, limited protection of workers through collective bargaining, and a culture of households working long hours combined with a high level of work effort. On the other hand, several features are distinctive to the United Kingdom labor market. Unlike the United States, Britain made an explicit effort to increase the relative value of the NMW during the period 2003 to 2006. Also, it is clear that the conditions that accompany low-wage work are less severe in the United Kingdom. For example, while lack of good health insurance is a prime determinant of a "bad" job in the United States (Kalleberg, Reskin, and Hudson 2000), in the United Kingdom all workers benefit from universal provision of free health care funded by taxation. And importantly, while there is no statutory provision for minimum annual leave in the United States, such provision has been made for employees in the United Kingdom as a result of EU legislation. These differences are starkly illustrated in Barbara Ehrenreich's (2001) and Polly Toynbee's (2003) journalistic investigations of low-wage work in the United States and Britain. While Toynbee had Kafkaesque meetings with welfare officials, at least her experiences demonstrated the functioning of a state-provided safety net in the United Kingdom. By contrast, lacking state provision and unable to afford personal insurance, Ehrenreich's U.S. coworkers were frequently found sleeping in car parks or suffering untreated ill health.

Our research has identified six key institutional features of the United Kingdom labor market that have affected the organization of low-wage work and the way in which distributional bargains have been designed or contested at a firm and industry level:

1.  Minimum wage legislation

2.  The regulation of working time

3.  Employment protection for temporary agency workers

4.  The regulation of interorganizational employment relations

5.  Provisions for trade union organization

6.  Policies that increase the supply of labor for low-wage jobs

## MINIMUM WAGE LEGISLATION

The introduction and subsequent annual upratings of the NMW represent perhaps the most important sustained institutional effect on the low-wage labor market in the United Kingdom (see chapter 2). Across the five industries and in many of the thirty-seven organizations investigated in this volume, the NMW has played a role in either raising or sustaining wage levels in the face of pressures to cut costs. Three main distributive outcomes can be detected. First, the minimum wage has established an agreed-upon wage floor against which employers, acting unilaterally or jointly with trade unions, can benchmark pay rates. For example, five of the six food-processing companies paid entry wage rates above the minimum, thus giving managers and employees a sense of relative value and also protecting employees from cost-cutting strategies. Also, in negotiating the new national pay structure for public hospitals, trade unions were able to boost basic pay rates for the lowest-paid by striving for a collectively negotiated minimum significantly above the national wage floor.

However, this positive distributional outcome contrasts with a second outcome caused by employers using the NMW as the "going rate." Among hotels, retail firms, and agency workers in food-processing plants, the chapters here show that this practice was common. Six of the eight hotels paid room attendants at or slightly above the NMW, four of the eight retail firms set entry pay at just a few pence above the NMW, and all six food-processing firms paid agency workers at the minimum wage or only slightly higher. Wider national surveys confirm these findings, showing that three-quarters of pubs and restaurants, for example, paid new recruits the minimum wage, that the median starting rate for a nursery assistant in 2001 and again in 2003 was the equivalent of the minimum wage, and that many leisure services firms have shifted from a strategy of paying well above the minimum wage to using the minimum wage as a starting rate (IDS 2004). The increase in the number of minimum wage workers has been associated in some of the retail case studies (see chapter 4) with revised employment contracts that reduce opportunities for pay enhancements through bonuses or higher rates for working weekends and public holidays.

A third distributional outcome concerns the level of the NMW. Despite improvements in the relative level of the minimum wage during the period 2003 to 2006 (following a fall in relative value during the period 1999 to 2003), it remains low compared to estimates by the Living Wage Unit (2006) of a living wage (£5.35 (US$10.91) per hour from October 2006, compared to the London living wage campaign estimate of £7.05 (US$14.38) in 2005–2006).[1] Our case studies suggest that even those workers paid at around the low pay threshold of £6.35 ($12.95) per hour (25 percent more than the NMW) found that their weekly income was not sufficient to establish financial independence. Many chose to work two or more jobs (in hotels, for example) or work long overtime hours (especially in the food-processing firms), and relied on state benefits (in the form of tax credits). The idea that the relative level of the minimum ought to reflect, in part, social norms of fairness or justice—as reflected in the growing number of living wage and trade union campaigns to boost low pay—is not part of the terms of reference of the Low Pay Commission, despite evidence that all wages are, to a greater or lesser extent, the result of the combined influences of social, political, and economic factors (Figart, Mutari, and Power 2002; Grimshaw and Rubery 2003; Rubery 1997).

## THE REGULATION OF WORKING TIME

The regulation of working time constitutes a second important institutional effect on the distributional outcome for low-wage workers. As chapter 2 details, because the United Kingdom uses a voluntary opt-out from the European Union directive regarding the forty-eight-hour working week, workers enjoy far less protection than their counterparts in most continental European countries. Moreover, research shows that for many employers, the opt-out is unnecessary because of the diluted nature of the regulations as applied in the United Kingdom (Hurrell 2005).[2] It is unsurprising, therefore, that in several case study organizations workers reported long hours of work—especially in food processing, where industry data show that one in five men work more than forty-eight hours per week. At four of the six case study establishments, overtime was common and many operatives had signed the opt-out.

Nevertheless, while the legislative protection for working time is relatively weak, many organizations are still bound by strong industrial relations custom and practice that protect standard hours and maintain enhanced pay for unsocial and overtime hours. This traditional industrial relations model of working time is especially associated with unionized manufacturing and public sector workplaces and can be argued to generate additional pressures for long working hours as a means for workers to earn a decent weekly wage by earning enhanced pay (Rubery et al. 2005). Thus, the situation in the food-processing firms results from a dual-pronged institutional effect reflecting the ability of employers, on the one hand, to extend the hours of full-time workers and, on the other, the success of unionized low-wage workers to defend the time-and-a-half premium for over-time working. In the public sector hospitals, unions resisted efforts by employers to cut unsocial hours premiums, and in our case studies employees defended the customary principle of time-and-a-half and double-time pay enhancements. However, the evidence also warns of the risks of long working hours, including the threat to workers' health and safety, as well as the problem of establishing a lifestyle based on an enhanced pay packet that might be unexpectedly reduced when, for example, supermarkets cut product orders and food-processing employers respond by abolishing overtime hours. Outside manufacturing and public sector workplaces, evidence of enhanced pay for unsocial and overtime hours is more limited. For example, while unsocial hours wage premiums were once an accepted feature of the retail industry, this convention has been steadily eroded. Also, most of the call centers and all of the hotel case studies provided no additional payments for weekend or evening work.

A dimension of working time that strongly distinguishes the United Kingdom from the United States concerns time off from work. At the time of our research, the United Kingdom set a statutory level of paid holiday entitlement at twenty days per year, following the incorporation of the European Union "Working Time Directive" in 1998. The government has announced that the statutory level will increase to twenty-eight days after October 2008 (DTI 2007). A notable finding from three of the industries (call centers, food processing, and hospitals) was that the targeted occupations already benefited from annual leave entitlement that was at least as generous as the future 2008 statutory level. For example, most food-processing firms offered a minimum of twenty days plus eight public holidays to all new employees, with an additional five days after five years' service. In the public hospitals, cleaners and assistant nurses enjoyed twenty-seven days plus eight public holidays, and their time off rose to thirty-three days plus eight public holidays after ten years' service. In contrast, provision in retail firms and hotels was close to the statutory minimum, with the consequence that those workers who were in the lowest-paying occupations in the study also received the fewest benefits.

## Employment Protection for Temporary Agency Workers

In line with its flexible labor market philosophy, the United Kingdom government imposes only a few restrictions on the use of agency workers. (For example, it prohibits their use to replace striking workers.) While most member states of the European Union have legislation (or legally binding collective agreements) to ensure that temporary agency workers earn the same pay as directly employed workers doing comparable jobs, the United Kingdom does not require such pay parity. Donald Storrie (2002) found that wages were "the biggest area of complaint" for temporary agency workers, who earned just 68 percent of the average weekly income of all employees. Moreover, the vulnerable status of agency workers in the United Kingdom is underlined by the absence of any legal requirement for them to be employed by either the agency or the client organization. Without the status of "employee," an agency worker is not entitled to the full range of employment rights, including, for example, protection against unfair dismissal, sick pay, and occupational pension schemes (TUC 2005).

Our research shows that the use of agency workers is very common in low-wage labor markets. Only in retail and among hospital cleaners did we find their use to be very limited. The weakness of legal restrictions clearly makes agency use a practical option for employers wishing to act quickly to meet uncertain production demand or to cut labor costs (Storrie 2002). In chapter 6, the manager of one of the food-processing firms, PoultryCo, memorably described agency use as "just an easy turn-on of the tap." Our research also shows that most agency workers receive only the statutory minimum in relation to holiday and sick pay. Agency use provides not only a flexible pool of labor but also a wider pool of labor often willing to work for inferior terms and conditions of employment. In the London hotels and the food-processing firms, the evidence shows that agencies have successfully drawn on groups of migrant labor from the new member states of the European Union.

Significantly, the research also suggests that there may be hidden organizational costs to high use of agency workers. Two call centers had started to rely on them less following the inability of temporary agencies to recruit people who could complete the required induction training or maintain adequate quality standards within the job.

In one of the upper market hotels, remedial training had to be provided to ensure quality standards. Thus, despite reduced labor costs, managers argued that such problems made very high levels of agency use a nonviable strategy, or at least problematic. In the public hospitals, a new national not-for-profit temporary work agency has been established in direct response to an exponential rise in agency spending to cover nursing positions. This new agency deploys information about staffing in hospital wards with the explicit aim of saving hospitals money: it charges half the fee compared to for-profit agencies and, crucially, extends the full range of employment terms and conditions enjoyed by directly employed public hospital workers to agency workers, including the final salary pension scheme. By contrast, for-profit agencies attempt to increase the market for temps and to maximize fees, while continuing to lobby against equal protection for agency workers.

## The Regulation of Interorganizational Employment Relations

A fourth institutional effect concerns an increasingly important dimension of low-wage work—the employment consequences of interorganizational production or supply chains. There are two relevant components: working in an organization that is squeezed by a powerful customer or client, and changes to employment caused by outsourcing.

Evidence from the Workplace Employee Relations Survey (WERS) shows that, after controlling for workplace and individual characteristics, workers' pay is depressed by 5 percent when they are employed in a workplace characterized by high competition and dependence on a large customer (for more than 10 percent of output) (Forth and Millward 2001, table 3). This significant finding is reflected in the case studies in this volume (see also Grimshaw and Carroll 2006). In particular, each of the meat-processing firms investigated had strongly dependent relations with one or two of the top four supermarket chains. The result was that supermarkets could "put the thumbscrews on," as one of the factory managers put it, by dictating prices as well as other terms governing production and delivery standards. In the absence of strengthened regulation that protects weak firms from powerful customers, it is likely that workers will continue to bear the brunt of such pressures on costs. At present, there is a statutory coded practice for the larger supermarkets, but it has been heavily criticized for being ineffective. In response, the Office of Fair Trading in 2006 referred supermarkets to the Competition Commission (for the second time in less than a decade) for an investigation into their dealings with suppliers.

The other employment dimension to supply chains involves the outsourcing of work. Workers who are transferred from one employer to another following the outsourcing of tasks to a subcontracting firm enjoy very limited protection under United Kingdom legislation. The Transfer of Undertakings (Protection of Employment) (TUPE) regulations provide for the employment conditions set by one employer to be carried over to another employer following outsourcing.[3] TUPE has no procedures, however, for coordinating terms and conditions over time after the point of transfer; as a result, transferred employees face the risk of deteriorating conditions. Also, other workers recruited directly to the subcontracting firm may be offered very different employment conditions, leading to a two-tier workforce of individuals who may be carrying out similar tasks. In the absence of stronger legal protection, our research evidence suggests that employers will continue to use outsourcing primarily as a means of reducing labor costs. There is, however, one notable example of an institutional innovation in this area that has considerably strengthened workers' protection. In March 2005, following a lengthy trade union campaign, the government introduced a two-tier code to ensure that new recruits to subcontractor firms providing public services receive treatment comparable to conditions for staff transferred from the public sector. In the National Health Service (NHS), the government set aside £75 million (US $153 million) for implementing the new policy and encouraged hospitals to renegotiate contracts with private subcontracting firms to pay for improved employment conditions. There appears to be no intention, however, of rolling out the policy to cover outsourcing deals in the private sector.

Even with improved protection for outsourced workers, the research in public hospitals suggests that the continued pressure by government to outsource low-wage jobs hampers improvements in job quality. Government policy is not supported by evidence showing that outsourcing generates organizational efficiencies or improves the quality of services. Moreover, the evidence from public sector hospitals suggests that outsourcing is fragmenting internal job ladders and putting obstacles in the way of cleaners who hope to progress to supervisory jobs or apply for an assistant nurse post.

## Provisions for Trade Union Organization

A fifth institutional effect on the United Kingdom's low-wage labor market derives from institutions for the collective representation of workers, which are the most important historical means for improving the jobs of workers at the lower end of the labor market. With the dramatic decline in union membership over the last twenty-five years, the representation of low-wage workers has fallen to particularly low levels in the United Kingdom. In 2003 just 15 percent of workers earning £6 (US$12.23) an hour or less were union members, compared to 40 percent among workers earning between £10 and £20 (US$20.40 and US$40.79) per hour (Howarth and Kenway 2004, 32). Moreover, the positive impact of unionization on pay has declined in recent years. Drawing on Labour Force Survey (LFS) data, David Blanchflower and Alex Bryson (2004) show that the union wage premium in the United Kingdom declined during the period 1994 to 2000 and that it fell to a nonsignificant level for manufacturing workers, men, private sector workers, and nonwhites. Declines in the wage premium were also substantial for the less-educated and for women, "raising questions about unions' ability to bid up the wages of those with lower marginal productivity and those who may be earning below their marginal product as a result of discrimination or labor market segmentation" (Blanchflower and Bryson 2004, 18).

Around half of the workplaces studied in this volume were unionized, predominantly in food processing, hospitals, and call centers. In these three industries, unions negotiated with management over pay and conditions. However, bargaining power was severely limited in food processing by weak union organization, high levels of use of agency workers, and the lack of supportive labor market pressures. Nevertheless, unions did play a positive role, particularly in the areas of working time and health and safety and in defending, to some extent, preexisting rights. In one case, an active shop-floor union representative successfully pressed managers to raise overtime enhancements for both agency workers and direct employees. In call centers, unions found it hard to organize in the face of high levels of turnover and use of temporary agency workers. With terms and conditions often determined at the division or company level, local representatives tended to have a more marginal role. Unions representing cleaners and assistant nurses in the public hospitals could claim a far more significant effect in improving employment conditions. Their long-running campaigns against the two-tier workforce, low pay in the public sector, and exploitative temporary work agencies have all led to U-turns in government policy, albeit after several years of struggle.

In the other two industries, retail and hotels, unions were severely marginalized. Labour Force Survey data for 2006 show union density levels of just 5.6 percent in hotels and restaurants and 11.1 percent in the wholesale, retail, and motor trade sectors (Grainger and Crowther 2007, table 10). Several factors have contributed to unions' failure to organize effectively within the hotel industry: the characteristics of workers and workplaces, employer hostility, and unions' own organizational and strategic inadequacies. In retail, the one case study firm that recognized a union granted it no role in pay-setting. As a manager from the headquarters office bluntly put it: "We let [the union] know things, but they don't have any rights." In the non-unionized retail firms, there were consultative committees for workers to air their grievances, but the research suggests that these had limited effectiveness.

## POLICIES THAT INCREASE THE SUPPLY OF LABOR FOR LOW-WAGE JOBS

The sixth institutional effect on the United Kingdom's low-wage labor market concerns the construction of an available pool of labor for low-paid jobs. The regulation of migrant workers plays a key role here. Since the late 1990s, government policy has encouraged workers to enter the United Kingdom to undertake low-skilled jobs in industries where employers have experienced recruitment difficulties. This use of an external pool of labor, augmented since 2004 by workers from the accession countries (particularly from Central and Eastern Europe) has relieved labor market pressures that would undoubtedly have hit the hotel and food-processing industries (see Murphy 2006). In particular, for jobs that require minimal English-language ability because of limited interaction with customers, the wide potential net for recruitment enabled managers not only to keep the wage levels of direct employees low but also to undercut them through the use of lower-paid agency workers.

In those industries that require a relative fluency in English because of direct employee-customer interaction, employers drew on a number of different labor market segments. One notable group that has increased significantly in recent years is young people seeking part-time work. Over one million students were active in the labor market in 2000, with further increases to 2011 expected as government pursues its targets for expanding higher education (Curtis and Lucas 2001). The introduction of tuition fees, the abolition of the student grant entitlements, and increased personal debt have given students strong financial incentives to work (Furlong and Cartmel 2005; Ward 2004). Consequently, students have become a structural feature of the labor market. However, a "coincidence of needs" is being established between employers and students, according to Susan Curtis and Rosemary Lucas (2001). Students seem willing and available to work flexibly for low wages, and employers perceive them to have good "social skills" (Nickson et al. 2004). Indeed, some supermarket retailers in the United Kingdom are now deliberately and actively recruiting on university campuses and offering employment contracts that wrap around study commitments (Dutton et al. 2005). This latter point is important since student employment is concentrated by industry and occupation. Nearly three-quarters of all working students are employed in routine interactive services, such as retail and hospitality and in jobs such as checkout operators and bar and waiting staff (Canny 2002; Curtis and Lucas 2001).

A further pool of available labor is represented by women with young children, who have been encouraged by government to return to work through higher levels of in-work benefits, financial support for child care, and government schemes such as the New Deal for Lone Parents. Again, many such women, particularly lone parents, are being directed toward routine interactive services (see, for example, Dutton et al. 2005). The high price of child care and the lack of provision for school-age children ensure that for many women at the bottom of the labor market there is no option but part-time work. Moreover, different government policies conflict with each other. Because of the high cost of child care, many low-paid women use their child's retired grandparents to provide "no-cost" child care. A new government policy to raise the age of retirement with a view to possibly abolishing a formal retirement age could undermine the employment possibilities for such women.

Most of our case study organizations in the retail, hotel, and hospital industries were found to have an abundant supply of workers willing to take on low-paid jobs on a part-time basis. These labor market supply factors consequently had a restraining influence on wages and conditions, in the context of relatively low official rates of unemployment. In contrast, recruitment shortages that could not be easily met by migrant labor or part-time workers were found to have led to improvements in some aspects of job quality within a number of the call centers.

Overall, therefore, the institutions that shape the United Kingdom's low-wage labor market have had a mixed effect. The NMW and rights to paid time off have improved the position of those at the very bottom of the (formal) labor market, although the relative level of the NMW has not improved sufficiently to reduce the proportion of low-paid workers (see chapter 2). Limited regulation of the employment conditions of agency workers and those subject to outsourcing or corporate takeover have enabled some companies to take advantage of a cheaper source of alternative labor. An expansion in labor supply, particularly at the lower end of the labor market, has also dampened wage pressures. Trade unions have been able to play some role in improving wages and conditions, but tend to lack organizational strength and the ability to recruit members and secure recognition rights in most low-wage industries.

## A POLICY AGENDA

The above assessment demonstrates that the quality of low-wage work in the United Kingdom is shaped by the particular configuration of institutions, especially those related to the minimum wage, working time, agency workers, outsourcing, trade unions and the supply of available labor, including mothers/returners, students and migrant workers. This focus on institutions opens up the potential for exploring alternative policy interventions both to reduce the numbers of low-wage workers in the United Kingdom and to improve the quality of low-wage work. In this section, we consider what policy options exist and what are the prospects for such a new agenda to emerge.

### WHY LOW-WAGE WORK IS A PROBLEM

The existence of large numbers of low-wage workers within the United Kingdom has a number of consequences for individuals, for society, and for the economy. Low-wage work is insufficient to provide a decent or, in some localities, even a basic standard of living, and it threatens to stretch and shred the social fabric if income inequalities become unsustainably great and those on the lowest incomes disengage from the rest of society (Toynbee 2003). The government has attempted to tackle income inequalities through limited remedial actions, such as providing tax credits for low-income families. Workers unwilling to take up government welfare support—or who are ineligible for it—have to rely either on liberal credit facilities through which they may incur substantial personal debts (a feature of the United Kingdom that is increasingly coming under critical scrutiny) or on supplementary sources of income, such as working long hours or taking second jobs. As chapter 1 shows, most low-wage workers are not members of poor households, because they live with others who are working or they receive state income transfers. However, over half of all poor households and nearly half of the three million children living in poverty have at least one person working in their household (Harker 2006). In addition, many of those working long-term in low-wage jobs may escape household poverty during their working lives, but once retired, they are more likely to end up in poverty owing to lack of an occupational pension and limited opportunities for saving (Bardasi and Jenkins 2002).

The problems of poverty not only involve direct personal and family material hardship but also poor diet and health and social exclusion. As Helen Masterman-Smith and her colleagues (2006, 6) state: "For many, living in a low wage household means going without meals, home heating, clothing, healthcare and medicine, transportation, house repairs, sport, holidays, basic leisure activities and educational opportunities." As chapter 2 shows, for workers in age groups above the age of twenty-five, low pay is most often not a short, transitory phase but a long-term experience and so has lasting effects. Most childhood poverty is not transitory. In Donald Hirsch's (2006) study, for example, two-thirds of children living in poverty had been poor in three out of the four previous years. There is also an intergenerational "knock-on" effect that is becoming more persistent, with poverty enduring from childhood to middle age (Blanden and Gibbons 2006). Current government measures aimed at cutting levels of poverty appear to have stalled, while income inequality has recently begun to rise again (Brewer et al. 2007). A number of commentators have argued that the gains to be made through reducing the number of workless households are now limited and that the focus should shift toward reducing poverty for those who are working (Brewer and Shephard 2004; Hirsch 2006). However, relying on tax incentives and in-work benefits to "make work pay" and to reduce poverty levels is a costly option that may involve continued and increasing levels of subsidies to low-paying employers (Prasch 2002).

Not only are low wages a problem for individuals and for social cohesion, but they also form part of a structure of economic incentives that underpins many firms' business strategies in the United Kingdom (see chapter 2). While the United Kingdom has enjoyed great improvements in economic performance since the late 1990s—job growth, low unemployment, economic growth, and low inflation—it is still plagued by relatively poor productivity performance, low levels of research and development and investment in physical capital, and too many firms producing low-specification products or services in price-competitive markets (Coffield 2004; Delbridge et al. 2006; Finegold and Soskice 1988; Keep and Mayhew 1998; Lloyd and Payne 2002). It is also the case that while low-cost products, such as cheap food and clothes, are all that some consumers can afford, other consumers have become accustomed to and like low-cost offerings, as the boom in "no-frills" cheap flights demonstrates. Government-commissioned reports assert that low-cost, low-skill product strategies are no longer sustainable and that more firms will need to compete in innovative, quality-based markets utilizing highly skilled workers (see, for example, Porter and Ketels 2003). Thus, although a low-wage, flexible labor market has been integral to how many firms compete, what is required if the incidence of low pay is to be reduced is a systematic response that addresses firms' business strategies as well as the United Kingdom's institutional and regulatory framework, which shapes the quality of jobs and the management of employees.

## RECOGNIZING THAT ESCAPE HATCHES EXIST

The existence of differences among European countries in the extent of low-wage work and our earlier brief comparison of the United Kingdom's and the United States' economies suggest that outcomes are not predetermined and that there remains scope for political choice about the distribution of gains and losses. This view is supported by Andrew Glyn (2006, 175) who, reflecting on trends in welfare and income inequality among the most developed economies, argues:

> Thus far there seems no clear tendency for the differences [in income inequality] between countries to be eroded by a scramble to the bottom.... Even with capitalism off the leash, it has still been possible to significantly affect the most fundamental of all economic outcomes—who gets what.

Compared with other European countries, the United Kingdom lacks many institutional features that would help to reduce the number of low-wage workers: sectoral or industry-level collective bargaining, a relatively high minimum wage, and strong labor market regulation. The UK also lacks an assortment of institutional arrangements and supports that, in several other countries, have helped to improve the market position of organizations, such as strong local employer associations and networks and targeted national and local industrial policies. In this alternative context, firms have learned to cope with a higher-cost and less numerically flexible labor force by, for example, utilizing more technology, developing quality-based business approaches, and passing on higher costs of services to consumers or the state (see Hall and Soskice 2001; Streeck 1997).

Although the United Kingdom government recognizes that many businesses need to shift away from cost-based competition, it is inclined to perceive the issue not as systemic but as a failure of individual firms (Coffield 2004). The response then lies in persuading organizations to "change their ways," primarily through exhortation, some very limited tax incentives, and provision of a more highly qualified workforce. This approach appears to have had little effect, while other policies, such as providing subsidies via the tax credit system for families and expanding the supply of labor at the bottom end, help shore up low-cost, labor-intensive competitive strategies. Little heed has been paid to other forms of intervention that might encourage alternative business approaches based on innovation and investment in new technology, products, and services (Coffield 2004; Delbridge et al. 2006; Edwards, Geary, and Sisson 2002; Keep 2000; Lloyd and Payne 2002; Shah and McIvor 2006).

While a low-value-added strategy may set bounds to wages, many firms that employ low-wage workers are highly profitable (as evidenced in our hotel, call center, and retail case studies and affirmed in other services research; see Lloyd 2005a). The issue is thus not ability to pay but rather employers' unwillingness to pay, reflecting their relative power within the local labor market. Moreover, for those firms that do attempt to move "up-market" in terms of product quality, the end of low wages is not guaranteed. Substantive parallel changes to the United Kingdom's institutional configuration and regulatory framework are required that, for example, would begin to rebuild employers' associations and trade unions and encourage their mutual engagement so as to better coordinate firms' approaches to pay, skill development, and industrial policy (Edwards et al. 2002).

The problem is that these types of wholesale change, while desirable and necessary, are inevitably longer-term objectives. An alternative, more feasible approach in the short term is to reconfigure current policies with a view to improving the terms and conditions of employment in low-wage jobs, especially as they relate to pay and career development. The next section focuses on four areas for action: raising the NMW, improving child care provision, utilizing the public sector as a model employer, and encouraging higher investment in training. All of these actions are consistent with maintaining current high employment rates in the UK (and indeed improvements in child care would help increase women's emploment rate). Although not a systemic response, together these interventions could offer a New Deal for the Low-Waged.

## POLICY OPTIONS

*Raise and Enforce the National Minimum Wage*    Despite initial employer hostility, the NMW has now become an accepted feature of the institutional framework of the United Kingdom's economy. Nonetheless, as chapter 2 highlighted, the NMW may have helped to shore up wages at the bottom end of the labor market, but it has failed to reduce the proportion of low-wage workers. Moreover, official data reveal that 1.3 percent of the workforce (336,000 workers) are still paid below the NMW, both legally and illegally (National Statistics 2006).

What is needed is a sustained effort to raise the NMW to a suitable level in relation to the median wage for all workers. There are different perspectives on defining what is meant by a "suitable level"—for example, there is an economic point of view, and then there is a sociological point of view—yet the evidence at present is generally supportive of the claim that the current level is too low. From an economics perspective, a suitable level is reached when the costs outweigh the benefits. Regarding employment effects, a recent careful assessment by David Metcalf (2006), a member of the Low Pay Commission, has shown that job losses resulting from the NMW have been "small or non-existent" to date. Regarding wage pressures on inflation, the introduction of the NMW does not seem to have detracted from the United Kingdom's experience of relatively low inflation combined with moderate unemployment since 1999 (chapter 1). Regarding taxes, a raised NMW (holding other factors constant) would reduce government expenditure on tax credits. The final issue concerns the potential squeeze on profits. In a static economy, raising the NMW would lead to a one-off redistribution from employers to low-wage workers, but in the real-world dynamic economy, many firms have scope to respond to higher wage rates by making appropriate changes to their product market and human resource strategies.

From a sociological perspective, a suitable level of the NMW must accord with notions of fairness. The case studies show that, despite workers' resilience when faced with demands for hard work at low rates of pay, the level of the NMW did not meet their notions of a fair wage for their effort. Such norms overlap strongly with gender relations. Wages are in part a social practice that establishes and reinforces what men and women should be doing and how they should live (Figart et al. 2002). Given the concentration of women among low-wage workers in the United Kingdom, a higher NMW would help overturn the persistent discriminatory belief that many women (especially those in part-time jobs) work in low-wage jobs for "pin money" (for evidence, see Grant, Yeandle, and Buckner 2005). Furthermore, given evidence of the undervaluation of women's work in many low-wage industries, such that pay does not reflect the quality of work (whether measured by skill, service quality, or qualification; see Grimshaw and Rubery 2007), a higher NMW would contribute to wider efforts to overturn sex discrimination at work.

Whichever perspective is adopted, therefore, we can see that the NMW is not yet at a suitable level. From 2003 to 2006, the Low Pay Commission argued for a gradual increase in the NMW relative to median earnings. We believe that this position ought to be renewed. The commission should also reorient its framework of analysis to include social norms of fairness and justice as well as economic conditions. The government might also widen its terms of reference to examine a range of factors shaping the low-wage economy, such as the impact of increasing wage inequality at the top on inflation, access to housing markets, and norms of fairness, or the downward pressures of inward labor migration on pay rates in specific industries (Toynbee 2006). Evidence relating to employment effects must still figure centrally in a new analytical framework, but this should be supplemented by detailed investigation into the labor market transitions of any low-wage workers who lose their jobs as a result of hikes in the NMW.

The government must also ensure that the NMW is being properly enforced. Recognizing that some employers in industries that employ significant numbers of migrant workers attempt to circumvent regulations, the Low Pay Commission (2006) recommended better enforcement. Currently, enforcement is weak owing to lack of inspection, employers "miscalculating" piecework pay where union protection is absent, workers being unaware of their rights, and some employers seemingly misunderstanding the legislation (Croucher and White 2004). A single NMW regardless of worker age would be easier for employers to implement and simpler to enforce. Trade unions could play a key role in the enforcement process by providing advice and monitoring the application of the NMW by employers. Such a position would not only directly help underpaid workers but could also provide unions with key openings into areas that have traditionally been devoid of organization.

*Improve Child Care Provision*    Working mothers are especially at risk in the United Kingdom's low-wage labor market. Women returning to work after having children are very likely to interrupt their careers, switch jobs, and/or move into part-time employment. While some argue that such decisions reflect mothers' preferences for being a "homemaker" and lesser commitment to paid work (see, for example, Hakim 1991), the evidence for the United Kingdom (and also for the United States) suggests that the jobs that mothers take are not more family-friendly than other jobs (England 2005; Tomlinson et al. 2005). Women returners tend to underutilize their previous training and skills, especially in caring jobs, sales, and customer services. In particular, for women returning to part-time work, there is a wage penalty of 17 percent per hour after controlling for human capital characteristics (for a review, see Grimshaw and Rubery 2007).

Many low-wage women workers are thus shouldering disproportionate costs following their decision to have children and face a restricted set of labor market options. The evidence strongly suggests that lack of affordable child care is a key part of the problem (Fox, Pascall, and Warren 2007). What would help is childcare that enables those women who wish to do so to move into full-time jobs. As with other areas of proposed reform, the government has recognized this need and made a start in expanding and improving child care. As then-Chancellor of the Exchequer Gordon Brown stated in 2004:

> While the nineteenth century was distinguished by the introduction of primary education for all and the twentieth century by the introduction of secondary education for all, so the early twenty first century should be marked by the introduction of pre-school provision for the under-5s and childcare available for all. (quoted in McLaren 2005, 45)

In 2006, free places were available in nurseries for three- and four-year-old children, but because they are limited to twelve and a half hours per week and restricted to school term times, they were unlikely to allow parents time to work. The child care subsidies introduced through the tax credit system can be relatively substantial for low-income families, yet parents still pay around three-quarters of the costs. However, it is not just issues of cost that restrict access to provision but location, concerns about the quality of staff and facilities, and availability at suitable hours (NAO 2004). Once children reach school age, provision is extremely restricted outside school hours and during holidays.

More government-subsidized child care hours are needed, with better-quality provision. Trade unions can play a role in pressing for more employer involvement. The public sector trade union Unison, for example, launched a strategy in 2004 to bargain for improved child care, arguing the case for both workers and business. Improved child care would deepen the labor market participation of a key group of low-wage workers and allow working mothers to undertake more full-time employment and gain access to better opportunities for career development (Unison 2004).

*Promote the Public Sector as a Model Employer*   As noted in chapter 5, low pay is not just a private sector phenomenon. Government employs many workers in health, education, and other jobs who are low-waged. Some of these public sector workers, particularly women part-timers, have received a boost in wages as a result of job evaluations within single-status agreements between unions and local government, allied to equal value claims championed by the Equal Opportunities Commission (see, for example, EOC 2007). These developments have sometimes featured lengthy, difficult negotiations (*Labour Research* 2006), as well as bitter disputes. In 2004 nursery nurses in Scotland, with average annual earnings of around £13,000 (US$26,516), were involved in the longest strike in the United Kingdom since the 1984–85 miners' strike (BBC News 2004; Unison 2003).

The government could therefore build a positive reputation as a "model employer" by offering better pay, working conditions, and progression opportunities (Coffield 2004; Keep 2000). Some notable improvements have already been made (as highlighted in chapter 5), following sustained pressure from trade unions. The new national pay structure in the NHS has boosted pay for the lowest grades and, with the agreement on a new two-tier code, the government has passed a de facto wage extension agreement to workers engaged in subcontractor private sector firms. This approach could be taken further by applying it to all parts of the public sector and ensuring that all suppliers meet a rigorous set of employment standards through contract compliance—a position adopted in all but name in 2007 by Glasgow City Council, the largest local authority in Scotland. These improvements ought to have positive spillover effects in the wider labor market, as the public sector would then provide a new benchmark to encourage private sector employers, who often compete for the same workers, to improve wages (Rutherford and Shah 2006).

*Increase Training Investment*   Significantly, one area in which government has been prepared to invest considerable sums of money is in training for the low-skilled. In 2006 the HM Treasury–commissioned *Leitch Review of Skills* set a target to raise the percentage of adults qualified to at least level 2 from 69 to 90 percent by 2020 (Leitch 2006).[4] Funding for this training is expected to be provided by the government, yet it is unclear as to whether this initiative will assist those employers who are currently not training workers or the low-waged themselves. There is also a significant problem here for low-wage workers. For the jobs covered in our research, employers were often more concerned with workers' personal qualities—being hardworking, a team worker, flexible, punctual, friendly, having a comprehensible accent, being visually presentable—than with their qualifications (see Grugulis, Warhurst, and Keep 2004). The jobs typically required no qualifications on entry. Moreover, evidence suggests that on average workers make little or no monetary gain by possessing vocational qualifications at levels 1 and 2 (Dearden, McGranahan, and Sianesi 2004; Felstead, Gallie, and Green 2002).

One way that jobs might be improved is through a license to practice; this regulatory mechanism, which is widespread in Germany and in a number of U.S. states, has been shown to have a positive impact on wages. A license to practice might be implemented as a statutory mechanism through which employers would have to train employees to a national standard, with approved qualifications as a compulsory requirement for being able to deliver goods or services in a particular trade or occupation. Such licenses would also offer some product quality assurance for consumers. Their recent introduction for some lower-skilled occupations—for example, care workers and nightclub bouncers (Lloyd 2005b; Nickson et al. 2008)—might indicate a willingness on the part of the government to extend this practice. However, the *Leitch Review* failed to recommend the wider use of licensing.

An additional option is the Union Learning Fund (ULF). ULF and its Scottish variant (SULF) were introduced by the Labour government to address perceived skill deficiencies, particularly basic skills, as a means to enhance employer productivity and competitiveness and increase employability.[5] Through the fund, workplace learning projects are encouraged that involve employers but are driven by trade unions, since unions can more easily reach those workers whose formal qualifications are low or lacking and who, along with migrant workers, populate the type of low-wage jobs included in our case studies (Findlay et al. 2006; Warhurst, Findlay, and Thompson 2006). The evidence to date suggests that the projects have met a latent demand for learning among these workers and have stimulated further demand, with workers associating improved learning with opportunities for pay advancement (Findlay, Findlay, and Warhurst 2007). Through their acquisition of qualifications, ULF can also provide workers with a "job escalator"—for example, hospital cleaners could progress into better jobs in the same department or in other occupations, such as nursing (Warhurst et al. 2006). The government has indicated its continued short-term support for the fund. However, there is concern among unions about the impact of a change of government and the need for statutory support for learning as part of union bargaining rights and for employees to have a statutory right to allow paid learning at work (Findlay et al. 2006). Moreover, ULF only applies to workplaces with union presence, and the overwhelming majority of low-wage workers are in workplaces without unions.

In principle, such an approach might provide some workers with an exit route out of low-wage work, though the initiative has been so recently introduced that it is still too soon to tell. Even so, two questions remain about how far and in what ways this type of learning can improve job quality. First, some individuals will be able to move on to better-paying jobs, but as long as other workers are available to fill their positions—migrant workers, students, and those returning to the labor market—the initiative is unlikely to have any knock-on effect on the quality of the jobs they leave behind. Second, as our research indicates, lack of training was rarely the main reason progression was restricted for low-wage workers; rather, it was the limited availability of higher-level jobs, particularly for those working part-time. Across the economy, there is little evidence that the increased supply of better-qualified workers is being met with a reciprocal demand for such workers from employers. Rather, research indicates that there continues to be a substantial number of jobs that require no qualification for entry and growing levels of overqualification and underemployment of workers (Grant et al. 2005; Green 2006; Keep 2006; Warhurst and Thompson 2006).

Learning in itself is unlikely to reduce the number or improve the quality of low-wage jobs, but it may provide an indirect lever, as evidence indicates that union learning initiatives can have a positive impact on union recruitment and organizing in the industries that feature in our research (Findlay et al. 2006; Warhurst et al. 2006). More generally, upward pressure on wages in low-paying jobs through the NMW should increase the incentives for many employers to try to increase worker productivity by investing more in training and in more skill-intensive forms of work organization.

## CONCLUSIONS

The United Kingdom has one of the highest rates of low-wage workers among the European Union countries, with low pay now affecting 22 percent of workers in paid employment. With government attention focused on shoring up the supply side of the labor market by attempting to improve the stock of skills and qualifications among the workforce, little attention has been paid to date on the demand side: what employers want from workers, and how they deploy them. This neglect is particularly true of low-wage work, whether in the United Kingdom or elsewhere. As Elisabeth Wynhausen (2005, 234) noted in her journalistic sampling of low-wage work: "In my experience as a low wage worker, the jobs all had one thing in common: I no sooner took them on than I, like my fellow employees, seemed to be rendered invisible."

The research in this volume examined low-wage jobs in five industries in the United Kingdom: retail, food processing, hospitals, hotels, and call centers. Ranging across the public and private sectors, manufacturing and services, these jobs revealed the varied effects of organizations' attempts to control costs in competitive conditions. Negative trends in job quality included more precarious contract status, reduced pay prospects, more erratic working time schedules, increased work effort, and job insecurity caused by outsourcing. In all but one of the target occupations, a high proportion of workers were earning below the low pay threshold, and pay rates at minimum wage levels were common in retail, hotels, and food processing.

These outcomes are understandable given the institutional context of low-wage work in the United Kingdom—most notably, light regulation, flexible labor markets, weakened trade unions, and a useful but low-level NMW. Nevertheless, as we have argued, the extent and nature of low-wage work is not fixed but is the outcome of policies made within political constraints. As Toynbee (2003, 211) asserts, "Nations make their own destinies. They can decide how fair or unfair they will be." There are a range of alternative policy options available, from radical institutional rebuilding to more gradualist proposals that build on existing policy interventions. Any change, however, will require sustained pressure on government from trade unions and community groups. Drawing on ideas from the United States, a living wage campaign that includes trade unions and provides a bridge to trade union affiliation and activism has had a number of successes in London: for example, pay has improved for low-wage workers contracted to work for financial services, hospitals, and local government (see chapter 3).

It is essential that concerted efforts be made to raise the profile of low-wage work and that these efforts highlight not just the problems for workers but also those created in the longer term for employers, the United Kingdom's economy as a whole, and wider society. This recognition is the first step to giving the low-waged greater visibility. Only then can other steps be taken to provide or encourage the voice for the low-waged and stimulate the necessary political will to address the underlying issues of low-wage work.

## NOTES

1.  The estimates provided in the official report from the Low Pay Commission (2005, table 2.5) show that, relative to mean gross hourly earnings for all employees, the NMW dropped from 36.7 percent in 1999 to 34.2 percent in 2001 and then rose slightly to 35.7 percent by 2003.
2.  Derogations include exceptions for those workers who organize their own working time, exemptions from daily/weekly rests where a worker changes shift, and numerous "operational reasons" (see Hurrell 2005, 535).
3.  The TUPE regulations were introduced in 1981 to comply with European Union directives. These regulations are designed to protect employees' terms and conditions, excluding pensions, and to provide continuity of employment with any transfer of ownership.
4.  Level 2 is equivalent to five GCSEs at grade A* to C, which are normally taken at the end of compulsory schooling at age sixteen or their vocational equivalent, such as NVQ, level 2.
5.  Until 2007 the government in Scotland was a coalition of the Labour and the Liberal Democrat Parties, led by Labour.

## REFERENCES

Bardasi, Elena, and Stephen J. Jenkins. 2002. *Income in Later Life*. Bristol, U.K.: Policy Press.

BBC News. 2004. "Nursery Nurses in All-out Action." March 1. Accessed at www.news.bbc.co.uk/go/pr/fr/-/1/hi/scotland/3496192.stm.

Blanchflower, David G., and Alex Bryson. 2004. "The Union Wage Premium in the U.S. and the U.K." Discussion paper. London: London School of Economics, Centre for Economic Performance.

Blanden, Jo, and Steve Gibbons. 2006. *The Persistence of Poverty Across Generations*. Bristol, U.K.: Policy Press.

Brewer, Mike, Alissa Goodman, Alastair Muriel, and Luke Sibieta. 2007. *Poverty and Inequality in Britain: 2007*. London: IFS.

Brewer, Mike, and Andrew Shephard. 2004. *Has Labour Made Work Pay?* York, U.K.: Joseph Rowntree Foundation.

Canny, Angela. 2002. "Flexible Labor? The Growth of Student Employment in the U.K." *Journal of Education and Work* 15(3): 277–301.

Coffield, Frank. 2004. "Alternative Routes Out of the Low Skills Equilibrium: A Rejoinder to Lloyd and Payne." *Journal of Education Policy* 19(6): 733–40.

Croucher, Richard, and Geoff White. 2004. "Enforcing the Minimum Wage: The Experience of Workers and Employers." Research report for the Low Pay Commission, London: Low Pay Commission.

Curtis, Susan, and Rosemary Lucas. 2001. "A Coincidence of Needs? Employers and Full-time Students." *Employee Relations* 23(1): 38–54.

Dearden, Lorraine, Leslie McGranahan, and Barbara Sianesi. 2004. "An In-depth Analysis of the Returns to National Vocational Qualifications Obtained at Level 2." Discussion paper 46. London: London School of Economics, Centre for the Economics of Education.

Delbridge, Rick, Paul Edwards, John Forth, Peter Miskell, and Jonathan Payne. 2006. *The Organization of Productivity*. London: AIM.

Department of Trade and Industry (DTI). 2007. "Success at Work: Increasing the Holiday Entitlement: An Initial Consultation." London: DTI (January). Accessed at http://www.dti.gov.uk/files/file36448.pdf.

Dutton, Eli, Chris Warhurst, Dennis Nickson, and Cliff Lockyer. 2005. "Lone Parents, the New Deal, and the Opportunities and Barriers to Retail Employment." *Policy Studies* 26(1): 85–101.

Edwards, Paul, John Geary, and Keith Sisson. 2002. "New Forms of Work Organization in the Workplace: Transformative, Exploitative, or Limited and Controlled." In *Work and Employment Relations in the High-Performance Workplace*, edited by Gregory Murray, Jacques Bélanger, Anthony Kent Giles, and Paul-André Lapointe. London: Continuum.

Ehrenreich, Barbara. 2001. *Nickel and Dimed*. New York: Metropolitan.

England, Paula. 2005. "Gender Inequality in Labor Markets: The Role of Motherhood and Segregation." *Social Politics* 12(2): 264–88.

Equal Opportunities Commission (EOC). 2007. *Valuable Assets: A General Formal Investigation into the Role and Status of Classroom Assistants in Scottish Schools*. Glasgow: EOC.

Felstead, Alan, Duncan Gallie, and Francis Green. 2002. *Work Skills in Britain 1986–2001*. Nottingham, U.K.: DfES.

Figart, Deborah M., Ellen Mutari, and Marilyn Power. 2002. *Living Wages, Equal Wages*. London: Routledge.

Findlay, Jeanette, Patricia Findlay, and Chris Warhurst. 2007. *Estimating the Demand for Union-Led Learning in Scotland.* Glasgow: Scottish Trades Union Congress.

Findlay, Patricia, Robert Stewart, Eli Dutton, and Chris Warhurst. 2006. *Evaluation of the Scottish Union Learning Fund (SULF), 2000–2005.* Edinburgh: Scottish Executive Social Research (May). Accessed at http://www.scotland.gov.uk/Publications/2006/05/23131735/0.

Finegold, David, and David Soskice. 1988. "The Failure of Training in Britain: Analysis and Prescription." *Oxford Review of Economic Policy* 4(3): 21–53.

Forth, John, and Neil Millward. 2001. "The Low-Paid Worker and the Low-Paying Employer: Characterizations Using WERS98." Discussion paper 179. London: National Institute for Economic and Social Research.

Fox, Elizabeth, Gillian Pascall, and Tracey Warren. 2007. "Innovative Social Policies for Gender Equality at Work." Final report. Nottingham, U.K.: University of Nottingham.

Furlong, Andy, and Fred Cartmel. 2005. *Graduates from Disadvantaged Families.* Bristol, U.K.: Policy Press.

Glyn, Andrew. 2006. *Capitalism Unleashed.* Oxford: Oxford University Press.

Grainger, Heidi, and Martin Crowther. 2007. *Trade Union Membership 2006.* Accessed at http://www.dti.gov.uk/files/file39006.pdf.

Grant, Linda, Sue Yeandle, and Lisa Buckner. 2005. *Working Below Potential: Women and Part-time Work.* Working paper 40. London: Equal Opportunities Commission.

Green, Francis. 2006. *Demanding Work.* Princeton, N.J.: Princeton University Press.

Grimshaw, Damian. 2005. "Using Qualitative Data to Understand Employer Behavior in Low-Wage Labour Markets." In *Job Quality and Employer Behavior,* edited by Stephen Bazen, Claudio Lucifora, and Wiemer Salverda. London: Palgrave.

Grimshaw, Damian, and Marilyn Carroll. 2006. 'Adjusting to the National Minimum Wage: Constraints and Incentives to Change in Six Low-Paying Sectors." *Industrial Relations Journal* 37(1): 22–47.

Grimshaw, Damian, and Jill Rubery. 2003. "Economics and Industrial Relations." In *Understanding Work and Employment,* edited by Peter Ackers and Adrian Wilkinson. Oxford: Oxford University Press.

———. 2007. *The Undervaluing of Women's Work.* Manchester, U.K.: Equal Opportunities Commission.

Grugulis, Irena, Chris Warhurst, and Ewart Keep. 2004. "What's Happening to Skill?" In *The Skills That Matter,* edited by Chris Warhurst, Ewart Keep, and Irena Grugulis. London: Palgrave.

Hakim, Catherine. 1991. "Grateful Slaves and Self-made Women: Fact and

Fantasy in Women's Work Orientations." *European Sociological Review* 7(2): 101–21.

Hall, Peter A., and David Soskice, eds. *Varieties of Capitalism.* Oxford: Oxford University Press.

Harker, Lisa. 2006. *Delivering on Child Poverty.* London: HMSO.

Hirsch, Donald. 2006. *What Will It Take to End Child Poverty?* York, U.K.: Joseph Rowntree Foundation.

Howarth, Catherine, and Peter Kenway. 2004. *Why Worry Anymore About the Low-Paid?* London: New Policy Institute.

Hurrell, Scott A. 2005. "Dilute to Taste? The Impact of the Working Time Regulations in the Hospitality Industry." *Employee Relations* 27(5): 532–46.

Incomes Data Services (IDS). 2004. *Report to the Low Pay Commission on the Impact of the National Minimum Wage in 2003 and 2004.* London: IDS (September).

Kalleberg, Arne L., Barbara F. Reskin, and Ken Hudson. 2000. "Bad Jobs in America: Standard and Nonstandard Employment Relations and Job Quality in the United States." *American Sociological Review* 65(2): 256–78.

Keep, Ewart. 2000. *Upskilling Scotland.* A New Horizon Report. Edinburgh: Centre for Scottish Public Policy.

———. 2006. "Market Failure in Skills." *SSDA Catalyst,* issue 1. Wath-upon-Dearne, U.K.: Sector Skills Development Agency.

Keep, Ewart, and Ken Mayhew. 1998. "Was Ratner Right?" *Economic Report* (Employment Policy Institute) 12(3).

*Labour Research.* 2006. "Single Status Remains Paralyzed." *Labour Research* 95(12): 12, 4.

Leitch, Sandy. 2006. *Leitch Review of Skills.* London: HM Treasury.

Living Wage Unit. 2006. *A Fairer London.* London: GLA.

Lloyd, Caroline. 2005a. "Competitive Strategy and Skills: Working Out the Fit in the Fitness Industry." *Human Resource Management Journal* 15(2): 15–34.

———. 2005b. "The Regulation of the Fitness Industry: Training Standards as a Policy Option?" *Industrial Relations Journal* 365): 367–85.

Lloyd, Caroline, and Jonathan Payne. 2002. "On 'the Political Economy of Skill': Assessing the Possibilities for a Viable High Skills Project in the U.K." *New Political Economy* 7(3): 367–95.

Low Pay Commission. 2005. *The National Minimum Wage: Low Pay Commission Report 2005.* Norwich, U.K.: HMSO.

———. 2006. *National Minimum Wage: Low Pay Commission Report 2006.* Norwich, U.K.: HMSO.

Masterman-Smith, Helen, Robyn May, and Barbara Pocock. 2006. "Living Low-Paid: Some Experiences of Australian Child Care Workers and

Cleaners." Adelaide, Australia: University of South Australia, Centre for Applied Social Research, Royal Melbourne Institute of Technology, Centre for Work and Life.

Mayo, Elton. 1946. *Human Problems of an Industrialized Civilization*. New York: Macmillan.

McLaren John. 2005. *Soft Skills and Early Years*. Glasgow: Scottish Enterprise.

Metcalf, David. 2006. "On the Impact of the British National Minimum Wage on Pay and Employment." Accessed at http://cep.lse.ac.uk/research/labour/minimumwage/WP1481c.pdf.

Murphy, Neil. 2006. "Employing Migrant Workers." *IRS Employment Review* 844: 42–45.

National Audit Office (NAO). 2004. *Early Years: Progress in Developing High-Quality Child Care and Early Education Accessible to All*. London: HMSO.

National Statistics. 2006. "Low Pay Estimates: Spring 2006." London: National Statistics.

Nickson, Dennis, Chris Warhurst, Cliff Lockyer, and Eli Dutton. 2004. "Flexible Friends? Lone Parents and Retail Employment." *Employee Relations* 26(4): 255–73.

Nickson, Dennis, Chris Warhurst, Eli Dutton, and Scott A. Hurrell. 2008. "A Job to Believe In: Recruitment in the Scottish Voluntary Sector." *Human Resource Management Journal* 18(1): 18-33.

Office for National Statistics (ONS). 2006. *UK Input-Output Analyses: 2006 Edition*. London: Office for National Statistics.

Porter, Michael E., and Christian H. M. Ketels. 2003. *U.K. Competitiveness: Moving to the Next Stage*. London: Department of Trade and Industry.

Prasch, Robert E. 2002. "What Is Wrong with Wage Subsidies?" *Journal of Economic Issues* 36(2): 357–64.

Rubery, Jill. 1997. "Wages and the Labour Market." *British Journal of Industrial Relations* 35(3): 337–66.

Rubery, Jill, Kevin Ward, Damian Grimshaw, and Huw Beynon. 2005. "Working Time, Industrial Relations, and the Employment Relationship." *Time and Society* 14(1): 89–111.

Rutherford, Jonathan, and Hetan Shah, editors. 2006. *The Good Society*. London: Compass/Lawrence & Wishart.

Shah, Hetan, and Martin McIvor. 2006. *A New Political Economy*. London: Compass/Lawrence and Wishart.

Smith, David. 2007. "Social Exclusion, the Third Way, and the Reserve Army of Labor." *Sociology* 41(2): 365–72.

Storrie, Donald. 2002. *Temporary Agency Work in the European Union*. Dublin: European Foundation for the Improvement of Living and Working Conditions.

Streeck, Wolfgang. 1997. "Beneficial Constraints: On the Economic Limits of Rational Voluntarism." In *Contemporary Capitalism*, edited by J. Rogers Hollingsworth and Robert Boyer. New York: Cambridge University Press.

Taylor, Phil, and Peter Bain. 2005. "'India Calling to the Faraway Towns': The Call Center Labor Process and Globalization." *Work, Employment, and Society* 19(2): 261–82.

Tomlinson, Jennie, Wendy Olsen, Daniel Neff, Kingsley Purdam, and Smita Mehta. 2005. *Examining the Potential for Women Returners to Work in Areas of High Occupational Segregation*. London: Department of Trade and Industry.

Toynbee, Polly. 2003. *Hard Work*. London: Bloomsbury.

———. 2006. "Imagine What Might Be, if Labour Only Dared." *The Guardian*, December 29, 2006: 23.

Trades Union Congress (TUC). 2005. *The EU Temp Trade: Temporary Agency Work Across the European Union*. London: TUC.

Unison. 2003. "Nursery nurse dispute briefing." Glasgow: Unison (September 23).

———. 2004. "Bargaining for Child Care." *Unison Bargaining Support Guide*. Accessed at http://www.unison.org.uk/acrobat/14001.pdf.

Ward, Lucy. 2004. "Student Debt Hits £12,000, Says Study." *The Guardian*, August 11.

Warhurst, Chris, Patricia Findlay, and Paul Thompson. 2006. "Organizing to Learn/Learning to Organize: Three Case Studies on the Effects of Union-Led Workplace Learning." Research paper 68. Universities of Oxford and Cardiff: Economic and Social Research Council (ESRC) Centre on Skills, Knowledge, and Organizational Performance (SKOPE).

Warhurst, Chris, and Paul Thompson. 2006. "Mapping Knowledge in Work: Proxies or Practices?" *Work, Employment, and Society* 20(4): 787–800.

Wynhausen, Elisabeth. 2005. *Dirty Work*. Sydney, Australia: Pan Macmillan.

# Index